RE-READING THE MANUAL OF TRAVELLING EXHIBITIONS, UNESCO, 1953

TABLE OF CONTENTS

MANUAL OF TRAVELLING EXHIBITIONS

BY ELODIE COURTER OSBORN

READING NOTES

On the margins of the following pages, a series of comments accompany the reprint of a book. They are the result of a careful reading of the texts, drawings, diagrams and images, the layout and typesetting, the paper and binding, which in combination constitute the *Manual of Travelling Exhibitions* as a material object. The notes by Kurt Eckert, Moritz Küng and Andreas Müller document three respective readings of the *Manual,* from the perspectives of graphic design and book making (KE), curating and exhibition making (MK), and exhibition design (AM). The comments make visible the act of re-reading, an intellectual appropriation, transformation, and co-production of the historic book.

The quotes found on the bottom centre of the reprint are part of Moritz Küng's commentary and an attempt to comment on a book as such. They are transcribed from the book project of Fluxus artist George Brecht, *Book,* originally conceived in 1964, and first published in 1972.

01 KE Published in 1953. Pale and exquisite, handy and vulnerable; its pages hang somewhat loosely from the thread. White gloves seem necessary to handle it.

02 MK What I am looking at, reading, and commenting on is not a book, but a PDF reproduction of a book. Accordingly, it has no physical or tactile qualities, has no pages to turn, and doesn't have a smell. It is flat and aseptic, and its contents are not read by light but as light. As intangible, it seems to be a book without properties. Besides my own remarks, in which I also refer to other (predominantly artists'-) books, I have also inserted the complete text from *Book (This is the cover of the Book)* by the American Fluxus artist George Brecht (1926–2008) as a kind of meta-comment. Conceived in 1964 and published in 1972 by Michael Werner Gallery in Cologne as a 28-page hard cover volume with a limited run of 50 numbered copies, it remarks on the role and qualities of each of the book's own pages in 20 concise formulations. The tautological and self-referential Brecht quotes make the book at hand into a twofold study object. *Book (This is the cover of the Book)* was reprinted as a soft-cover facsimile in an edition of 250 copies (IF-Publications, Barcelona 2017) to accompany the artists' book exhibition *Selección Natural–This is the cover of the Book* (Madrid and Gent, 2017, curated by Küng).

03 KE The typeset comprising the headline was made of lead, it was both durable and combinable, but also vulnerable, and is thus a treasured feature of the typesetter's inventory. So it comes as no surprise that the cover characters of the UNESCO edition had already made an appearance in another performance—like actors in a theatre group. In the web-archive of the *Imprimerie Union* (founded by Russian emigrants in 1909, initially the printers of the Russian exile community in Paris) there is actually a typographical double. The jacket of a 24-page brochure shows an identical two-liner, with comparable rhetoric, and characters with equally careless kerning. Title: *Rupture inaugurale.* Publication series: Editions surréalistes. Subtitle: *Déclaration/Adoptée le 21 juin 1947 par le groupe en France pour définir son attitude préjudicielle a l'égard de toute politique partisane.*[1]

04 AM Elodie Courter Osborn (1911–1994) professionalised travelling exhibitions through her work at the Museum of Modern Art, New York, as well as her involvement with UNESCO and the American Federation of Arts. After receiving her degree in art history in 1933, Osborn joined MoMA's newly founded Department of Circulating Exhibitions as a volunteer. She became the programme's secretary in 1935 and was named Director in 1939, a position she held to 1947. Osborn developed the programme's domestic agenda and was involved in all of its aspects, from overall direction to budget to curatorial negotiations to copy editing. Between 1932 and at the apex of the programme in 1954, MoMA circulated 461 exhibitions among 3.700 venues including schools, colleges, clubs, military installations, and department stores. In Osborn's era, exhibitions circulated internationally but the majority were designed for an American audience.

05 AM In November 1945 a United Nations Conference for the establishment of an educational and cultural organisation was convened in London with 44 governments represented. At the London Conference, the Constitution of UNESCO was introduced and signed by 37 countries. It came into force on November 4th, 1946 after ratification by twenty countries: Australia, Brazil, Canada, China, Czechoslovakia, Denmark, the Dominican Republic, Egypt, France, Greece, India, Lebanon, Mexico, New Zealand, Norway, Saudi Arabia, South Africa, Turkey, the United Kingdom, and the United States. The first General Conference took place from November 19th to December 10th 1946, and elected Dr. Julian Huxley as the Director-General.

01 KE
02 MK

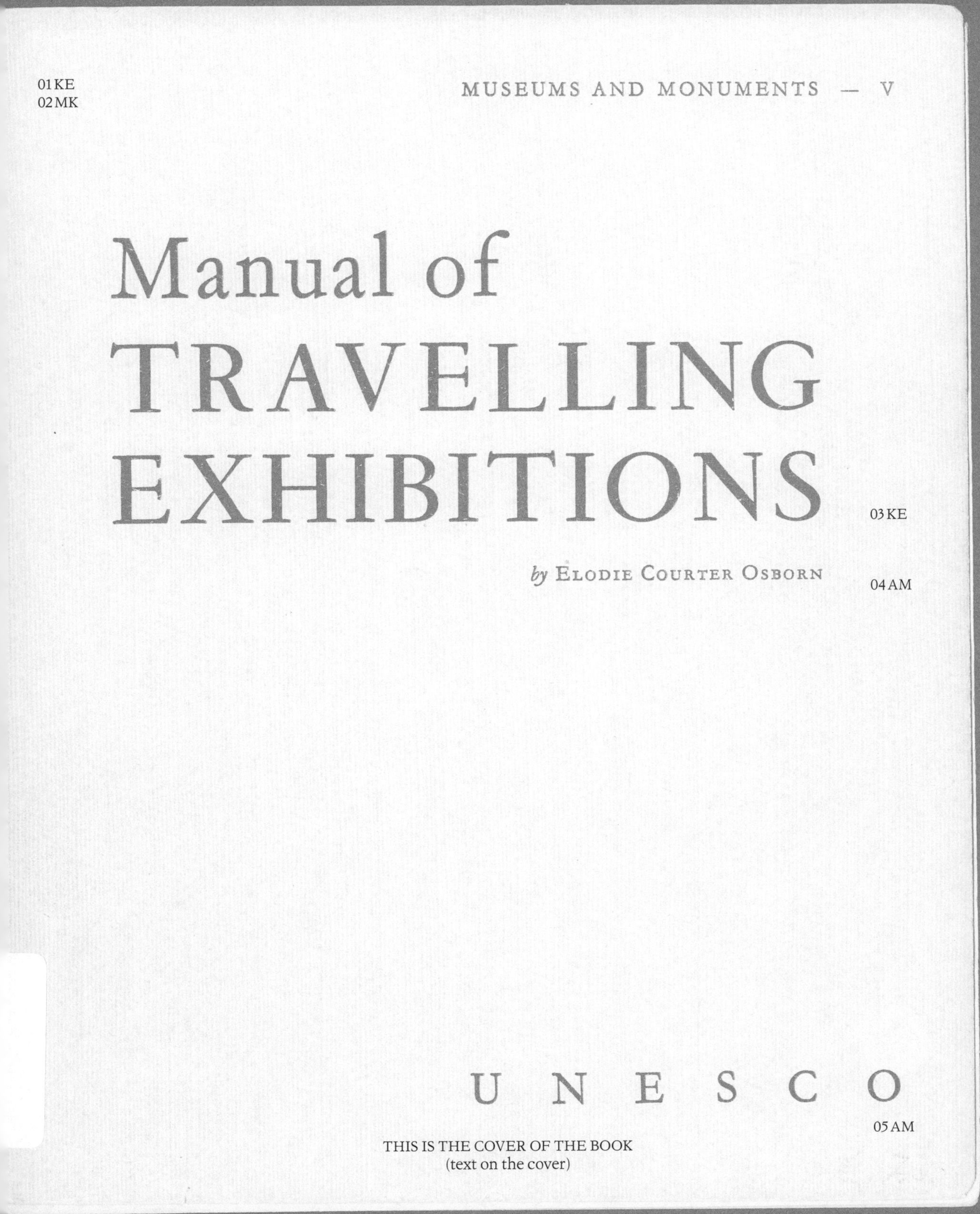

MUSEUMS AND MONUMENTS — V

Manual of
TRAVELLING
EXHIBITIONS

03 KE

by ELODIE COURTER OSBORN

04 AM

UNESCO

05 AM

THIS IS THE COVER OF THE BOOK
(text on the cover)

↳129 THE HISTORY OF THE UNESCO LOGO
↳131 READ CAREFULLY AND FOLLOW THE ATTACHED INSTRUCTIONS

06KE The publication features a bluish-green linen embossed cardstock cover. The contents are comprised of two parts: porous, wood-containing paper for the text and drawings, browned like an aged newspaper; and a light, matte finished paper for the section containing the photographic images, with no signs of aging. The grammages: 80 and 90 g/m². A simple pamphlet stitch holds together the seven sections, 112 pages in total. The inside of the cover spine is glued to the back of the book block. Interim binding, to use the language of bookbinders, dispenses with endpapers. Signs of letterpress printing and hot metal setting are evident: a fine surface embossing can be seen under a sidelight; the squeezed edges of the letters are visible under a linen tester; and the font is one of the canonised typefaces – Monotype Garamond.

06KE

MUSEUMS AND MONUMENTS — V

THESE ARE THE END PAPERS OF THE BOOK
(text on the inside cover and p. 1)

07KE A few basics over typographic technicalities: The Gutenberg era and the Imprimerie Union used the units cicero and point—1 point = 0,376 mm, 12 points = 1 cicero. The measurement system is duodecimal based.[2]

08AM The choice of the topics amongst the first titles for the *Museums and Monuments* series is interesting. It is about the care of paintings, the reconstruction of a town, the restoration of monuments, and the preservation of frescoes. The *Manual of Travelling Exhibitions* at first seems out of this range of topics, as it addresses questions of information, communication, and education.

07KE

Series: Museums and Monuments / Série: Musées et Monuments

I (af)	Sites & Monuments, problèmes actuels/problems of today. *Réimpression/Second edition (1953).*	$3.00	16/6	800 fr.	
II (af)	The Care of Paintings / Le traitement des peintures. *Réimpression/Second edition (1952).*	$2.25	14/6	700 fr.	
III (a)	Cuzco: Reconstruction of the Town and Restoration of its Monuments *(1952).*	$1.50	8/6	400 fr.	
III (f)	Cuzco, la reconstruction de la ville et la restauration de ses monuments *(1953).*	$1.50	8/6	400 fr.	
III (s)	Cuzco, Reconstrucción de la ciudad y restauración de sus monumentos *(1953).*	En preparación			
IV (a)	Saint Sophia of Ochrida, Preservation and Restoration of the Building and its Frescoes *(1953).*	$1.00	5/-	250 fr.	
IV (f)	Sainte-Sophie d'Ochrida, la conservation et la restauration de l'édifice et de ses fresques *(1953).*	$1.00	5/-	250 fr.	
V (a)	Manual of Travelling Exhibitions *(1953).*	$1.75	10/6	500 fr.	08AM

THIS IS THE PAGE BEFORE THE TITLE PAGE
OF THE BOOK THAT TELLS YOU WHAT THE
TITLE IS OR WAS, OR IS GOING TO BE.
(text on p. 3)

09KE The typesetting of the *Manual* was made on the Monotype hot metal typesetting machine. Except for the manual text input, punched tapes direct the typecasting. The compressed air-driven Monotype formatting the tapes, the drum to calculate word spacing in justified text, the caster, and the character set of the matrix cases are all components of the individual letter casting. In contrast to the largely mechanised typesetting production, the cover title, title pages, and chapter titles were all set by the hand of a typographer. They are responsible for assembling the page markups—including the formatting, merging the text layers and images, lines, gutters, blank lines and empty spaces.[3]

10KE A flashback to the 1920s: Under the art direction of Stanley Morison, the British branch of the Monotype Corporation brought a range of historical font revivals onto the market: Garamond, Bodoni, Baskerville, Poliphilus, Fournier, Perpetua, Bembo, and many more. A competitive field, even within the Monotype Corporation itself. As a response to the American Monotype variant by the name of Garamont (1921), designed by Frederic Goudy, Morison countered with his interpretation, realised with the draftsman Fritz Stelzer (1923—contemporaneous with László Moholy-Nagy's Bauhaus essay "typophoto", published in Weimar). Garamond as a brand is based on an error, which Beatrice Warde, the typographic eminence at Morison's side, uncovered two years after its release: she identified the templates created by the punchcutter and printer Jean Jannon, which were published in 1640, over 90 years after Claude Garamond had been active.

A historical aside: Jannon was a Calvinist and printed for the Huguenots, who were subject to the Inquisition. Cardinal Richelieu had Jannon arrested and his tools and molds confiscated and used them for his own ends. Today, Jannon's matrices and molds belong to the archives of the Imprimerie Nationale in Paris.[4]

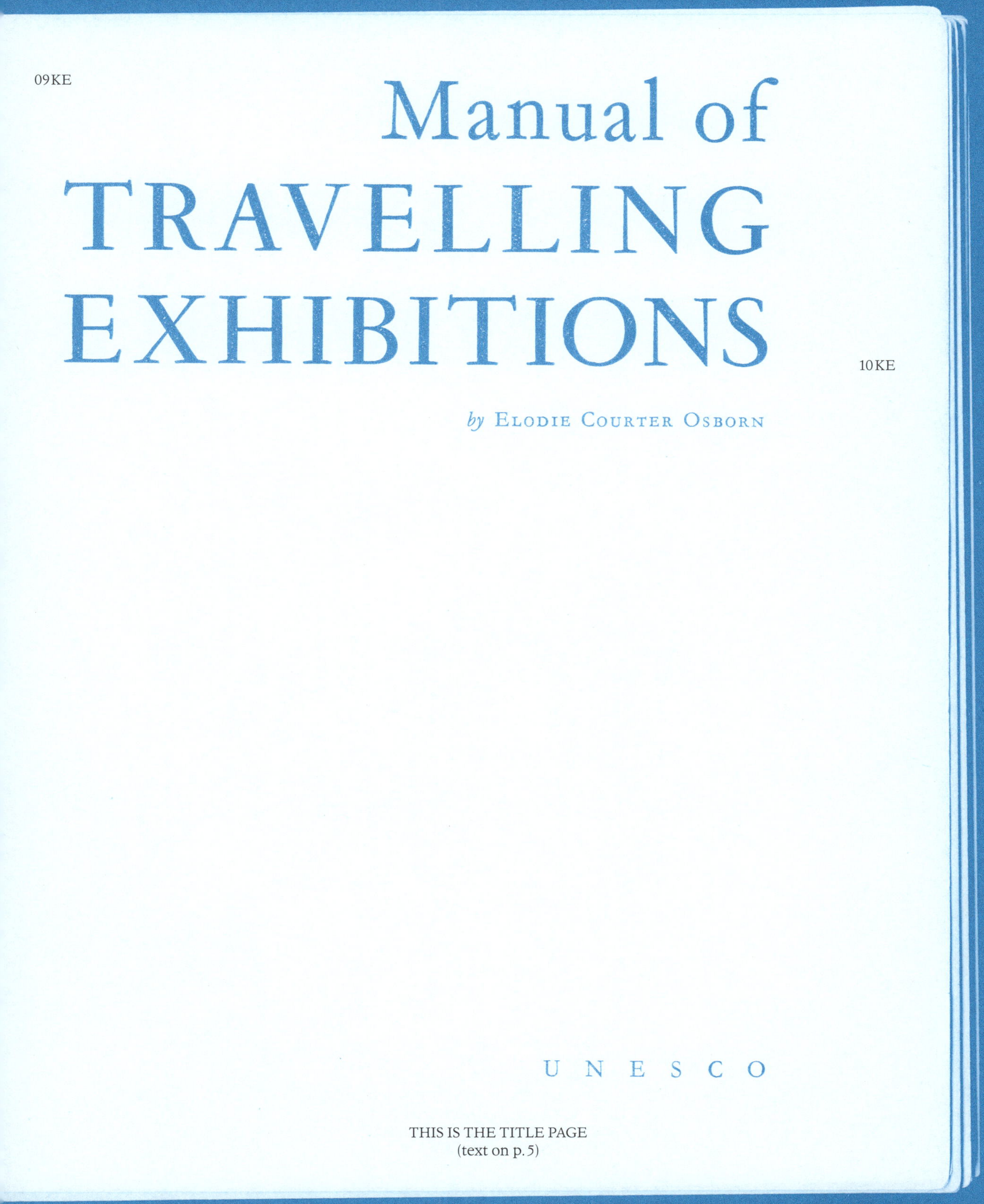
09KE

Manual of
TRAVELLING
EXHIBITIONS

by Elodie Courter Osborn

U N E S C O

10KE

THIS IS THE TITLE PAGE
(text on p. 5)

11 AM "UNESCO was then a small organisation located in a former luxury hotel, the Hotel Majestic, near the Étoile on the Avenue Kléber, which had been used by German forces during the Occupation. Next door was a massive reinforced concrete building which had housed their communications equipment. The main building still bore the traces of its hotel past. Former bedrooms and bathrooms became offices decorated with coloured tiles and remnants of luxury apartments such as light fixtures, a striking contrast to the bleak appearance and utilitarian furniture found in most offices. The largest bedrooms were shared by several secretaries who stored their files in the wardrobes, while middle grade professionals were put in disused bathrooms, using the bathtubs to store their papers. But despite the less than ideal working conditions, UNESCO's small staff all knew each other and worked together on co-operative projects."[5]

12 AM The Imprimerie Union has an interesting history. Founded in 1909 by Russian immigrants, who had previously worked in the printing office of the Social Democratic Party of Lenin, which was in Paris until 1912, it changed its name from Kooperativnaïa typografia soïouz to the French Imprimerie Union in 1913. The first ten years were mainly devoted to the printing of newspapers of the different political tendencies of the Russian community in Paris. From the 1920s on, Imprimerie Union printed the main art magazines of the period: *Les Arts à Paris* by Paul Guillaume (1918–1935), *Action* by Florent Fels and Marcel Sauvage (1920–1922), *Oudar* by Serge Romoff (1922–1924), *Les Cahiers d'art* by Christian Zervos (1926–1933). The Surrealists regularly used the printing presses from the last issue of *La Révolution Surréaliste* (December 1929), and the whole of *Surréalisme au service de la révolution*, as well as half the editions of *Minotaure* magazine, were printed there.[6]

11 AM

Published in 1953 by the United Nations
Educational, Scientific and Cultural Organization
19 avenue Kléber, Paris-16e
Printed by Imprimerie Union, Paris

12 AM

Printed in France
CUA. 52. X. 5 A

THIS IS THE OTHER SIDE OF THE
TITLE PAGE, THAT GIVES YOU INFORMATION
LIKE WHO PUBLISHED IT AND WHEN,
IF IT'S COPYRIGHTED OR NOT, AND WHERE
OR WHEN MAYBE, AND PERHAPS A
REFERENCE NUMBER, IF NOT MORE
(text on p. 6)

13KE Logistics. The foreword creates impact. The authors have their fingers on the pulse. The *Manual* is underpinned by an educational credo. The contents page promises scientific fastidiousness, its tabs reveal a regulative authority. The typography of the text section is enunciated by a slender scale of nuances – the typographic consistency is based on density, expediency, orientation.

14AM *"Australian Aboriginal Culture,* the first exhibition prepared by a member state and offered through UNESCO for circulation to its other member states, began its two-year tour of the United States of America, the first country it is arranged to visit, in June 1953. It opened at the Buffalo Museum of Science, at the time of the American Association of Museums annual meeting. More than 300 museum workers, attending that conference from all parts of the United States of America and Canada, found the exhibition interesting alike for its contents and for the care and ingenuity with which it had been designed for travelling. [...] The exhibition consists of twenty-four panels, each one is six feet wide by four feet tall. Every panel has a frame, which is shallow at the top and sloping at the bottom to form a ten-inch shelf for the display of three-dimensional objects and to protect the projecting material mounted elsewhere on the panels. Directions are furnished for packing the panels face to face in designated pairs to form strong boxes 6"x4"x10", of which each two fit snugly into a heavy packing case for shipment. The panels are easily and quickly installed for exhibiting by being screwed on the light but sturdy tubular steel stands provided. They may be arranged in various ways to suit the space available, against a wall, in a free standing line, in pairs facing in one direction, or back to back according to convenience. They are attractively coloured flat grey mounted with sepia toned photographs for the panels, glossy grey for the inner surface of the frames and green on all exterior surfaces".[7]

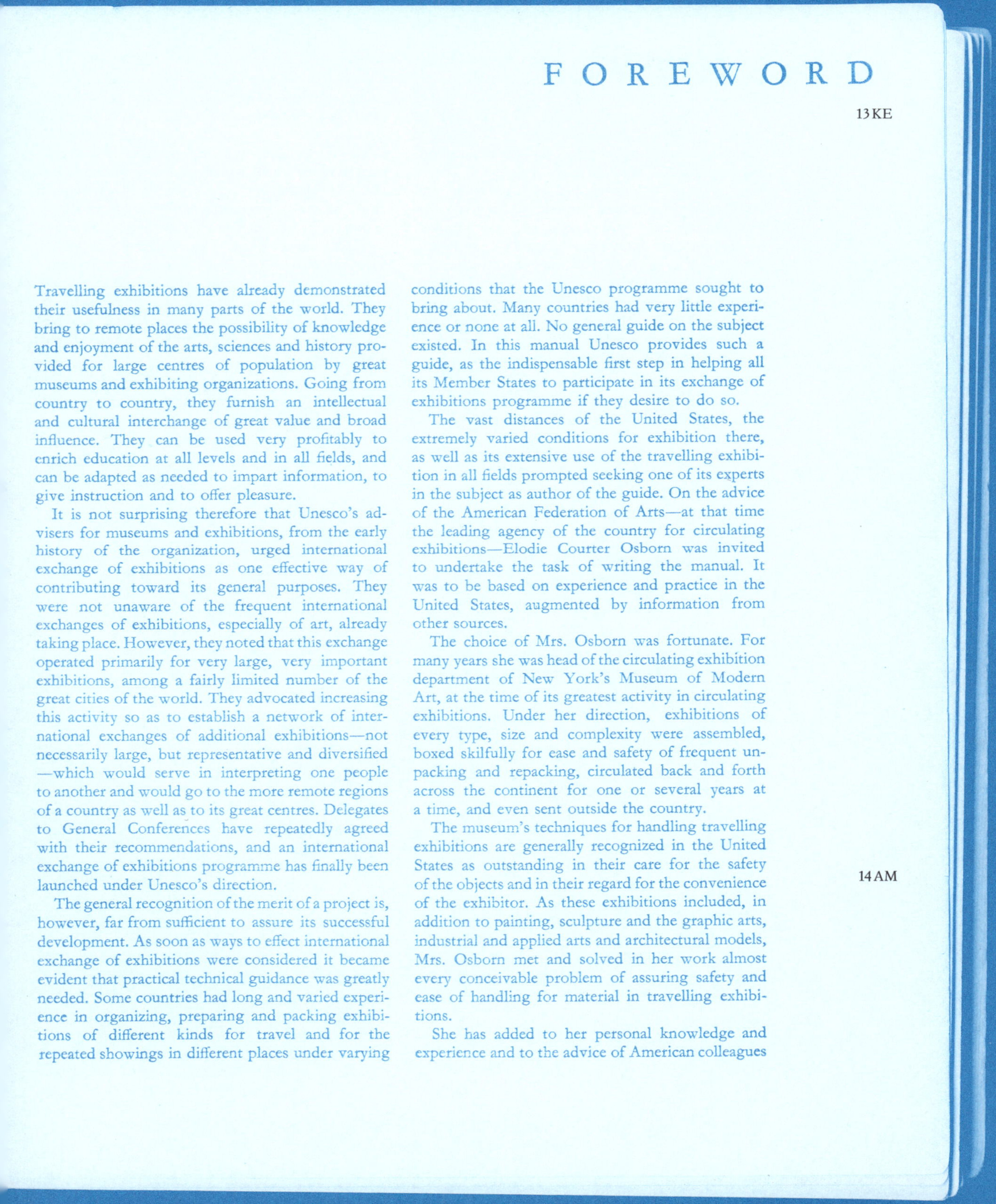

FOREWORD

13KE

Travelling exhibitions have already demonstrated their usefulness in many parts of the world. They bring to remote places the possibility of knowledge and enjoyment of the arts, sciences and history provided for large centres of population by great museums and exhibiting organizations. Going from country to country, they furnish an intellectual and cultural interchange of great value and broad influence. They can be used very profitably to enrich education at all levels and in all fields, and can be adapted as needed to impart information, to give instruction and to offer pleasure.

It is not surprising therefore that Unesco's advisers for museums and exhibitions, from the early history of the organization, urged international exchange of exhibitions as one effective way of contributing toward its general purposes. They were not unaware of the frequent international exchanges of exhibitions, especially of art, already taking place. However, they noted that this exchange operated primarily for very large, very important exhibitions, among a fairly limited number of the great cities of the world. They advocated increasing this activity so as to establish a network of international exchanges of additional exhibitions—not necessarily large, but representative and diversified —which would serve in interpreting one people to another and would go to the more remote regions of a country as well as to its great centres. Delegates to General Conferences have repeatedly agreed with their recommendations, and an international exchange of exhibitions programme has finally been launched under Unesco's direction.

The general recognition of the merit of a project is, however, far from sufficient to assure its successful development. As soon as ways to effect international exchange of exhibitions were considered it became evident that practical technical guidance was greatly needed. Some countries had long and varied experience in organizing, preparing and packing exhibitions of different kinds for travel and for the repeated showings in different places under varying conditions that the Unesco programme sought to bring about. Many countries had very little experience or none at all. No general guide on the subject existed. In this manual Unesco provides such a guide, as the indispensable first step in helping all its Member States to participate in its exchange of exhibitions programme if they desire to do so.

The vast distances of the United States, the extremely varied conditions for exhibition there, as well as its extensive use of the travelling exhibition in all fields prompted seeking one of its experts in the subject as author of the guide. On the advice of the American Federation of Arts—at that time the leading agency of the country for circulating exhibitions—Elodie Courter Osborn was invited to undertake the task of writing the manual. It was to be based on experience and practice in the United States, augmented by information from other sources.

The choice of Mrs. Osborn was fortunate. For many years she was head of the circulating exhibition department of New York's Museum of Modern Art, at the time of its greatest activity in circulating exhibitions. Under her direction, exhibitions of every type, size and complexity were assembled, boxed skilfully for ease and safety of frequent unpacking and repacking, circulated back and forth across the continent for one or several years at a time, and even sent outside the country.

The museum's techniques for handling travelling exhibitions are generally recognized in the United States as outstanding in their care for the safety of the objects and in their regard for the convenience of the exhibitor. As these exhibitions included, in addition to painting, sculpture and the graphic arts, industrial and applied arts and architectural models, Mrs. Osborn met and solved in her work almost every conceivable problem of assuring safety and ease of handling for material in travelling exhibitions. 14AM

She has added to her personal knowledge and experience and to the advice of American colleagues

15 AM "The programme of the Museums and Monuments Division (later known as the Division for Cultural Property and currently the Division of Cultural Heritage) included several new projects. One was the publication of the 'Museums and Monuments' series".[8]

16 AM "Grace McCann Morley was the founding director of the San Francisco Museum of Art in 1935, the country's second museum devoted solely to modern art. In 1945, the San Francisco Museum of Art was the place of the United Nations Conference on International Organisation at which the United Nations Charter was signed. During the two month long conference, the museum was obliged to move to a temporary facility and returned to its original location upon the signing of the United Nations Charter. In 1946, Morley was asked by the State Department to serve on the UNESCO Secretariat as a consultant on museums and libraries for the charter meeting in Paris. For the next three years, she worked for UNESCO, travelling to Germany to consult with French, British and American authorities about the return of stolen artworks."[9]

as much information on the subject as she and the officials of Unesco's Division of Museums and Historic Monuments could gather from other sources throughout the world. This manual is, therefore, the most complete survey of all aspects of travelling exhibitions yet made, though Mrs. Osborn has emphasized that it is to be considered only a first statement which should be augmented and supplemented as others provide additional information, comment and suggestions. It supplies, however, a thoroughly practical guide for travelling exhibitions in general, with the special attention to their international movement that Unesco's concern with the problems of crossing frontiers prompts. Though the majority of examples used are drawn from the field of the arts, the principles, as Mrs. Osborn herself states, are applicable to all objects that can be used in exhibitions. Their success for the safe and efficient handling of art objects, generally likely to be fragile and of great value, assures their usefulness for other fields where loss or damage is perhaps not as tragic but is equally to be avoided. This manual, therefore, will greatly help all those who organize exhibitions of any kind. Museum experts who already are familiar with most or all of the techniques described have reason to rejoice that the benefits of travelling exhibitions, within frontiers as well as across them, will become more accessible to their colleagues everywhere under this practical guidance. Everyone, indeed, concerned with exhibitions will be grateful to Unesco for making generally available the best information on the subject by producing this publication.

GRACE L. MCCANN MORLEY
San Francisco Museum of Art

15 AM
16 AM

This tells who the book is dedicated to.
(text on p. 7)

CONTENTS

THIS COULD BE THE CONTENTS PAGE, UNLESS THERE'S ONE LATER
(text on p. 9)

17KE Communication vessels. Despite its dense design and diminutive typography, a breeze of mobility, expansion, and enterprise is carried throughout the *Manual*. Viewed typologically it is a compendium with a small-print character, and invites comparisons with Marcel Duchamp's portable monograph *Boîtes-en-valise* (see also *You and Your Neighbourhood*, ↪ 103). The leap into the next dimension—a rezoom such as in *Powers of Ten* by Ray and Charles Eames—is marked by the table of the UNESCO National Distributors, which spans 75 cities across 6 continents ↪ 120.

Between the foreword and the introduction, the *Manual* grants a prominent place to its prestigious collaborators: in the acknowledgments sections, the author specifically mentions the contributions of her five closest consultants. With them she emphasises the California—New York—France axis: the illustrious addresses of the San Francisco Museum of Art, the Metropolitan Museum of Art, New York, the Museum of Modern Art, New York, and UNESCO, Paris. She lists over 20 contributors and their affiliated institutions (all but two are US-based) who contributed information, photographs, or diagrams, and documents that connected UNESCO (outside of the USA) with ministries, museums and galleries in locations from Glasgow to Zurich, via London, Melbourne, Paris, Peshawar, Reims, Rome, São Paolo, and Warsaw.

18AM Out of the 27 named individuals, 23 worked for US American companies or art institutions, the majority of which were based in New York. Only three represented European museums: Douglas Allen, the director of the Royal Scottish Museum, Edinburgh, who organised the UNESCO workshop *The Role of Museums in Education*, 1952 in New York, Torsten Althin, the Director of the Swedish National Museum of Science and Technology, and Peter Floud, Keeper of Circulation at the Victoria and Albert Museum, London. Any expertise from other parts of the world was absent. An internationalist position was taken by Raymonde Frin, who was the very first editor of *Museum*, presiding over its destiny from its founding in 1948 until her retirement from UNESCO in 1972. Several technical and administrative questions were covered by registrars like Robert P. Sugden from the Metropolitan Museum of Art, New York, who wrote two books on handling and safeguarding works of art, and Dorothy Dudley from the MoMA, who was involved in the drafting of an amendment to the Tariff Law that facilitated the free import of art works. Leslie Cheek, Director of the Virginia Museum of Fine Arts, transformed the museum from a small local gallery to a nationally known cultural centre. Cheek's innovations included, in 1953, the world's first *Artmobile*, a mobile tractor-trailer that housed exhibits with the purpose of reaching rural areas.

A number of prominent designers stood out among those acknowledged, e.g. Herbert Bayer, who was an important figure in the dissemination of Bauhaus Modernism in the USA, especially through his design of the first Bauhaus exhibition at MoMA in 1938. He relocated to Aspen in 1946, building the Aspen Design Institute together with businessman and philanthropist Walter Paepcke and also with designer and expert in colour theory Egbert Jacobson.

An influential figure from MoMA was Edgar Kaufmann, an architectural historian, curator and philanthropist. He was an apprentice in Frank Lloyd Wright's Taliesin Fellowship before he joined the Museum of Modern Art, where he served for several years as director of the Department of Industrial Design. He was particularly interested in the relationship between design and everyday life, and took charge of the museum's series of exhibitions of household objects of high quality design. Kaufmann's father, the owner of the prominent Kaufmann's Department Store in Pittsburgh, commissioned two modern architectural masterpieces, Fallingwater, designed by Frank Lloyd Wright and the Kaufmann House in Palm Springs, designed by Richard Neutra.

17KE
18AM

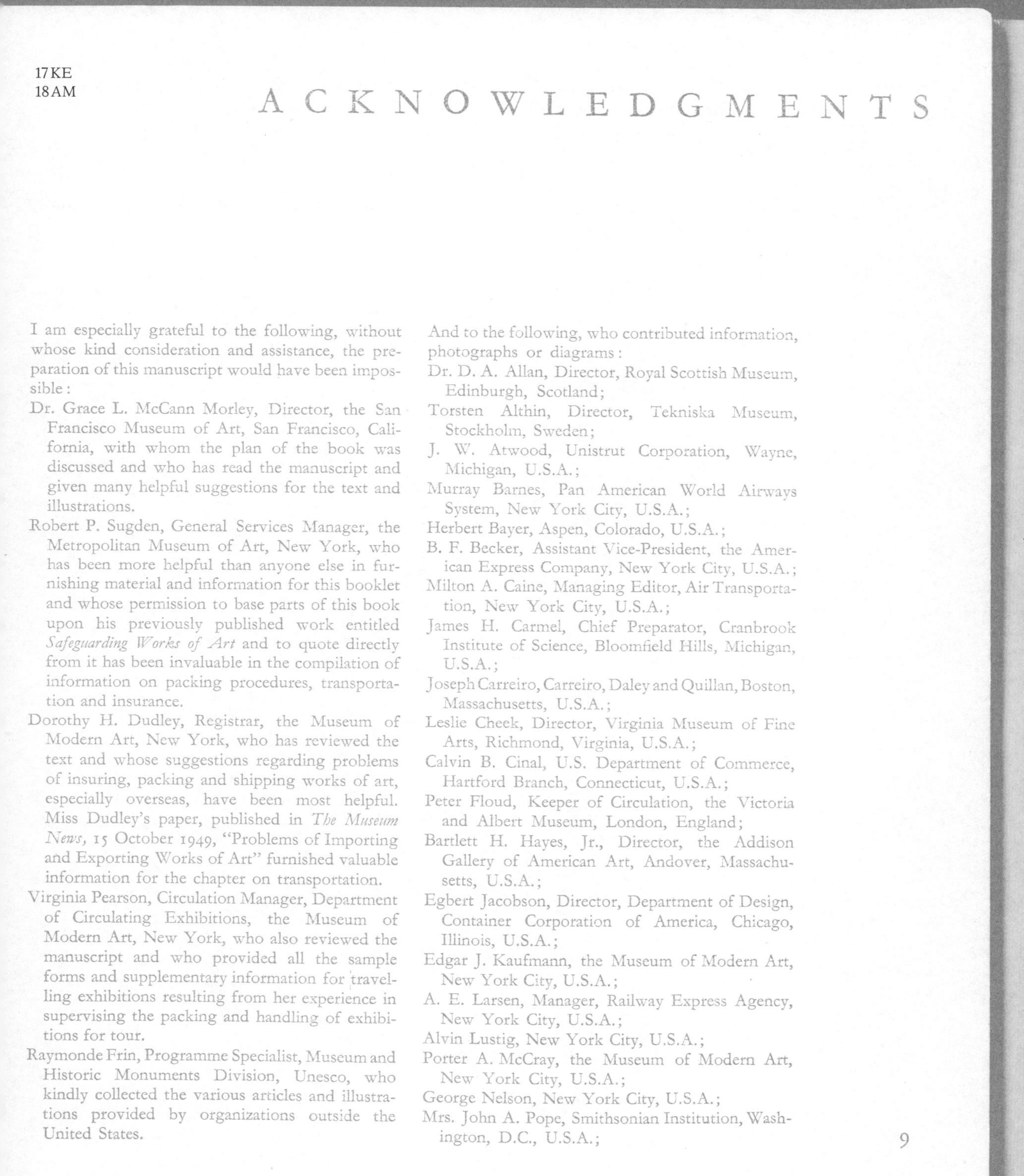

ACKNOWLEDGMENTS

I am especially grateful to the following, without whose kind consideration and assistance, the preparation of this manuscript would have been impossible:

Dr. Grace L. McCann Morley, Director, the San Francisco Museum of Art, San Francisco, California, with whom the plan of the book was discussed and who has read the manuscript and given many helpful suggestions for the text and illustrations.

Robert P. Sugden, General Services Manager, the Metropolitan Museum of Art, New York, who has been more helpful than anyone else in furnishing material and information for this booklet and whose permission to base parts of this book upon his previously published work entitled *Safeguarding Works of Art* and to quote directly from it has been invaluable in the compilation of information on packing procedures, transportation and insurance.

Dorothy H. Dudley, Registrar, the Museum of Modern Art, New York, who has reviewed the text and whose suggestions regarding problems of insuring, packing and shipping works of art, especially overseas, have been most helpful. Miss Dudley's paper, published in *The Museum News*, 15 October 1949, "Problems of Importing and Exporting Works of Art" furnished valuable information for the chapter on transportation.

Virginia Pearson, Circulation Manager, Department of Circulating Exhibitions, the Museum of Modern Art, New York, who also reviewed the manuscript and who provided all the sample forms and supplementary information for travelling exhibitions resulting from her experience in supervising the packing and handling of exhibitions for tour.

Raymonde Frin, Programme Specialist, Museum and Historic Monuments Division, Unesco, who kindly collected the various articles and illustrations provided by organizations outside the United States.

And to the following, who contributed information, photographs or diagrams:

Dr. D. A. Allan, Director, Royal Scottish Museum, Edinburgh, Scotland;

Torsten Althin, Director, Tekniska Museum, Stockholm, Sweden;

J. W. Atwood, Unistrut Corporation, Wayne, Michigan, U.S.A.;

Murray Barnes, Pan American World Airways System, New York City, U.S.A.;

Herbert Bayer, Aspen, Colorado, U.S.A.;

B. F. Becker, Assistant Vice-President, the American Express Company, New York City, U.S.A.;

Milton A. Caine, Managing Editor, Air Transportation, New York City, U.S.A.;

James H. Carmel, Chief Preparator, Cranbrook Institute of Science, Bloomfield Hills, Michigan, U.S.A.;

Joseph Carreiro, Carreiro, Daley and Quillan, Boston, Massachusetts, U.S.A.;

Leslie Cheek, Director, Virginia Museum of Fine Arts, Richmond, Virginia, U.S.A.;

Calvin B. Cinal, U.S. Department of Commerce, Hartford Branch, Connecticut, U.S.A.;

Peter Floud, Keeper of Circulation, the Victoria and Albert Museum, London, England;

Bartlett H. Hayes, Jr., Director, the Addison Gallery of American Art, Andover, Massachusetts, U.S.A.;

Egbert Jacobson, Director, Department of Design, Container Corporation of America, Chicago, Illinois, U.S.A.;

Edgar J. Kaufmann, the Museum of Modern Art, New York City, U.S.A.;

A. E. Larsen, Manager, Railway Express Agency, New York City, U.S.A.;

Alvin Lustig, New York City, U.S.A.;

Porter A. McCray, the Museum of Modern Art, New York City, U.S.A.;

George Nelson, New York City, U.S.A.;

Mrs. John A. Pope, Smithsonian Institution, Washington, D.C., U.S.A.;

9

Edgar P. Richardson, Director, the Detroit Institute of Arts, Detroit, Michigan, U.S.A.;
Mrs. Emily Tremaine, the Miller Company, Meriden, Connecticut, U.S.A.

The Arts Council of Great Britain;
Glasgow Art Gallery and Museums;
Kunstgewerbe Museum, Zürich, Switzerland;
The Museum of Modern Art, São Paulo, Brazil;
Ministry of Public Instruction, Rome, Italy;
Muzeum Narodowe, Warsaw, Poland;
Museum of Rheims, France;
National Gallery of Victoria, Melbourne, Australia;
Palais de la découverte, Paris, France;
Peshawar Museum, North-West Frontier Province, Pakistan.

19AM Is "vigorous exchange of cultural material" a euphemism for the looting and capturing of artworks during the Second World War? In a very cynical sense, both the measures of safeguarding works from being damaged in acts of war and the stealing of captured artworks from museums in occupied countries were logistical challenges that contributed to the pragmatic knowledge about the transport of fragile goods.

20AM The idea of communication based on visual means rather than on language was a convenient fit for the internationalist agenda of UNESCO in the early 1950s. Visual communication was considered a universal form of communication, which could overcome conventional language barriers. This optimism about visual communication shared by UNESCO was based on the problematic assumption that unlike language, visual signs would be universally understood and interpreted in the same way. A pioneering work of visual communication was György Kepes, *Language of Vision*, published in 1944. It stated that "Visual communication is universal and international; it knows no limits of tongue, vocabulary, or grammar, and it can be perceived by the illiterate as well as by the literate." The book predated three other influential texts on the same subject: Paul Rand, *Thoughts on Design* (1946); László Moholy-Nagy, *Vision in Motion* (1947); and Rudolf Arnheim; *Art and Visual Perception* (1954).

INTRODUCTION

We tend to think of museums solely as repositories for works of art, principally those of the past, and yet today many of these institutions, both large and small, share their collections with other museums, art galleries, public libraries, universities and schools. Nor do they rest on their laurels of displaying permanent collections alone, but often introduce into their galleries travelling exhibitions which bring their own activities into closer contact with their communities. Exhibitions which travel have become more and more popular, particularly during the last two decades, and since the close of the war in 1945 this activity has increased and spread internationally.

While its development has taken place recently, the idea is over a century old and its originator one of the leading museums of Great Britain, the Victoria and Albert in London. Similar activity dates in Canada from the early 20's; travelling exhibitions have been employed in the United States for the past 25 years and they have become a general policy in South Africa and Australia within the last 20 years. Museums in the following countries all make use of travelling exhibitions and the majority can report some exchange of material as well: Australia, Austria, Brazil, Canada, Czechoslovakia, Denmark, England, France, India, Ireland, Israel, Italy, Lebanon, Mexico, Netherlands, Norway, Pakistan, Poland, Scotland, Sweden, Switzerland, the United States of America, the Union of South Africa and Wales.

The prototype in England was launched in 1850 with loans of works of art from the original Victoria and Albert to the Central School of Design at Somerset House, and during the following two years the exhibition was successively shown at various provincial schools. From 1852 onwards these loan activities were directed by a separate Circulation Department. Its first efforts were concerned with the preparation of a comprehensive circulating museum comprising nearly 600 objects which toured for more than four years and was seen by no fewer than 307,000 people. After a second similar circulating museum was started on an even larger scale, the work of the department was concentrated on serving the needs of art students rather than the general public. Loans were made primarily to provincial art schools but the general demand for expansion of this service soon led the department to again undertake loans to museums and art galleries. The principle of lending a part of its treasures to the provinces has persisted ever since and today the Victoria and Albert boasts the most comprehensive facilities for this purpose. Moreover, no limitation of value, fragility or rarity is placed upon the objects which are circulated; only those items which are defined as "strictly unique and of international importance" are excluded from the loan collections. Such an example on the part of one of the principal museums of the world is an inspiration to other institutions to create educational programmes of similar merit.

It is somewhat ironic that the war years produced the most vigorous exchange of cultural materials between countries. Surely a deeper understanding 19AM
between peoples should assist in lessening tensions which ultimately flare into international conflicts. Presentation of the visual arts, the handicrafts, architecture, civic planning, scientific discoveries and achievements,[1] the history of different countries offers a means of better understanding the aspirations, customs and character of different peoples. Moreover, the diffusion of knowledge for education in all fields—natural science, history, health, science, art, etc.—can be accomplished effectively through exhibitions. Visual presentation offers an international means of communication in which 20AM
language barriers begin to disappear. Information can be exchanged, problems and subjects common to several nations can be studied and through such exhibitions gain wide public attention. It is hoped that a greatly expanded programme of exchange of

[1] See fig. 1, page 73.

11

THIS IS THE FIRST PAGE OF THE BOOK.
(text on p. 11)

↩145 THE PROTOTYPE: THE V&A DEPARTMENT OF CIRCULATION
↩149 DRAFT SCRIPT OF A RADIO: INTERVIEW WITH PETER FLOUD
↩155 THE LANGUAGE OF THE WORLD MUSEUM

21 AM ICOM, the International Council of Museums, was founded in 1946 as a reaction to the damage and loss of cultural goods during the Second World War. It is a non-governmental organisation maintaining formal relations with UNESCO. The joint UNESCO-ICOM Information Centre, created in 1946, is situated in the UNESCO headquarters in Paris. The collections consist of the publications by ICOM and UNESCO—in particular those that concern the protection of cultural heritage. In addition, the centre holds national legislations on the protection of cultural heritage, international and national museum directories, publications related to illicit traffic of cultural property and reports, as well as publications on endangered heritage in emergency situations.

exhibitions may be fostered through the offices of the United Nations Educational, Scientific and Cultural Organization (Unesco). In each of its programmes since its inception, resolutions have been adopted designed to encourage exchange of exhibitions between Member States.[1] While Unesco is unable to undertake financial or other responsibilities of selection, securing, preparing and circulating exhibitions, it is allowed full scope in promoting exhibition exchange by lending whatever aid and facilities its international connexions in the museum world may provide. Assisted by the International Council of Museums (ICOM), Unesco is also able to furnish considerable technical information.

21 AM

One important development which has taken place since the museum loan service was introduced a hundred years ago is the completely "packaged" travelling exhibition. This type of exhibition arrives with its own installation units ready to set up, its labels properly attached and its component parts easily removable from packing cases requiring a minimum of effort from the host museum staff. The sudden expansion of this type of service during the war, particularly through government agencies, points to sincere interest in exchange programmes, and many methods of achieving first-rate exhibitions without the use of valuable, rare or fragile articles have been devised. Such shows now originate in museums, in art galleries, art schools, universities, clubs, and in industrial organizations, and government agencies. They are often assembled by offices whose sole purpose is to collect material, prepare it for display and pack it for safe shipment.

Since the war there has been an increased awareness of the necessity and the moral obligation to extend educational opportunities and to make cultural values more readily accessible to all, without regard to social distinction or geographic isolation. There have been efforts to provide in newer countries which lack great accumulations of art and other cultural treasures, even for their outlying areas, the advantages which centres of older civilizations enjoy.[2] With this emphasis on the need for bringing fundamental education to all the peoples of the world, which Unesco has done much to contribute toward meeting, the usefulness of the travelling exhibition has been enormously broadened.

The possibility of even more widespread use of the travelling exhibition as a medium for the dissemination of information has prompted the publication of this book. While it is confined to methods of safely and effectively displaying objects in travelling exhibitions and to the systems which have proved successful to date of packing works of art or other material held by art museums, the principles may nevertheless apply to institutions and organizations whose collections cover other fields such as history, science or natural science.

The material contained in the following pages is in no sense representative of practices in use in all museums or circulating agencies, for it was necessary to rely upon the information which could be assembled in a short time to supplement the author's experience. It is to be hoped that publication of this material will encourage others whose experience offers equally effective and satisfactory methods to send information to Unesco's office in Paris as a basis for further, more complete and more inclusive studies in the same field.

---

1 Resolution 4.4232 of the Programme for 1952, authorized the Director-General:

"To encourage Member States to prepare and to circulate, in co-operation with the appropriate professional organizations, including the International Council of Museums (ICOM) and international organizations of artists, exhibitions to travel from country to country, especially exhibitions having an international appeal on account of their subject and character."

In response to a circular letter (CL/401 of August 1950), a considerable number of Member States listed exhibitions which they would undertake to prepare, or to have prepared, to be sent to other countries wishing to borrow them.

The above text is from the Annex to a circular letter to Member States (CL/589 of January 1952) entitled "Explanatory Note on Preparation and Circulation of Exhibitions by Member States" published by Unesco.

This letter has prompted further offers of specific exhibitions from Member States. By the end of 1952 some tours of internationally circulating exhibitions will be in operation.

2 The director of the National Art Gallery of New South Wales, Sydney, writes that pioneer efforts in Australia have been undertaken with government support since 1944 bringing exhibitions to remote country centres "to diffuse a knowledge of, and an interest in, the visual arts, and more particularly the Australian arts as they affect our people". During the first three years, exhibitions had to be accommodated in town halls, school assembly rooms, churches, stores, barber's shops, restaurants and other available spaces. After five years of this service, however, a number of the centres now plan to build art galleries to accommodate travelling exhibitions. The government plans also to provide railway carriages, stripped of their furnishings, to be used as travelling galleries to serve centres economically.

12

THIS IS THE FIRST PAGE OF THE BOOK.
(text on p. 12)

I. TRAVELLING EXHIBITIONS

ORIGINS

The circulating exhibition has come into being for two principal reasons: the usefulness of temporary exhibitions to museums and the educational opportunities offered by a concentrated collection of material on one or more related subjects. The value of loan collections to the provincial museums has been widely proclaimed.[1] They overcome the lack of space, funds and staff which, in the small museum, are handicaps to setting up a series of its own temporary exhibitions, and the continuous flow of first-rate material—whether of history, science or art—through its galleries provides a rich and varied programme far beyond any that could be provided by its own collections. And even for the large museums, with almost unlimited sources upon which to draw, temporary exhibitions present difficulty. Their staff, concentrating principally on the work of preservation, may lack the time or interest required to prepare a series of temporary exhibitions, for they demand considerable research, documentation and publicity as well as the physical work of setting up the objects for display *(figs. 1, 2 and 2a, pages 73, 74)*. Further, museums offer various specialities and no one museum can cover all subjects. Consequently the travelling exhibition organized by a number of participating museums according to their individual specializations permits more efficient use of scholarship and skills for the benefit of all. The introduction of temporary exhibitions into its programme may also create, among the staff as well as the public, a more awakened interest in the relationship between various civilizations of the past and that of our own time.

Up to the present, circulating exhibitions have been principally restricted to art, though many of the same principles could be applied to other fields—for example, science, history and natural science—in development of their own resources for educational purposes *(figs. 3, 3a, 4, pages 75, 76)*.

Travelling exhibitions may originate in various ways:

1. The richly endowed museum, overflowing with material, may wish to send out a series of travelling exhibitions which utilize a larger proportion of its permanent collections than can be displayed in its own galleries. They thus provide an active educational programme for its own staff and at the same time enrich the provincial museum or other organization to which they are dispatched. A community service is thus accomplished by both participating institutions to their mutual benefit.
2. A group of museums may collaborate in organizing an exhibition circulating it in turn among them. Often this type of co-operation is prompted by the difficulty of financing a large loan collection assembled from many distant points. The recent retrospective exhibitions of the work of Cézanne and Matisse in America, and of Monet in Europe, are examples of this kind of collaborative effort.[2]

   The participating museums share the benefits of assembling a unique collection and divide the costs of travel, research, transport, packing, insurance, catalogues or other incidental expenses between them. By sharing costs, exhibitions of higher quality, greater comprehensiveness and more thorough documentation may result. These collaborative exhibitions are usually undertaken among fairly large museums which normally have adequate staff capable of handling installations individually adapted to their own galleries,

---

[1] An excellent statement on the reliance of museums in the United Kingdom on the circulating exhibition is made by Dr. D. A. Allan in *Museum*, vol. III, No. 4, 1950, pp. 304-12.

[2] *Cézanne* shown in New York and Chicago; *Matisse* in Cleveland, Chicago, San Francisco and New York; *Monet* in Zürich, The Hague and Paris.

THIS IS THE PAGE WITH TEXT ON IT.
(text on p. 13)

22MK Although they have a determining influence on the project, production costs and exhibition budgets are often severely underestimated (see *Manual* p. 16: "Fee for exhibition $150"). As this important factor is often only discussed at the end of proceedings, it's all the more admirable and welcome that here in the *Manual* it is mentioned in a prominent position in the first chapter.

and therefore no packing or installation of the easily re-usable kind is employed. This kind of co-operative planning offers to the smaller museums possibilities for increasing their services as well as means of attaining more important exhibitions.

3. Sometimes the interest aroused in a large and important collection prompts a museum to prepare for circulation a similar exhibition composed of reproductions of the original material. Such exhibitions take advantage of the research necessitated by the original collections and many institutions other than museums find them useful to rent *(fig. 5, page 77)*. Schools and colleges in particular can thus supplement their courses or they may tie them in with special lectures or other events. The difficulties of exhibiting and handling valuable works of art or other treasures are avoided, and yet the stimulating experience of seeing first-rate works, even in reproduction, is always educationally worth while.
4. Finally, circulating exhibitions may be organized and circulated by an agency or museum specializing in this service.[1] To provide travelling exhibitions which maintain the standards set by museums and allow of installation with the least effort on the part of the subscribing institution demands well thought-out preparation on the part of the agency. Unable to call upon the services of a curatorial staff, or to take advantage of the research done for a museum exhibition, such agencies often employ experts to assemble, document and design their travelling exhibitions. In such cases, costs may run higher than for a similar show prepared by a museum whose staff can contribute valuable time. To avoid such added costs, agencies often take over an exhibition assembled by a museum, reorganize it and circulate it. Or, an agency may commission a museum to prepare an exhibition which it thinks would be widely used by other museums and like organizations.
5. Certain museums maintain a department of education whose staff is employed to assemble all types of materials for use by schools, clubs or other organizations. Interpretative exhibitions may be shown in the museum itself *(fig. 5a, page 78)* often based upon objects in the museum collection; travelling exhibitions, lectures, publications, slide-talks, filmstrips, motion pictures, radio and television programmes are prepared to permit the widest possible use of the educational material *(fig. 6, page 79)*.

COSTS

22MK

The costs of preparing and circulating travelling exhibitions may be divided among participating exhibitors in different ways. The most frequent methods are:

1. If an institution has developed a programme of circulating exhibitions as a part of its educational activities, the costs of curatorial and administrative time are not usually reflected in the rental fees charged to subscribers. Sometimes museums are even able to absorb costs of preparation as well. In such instances, costs of transport and insurance are usually the only expenses assumed by the borrowing institutions. In order to keep these at a minimum, the exhibition must be efficiently routed between exhibitors so that the shortest distances are traversed. Often exhibitors have to accept second or third choice of exhibition dates in order to enable the most economical tour to be arranged.
2. If an institution or agency's service of travelling exhibitions is organized on a self-supporting basis, all costs must be lumped together and a rental fee arrived at by dividing the number of possible showings into the total sum. An exhibition composed of photographs or other reproductions which have been purchased, rather than of originals on loan, can be extended over a longer period than is possible in the case of borrowed works, and longer than it is advisable to subject originals to the hazards of travel. Thus costs to subscribers may be substantially reduced.

SCHEDULING

In addition to finding a basis for loan fees, it is necessary to establish a schedule of exhibition dates

1 Several agencies exist in the United States: The American Federation of Arts, the Western Association of Art Museum Directors and the Museum of Modern Art among others. In England, the Arts Council and the British Council, with support from the government carry out a similar service abroad. Many museums in various countries including Australia, Brazil, Canada, England, France, Israel, Mexico, Pakistan, Poland, Scotland, Sweden and the United States prepare exhibitions for national or regional circulation.

14

23 MK The fact that the means of transport itself becomes the exhibition space – the *Manual* draws attention to a converted bus – is an inspired thought. It prompts my vague recollection of seeing a Mini Cooper parked in front of Art Basel in the 1990s, which was being used to showcase the programme of one of the galleries that hadn't been accepted to the fair. That vehicles had been used to instrumentalise artworks and exhibitions in a broader sense was nothing new. In 1975, for example, BMW launched a series of 18 so-called "art cars", whose bodies were painted by renowned artists (the first was by Alexander Calder, the most recent by John Baldessari in 2016). In turn, for the first Skulptur Projekte Münster, Michael Asher inconspicuously parked a 4,56-metre-long caravan with drawn curtains and closed doors in 19 different locations during the 19-week exhibition (something that was repeated during the four subsequent editions of this exhibition project). He stated: "It was intended to create the impression that the trailer was an integral part of its surroundings, rather than an entity in or of itself." Here, the caravan was an ambiguous placeholder: as both a sculpture in the public realm and as a temporal indicator of the duration of the exhibition. In the *Manual of Travelling Exhibitions*, the subject of travel itself (wandering, the route to art) is not covered in much depth, although this is sometimes of great relevance – as in the case of La Congiunta, a museum on the outskirts of the southern Swiss village of Giornico (first exit after the Gotthard Tunnel on the Ticino side). This extremely spartan building, designed by Peter Märkli and built using in-situ poured cement, solely exhibits bronze reliefs and sculptures by the sculptor Hans Josephsohn. The museum has no air conditioning, electric lighting, exact opening times, and no staff. To visit you have to first pick up the key from a nearby village bar. The journey through the tunnel, the Alpine landscape, the bar, and the museum architecture all have a significant influence on the nature of perception and the overall experience of the exhibition.

well in advance of a tour in order to offer exhibitors maximum service. Announcement by letter to probable exhibitors is the most frequent method of arranging a series of successive showings. It is well to have in mind approximate dates and to ask exhibitors to make several choices in order to arrange an efficient schedule. Generally, it is unwise to send a collection of valuable works of art on tour for more than six successive showings without having the exhibition returned to its source for thorough checking over of its contents, for repairs and for repacking when necessary. This applies, of course, only to somewhat fragile or to valuable materials. The period of the tour can be extended when materials can withstand continual shipping, or when arrangements can be made for thorough checking and reconditioning at a reliable institution on the schedule.

Normally, museums wish to schedule exhibitions for one month to six weeks at a time. Smaller organizations, taking less extensive collections, exhibit them for two weeks to one month. Sufficient time should be allowed between scheduled showings for packing, transport, unpacking and re-installation of collections. Factors which should be taken into account in determining the interval between showings are: size of the collection, complexities of installation, staff available for handling unpacking and installation, geographical location of showings scheduled.

Organizations offering numerous collections for tour usually issue an annual catalogue describing the exhibitions. Subjects are discussed, contents outlined, space and installation requirements listed, weight of packed show given, terms of rental and costs stated. From this descriptive material an exhibitor can usually judge the value of a collection for his own use. Fuller information, including photographs, is often available from the circulating agency. Some museums are able to exhibit their circulating collections during the summer months, allowing subscribers to register their choice of exhibitions and dates at that time.

To make clear the kind of material to be offered for international circulation among Member States, Unesco proposes to issue mimeographed texts describing not only the contents of the exhibition (listing works and artists) but also giving the texts of labels, biographies of artists, examples of publicity releases, instructions concerning preparation, packing, insurance or other pertinent details. As many illustrations as are deemed necessary to indicate the quality and type of material to be included will be reproduced either in 35 mm. photographic prints, on filmstrips or in printed plates from catalogues and included in the "prospectus" to be circulated to Member States. Full information is necessary when exhibitions are to be offered internationally, for while those who are considering exhibitions for use in their own countries may be expert in the general field, they may have little or no previous knowledge of the specific material proposed and they need to be thus informed if they are to judge its suitability and interest.

SUPERVISION OF TOUR

Since the principal problems in connexion with circulating exhibitions are packing, safe transport, the guarantee of arrival dates and assurance of practical and attractive installation under diverse conditions, constant assistance and supervision on the part of the circulating agency is required. The extent of this depends upon several factors: the staff available for this supervision; the value and rarity of the works of art on tour; the type of material to be displayed and the means of installation employed.

If the sponsoring institution has no staff member available to supervise the collection on tour, the exhibition may be turned over to an agency specializing in circulation problems.

Most subscribing institutions would prefer to have someone arrive with a loan collection, unpack and install it with a minimum of disturbance to their own routine. Such service is, however, not always feasible, although it is general practice among many museums in Europe and in Great Britain. Where distances between cities and towns are great, as in the United States, few museums can afford this procedure. In some countries government support supplies this service by paying the salaries and costs of travel for museum staff to accompany exhibitions on tour. Certain museums are not only able to send a member of their staff with a collection, but also maintain trucks which carry the collection from place to place on the circuit. Large vans have been equipped also with lighting and permanent display cases so that the means of transport becomes the exhibition hall itself *(fig. 7, page 80)*. The advantages are numerous. The tour can go to any area without fear of encountering staffs inexperienced in handling valuable works of art, the material itself has to be installed only once, the organizing institution is able to maintain a constant check on 23 MK

15

the condition of the material. The show is necessarily limited in scope, for the space inside a van is less than that offered by most galleries and the cost of equipping several such mobile galleries is considerable.

When it is impossible to send someone with the exhibition, the circulating agency should be able to prepare the exhibition in detail so that a minimum of work is required of the host museum staff. This is necessary, not only to allow the tour to run smoothly, but also to provide the circulating agency with a complete record of the location, the condition and the use to which the material is being put. For instance, the agency should be advised of each movement of the exhibition from one city to another. At each unpacking, or repacking of the material a thorough check of the condition of each object should be made and a report made to the agency.

As each new date on the tour approaches, the circulating agency may inform the gallery in which the collection is to be shown of the number of boxes to expect, the approximate date of arrival, the method of shipment. A thoroughly detailed list of contents as well as full instructions for hanging or other installation should be given well in advance of a scheduled date to prepare the participating institution for specific or unusual requirements. Photographs of the exhibition installed in various galleries are often helpful to exhibitors in planning spaces and methods of display for the travelling collection in their own institution. Sufficient flexibility should be allowed in chronological arrangement to permit the host museum staff to exercise its own judgment in arranging the display.

SCHEDULE SHEET

To keep all such details in order a schedule sheet for each exhibition may be found valuable. A sample form follows:

Name of exhibition

Total value for insurance	$50,000
Valuation per box for shipping purposes[1]	$50
Number of boxes in shipment	8
Weight of exhibition	1,200 lbs.
Fee for exhibition	$150
Period of rental	4 weeks
Number of items included	35 pictures
Space required	200 lineal feet

Showing scheduled:	Contract signed:	Form I sent:	Receipt rec'd:	Publicity sent:	Form II sent:	Shipment made:
Museum of Fine Arts Richmond, Virginia Dec. 10 to Jan. 12, 1953	Oct. 2 1952	Nov. 22	Dec. 5	8 photos 30 catalogs Dec. 7	Jan. 4	Jan. 14

With this information at hand, the circulating agency can keep a record of all data dispatched and keep in contact with each step of the work as it comes up. When an exhibition is dismantled, such a sheet offers a permanent file or index of the exhibition, number of catalogues sold, etc., for future reference.

EXHIBITION CONTRACT[2]

A contract is useful to bind agreements between the sponsoring institution or circulating agency and the exhibitor and to discourage last-minute cancellation of schedule dates. Exhibitors do not alter plans without consultation with the agency if they are bound to pay for an exhibition whether or not it is shown. The contract protects the circulating agency from loss of funds through fees calculated to pay the cost of assembling and circulating an exhibition. It is sometimes difficult or impossible to fill a cancelled engagement for an exhibition if the showing scheduled is not well in

[1] See page 49, "Transport".
[2] See Appendix A, page 57.

24MK Personally, I find labels at exhibitions often irritating. They either disturb the eye by their immediate proximity to the object, or cause confusion by being too far away. The same goes for long, descriptive texts on the wall that are awkward to read when standing. An alternative is the handout or brochure, which offers enough space for detailed information and can also be taken away. But, no rule is without its exception: for the exhibition on the Dutch graphic designers Mevis & Van Deursen and their catalogues, posters, and signage for museums at the 26th Brno Biennial in 2014, I massively expanded the content of the legend texts and enlarged them to several times that of the exhibits (80×150 cm). They not only contained information regarding title, format, year, and occasion, but also fonts used, type and thickness of paper, stitching techniques, amount of illustrations, printing methods and edition numbers, author names, publisher, printer, etc. – all details that ultimately defined the character of the printed material. This had the effect that not the printed matter itself but its characteristics came to the fore, thus becoming the actual exhibit, while the framed material became the image captions.

advance of the cancellation. (Conditions of the sample contract reproduced on page 57 include cancellation of showing at least six weeks before the scheduled opening date or the full rental fee is charged. This arrangement is for national circulation in the United States. Longer periods would be stipulated if a show were being circulated internationally.)

MAILING FORMS AND INSTRUCTIONS[1]

The mailing form (I) reproduced on page 57 is one now in use at the Museum of Modern Art, New York. It has been evolved over a number of years of experience in circulating many types of exhibitions. It obviates a long letter describing the contents in detail and gives the exhibitor a ready comprehension of the various lists enclosed.

A similar form (II) is sent prior to shipment of the exhibition to the next exhibitor and gives the institution which will ship the exhibition advance information about packing, addressing the boxes and arrangements to be made for transport.

Samples of other types of enclosures are also reproduced on pages 57-62 and their use described.

SUPPLEMENTARY INFORMATION

Labels[1]

24MK

Various types of labels useful for travelling shows have been evolved to replace catalogues published at considerable cost. Picture labels, or labels for small objects are usually merely identification tags. They may be quite concise giving only such data as—artist, dates, country of origin, title of work, medium and lender. If it is an original the name of the museum or person to whom it belongs is usually of interest.

Longer labels are indispensable for bringing out clearly the meaning or educational intention of any exhibition. They may contain biographical information, historial data or explanatory descriptions of material included. If the exhibition is composed of paintings, prints, sculpture, architectural models, or other separate objects, the labels are mounted for placing on the wall in the proper sequence referring to specific items. If the exhibition is composed of photographic or other flat material mounted on large panels, the labels may be incorporated upon the panels with the items to which they refer.

Primary considerations are *clarity of presentation* (typewritten labels can be photographed and enlarged to increase legibility; poster-size typewriters are also available with enlarged letter keys); *accuracy of information*; and *sufficient explanatory data* to supplement the visual material in the exhibition. Sponsoring institutions should realize that exhibitors who may be unfamiliar with the subjects treated in the travelling exhibition will appreciate the fullest information for use in publicity, for gallery lectures as well as for student visitors. Most circulating agencies request that their labels be hung with the exhibits as specified.

If labels are mounted on lightweight cardboard and provided with metal rings in the mounts for hanging, they can be used by each exhibitor on the circuit without having to be replaced during the tour.

Publicity

In addition to sending exhibitors suggested forms for newspaper release (Appendix A, *page 60*), it is often helpful to have other material on hand. Photographs of items included in an exhibition add interest to stories issued to newspapers and periodicals. Photographs can be taken by the circulating agency at the time the collection is assembled, the cost being included as an exhibition expense, a portion of which can be charged in the rental fee to each subscriber. If an exhibitor wishes a particular object photographed, however, such pictures are usually taken during his own showing. The usefulness of the particular picture may offset the additional expense involved. Many circulating agencies require that permission be requested before any object is photographed by exhibitors.

To make the greatest possible use of an exhibition, other means of publicity can be devised. The exhibitor may arrange a formal opening event for his own showing, planning it as a social occasion to bring in members of his own organization, or to increase the attendance at his museum by extending the invitation to other groups. He may plan a lecture related to the exhibition with slides which more fully explain the value of the material on exhibition. Many circulating agencies keep a file of slides to rent to subscribers, and often the agency can supply or suggest to lecturers motion pictures for special occasions.

Large placards designed for the travelling exhibition may be placed outside the museum or gallery in which they are to be displayed *(fig. 8, page 80)*. If funds permit, posters or handbills advertising

[1] See Appendix A, pages 57-62.

17

25 MK Catalogues are mostly conceived as an addition to an exhibition. They clarify contexts, further elucidate works, and give complementary information – and most of all appear when the budget allows. However, it is rarely the case that the catalogue is attributed its own artistic autonomy, and precisely this aspect interests me. The catalogue depicts a space with its own contentual criteria, artistic parameters, and the effects of its collaborative synergy. In the best-case scenario, it is a hybrid between an artist's book and an anthology – a book object – that could be defined as an artist's catalogue. This book typology is mostly encountered in the artist's monograph, like (from A to Z) *Michael Asher: Writings 1973–1983 On Works 1969–1979* (Halifax: The Press of the Nova Scotia College of Art and Design, 1983); *Daniel Buren: Mot á mot* (Paris: Éditions Xavier Barral, Éditions de La Martinière and Centre Pompidou, 2002) or *Heimo Zobernig: Books & Posters: Catalogue raisonné 1980–2015* (Malmö and Cologne: Malmö Konsthall, Verlag der Buchhandlung Walther König, 2016), edited by myself and Diana Baldon. In this respect, catalogues of group exhibitions become interesting when they are allowed more freedom – especially regarding the layout, as with *Live in Your Head: When Attitudes Become Form: Works – Concepts – Processes – Situations – Information* (Bern: Kunsthalle Bern, 1969, conceived as an in-progress ring-binder), *All Hawaii Entrées / Lunar Reggae* (Milano: Edizione Charta, 2006, solidly made but printed out-of-focus), or *Entropie: über das Verschwinden des Werkes* (Bolzano: Galerie Museum, 2004, with incorrectly assembled spreads whose contents are only fully readable after the book has been taken apart).

the exhibition can be printed and copies placed at various points throughout a town or city calling attention to the dates and place of exhibition.

25 MK

Catalogues

If catalogues have been published for the original showing, at least one copy should be mailed to each subscribing institution to help the exhibitor with his publicity or his labels. Some agencies send more than one copy.

In countries where costs of printing are high, the practice of preparing special catalogues for travelling exhibitions is less used. When a large loan collection is brought together, catalogues are usually published and the museum sending the exhibition on tour may offer the book to subscribing institutions on a consignment basis.[1] If the exhibition is not large, it is often preferable to document it sufficiently with wall labels so that the visitor need not buy a catalogue in order to identify objects or understand the message of the exhibition.

When an exhibition is jointly prepared by several institutions and then rotated among them, catalogues may be imprinted in advance with the names of the co-sponsors. If the order can be placed in advance of publication, each subscribing institution may have its own edition printed. In such instances, more copies are usually requested by each exhibitor. This is only possible, of course, if a tour is arranged in advance of preparing the exhibition itself.

ASSEMBLY AND DISPLAY

There are more steps in the preparation of an exhibition which will tour several cities than there are in assembling a collection for a single showing. Furthermore, the circulating agency is held responsible not only for the character of the collection on tour, but for the clarity of presentation and the safety of the contents. Individual subscribers may augment the original collection to add aesthetic enjoyment, to increase the educational value of the travelling unit, or to relate the exhibition to their own or local private or public collections, but the basic quality is established by the original institution. This institution has a responsibility to itself and also to those lending material for the travelling exhibition. It must also assume the responsibility for quality and presentation to those who subscribe to the exhibition without first examining its contents. It is interesting that the first institution to provide travelling exhibitions clearly feels this responsibility; it states that its circulation collection in no way represents "throw-outs, discarded as being unworthy of exhibition in London, or even second-class examples of lesser monetary value".[2]

The collections from the Victoria and Albert are normally circulated only in England and installed by their own staff in the provinces. Limitations might be imposed on material to be shipped overseas, or which had to be entrusted to less experienced hands. Still, the principle is maintained that it is better to substitute a photographic reproduction of a first-rate work of art than to assemble collections of second class material for tour. Many exhibitions of unusual merit and interest have been presented in photographic reproduction so that they could be shipped to institutions where expert and experienced staff are lacking.

Most circulating agencies divide their collections for tour into several groups. Exhibitors must comply with certain regulations to obtain collections in each class. One group may contain works of art of especial value for which exhibitors must guarantee particular care in handling. A second group, containing less valuable original works, may be available to schools, universities, libraries, etc. where trained personnel may not be available but where supervision will afford the necessary care in handling. Other groups will probably contain prints, photographs or other reproductions—replaceable materials—which may be offered to institutions with less experience in handling works of art.

Travelling exhibitions are generally unpacked and installed within a few days by persons unfamiliar with the contents, repacked and ready for shipment in the same time at the close of a showing. Methods of presentation vary considerably with the contents of an exhibition and must allow for adjustment to the types of spaces in which an exhibition is to be shown. The most useful kind of installation for travelling exhibitions is therefore the pre-fabricated type, adaptable to different spaces and lighting conditions. Weight, which adds

18

1 By this method the subscribing institution pays only the cost of copies sold. If unsold copies remain at the close of the exhibition, they may be returned for credit to the institution publishing the catalogues.

2 From an article entitled "The Circulation Department of the Victoria and Albert Museum" by Peter Floud in *Museum*, vol. III, no. 4, p. 300.

to shipping costs, places a limitation on the amount of supplementary material to be added to the exhibits themselves. Also, not all background features can be planned in advance. Lighting fixtures, for instance, are difficult to provide because they must conform to a variety of electrical currents, amperes, outlets, etc., in different areas where an exhibition may be scheduled. It is often necessary, therefore, to omit such fixtures and trust that the subscribing exhibitor will see that proper illumination is provided. If the type of electrical service available for an entire tour can be ascertained in advance, however, it is more effective when designing the exhibition to incorporate fixtures into the units where they are needed *(figs. 9, 9a, 9b,* and *10, pages 81, 82).*

Numerous solutions have been found for various problems related to the installation of travelling shows. Some of them, known to the author, will be illustrated in the following pages. For the sake of clarity and for reference purposes, exhibitions have been tabulated by media and suggestions for installation follow.

Extremely fragile glass, porcelain, pottery, old paintings, especially those on wood panels, old textiles, antique plaster and gilt frames and such items are usually eliminated from travelling exhibitions because such objects cannot sustain repeated handling or shipment.

PAINTINGS

Paintings are usually framed for exhibition and it has been found that they are safest in shipment when some type of frame is provided. The frames must have simple mouldings and be made of wood. The frame must project out from the surface of the canvas on all sides and on the back as well if no stretcher is provided.

It is never advisable to send on tour any type of carved plaster frame. They are too easily broken and may endanger the canvases if pieces become loosened in transit. If a frame of special value must accompany a picture, it should be packed separately, or be double-boxed (see packing instructions for paintings, *page 37,* and *diagram* L (c), *page 36*).

Frequently, special frames, simple, strong, good looking, which fit easily into slots in packing cases, are substituted for the permanent frames during the tour. They often add greatly to the appearance of a show as a whole for they give uniformity and so tend to put emphasis on the pictures.

WATERCOLOURS, DRAWINGS, PRINTS, PHOTOGRAPHS OR OTHER WORKS ON PAPER

If framed, the simplest narrow mouldings (one-half to one inch) round or flat wood, strong enough to withstand repeated packing and shipping should be used. For packing arrangements, it is advantageous to use uniform sizes of mats and frames. Oversize pictures should be framed in heavier mouldings. If presented in frames, exhibitions containing these works are usually hung on walls or screens like exhibitions of painting. The latter arrangement is necessary in many museums where plaster walls, not equipped with picture mouldings, do not permit the direct application of picture hooks or nails to walls or mouldings.

Such items can be matted to save the expense of wooden frames and cost of transportation. They may be matted individually or in groups, depending on their size and the character of the exhibition.

Even fragile and rare items may be treated in this way and, in fact, are often safer than when framed with breakable glass. Two methods of matting which have been found most successful are described:

1. If the work is unmounted, place the watercolour, print or drawing upon a large sheet of cardboard. The cardboard mount should extend at least four inches beyond the edge of the work on paper *(diagram A, page 20).*

   (Fasten the watercolour to the cardboard backing by attaching a fibrous paper such as Chinese rice paper to the top corners of the back of the watercolour. The rice paper tabs should be affixed with an adhesive which will not stain through; library flour paste appears to be the most satisfactory. Join the rice paper to the backing mount with the paste. This is done so that the watercolour or drawings will not slip away from the backing mount. If such materials cannot be used, this step may be omitted altogether because the covering mat tends to hold the work in place sufficiently.)

   Then cut a piece of celluloid (clear acetate) slightly larger (not more than one inch) than the drawing and attach this protective covering to the cardboard mount by means of cellulose "masking" tape.[1] Cut a mat with a window in it

[1] Cellulose "masking" tape is a paper product available in rolls of various widths. One side is covered with a non-water soluble adhesive with

Diagram A. MATTING A WATERCOLOUR WITH CELLULOID COVERING SHEET.

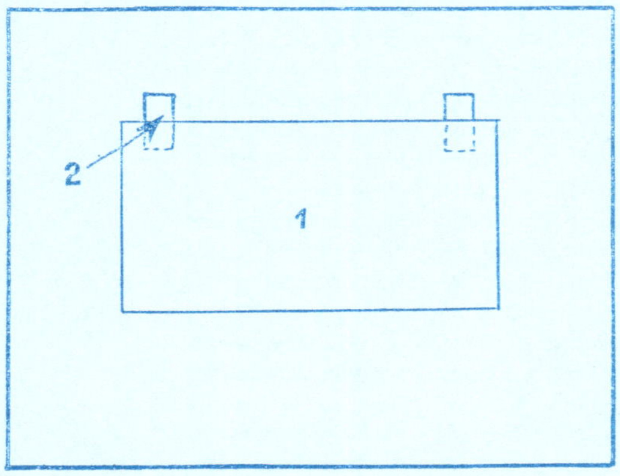

Step 1. Fasten the watercolour (1) to backing mount with rice paper tabs (2).

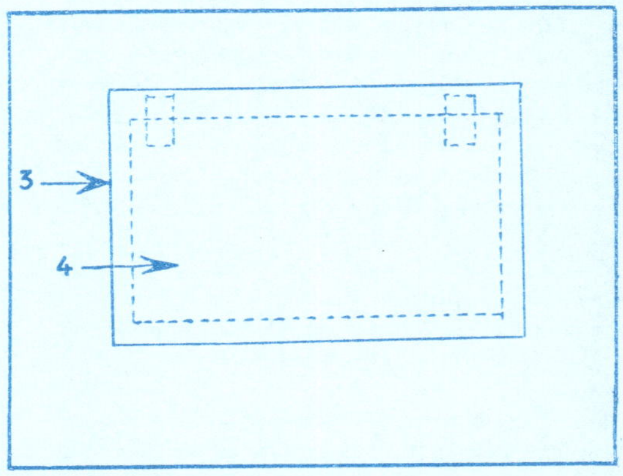

Step 2. Cut celluloid sheet (3) slightly larger than watercolour (4).

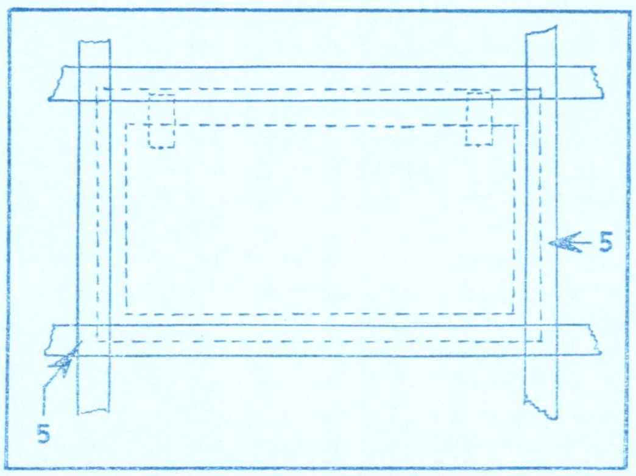

Step 3. Attach celluloid to mount with "masking" tape (5).

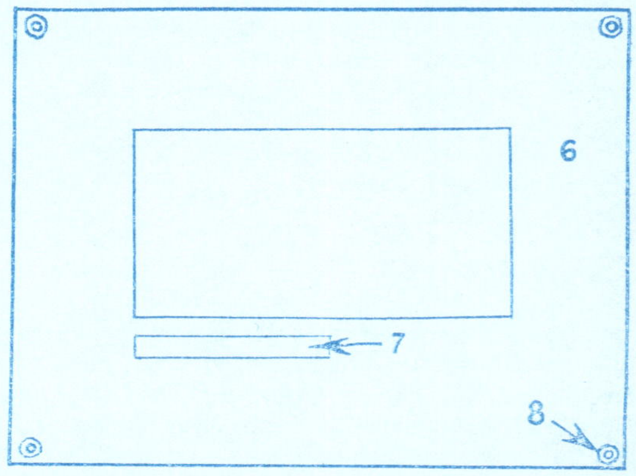

Step 4. Cut covering mat (6) size of watercolour and paste to backing mount; (7) label; (8) metal rings or "grommets".

---

strong binding qualities. Similar tapes are available in plastics. The most useful commercial product is made by the Minnesota Mining and Manufacturing Company at St. Paul, Minnesota, U.S.A. and is called Scotch Wetordry Masking Tape.

20

(fig.)
(text on p. 14)

the size of the watercolour exhibited and large enough to extend to the edges of the cardboard backing mount. Affix the window mat to the backing mount with paste so that the work of art will be "sandwiched" in between the covering mat and the cardboard backing, its surface covered with celluloid.

The celluloid must be rigid enough (thick enough) not to tear easily. The only disadvantage in this material is that some celluloids are not absolutely clear and a slight discoloration toward yellow or grey is noticeable against the work of art. The best quality of celluloid will not noticeably affect the colour of the paper and the advantage of having the work "sealed" into place for the duration of the tour may offset the slight colour disadvantage if high-grade material cannot be procured.

When the work returns from the tour, the mat can be cut apart and the drawing removed without injuring or soiling its surface in any manner. The use of thin rice paper tabs to affix the drawings to the backing mount makes it possible to lift the watercolour or drawing from the mount without tearing the work on paper itself. Tiny fibres of the rice paper may adhere to the back of the watercolour paper, but their presence is in no way injurious to the work of art. This type of mounting, recommended by museum print departments, requires skilled technicians to cut the mats cleanly and to mount the work of art carefully. It is not advisable to entrust this work to inexperienced hands.

Picture labels can often be incorporated at the lower left-hand corner or along the bottom of these mats, giving the show a neat appearance and saving exhibitors the nuisance of matching and hanging separate labels with individual works.

2. A similar method has been devised for mats which are white or light in colour and which might be soiled by handling. The celluloid is placed over the entire surface, covering mat as well as the watercolour which is mounted on a backing sheet and covered with a window mat in the same manner as described above. The celluloid is fixed to the covering mat by means of a linen, plastic or other adhesive tape which binds all three surfaces together around the edges. The work of art is again "sealed" in a dust-proof "sandwich" *(diagram A, page 20,* and *figs. 14, 14a, page 85).*

If a clear plastic is not available, glass may be substituted but great care must be taken to fasten it into place thoroughly around the edges with the binding tape. Otherwise it is safer to return to the conventional method of framing with narrow wooden mouldings.

If bindings are used around the edges, means must be provided for hanging the mounted works. Metal "grommets" (small metal eyelets or rings) can be punched through the surface of the mats. These provide places for tacks, nails, picture wire or cord to pass through without injuring the mats. If such fasteners are not available, linen tabs may be devised by gluing together several sheets of linen (or any closely-woven fabric) and cutting them into strips. The strips are then glued to the upper corners of the mats, preferably so that they do not show above the corners. These strips may be flat for use as a tacking surface, or looped if exhibitors need to hang with picture wire or cord. This form of hanger is not as durable as the metal "grommets"; often the strips pull loose from the back of the mat if they are not handled with care. But they serve the purpose if better means cannot be found and they can be replaced easily.

3. If several works of art of different sizes are to be mounted for hanging, the method described in diagram A, page 20, can also be used effectively *(fig. 13, page 84).* Labels can be mounted directly upon the mat surface. The use of painted paper or cloth letters for titles adds to the clarity of the presentation. Numerous small items can thus be grouped together for more effective display and more efficient packing.

4. A variation on this method has been carried out with sheets of heavy plastic (one-eighth to three-sixteenths of an inch plexiglas).[1] The watercolour in its mat is placed between two rigid clear plastic sheets which project beyond the outside edge of the mat on all sides. A plastic (plexiglas) filler strip three-quarters of an inch wide and the exact thickness of the mat, watercolour and backboard is inserted on all four sides. This assembly must be carried on in a room in which the relative humidity is not more than 20° to 68°. The filler strip is then cemented to the front and back plastic sheets making an entire plastic envelope impervious to dust, water and humidity[2] *(figs. 14, 14a, page 85).*

---

[1] Plexiglas is a trade name for a heavy, unbreakable, clear plastic resembling glass made by Rhom and Haas, Philadelphia, Pennsylvania, U.S.A.

[2] The method described above was an experiment carried out by the Walker Art Center, Minneapolis, Minnesota, U.S.A. for an exhibition to be

5. Enlarged photographs, made from available negatives need less protection than the previously described methods of mounting afford. Photographs may be directly attached individually or in groups, on to heavy cardboard, wood, composition board or other rigid panels. If mounted individually, it is often advisable to extend the enlarging paper beyond the edge of the mount, wrapping it around the edges and fastening it to the back of the mount. This eliminates the possibility of the edges of the photograph lifting or tearing loose from the backing mount. Rounding the corners of mounts or panels to which photographs are fixed will reduce damage to corners in handling and packing *(fig. 15, page 86)*.

SCULPTURE

The travelling exhibition of sculpture always presents problems of display because the exhibitor must have on hand enough pedestals the right size and height to show the pieces to advantage, or the circulating agency must provide them. The latter is difficult and expensive unless means can be found to transport the exhibition by van. Collapsible pedestals have been designed but even these made of plywood are expensive to construct and ship *(diagram B, page 23)*. Any lighter weight material is apt to bend or buckle with successive handling and packing and is therefore not advisable. Sometimes the exhibitors build simple pedestals made of inexpensive lightweight wood frames to which cardboard can be nailed, but they must be made sturdily to support the sculptures. They are not advisable as travelling exhibition pedestals unless the sculpture included is limited to exceedingly lightweight materials such as hollow clay, plaster casts, papier maché or some of the least dense woods.

Metal stands, collapsible for packing, such as tripods used by photographers, might be experimented with for tour. They would not be advisable, however, for sculpture of any great weight, rarity or fragility. The possibility of their tipping over or being knocked into by visitors is too great a risk to recommend their use except in special cases such as educational exhibits in which only replaceable items of no great value are used.

Very small sculptures may be mounted upon small blocks of wood which are then fastened to a wall panel, but such installations involve risks to which owners must agree before lending. The sculpture should be packed separately, the block installed on a wall panel or screen by screws attached through the back of the panel. The sculpture should be wired to the block so that there is no danger of its being removed during exhibition.

Small sculpture can be further protected in this manner by attaching a heavy plastic "vitrine" (a transparent case) to the surface of the panel. Or the panel can be converted into a wall case, with a plastic or glass face, the sculptures attached to the back of the case.

TEXTILES AND COSTUMES

Many means have been devised for exhibiting textiles but it is always difficult to show them to real advantage. Fortunately fabrics are fairly adaptable to different forms of presentation and they can also be shipped easily if they are not in any way fragile.

Large pieces, either rugs, bed coverings, table linens or wall hangings may be mounted on long wooden poles or boards which can then be hung from ceilings or walls by means of picture wire. It is important that such textiles be mounted on the poles or wooden strips by sewing loops or tape at close intervals on the back of the textile through which the wood piece may be slipped. Smaller pieces may be similarly fixed to dowels or sticks

---

sent to tropical countries in South America. It is an expensive solution, but worth noting because it affords certain protection against insect damage, dust, water or humidity, all of which are hazards in hot climates. Moreover, including the packing it produces a lightweight shipment for use in air transport. It was subjected to the following tests:

Immersed in water for two weeks. Careful weighing before and after showed no water absorption.

Immediately following immersion and weighing, the units were refrigerated to 70° below zero in an effort to produce interior condensation. No condensation occurred.

The units were heated to 180° to check against discolouration and warping. Neither occurred.

The units were breakage-tested by dropping on a concrete floor from a height of five feet. The first small fissure appeared on the eighth drop. No serious breakage occurred until the units were forcibly thrown face downward on the floor. Breakage by any method including striking with a hammer did not produce splinters or small pieces which might injure the watercolo

26MK The depiction of the demountable pedestal reminds me of the assembly plan that Martin Kippenberger enclosed with his work *Don Quijote de la Mancha* (s.l.: Martin Kippenberger, 1989, in: Uwe Koch, *Kommentiertes Werkverzeichnis der Bücher von/Annotated catalogue raisonné of the books by Martin Kippenberger 1977–1997,* Nr. 80). A colour-printed cork shell in the guise of a book, its contents reveal around 50 colour photographs (snapshots of friends, parties, exhibition openings, etc.). In addition to these images is a sketch for the construction of a pedestal, which features a hollowed space that the book can be placed in and covered with a glass pane. In this way the pedestal, which the buyer must make themselves, mutates from the display unit to the actual artifact.

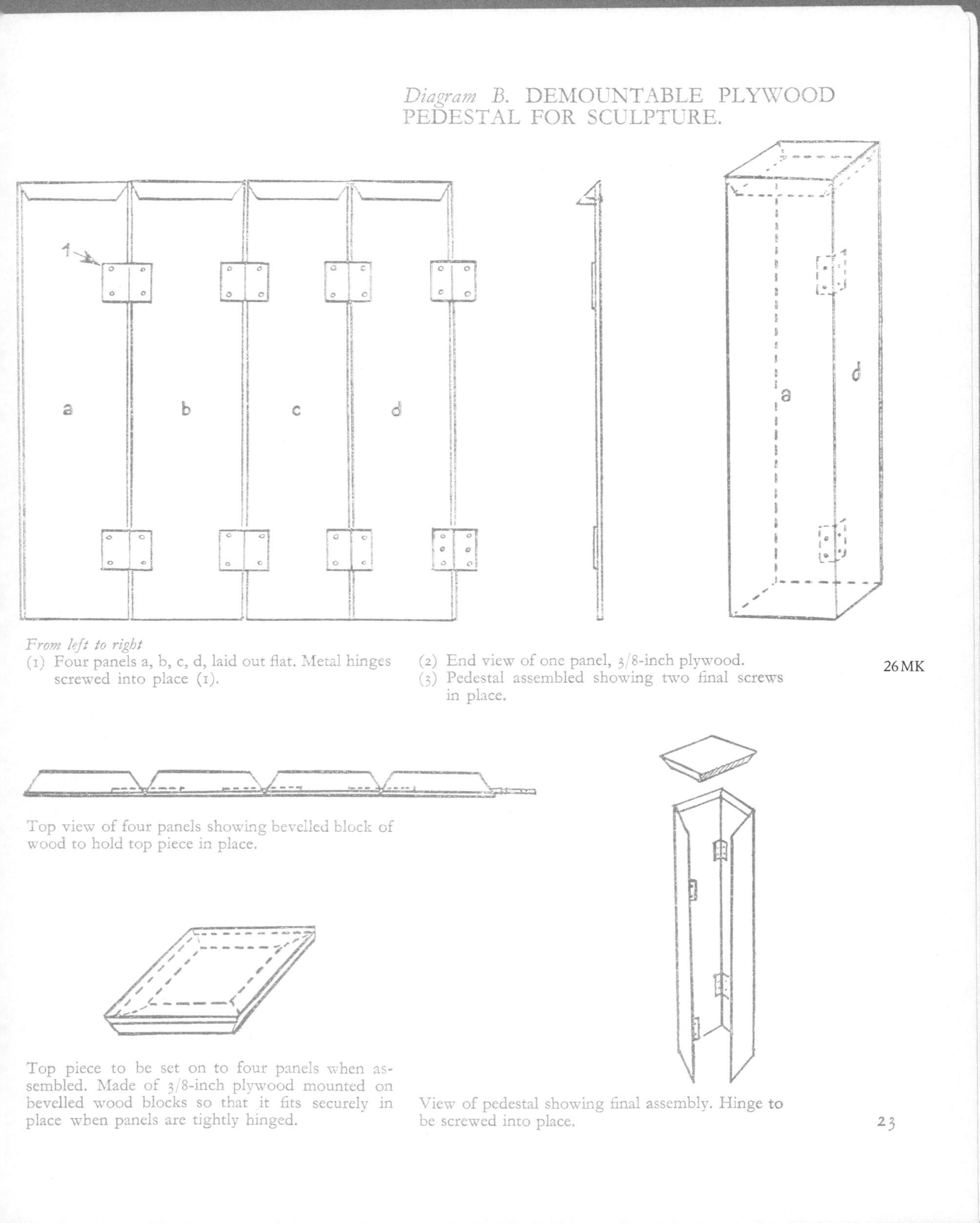

Diagram B. DEMOUNTABLE PLYWOOD PEDESTAL FOR SCULPTURE.

From left to right
(1) Four panels a, b, c, d, laid out flat. Metal hinges screwed into place (1).
(2) End view of one panel, 3/8-inch plywood.
(3) Pedestal assembled showing two final screws in place.

26MK

Top view of four panels showing bevelled block of wood to hold top piece in place.

Top piece to be set on to four panels when assembled. Made of 3/8-inch plywood mounted on bevelled wood blocks so that it fits securely in place when panels are tightly hinged.

View of pedestal showing final assembly. Hinge to be screwed into place.

23

27 MK The exhibiting of books – often in vitrines or under glass – seems to go against the very nature of reading. But even books with high print runs will one day be a rarity and therefore are predestined for exhibiting. But how do you exhibit a book accurately? In an interview with the artist Jonathan Monk, Seth Siegelaub said: "Why exhibit a book enclosed within a glass case in a museum and thus untouchable? When photocopies are made from our original publications, it doesn't decrease the importance of the book as a document, especially my publications which never, or hardly ever, have anything to do with great photographs or colour illustrations" (Jonathan Monk, *Cover Version*, Book Works, London 2004). This very pragmatic approach to books reminds me of a statement by the American artist Peter Downsbrough, who since 1972 has published over 113 artist books and seeks to deconstruct their status: "'Artists' books, I don't like the term. I prefer to call them simply 'books'!" Still, how do you deal with books that have suddenly become a rarity? Do you fetishise them and banish them to a lightproof vault? Protect them as trophies, guarded from dust behind glass? The best that can happen to books is that they are read. Over the course of time, however, this leaves traces, such as stains, scuffs, dents, dog-ears, and inscriptions. But isn't it exactly these signs of wear and tear that make a book into a fetish object?

attached to both top and bottom edges to hold the fabric flat *(figs. 16* and *17, pages 86, 87,* and *diagram C, page 26)*. If both sides of a fabric are to be shown, the piece may be mounted between two narrow wood frames and these frames hung from the ceiling or placed on simple wood stands like screens.

Costumes are usually best displayed on simulated figures to show the way a type of dress is worn. The figure may be made of demountable pieces so that it can be packed flat. Often, however, they are displayed on walls or attached to panels to simplify packing arrangements *(fig. 18, page 88)*.

Fragile, rare or unique items should be treated like paintings or drawings; mounted under glass, rigid plastic sheets or heavy celluloid in frames or mats. An attractive method of mounting very small and rare or fragile items, such as examples of ancient weaving from Egypt or Peru, is to place them between two pieces of celluloid, sewing the celluloid sheets together at intervals around the textile samples *(diagram C, page 25)*.

THREE-DIMENSIONAL OBJECTS

(In this category are small items such as tableware, silver, pottery, small carvings, decorative objects, toys, jewellery, ivories, industrial design, etc.)

Such items can be well displayed in many ways, depending upon the size, value and fragility of the object.

On Wall Panels. Some items can be mounted directly on panels, the panels to be hung like pictures from a wall *(fig. 11a, page 83)*. If valuable items are mounted on the panel, they may be wired to the surface, and protected by attaching a sheet of heavy plastic (plexiglas or lucite) of equal size two or three inches away from the surface of the panel. The protective sheet is bolted into the four corners of the panel with metal posts *(fig. 19, page 88)*. The panel affords the protection of a wall case, is simpler to construct and lighter in weight.

To accommodate three-dimensional objects, hinged shelves can be attached so that they fold flat for shipping *(fig. 20, page 88)*.

Another variation is a panel which has a protecting frame fastened on a slant so that at the top it is perhaps an inch deep and at the bottom seven or eight, forming space above for flat material and below a shelf for objects in the round. Such frames can be planned so that they fit one against the other to make a rectangular box which fits snugly into a shipping case *(diagram D, page 26)*.

On Demountable Tables. Objects may be affixed to the table tops or packed separately and placed thereon by each exhibitor. The method depends upon the size and nature of the objects *(fig. 21, page 89)*.

In Demountable Cases, or Wall Cases. This method is best for objects which must be protected by glass or heavy plastic covering. Such cases are usually small for ease of handling and for safety in shipment *(fig. 22, page 89)*. The table cases are usually made of lightweight woods, the surface on which the objects are displayed being polished, covered with a fabric or painted—whatever best sets off the items exhibited. If the specimens need to be protected by glass covering during exhibition only, a sheet, shipped separately, can be set into a recessed edge formed by the sides of the case *(diagram E, page 27)*.

Demountable Installation Units. The manufacture of unit systems of posts, shelves, panels or table surfaces which can be assembled by each exhibitor into a completely free-standing structure will be more fully discussed under "Panels and free-standing display units" (page 28). Excellent organization of an exhibition can be effected by means of such units, lighting incorporated, so that an entire room seems to be created quite independently of the space in which it exists.

Attention is called to this type of display for small objects because it permits the maximum of flexibility in various galleries and provides the combination of means afforded by tables and wall panels *(fig. 23, page 90)*.

Glass Cases or "vitrines". When trucking is available for transport, glass cases may be safely used for travelling collections. Handsome cases, easy to install, have been developed for small objects by numerous agencies, especially those in Europe and in Great Britain where a lorry is the usual means of transport. A particularly effective case is that designed by S. Jasievicz of Poland *(fig. 24, page 90)*, and another included in the travelling exhibition of Yugoslav Folk Art *(fig. 25, page 91)*.

BOOKS 27 MK

Depending upon their rarity value, books may be treated like small objects—mounted upon rigid panels, placed in demountable table or wall cases, or framed like pictures protected with glass *(fig. 26, page 91)*.

24

Diagram C. SUGGESTED METHODS OF DISPLAYING TEXTILES.

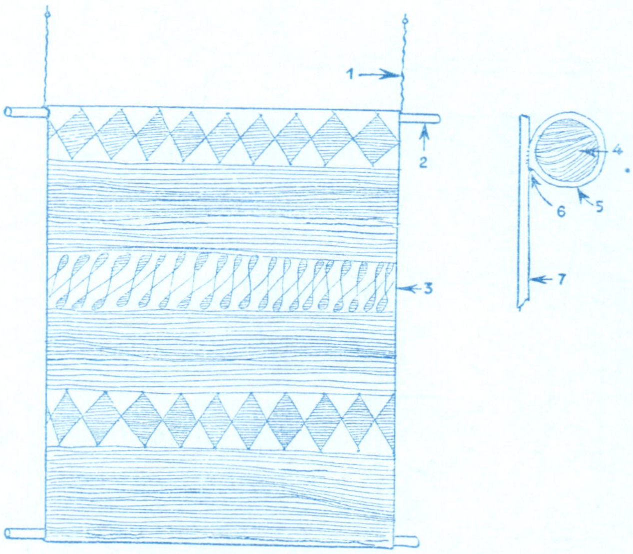

(1) Wire.
(2) Pole or dowel.
(3) Textile.
(4) Dowel.
(5) Tape loop.
(6) Sewing.
(7) Textile.

(8) Dowel or strip of wood.
(9) Textile looped on to dowels or strips.
(10) Label.

(11) Thin wire through celluloid.
(12) Sewing.
(13) Two sheets of celluloid.
(14) Textile.

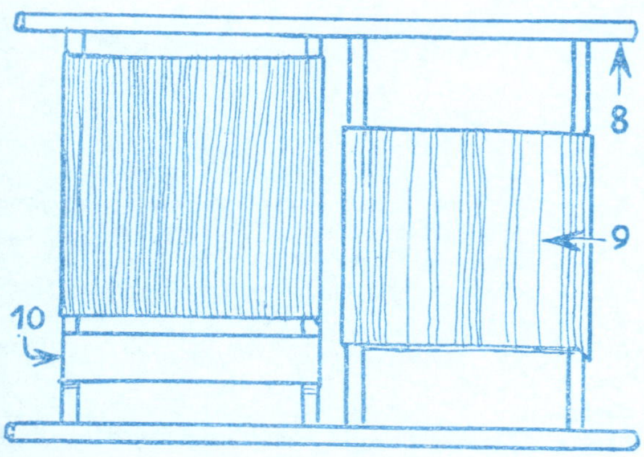

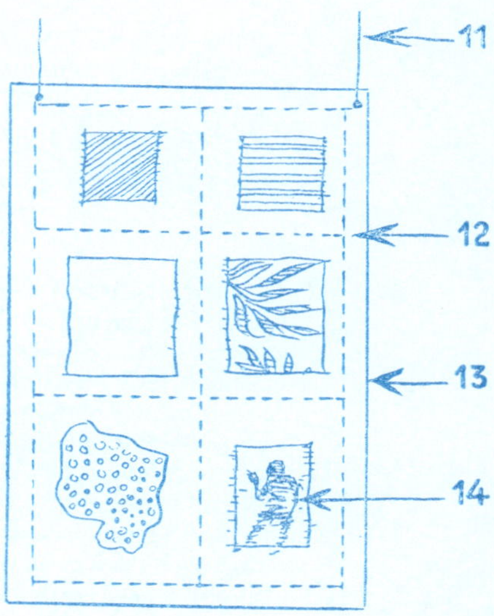

28KE The ink drawings hit the mark in an unforced manner. In addition to more elaborate depictions, crude outlines do justice to their subjects with impressive simplicity. Or is their charm due to the non-industrial construction of the wooden receptacles, far removed from the age of automation and machine art?

28KE *Diagram D.* WALL PANEL FOR DISPLAYING THREE-DIMENSIONAL OBJECTS.

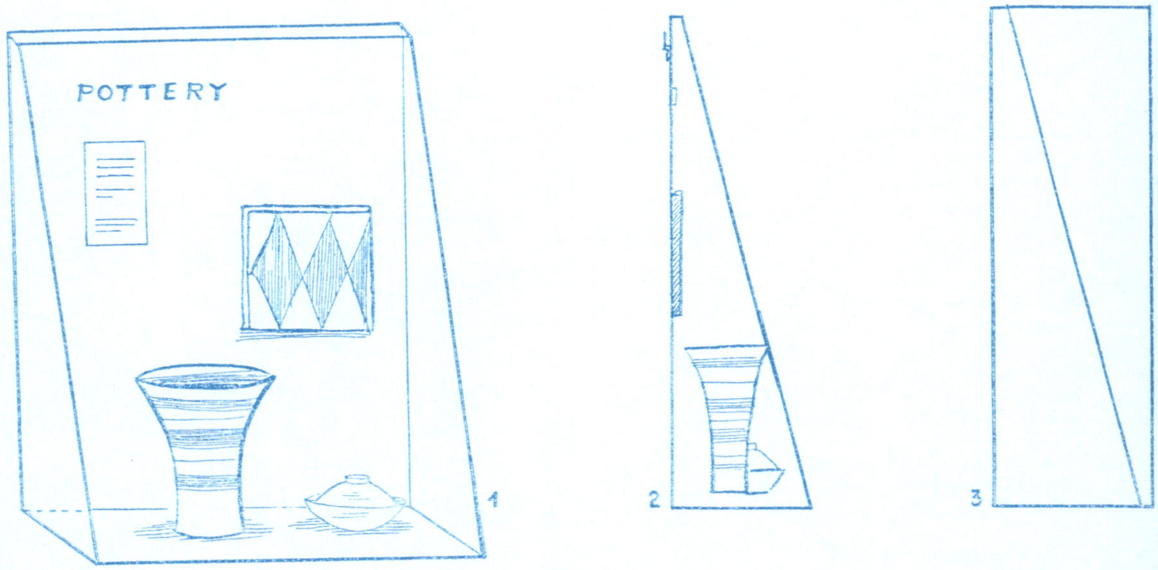

(1) Frame showing objects on base. Label, letters and flat objects on back panel.

(2) End view (transparent).
(3) Two frames placed together for packing.

If it is possible to display unbound pages of a book, these pages may be treated like watercolours or other works on paper, and framed with glass or mounted with celluloid coverings in mats. An effective method of displaying a series of pages from a single book is to mount each page against a cardboard background, cover it with celluloid and bind together the edges with adhesive tape. Then attach the mounts together at one edge by means of heavy canvas tape glued to adjoining mounts and display them like an accordian folder upon a shelf *(fig. 27, page 92)*.

If bindings are to be displayed, they should be exhibited in table cases. Small containers of water should be placed inside the case to insure sufficient moisture content so that bindings will not crack or flake from drying out.

26

POSTERS

Four methods have been found equally satisfactory for displaying posters. The choice is again made according to the value of the work. Means of exhibiting and weight of shipment are also factors.

For Unique and Valuable Examples of Poster Art

The poster may be framed with glass as if it were a painting. Usually a mat is omitted to reduce the size of glass required.

To decrease the weight of a shipment and avoid the hazard of using glass, the poster may be covered with a sheet of clear celluloid (acetate). The poster is placed on a sheet of cardboard of equal size, and

Diagram E. TABLE CASE WITH REMOVABLE GLASS.

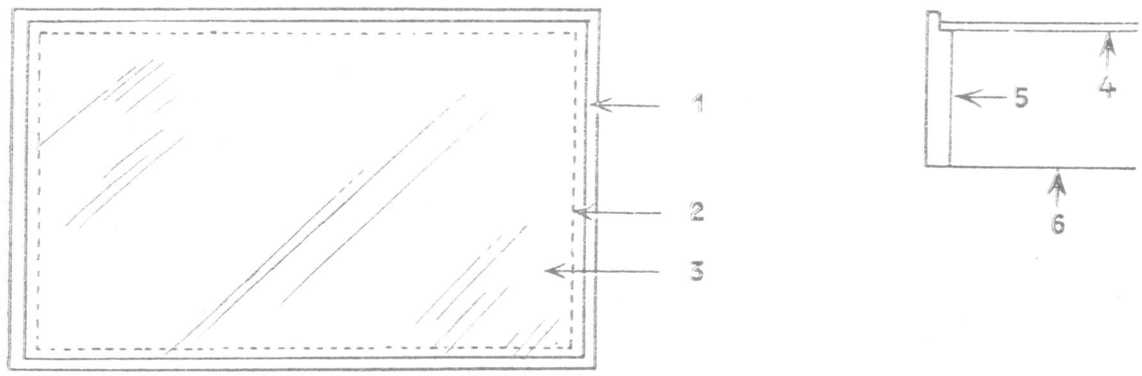

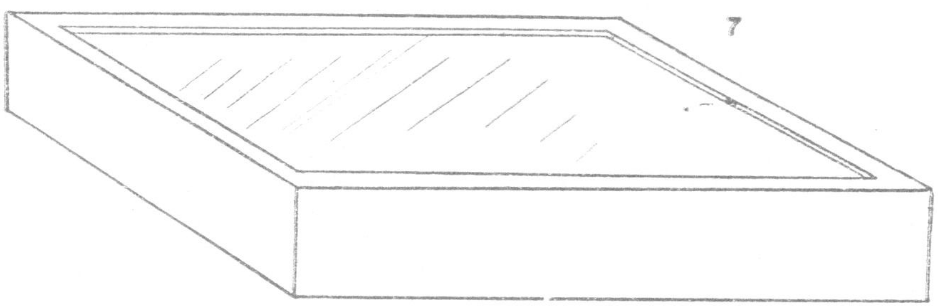

(1) Top of frame.
(2) Projecting edge of frame to hold glass.
(3) Glass.
(4) Glass.
(5) Profile of side of case.
(6) Bottom panel.
(7) Three-quarter view of table case.

the entire surface covered with the plastic sheet. Edges are bound together with strong adhesive tape. Linen tabs or metal rings may be affixed to the back of the mounted poster to afford an easy method of hanging from wall or picture moulding. If a poster is very large this method is not advisable because the celluloid in a large sheet is apt to buckle and pull away from the binding tape around the edges. It is better to resort to one of the following methods if the poster is over three by four feet.

For Contemporary Posters which can be replaced

A simple and economical method is to mount the poster on heavy cardboard or composition board. Metal "grommets" or rings placed in the corners enable exhibitors to hang them easily from picture mouldings or tack them to the walls. Sometimes collapsible framing systems are sent with posters in order to display them independently of wall surfaces *(fig. 28, page 92)*.

In order to decrease the weight and bulk of a shipment of posters, they may be mounted on heavy linen or canvas. The edge of the cloth should project an inch or more at top and bottom to permit insertion of the hangers without damaging the surface of the poster itself. The use of cloth backing permits the poster to be rolled for shipment so that only a small packing case is required. The posters can be tacked to walls, hung from picture wire or attached to free-standing framing systems with cord looped

27

29MK Similar to the displaying of books is the exhibiting of architecture, the perception and analysis of which can only be based on an actual physical interaction – walking through and around a building. It is this movement alone that reveals the multi-dimensional complexity between place, setting, topography, and genius loci: in short, the architectural context. To be able to understand architecture, you need to be able to travel. Most architecture exhibitions only show isolated aspects, be it sketches, plans, models, miniatures, photographs, renderings, animations, or mock-ups. And while this represents a part of the whole, it is never the holistic entity. Precisely because architecture yearns to be built rather than exhibited, architecture exhibitions should show it true to scale and anchored in the surroundings.

through the metal rings and pulled taut so that the poster remains flat *(diagram F, page 29)*.

FURNITURE

In general, furniture has to be treated like sculpture, mounted by each successive exhibitor on platforms, pedestals or directly upon the floor. Lightweight modern chairs of a durable character can sometimes be mounted directly upon wall panels to call attention to some special construction feature.

More often, exhibitions of furniture design are composed of enlarged photographs, supplemented by only a single piece, or at best a few small pieces, of furniture neither too fragile nor too bulky for easy shipping. Shipment by truck or lorry permits the inclusion of large pieces which do not require boxing, but for shipments by rail, boat or airship, large pieces are usually eliminated.

Model rooms have been devised with miniature pieces of furniture exemplifying the character of a given period of design. Such collections are often fragile and someone is needed to accompany the exhibition to make repairs, to supervise all packing and handling and to properly install the model rooms. These exhibitions have been remarkably successful, however, the additional cost of preparation and maintenance having been partially balanced by entrance fees paid by visitors.

29MK

ARCHITECTURE AND CIVIC PLANNING

Careful reproductions of buildings on a small scale are often used for exhibition purposes in the same way that model rooms are used to give a sense of the architectural style of a period. As such models are usually fragile and difficult to repair, their use in travelling exhibitions is restricted.

Pedestals on which models can be shown must be devised by each exhibitor. Scaffold frames may be constructed and covered with cardboard, paper or cloth. Packing-cases are often suggested by the circulating agency, a cloth covering being included for use when the models are displayed. The disadvantage of this method is that the model rarely stands at the proper eye level from which a building should be seen.

Small, lightweight models can be shown on shelves fixed by braces to a wall. Shelves and braces may be shipped in the case with the model. Free-standing display methods are usually preferable, however, because many museums cannot nail braces against their walls *(figs. 29, 29a, page 93)*.

Sometimes it is necessary to protect the model from curious fingers by covering it with a glass or heavy plastic vitrine or box. Again, it is difficult to ship such items by rail. Their use is usually avoided unless shipment can be made by van.

Architectural exhibitions may also be composed of enlarged photographs, labels, maps, etc. Small sections of buildings, structural features or samples of materials can be mounted directly upon wall panels *(fig. 30, page 94)*. Civic planning can be demonstrated with small block units resembling various types of buildings. Such educational shows containing photographs and diagrams as well can be conveniently packed in boxes which open like closets, fitted with shelves *(figs. 31, 31a, 31b, page 95)*.

Large models used to display designs for whole areas, such as civic planning exhibitions, are often made in sections for ease in shipping. They can be displayed as a mural, the sections hung against or mounted upon a wall panel, or shown flat on a table base or on the floor *(fig. 32, page 96)*.

PANELS AND FREE-STANDING DISPLAY UNITS

Like architecture, many subjects for display can be treated in photographs, colour reproductions or small three-dimensional objects mounted directly upon panels. Because so many museums were built to house only permanent collections, little thought being given by their builders to providing continuous wall space for the temporary presentation of two-dimensional material on loan, it has been difficult for many museums to take advantage of travelling exhibitions. The general need for systems of displaying material which are independent of the spaces in which such exhibitions are shown has prompted a series of ingenious solutions, primarily designed by architects. All are based upon methods of creating free-standing walls, cases, pedestals, panels, shelves or tables on which exhibitions may be presented.

While panels can, of course, be hung like pictures against a wall, it is often difficult for an institution to provide sufficient unbroken wall space to allow for the proper circulation of visitors from the beginning to the end of an exhibition, especially when a particular sequence of panels must be maintained. For such exhibitions, panels mounted on vertical supports which can be set up in open spaces, are more useful. The exhibitor can place the exhibi-

28

Diagram F. METHODS OF ATTACHING LINEN-BACKED POSTERS TO FRAME.

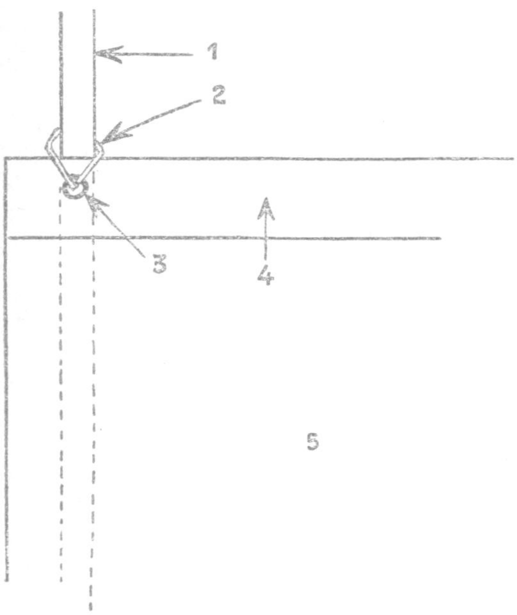

Detail showing poster attached to support at top.
(1) Vertical support.
(2) Cord.
(3) Metal ring or "grommet".
(4) Linen mount.
(5) Poster.

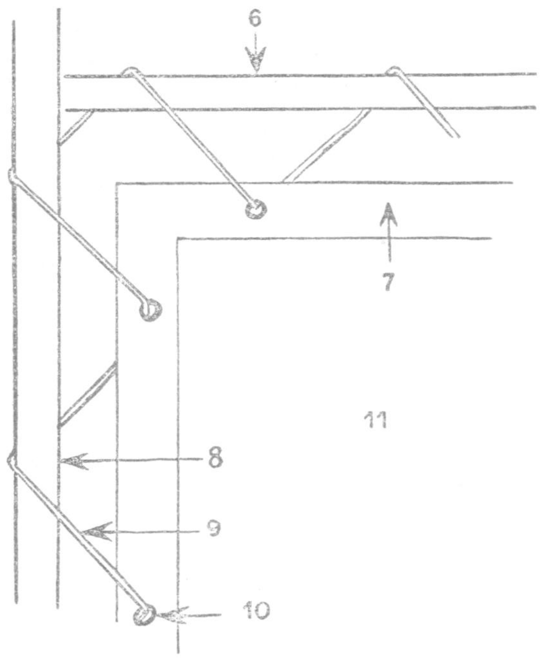

Detail showing poster attached to support at side and top of free-standing frame. Linen mount projects at side and top of poster.
(6) Horizontal support.
(7) Linen mount.
(8) Vertical support.
(9) Cord.
(10) Metal ring or "grommet".
(11) Poster.

tion so that some flexibility is allowed in the sequence of panels to accommodate entrances, exits, patrols of guards and to create open spaces in which groups may gather for talks or lectures on the materials displayed.

In designing portable installation units consideration must be given to ease of packing and lightness for shipping, speed of assembling and dismantling as well as maintenance *(figs. 33, 33a, 33b, page 97)*. But as one architect has pointed out, most exhibition units are "designed primarily from the standpoint of the materials to be exhibited and not from the conditions under which they are to be shown".[1] Architects have therefore given particular thought to designing unit structures which will be capable of presenting a variety of exhibitions under a variable number of physical conditions. A number of these solutions are illustrated on the pages following. Some of these systems are now being manufactured in the United States so that units can be purchased by an exhibitor or circulating agency and put together in whatever groupings the exhibitor needs to accommodate his display. Moreover they can be used in different combinations for various exhibitions so the purchase of a set of units may serve for successive exhibitions sent out over a period of years *(figs. 34, 34a, page 98* and *diagram G, page 30)*.

[1] Joseph Carreiro, William Daley, Charles Quillan on "Flexible Display".

Panels are usually made of plywood, pressed wood, composition board or other lightweight material painted in attractive colours, perforated or covered with cloth. Exhibitors can display pictures, photographs, posters or other flat materials on the panels. Architectural models, sculpture, books or other three-dimensional objects of various kinds can be packed separately and hooked on to panels, or they may be shipped as an integral part of the panel if their condition so warrants.

Some systems provide for the arrangement of shelves or table display by locking horizontal members into vertical supports. One of the prefabricated display systems is prepared in three-dimensional units which are not demountable, but nest into each other. The difference in size of units is so small it is unnoticeable, yet it permits stacking for shipping *(fig. 35, page 99)*. Some units can be set up so that whole rooms are created in which to show furniture, fabrics or other decorative objects *(fig. 36, page 100)*.

Certain imaginative designers have combined units manufactured for entirely different purposes into display systems for exhibitions at very moderate cost. The success of such efforts and the fact that structural units for display purposes are now being manufactured marks a step in advance toward ease in assembling and packing travelling installation as well as the objects themselves. It is possible that in the future many more exhibitions will be organized by museums for circulation if such materials can be made available at reasonable cost.

Diagram G. "STRUC-TUBE", A DEMOUNTABLE FRAMEWORK designed by George Nelson and manufactured by Affiliated Machine and Tool Company, New York. *(see figs. 34, 34a, page 98).*

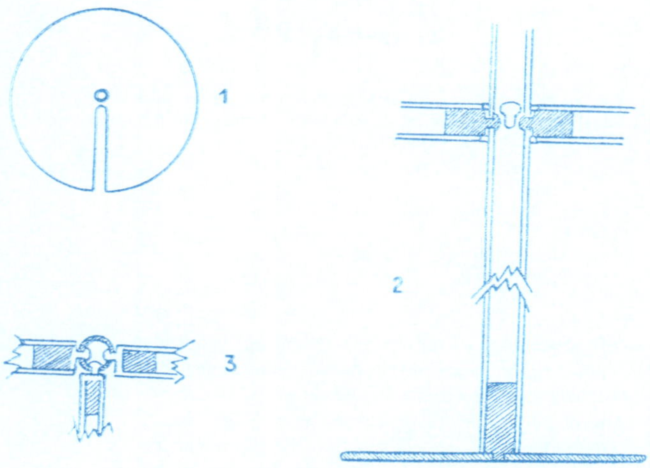

(1) Plan of base.
(2) Vertical section. Hollow tube fits over centre post attached to base.
(3) Section of centre post showing how horizontal tubes are joined to post.

30

30 MK I can only say 'Amen' to these two maxims: a) "it is impossible to set down rules which can be followed with complete success in every instance". No rule is without exception, which is also valid for curating exhibitions; b) "The printed word is no substitute for actual experience". Reviews, catalogues, and websites are all unable to communicate the physical idea of an exhibition.

II. PACKING WORKS OF ART FOR TOUR

Because the protection of every work of art is an individual matter, it is impossible to set down rules which can be followed with complete success in every instance. There are, however, certain general principles which apply to packing all materials for continued travelling; a brief outline of them follows summarizing the provisions which experienced packers have agreed upon as being essential. Only experience and the knowledge required to put good packing into effect can guarantee to any extent the results of following these suggestions. A general programme of training personnel in the problems of packing, handling and transporting works of art could accomplish much more than any manual of instructions, however detailed and elaborate. The printed word is no substitute for actual experience.

Since objects that are transported have to be unpacked, handled, and repacked by persons unacquainted with the particular items, standard methods, if they can be devised, are much to be desired. This outline of packing procedures has been based upon an article entitled "Packing Problems and Procedures"[1] by Robert G. Rosegrant which appeared in the January 1942 issue of *Technical Studies in the Field of the Fine Arts,* a journal no longer issued, which was published by the Fogg Art Museum, Harvard University, Cambridge, Massachusetts, U.S.A. This was in turn used for the excellent book entitled *Safeguarding Works of Art* by Robert P. Sugden of the Metropolitan Museum of Art, New York, and published by that institution.

In order to try to fit packing procedures into categories already in use by a number of museums, I have divided the media included in travelling exhibitions into the seven classifications set down in these previously published outlines. Procedures have been modified to apply more directly to travelling exhibitions than to shipments of single works of art on loan, going to and from a single destination. Each classification requires a somewhat different packing procedure, but the following general rules apply to all objects. 30 MK

GENERAL RULES

(The form for the outline of general rules has been taken from a report prepared by a committee of the American Association of Museums on Packing and Handling of Objects. Technical information on construction of containers has been further amplified by data supplied by the U.S. Department of Commerce in their publication *Modern Export Packing.*)

CASES

Construction

Seasoned (air-dried) wood, aged to a state of maximum stability, seven-eighths to one inch in thickness, free of bad cross grain or knots is recommended for construction of shipping containers to travel by rail or boat. Open crates are never used for shipping works of art. Containers must be solidly constructed; lumber should be tongued and grooved or otherwise matched *(diagram H, page 32).*

Interior dimensions should be from four to six inches larger than packaged contents to provide space for resilient padding. The exterior of the case should be reinforced by cleats and riding battens *(diagram I, page 33).* Cement-coated nails should be used since they have a greater resistance to withdrawal from wood than untreated nails. Wood may

[1] Written as a guide for packing works of art during wartime when many museums in the United States shipped valuable items from their collection to places of relative safety.

31

Diagram H. JOINTS USED IN BOX CONSTRUCTION.

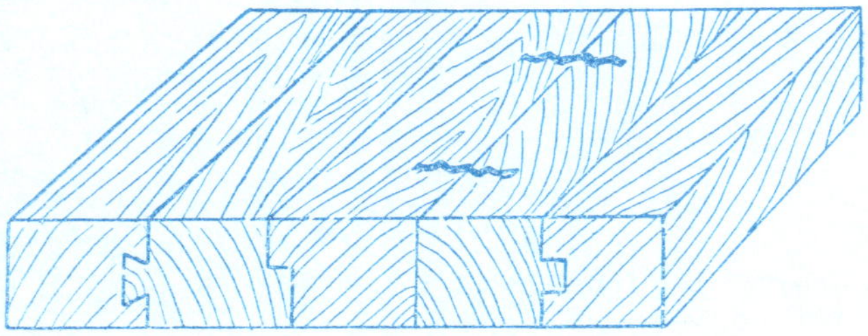

From left to right: Linderman joint, ship lap joint, butt joint, tongue and groove joint.

be coated with paraffin to prevent moisture escaping when humidity changes take place.

Small cases for lightweight pieces may be made of one-quarter to one-half inch plywood with heavier lumber reinforcements, particularly on the ends *(diagram J, page 34)*. Unless exhibits are heavy, such boxes are usually used for shipments travelling by air.

Cover Attachment

Screws should be used where cases are constructed for only a few trips; bolts are preferable for cover attachment when a container is to be used for many successive shipments. *Nails must never be used to attach covers of cases for travelling exhibitions.* Sucesssive nailings tend to split the wood and weaken the construction of the packing case. If shipments are to be sent overseas, some type of lock may be found to secure the case in transit. Metal strap sealing is also advised for shipping cases overseas. The straps hold the box parts in place, and help to distribute shock which would otherwise be absorbed locally *(diagram of methods of applying metal straps K, page 35)*.

Waterproofing

All containers should be lined with waterproof paper tacked or stapled down, all joints overlapping and sealed into place with gummed tape. Side and end papers should be left long enough to fold over to form a cover for contents.

Interior Partitions

Separation battens should be used when more than one object is packed in a single box. They may be made of corrugated board or heavy lumber, depending upon the weight and shape of the objects enclosed. These battens provide interior reinforcement and a partial floor or wall for the different objects so that they cannot shift about when the container is moved *(diagram L(a), page 36* and *fig. 37, page 100)*.

Board battens should have cleats attached to them at each end. The cleat furnishes a means of attaching the batten to the outer container without nailing the batten directly to the wall of the packing case. By nailing through the cleat the distribution of shock becomes less directly carried to the object protected by the batten *(diagram L(b) page 36)*.

If used to hold paintings in place, battens should be padded with excelsior pads and not nailed or otherwise directly attached to the picture frames. When board battens are used to support paintings, heavy corrugated board equal in size to the inside case dimensions should be placed either over or under the battens. A separator sheet should also be placed beneath the first object packed and over the last one in the case *(diagram N, page 39)*. When used to support heavy objects (sculpture, furniture, etc.) the batten should be padded with excelsior padding, sponge-rubber or felt, wherever it comes in contact with the object.

Size

Risks increase as the number of objects in each case is increased. Boxes should not be heavier than one man can lift. This is important unless the circulating agency knows that each exhibitor has sufficient staff or equipment to handle heavier cases. Cases must be strong enough, however, to carry the loads intended for them. It is better to make additional cases than to make a few overloaded ones. Attachment of handles of metal or strong rope are advised for safety and convenience in handling.

Padding and Wrapping

Paramount in importance and a rule to which all museums and packing experts agree, is that objects must "float" in the packing cases. Objects packed within a shipping container must ride free of contact with any walls or other object. This is to prevent the transmission of vibration or shock from the outside container to the packed object. For this reason, battens or braces to hold objects in place must not be directly attached to any item, but always separated from it by some shock-absorbing material such as excelsior padding, sponge rubber, felt or other resilient lining. The padding material should always be firmly affixed. If tacks are used, they must be long enough so that they will not work out of place during shipment. Loose tacks or other pointed objects should never be present in containers. It is better to staple[1] pads, or to attach them with adhesive tape than to risk using tacks which might become loosened. From four to six inches of padding should always be placed between objects and the wall of the packing case. The padding (such as excelsior) must be packed in tightly enough so that it cannot settle toward any one side of the case.

All padding material should be used in self-contained units, wrapped or sealed. The use of loose excelsior, cotton or other padding is permissible only when objects are already boxed or wrapped in heavy paper or cloth.

The padding material must be resilient. If shipments are being made only once, shredded newsprint or waxed paper is sometimes used, but these materials are not recommended for travelling exhibitions because they tend to absorb moisture and to mat, losing their resiliency after several trips. The

[1] A staple is a bent metal pin with two pointed ends. It can be driven into wood, both ends entering at once, so that it holds material securely in place.

Diagram I. TYPICAL BOX CONSTRUCTION.

a

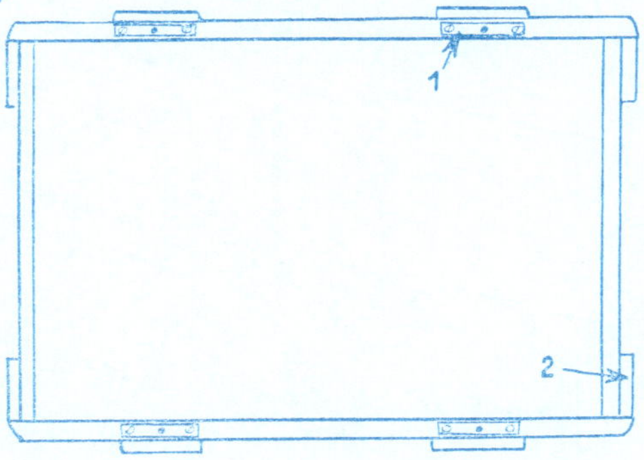

b

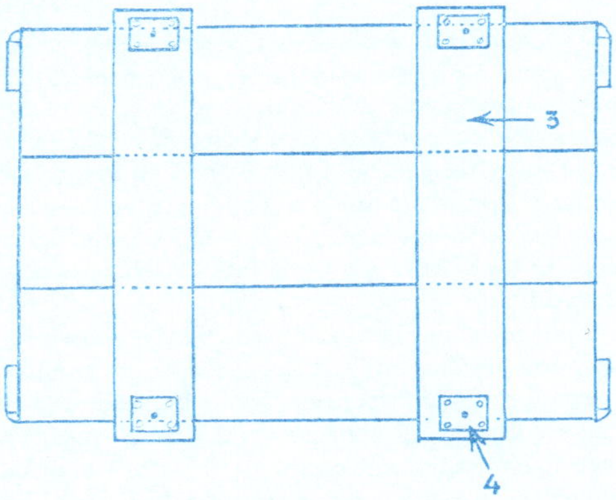

c

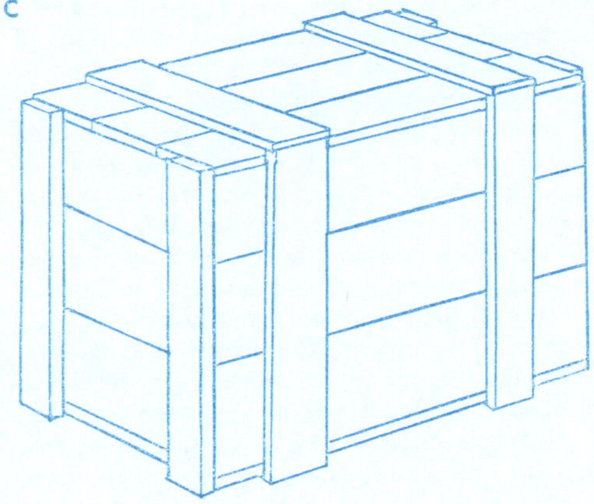

(a) Top view, case open. Metal plate screwed into side (1). Hole in centre to receive bolt attached though cover plate. Batten (2).
(b) Top view, cover in place. Batten (3). Metal plates to fasten cover (4).
(c) Three-quarter view of case showing siding battens and reinforcing battens.

Diagram J. THREE TYPES OF PLYWOOD CASES WITH REINFORCING BATTENS OF HEAVIER LUMBER.

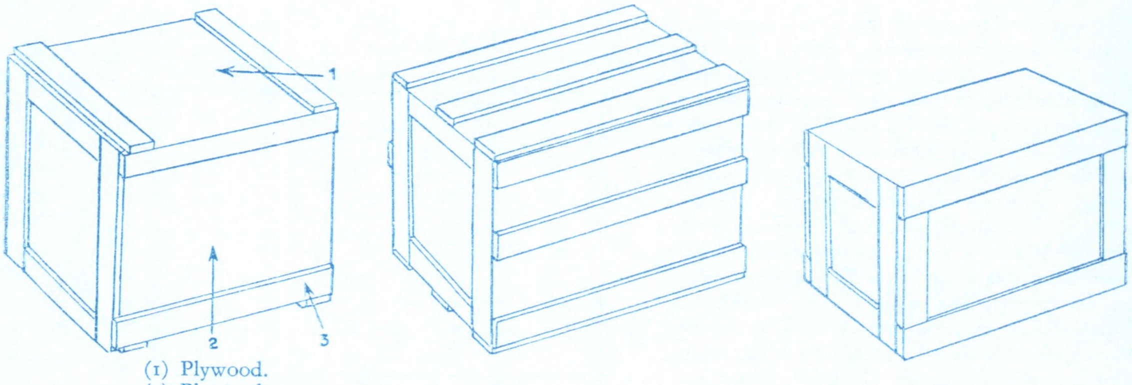

(1) Plywood.
(2) Plywood.
(3) Heavy lumber batten.

use of straw and sawdust, which also absorb moisture easily, is to be avoided and their presence in packing containers is forbidden at ports of entry to many countries. Excelsior seems to be the most satisfactory for general use; it is the least expensive, endures continued use over an extended period and retains its resiliency. It should be fresh, however, at the start of a tour so that its resilience is at a maximum.

Sponge-rubber has been used effectively for padding but it often needs the protective covering of muslin or other inexpensive cloth. If it is allowed to come into direct contact with certain polished metals, it is capable of creating a stain on the metal which is difficult and sometimes impossible to remove. It may also stick to a delicately encrusted surface, such as old glass, and remove small particles causing injury to the surface. Unless it is used in great quantity, it is not satisfactory for heavy items. A shock against the outside container will be transmitted directly to a heavy object packed only in sponge rubber. Its use, to the exclusion of excelsior should be carefully considered in relation to the weight of the objects packed. It is also more expensive than excelsior, though purchase of it may be justified since it is possible to re-use it. Its chief use is as padding on braces for paintings, sculpture or other heavy objects. The brace acts as the support, however, the rubber creating a condition of suspension for objects packed within the container.

All fragile surfaces, such as varnish, paint, etc., should be protected against contact with any loose padding material. Paper-wrapped pads are equally injurious to such surfaces. An interior package, dust-tight, moisture resistant, rigid and free of fragile surfaces should be made for any object of this kind.

It is suggested that only tissue paper, waxed paper, mulberry paper or soft cloth be used to wrap delicate objects such as jewellery, old glass, ivories, painted potteries, etc. Cotton batting is unsatisfactory because it is apt to become involved with a delicate surface and damage the object when it is removed. After the surface has been protected with one of the smooth papers, it can be wrapped in cotton batting to create a protective covering around the object when it is placed in the packing container (see description of packing small fragiles, page 43).

Mineral wool, a non-combustible material made of asbestos or gypsum is less frequently used, but entirely satisfactory.

Pictures covered with Glass

If glass must be left on pictures such as pastels, drawings, prints, watercolours or other works on paper, it should be protected by affixing strips of cellulose "masking" tape[1] to the surface in criss-

[1] The advantage of this "masking" tape is that it can be removed easily by merely pulling one end away from the surface to which it is attached, and it can be used over again. It leaves no mark on the surface of the glass, nor does it dry out

Diagram K. METHODS OF APPLYING METAL STRAPS.

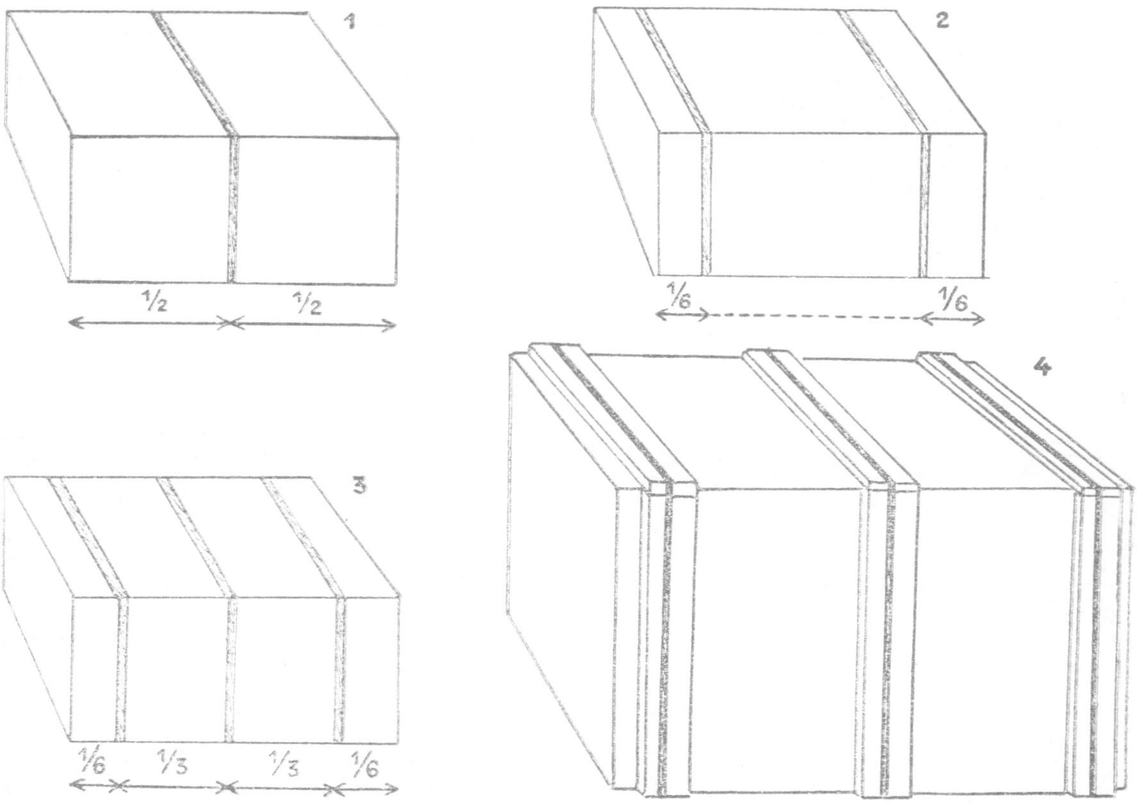

(1) One strap: place at centre of length.
(2) Two straps: place one-sixth of length from each end.
(3) Three straps: place centre one equal distance from two end ones, latter placed one-sixth of length from ends.

(4) Metal straps placed over battens.
Metal bindings act perpendicularly to the grain in the sides, top and bottom of a case. They should be placed tightly enough to cut into the wood so they will not loosen if the box shrinks.

crossed pattern or, better, in horizontal strips one-quarter of an inch apart. The strips are applied to hold small fragments of glass together should any breakage occur in transit. It has been found that paper or cloth glued to the glass is unsatisfactory because many packers are careless in removing it with water. Moisture penetrating under the glass can cause serious and sometimes irreparable damage to a drawing or watercolour.

When glass measures over 24 by 30 inches, it should be removed and packed separately in a compartment at the bottom or side of the container; alternatively, the picture can be removed and packed separately and glass taped and packed within the picture frame. It is always preferable to ship pictures without glass covering in travelling exhibitions.

or come loose from the glass, until it has been re-used many times. It is manufactured by the Minnesota Mining and Manufacturing Company, St. Paul, Minnesota, U.S.A. and is called Scotch Wetordry Masking Tape.

Diagram L. INTERIOR PARTITIONS.

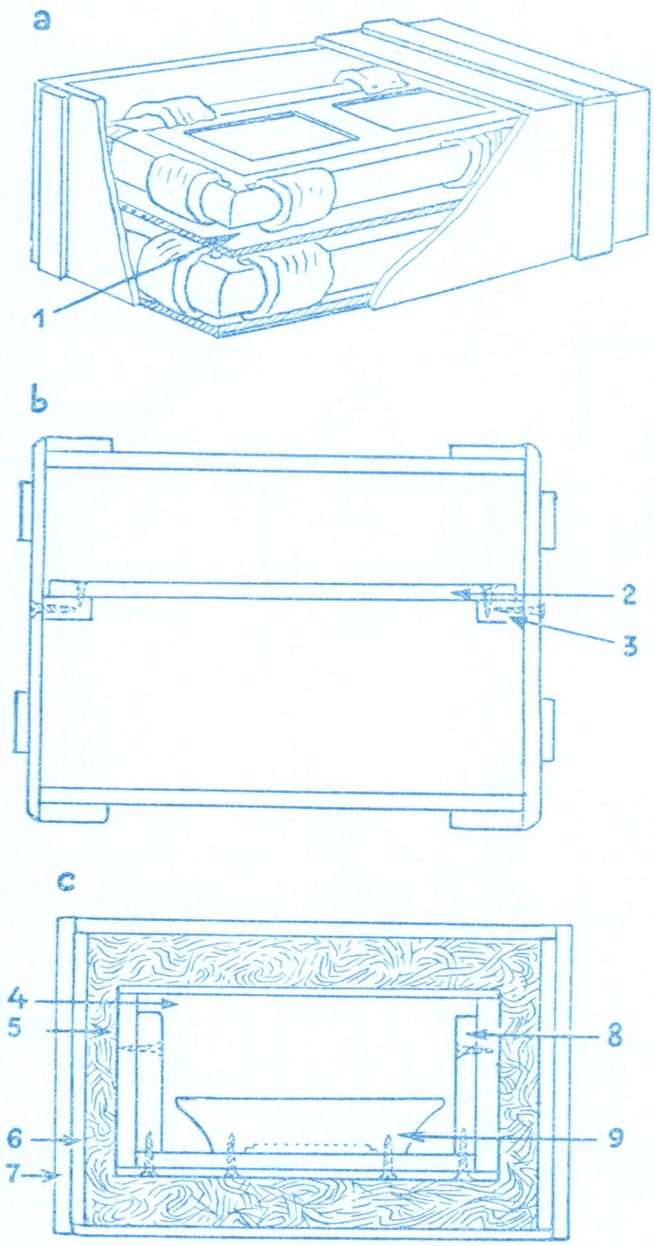

CONDITION OF OBJECTS

Paintings and other highly valued works of art in poor condition should not be subjected to the hazards of shipment. All works should be carefully examined prior to shipment and a record made of their condition (see suggested condition report reproduced in Appendix A, page 61). If possible, photographs should be taken for "before and after" comparison of any questionable items. These are invaluable should a claim for insurance be necessary.

MARKING CASES

All shipping cases should be clearly marked in stencilled letters at least two inches high in black indelible ink to assure careful handling and indicate shipping destinations during a tour. Words such as FRAGILE, HANDLE WITH CARE, should be painted on the outside of the box in bold letters. An international symbol for a work of art (such as an artist's palette) might be agreed upon so that every case containing a valuable work of art would be clearly stencilled with this sign. Shippers remark that the goblet, used to signify fragile materials such as glass or china, is recognizable to all who handle packing cases. Carriers might learn to recognize the nature and value of the contents of packing cases containing works of art or other treasures and perhaps exercise more caution than is customary in handling large boxes. Often language difficulties make the printed words useless, but until such a symbol is arrived at, it is wise to print on the box in large letters WORKS OF ART, or PAINTING or SCULPTURE, in whatever languages may be necessary during a tour.

It is also necessary to mark on the box for each exhibitor to recognize readily, the screws or bolts which should be removed to open the case and

(a) Corrugated board batten. Box cut away to show corrugated board battens (1) between pictures.
(b) Top view, box open. Lumber batten or brace (2) screwed to cleat. Cleat (3) screwed to wall of box.
(c) Side view showing fragile frame and painting in inner box "floated" in excelsior (4). Inner box set in excelsior (5). Outer box (6). Batten (7). Cleat screwed to box (8). Frame screwed to cleat (9).

saved for use in reshipment. The box should be marked OPEN HERE and to facilitate better handling of material which should remain in one position, the box should also bear the message THIS SIDE UP. Sometimes exhibitors place "fins" on all sides except the bottom so that the case will stand in a stable position on only one side *(fig. 38, page 101)*.

REPLACING PACKING MATERIALS

Altough mentioned elsewhere in the text it is important enough to mention as a general rule in packing an exhibition which will travel to a group of institutions, that loose packing material be avoided. If it is absolutely necessary, as in the case of some sculptures or small fragile objects which need excelsior and cotton surrounding the pieces, it should be clearly indicated on the packing and unpacking instructions and marked in bold painted letters on the inside of the packing case, that these materials are to be saved for use in repacking and that, if any has become damaged during the tour, this fact be reported to the circulating agency. It should then be replaced at once, either by the agency or the exhibitor.

SPECIAL INSTRUCTIONS

PICTURES

Oils, Temperas, etc.

It is advisable to limit the number of pictures to be placed in a packing case to the weight one man can handle. This stipulation is repeated because most damages to pictures occur when cases are too heavy to be easily managed by those who must move them in and out of galleries, storage rooms, off railroad platforms or trucks. Sometimes pictures are large and several must be packed together to save costs of labour and materials in boxing. When this is necessary, exhibitors should be warned in advance that two or more men will be needed to move the boxes from one place to another. The use of "dollies" (flat platforms on casters) makes it possible for one man to move large cases more easily and safely.

It is wise also to limit the size of pictures included in travelling exhibitions. A similar guide pertains to individual paintings—the size one man can carry safely. If larger paintings are included, exhibitors should be told in advance so that two men will be available for unpacking.

A painting protected by glass is a special problem. If measuring more than 24 by 30 inches, the glass should be removed and packed separately. (The larger the glass, the more likely it is to be shattered.) The glass should be stripped with "masking" tape (see footnote page 34) and placed in a compartment at the side of the box. Or, conversely, the picture can be packed separately, the glass left in the picture frame. In either case, the glass should be taped. By separating glass from painting, there is less risk of damage to the surface of the picture. Such arrangements should be made only with the consent of the owner. (For ocean voyages, it is not wise to remove glass from a canvas. The change in humidity may cause damage to the painted surface.) The substitution of heavy, rigid plastic (such as plexiglas or lucite) for the breakable glass may reduce the risk of damage in transit.

Shadow boxes should be eliminated, if possible, from travelling exhibitions. Glass placed away from a backing, as it is in a shadow box, is more easily broken than glass backed against a rigid support. If shadow boxes must be included, they should be packed separately from other pictures, in a special case built to house the shadow box.

Screw eyes should not be left on frames while in transit. They are apt to come loose and the pointed end may constitute a hazard, causing damage to frames or pictures. Their projection also increases hazards of damage to other works with which they are associated. They may be replaced with small metal plates which can be fastened tightly into picture frames with small screws *(diagram M, page 38)*. There is little risk of such plates coming loose because the stress from the picture wire is placed upon the opening in the metal plate, not upon the screws.

Canvases mounted on stretchers, and panel paintings, should be firmly fixed in their frames before packing. Nails are not satisfactory for this purpose. The stretchers should be attached to the frames by means of metal plates or "straps" screwed into place *(diagram M, page 38)*.

There are several satisfactory methods of packing paintings. The choice of method depends upon material available, cost and the amount of risk involved.

Pads and Separation Sheets. The simplest method of packing pictures is one which has been accepted

Diagram M. METAL STRAPS AND PLATES.

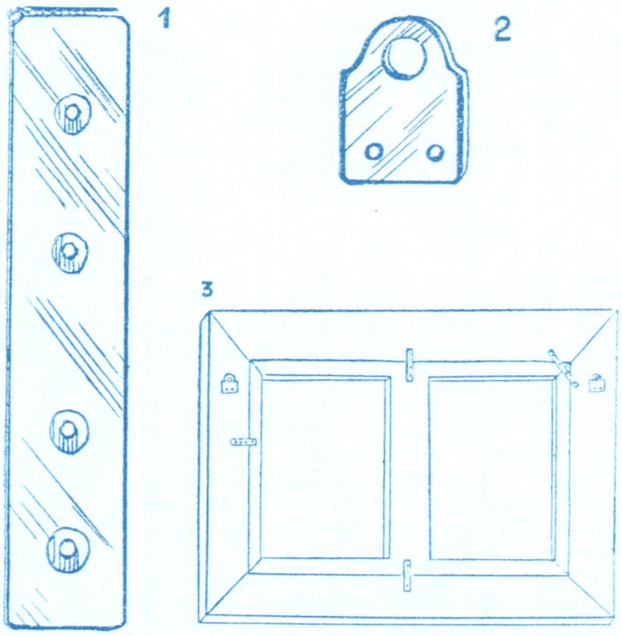

(1) Metal strap, actual size.
(2) Picture wire plate, actual size.
(3) Straps and plates in place.

as standard for single shipments for some time. It is *not* recommended, however, for travelling exhibitions unless an exhibitor cannot achieve packing in any other way. It may be employed with comparative safety if shipments are to be made from one museum to another and then returned; for successive shipments, there is too great risk of damage owing to pads breaking open after they have been used several times, or coming loose from the corners of the frames.

1. Group together pictures of equal size and place them face to face and back to back.
2. Tack, staple or fasten with adhesive, excelsior pads on to the corners of each frame. (Excelsior pads are made by taking strong, heavy wrapping paper, placing excelsior across the centre of the sheet and rolling the sheet of paper to enclose the excelsior. The open ends should be folded back and fastened together with gummed paper so that no excelsior will escape during transit.) These rolls become cushions on the corners of the frames to mitigate any shock which may occur to the outer container *(diagram N, page 39)*.
3. Place separation sheets of corrugated board or heavy cardboard between each picture. The separation board should be cut the size of the packing case, not the size of the picture.
4. Place padded braces wherever they are needed to separate paintings of different sizes so that they will ride firmly in the box during transit *(fig. 41, page 103)*.
5. Line up pictures at one side of the case, filling in spaces left at the opposite side and at the top with excelsior pads. Fill in with pads about four inches of space between the picture frames and the side of the case against which they are lined up *(diagram N, page 39)*.

Packages. This method is usually used for small unframed pictures; it can be used also for small framed pictures, panels or works on paper.

1. Wrap the picture in waxed or tissue paper.
2. Place corrugated board or composition board at the back and over the face of the wrapped picture. The boards should be cut just slightly larger than the size of the picture so that corner will be fully protected. Fasten these pro-

Diagram N. EXCELSIOR PADS.

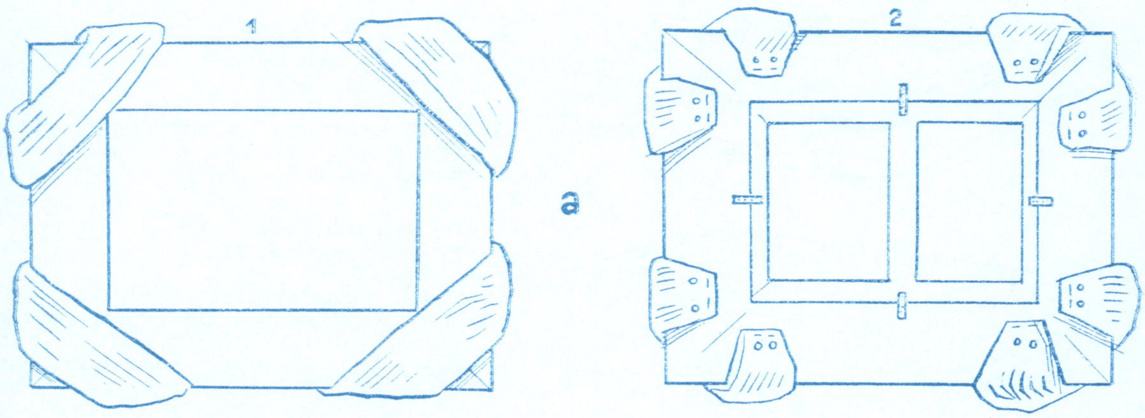

b
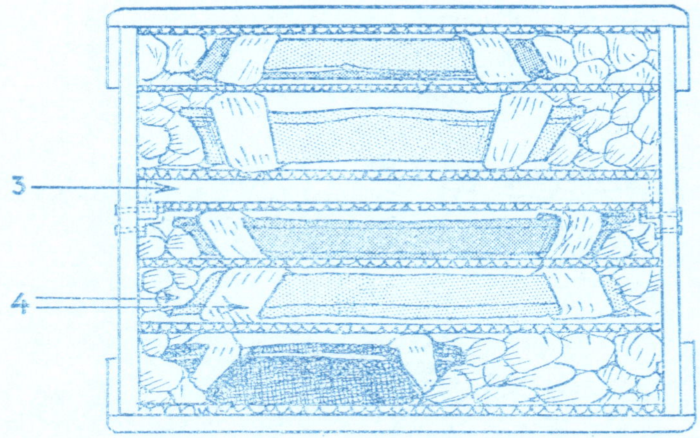

(a) Excelsior pads. (1) Front of picture, pads in place. (2) Back of picture, pads in place.

(b) Box showing pictures packed with excelsior pads and corrugated board separation sheets. (3) Batten or brace. (4) Excelsior pads.

tective boards in place by means of twine or gummed paper strips, being careful not to attach it to the tissue, or to pull the twine so tight that it will rub against the wrapped picture *(diagram O, page 40)*.

3. If pictures are small, several can be packed together in this manner. Each picture should be wrapped first in waxed or tissue paper, corrugated or composition board (any rigid material which will not puncture or bend easily) placed between pictures and the group then bound together with heavy wrapping paper. The pictures are packed face to face. Unframed pictures may be packed together in this manner if the decorated surfaces are in good condition and if the painted surface is level.

Envelopes or Inner Cases. This method may be used for small unframed pictures or for framed pictures of nearly the same size. If pictures differ widely in

Diagram O. PAINTINGS WRAPPED FOR SHIPMENT.

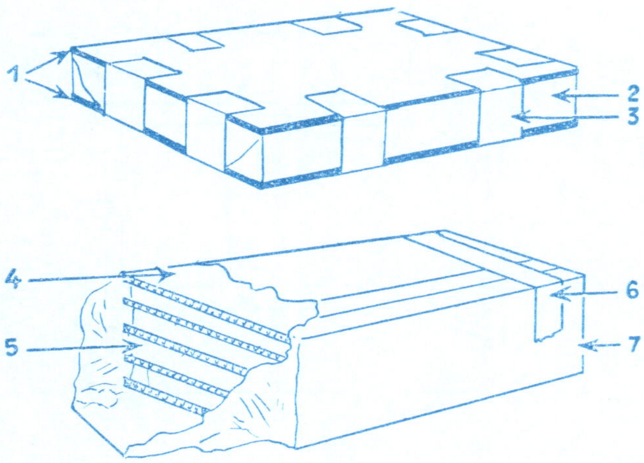

(1) Heavy composition boards.
(2) Wrapping paper.
(3) Gummed tape.
Heavy composition board prevents punctures in transit. The painting is wrapped first in tissue. The boards are held in place with tape or twine.

(4) Corrugated board,
(5) Tissue-wrapped pictures.
(6) Gummed tape.
(7) Wrapping paper.
Framed or unframed pictures of the same size wrapped together for shipment. Each picture is wrapped first with tissue or waxed paper, then separated from the others with sheets of corrugated board. The packages are then "floated" in excelsior in the packing case.

Diagram P. ENVELOPES OR INNER CASES.

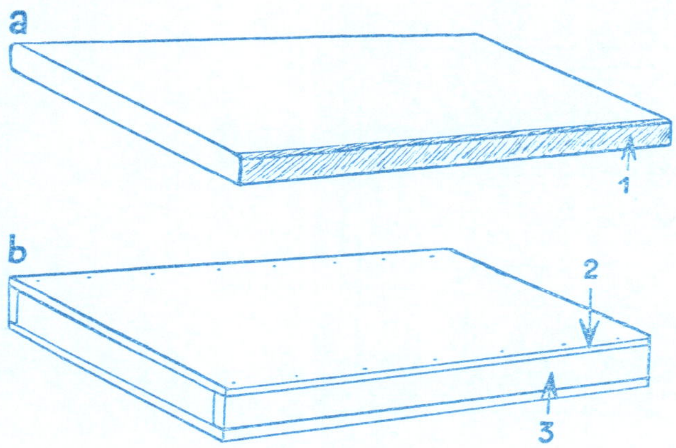

(a) Cardboard envelope for framed picture. (1) Canvas tape on cardboard.

(b) Plywood envelope for unframed pictures. The picture must be wrapped before placing in envelope. (2) Plywood. (3) 7/8-inch lumber.

size, it is better to use the package method described above.

1. A small box, made of cardboard or composition board may be constructed with one end left open. It is made by cutting the boards the size of the picture and taping the edges together with heavy canvas. Into this "envelope" is slipped the picture, wrapped first in tissue or waxed paper. If framed watercolours, drawings or prints are packed in this manner, it is not necessary to wrap them first in tissue *(diagram P, above)*.
2. The shipping box should be lined with thick sponge-rubber pads to prevent shocks sustained during travels from being transmitted to the inner cases and thus to glass or painting surface. An excellent method of holding envelopes in place is to put a sheet of heavy composition board over the sponge-rubber pads so that the group of envelopes ride together on one cushioned surface, thus distributing the weight of the group. The sheet of composition board is separated from the outer shipping case by the sponge-rubber pads. If different sized envelopes are contained in the same case, spaces at the

sides and top should be filled in with thick excelsior pads, pieces of sponge-rubber or several sheets of corrugated board taped together *(fig. 39, page 102)*.

Cases with Fitted Grooves for Pictures. This method has proved most successful in the United States where it has been used to a great extent over the past 10 years. It was arrived at after several related experiments to avoid sending *any* loose packing material with travelling exhibitions. The problem was to construct a shipping box which would fully protect the pictures from shock and yet allow exhibitors to remove and replace the pictures in their shipping containers with the least amount of effort. Furthermore, the need seemed to be for a "foolproof" method—a way of packing which would permit no alterations in the box or packing method during a tour. It was therefore necessary to design a case which would hold various pictures in only one way; inexperienced packers could not repack the box incorrectly.

Individual grooves are constructed so that each picture slides into its own compartment, clearly marked from the end which remains open. This method is the most expensive since it involves a great deal of labour to fit the pictures carefully into individually-constructed grooves. It has proved its worth, however, in that pictures seem to be able to travel indefinitely without sustaining damages. It eliminates many steps in packing and consequently pictures are handled less than by other methods. It can be managed, moreover, by less well-trained labour since there is little risk involved in sliding pictures in and out of padded grooves.

1. Construct a wooden rack slightly larger than the framed picture *(diagram Q, page 42,* and *fig. 40, page 103)*. Line the rack with felt at the sides which will cover the edges of the frame. At the bottom, place a piece of thick sponge-rubber so that the picture will be properly cushioned in transit.
2. Place the rack, padded with sponge-rubber at all critical points of contact, into a groove made of boards nailed into the side of the packing case.
3. Add sponge-rubber pads across the lid of the case so that the frames will touch the rubber pads here or at the bottom of the rack while riding.
4. Fasten cover in place by sinking three-inch bolts into holes provided in square metal plates, which are in turn screwed into the sides of the box with four-inch screws *(fig. 38, page 101)*.

The principle of this method is again to ' float" the picture in the packing cases. Therefore wherever picture or brace comes in contact with the walls of the case, it is cushioned against shock with sponge-rubber.

Trays. A similar arrangement has been worked out with a series of trays *(fig. 41, page 103)*. The packing box is built the size of the largest picture with padding placed on all four sides on which the picture rests. Smaller pictures are contained in a series of trays, the sides of which are extended to the proportions of the box. The interior of each tray is padded with felt so that no wrapping of pictures is necessary.

Although the photograph does not show this, the presence of sheets of corrugated board placed in the tray before laying the picture in place, as well as over the back of the canvas, adds fuller protection should any loose object, like a splinter of wood, become detached during transit.

Framed Watercolours, Drawings, Prints, Photographs

In general, works in these media are treated like paintings and packed according to one of the methods described above, the choice being based upon the size of the picture and the cost involved.

1. All pictures covered with glass must be protected against breakage of glass in transit (see General Rules, page 31). The best method, as heretofore described, is to strip gummed tape which is not water soluble at horizontal intervals of one-quarter of an inch across the entire surface of glass. If such material cannot be procured, the glass may be covered with a sheet of heavy wrapping paper or inexpensive cloth pasted on to its surface. (Note, however, that this method is not advisable if any other means can be found.) The substance attaching paper or cloth to the glass should, if possible, be a rubber-based adhesive. Paste or other water-soluble adhesives are hazardous because of the risk of water running to the edge of the glass and penetrating beneath, causing serious damage to the picture surface. If it is impossible to procure any substance except paste, cut the paper or cloth somewhat larger than the frame of the picture and attach the paste to the glass leaving at least an inch of glass free of paste where the glass meets the frame. When the paper or cloth is removed, there will be less danger of water seeping under the glass. The extra width of paper or cloth helps to give a strong surface to grasp and pull

Diagram Q. PACKING-CASE WITH FITTED GROOVES FOR PAINTINGS.

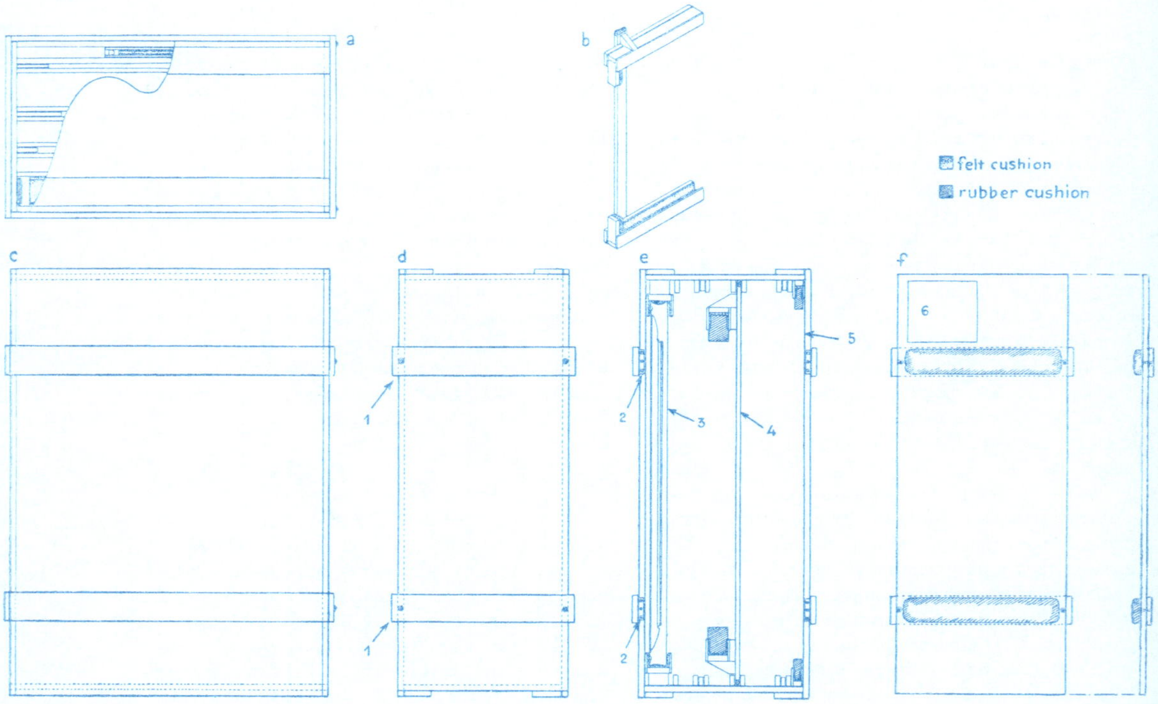

(a) Top exterior, cut away to show rack adjustment.
(b) Section of separate rack (half scale).
(c) Side exterior.
(d) Front exterior (removable). (1) Standard bolt and washers hardware.
(e) Interior with front removed. (2) Standard metal plates. (3) Packing shown in place. (4) One rack shown in place. (5) Waterproof paper covering entire inside of box.
(f) Inside of front panel. (6) Instruction label (packing and unpacking).

away from the glass. The glued portion of the paper need only be dampened with a wet cloth or sponge. Exhibitors should be clearly warned never to *soak* the paper or allow water to run across the surface of the glass.

2. Pack the picture by one of the methods described under the heading of oils. The most efficient method for travelling exhibitions seems to be that described under "Envelopes or inner cases" and illustrated in the photograph on page 102. The slip cases protect each individual picture from all others in the packing case.

If, for some reason, exhibitors cannot pack watercolours or drawings by any of the methods previously described, it is advisable to remove frames and glass before the exhibition is sent on tour. The pictures can be matted, the surfaces covered with heavy, clear plastic sheets (see description of mounting methods for watercolours, Chapter I, pages 19-21). They can then be shipped in inner cases, wrapped packages or "solander" boxes. (The latter are the stiff-sided boxes in which standard-sized matted prints are generally stored. The cover is hinged into place and drops over all four sides of the container.) Solander boxes should be wrapped in paper before being placed in packing-cases.

Oriental scroll-type watercolours should be rolled in tissue or waxed paper and placed in metal tubes or wooden boxes before being packed in outer containers. It is customary to keep such rolls in fine silk square wrappings in which they are placed diagonally and then wrapped before being placed in their boxes. Metal tubes are, of course, a modern device. If scrolls are to remain packed for any length of time, air-tight enclosures should be avoided.

Pastels

1. Do not remove glass or frame from pastels.
2. Protect the picture by affixing strips of gummed tape to the glass. Follow packing instructions under "Oils" for pictures covered with glass.
3. As pastels are particularly subject to damage in transit because the surface is so delicate, they are generally eliminated from travelling exhibitions.

Miniatures (on ivory, paper, wood, etc.)

1. Do not remove from frame or mount.
2. Cover with tissue, then wrap in cotton.
3. Double box, first in cardboard container, then in outer wooden case. Use generous amounts of dry excelsior padding between inner and outer boxes to absorb any shock.

Outer packing cases for all pictures should be constructed of strong matched lumber according to specifications given under General Rules, pages 31-33. All boxes should be lined with waterproof paper.

SMALL FRAGILES

(This classification includes ceramics, terracotta, glass, ivory, jewellery and small sculptures of wood, metal or stone.)

Protect the Surfaces

1. In preparation for packing, completely cover the surface of the delicate object with tissue, muslin or cheesecloth.
2. Wrap any projecting part such as a handle, arm, etc., carefully and independently of the body of the piece so that it is protected in itself from shock, then wrap the entire object so that the projecting part becomes an integral part of the whole. Tissue or shredded waxed paper are acceptable materials for wrapping projecting parts.

Protect the Entire Object

1. Place wrapped objects in small cardboard boxes. Surround object with sufficient tissue, cotton, or shredded paper so that no part of an object is without shock-absorbing support.
2. When placed in packing boxes, the inner boxes of cardboard should also be "floated" in packing material such as excelsior, but packed firmly enough so that they cannot shift position in transit.

SMALL NON-FRAGILES

(Objects in this class include small sculptures in marble, stone or bronze, silverware, coins, gems, etc.)

Packing

1. Treat such works as if they were small fragiles. In general, however, less surface protection will be required. The same amount of "floating" material will be needed to prevent shock within the shipping container. Heavy pieces should be packed in plywood, rather than cardboard inner boxes *(fig. 42, 43, page 104)*. Some objects normally classed as "non-fragiles" will have to be packed as fragiles because of deteriorated surface conditions, structural weakness or restoration.
2. Instead of separate cardboard or plywood containers, objects in this classification can also be packed in a compartment constructed inside the packing case. Each compartment, built to fit an individual object, can be filled with excelsior or lined with sponge-rubber or like padding sufficiently thick to cushion the object against shock. Fig. 44 on page 105 shows a combination of these methods. The interior boxes are lined with cloth-covered sponge-rubber fitted to the objects; the boxes are fixed in excelsior within the shipping container.

   Exhibitors[1] have also indicated the use of bed ticking (heavy canvas) to line a packing-case containing such objects. The canvas is nailed over excelsior padding to line the compartments inside the case. Instead of wrapping individual objects, small drawstring bags made of quilted cotton-filled cloth are constructed for each object. These arrangements are useful for travelling exhibitions because they eliminate loose packing material which may not be repacked with objects

[1] Used by the Addison Gallery of American Art, Andover, Massachusetts, for an exhibition of small stone sculptures.

each time they are shipped. Marked individual containers are always safer; the packer learns to look for a particular compartment or case for each object before packing it.

WORKS ON PAPER

(Objects in this category include prints, drawings, posters, manuscripts, pages from books, photographs, etc.)

Surface Protection

1. Place such works in window mats with celluloid covers if they are to be shipped unframed (see description for mounting watercolours, etc., Chapter I, Section 2 under "Assembly and Display", page 18).
2. If the work of art is not protected in this manner, it can be shipped safely by placing glassine or pure mulberry paper over the decorated surface. Sized paper should not be used and printed matter or poor quality papers should not be placed in direct contact with works in this group. It is not advisable to use this method for a travelling exhibition because the surface of the work is not fully protected at all times and it is subject to continued handling. There is risk of successive exhibitors losing protective papers and of mats becoming soiled and damaged by constant handling.

   It is mentioned here only for those who must avoid the added expense of encasing works in celluloid or plastic covers and who are willing to risk this method for several shipments. Valued works on paper should certainly not be sent on tour unless they can be sufficiently protected.

Outer Protection

1. Solander boxes—made for storage of standard-size mats—are recommended as the best type of inner packing box, especially when works are matted without a protective plastic sheet covering the surface.

   (If exhibitors would adopt the use of standard-size mats and solander boxes for storage of prints and drawings, shipping as well as display would be greatly facilitated. Museums could keep on hand standard-size frames so that unframed works could be easily framed on arrival for exhibition.)
2. Six to twelve items may be wrapped together with corrugated board, cut to size, placed at top and bottom of the group to prevent bending. Use strong wrapping paper to bind group together.
3. Sometimes these works are covered with glass, backed with heavy cardboard and "sealed" into place with adhesive tape around the edges. Works mounted in this manner may be slipped into narrow cardboard envelopes, or wrapped together (not more than six at a time) with corrugated board sheets between each item. If bound in this manner, it is not usually necessary to tape the glasses before packing *(diagram O, page 40)*.
4. Posters can be rolled and shipped in a cardboard or lightweight metal tube, or wooden box. They should be protected with sheets of tissue between the surfaces of each poster.
5. The outer box should be of wood construction, either plywood or seven-eighths of an inch lumber, depending on the weight of the packed items. It should be lined with waterproof paper, sealed into place. Sponge-rubber or excelsior-filled pads should be used to line outer cases to protect the solander boxes or wrapped packages from shock in transit.

BOOKS

Valuable Bindings

1. Books for which individual cover boxes are available should be placed in their boxes, then wrapped with brown paper.
2. Books without cover boxes should be wrapped in tissue, then in corrugated board. Inlaid or jewelled bindings should be treated as small fragiles.
3. For travelling exhibitions containing valuable bindings, exhibitors may provide glass or plastic enclosed cases. The bindings should never be attached to the display case in transit, however, but should be packed separately.

Books

1. Books of the same size may be wrapped together in tissue, then in heavy brown paper, and finally corrugated board. Books wrapped in paper only must not be tied tightly for if twine is used it will mar the bindings. Gummed tape is preferable to seal wrapped books.
2. Double packing will insure greater protection for all bindings and lessen movement in the outer packing boxes. The latter should be waterproofed. The packages of books should be "floated" in excelsior to prevent damage in transit.

This is the page
that rustles
when you turn it
[maybe]
(text on p. 15)

TEXTILES

(The fragility of textiles is not apparent on casual examination; accordingly, damage from creasing is a constant hazard. The entire thread structure may be endangered by improper folding.)

Surface Protection

1. Clean hands are essential when working with textiles. It has been found practical to send along with a textile exhibition at least two pairs of white cotton gloves requesting those who will handle the textiles to wear them.
   Fabric must be so wrapped that dust is excluded. Lay pieces of tissue on the surface of the cloth and roll the textile on to a drum, cardboard tube or round wooden pole. This method prevents creasing the fabric in folds.
2. If textiles must be folded to fit a package or container (costumes, bags, etc.) several layers of tissue should be placed in the folds to reduce creasing.

Outer Protection

For textiles mounted in frames, affixed to stretchers or to wall panels:

1. Use corrugated or composition board, cut to size, at front and back of each frame to stiffen the backing cloth to which the textile is attached. This will lessen vibration. Several framed textiles of the same size can be wrapped together in a single package.
   If the textile is framed with glass, treat as a picture, stripping the glass with "masking" tape at one-quarter of an inch intervals.
   If it is matted only, treat as a print or drawing, wrapping several together in a package.
   If textiles are mounted on frames, uncovered, wrap the surface of the textile in tissue, affixing the paper to the backing board with "masking" tape before packing frames in outer case. Be careful not to allow masking tape to touch the surface of the textile itself.
2. Place wrapped packages in wooden boxes large enough to allow for resilient padding between inner and outer containers. Cases should be lined with waterproof paper.

For unmounted textiles:

1. After placing tissue in folds, wrap textile in tissue, then in brown paper—or, as above, place tissue on surface and roll textile on to round support. Wrap outer surface exposed, first in tissue, then in brown paper.
2. If folded flat, pack with tissue in cardboard carton just tightly enough to prevent movement in transit. Packed cartons are then placed in wooden shipping boxes.
3. Wrapped packages or cardboard boxes should be cushioned with excelsior pads between each package when placed in outer packing case.

(Moths and other insects should be guarded against at all times. If textiles show evidence of insect attack, they should be fumigated before packing.)

LARGE OBJECTS

(This classification includes heavy sculpture, furniture, woodwork, etc. The danger in moving and packing any valuable object is increased by unusual size or weight. Each large object is a special problem in itself, requiring extra care in handling and packing. Exhibitors should be so warned prior to arrival of an exhibition so that sufficient staff is in attendance to assist in unpacking and handling.)

Sculpture

Each piece of sculpture must be carefully studied before arranging packing. The method of packing chosen will depend upon the medium, weight, fragility and the way the object is put together. Braces should not be attached, for instance, if there is danger of placing stress on a joint. Three methods have been worked out for safe shipment.

1. The first step is to protect the surface of the object. Wrap it in flannel or other soft cloth. The simplest method, used for non-fragile pieces which are not heavy, is to place the wrapped sculpture in a bedding of excelsior so that it will "float" in its container. Sufficient excelsior must be used to prevent any possibility of the sculpture coming in contact with the walls of the packing case. It is advisable to place pads on all projecting members, and to wrap pads at points of stress before placing the object in excelsior. Further protection may be gained by using double boxing placing excelsior again between inner and outer containers. Sufficient excelsior must be used to hold the object in place. Curatorial or conservatorial knowledge must be called upon to make the decision on boxing. Responsibility for handling and packing this type of material should never be delegated to packers alone.
2. If there is any question about the condition or fragility of a piece of sculpture, or if it is extremely heavy, it should be packed with padded

braces fitted to the object to reduce shock in transit *(fig. 45, 45a, pages 106, 107)*. If it is not a heavy piece, but a fragile one, it is wise to employ double boxing. Braces should be padded with heavy excelsior pads firmly attached to the braces, or better, with heavy felt or sponge-rubber pads covered with muslin or other inexpensive cloth. This prevents the sponge rubber from tearing apart, as well as eliminating any possibility of the rubber staining the polished surface of metal.

3. If the piece is large and heavy, a special case should be constructed to contain it. Again the surface is usually protected by being wrapped in cloth. Padded braces should be fitted to hold the sculpture in place in the packing container *(fig. 46, page 108)*. The container may be built in pyramidal form to command its riding on the base during transit, or the outside of the case may contain "fins" to force its riding on the base. The fins are merely large bars of wood, rounded at the ends, placed at the centre of each side of the box and on top. If a box is placed on one of these sides, it will not ride steadily and those transporting it will recognize at once that it must be placed on the flat base surface. The box should, of course, be marked TOP, BOTTOM, THIS SIDE UP, FRAGILE, etc. A rectangular box is more convenient for shippers than a pyramidal form though the latter might be necessary in certain instances where sculpture must retain a specific balance at all times.

Furniture

1. For small tables, benches, chairs, desks and items of like character which have been weakened by age, hard wear, dry rot or insects, "floating" the object in its container is essential. As advised for sculpture, large, heavy pieces of furniture must be braced in their shipping containers. An ornate table of any size would have considerable weight and only with braces can it be packed to prevent damage to lightly attached or weakened parts.
2. Braces must be placed so that they will bear the main weight of the piece without endangering its weak parts or decorative elements. Both table and brace should be heavily padded and the wider the brace, the less shock will be transmitted directly to any one portion of the object's framework.
3. As a general rule, objects for which bracing is required should be double-boxed. In this way the "floatation" material packed between inner and outer containers will reduce bracing shock to a minimum.
4. The fabric covering used on upholstery is frequently old and worn. It must be covered with muslin or wrapping paper to keep it clean and to preserve it, Arms and legs of chairs should be padded with packing cotton, fabric-covered sponge-rubber, felt or shredded paper in preference to kraft-type wrapping paper which, in shaping it to a curved member, will acquire creases sharp enough to scratch varnish. Pad arms and legs of chairs with excelsior-filled pads or heavy layers of sponge-rubber, covered with fabric.

Architectural Models, Stage Settings, etc.

No surface protection should be provided for models. So many parts are so extremely fragile, it is usually advisable to allow the model to ride without any packing material touching its surface. It should, however, be protected from shock by thick pieces of sponge-rubber or large excelsior pads placed around the base, against the sides of the packing box and beneath the model. Models are often fitted into sponge-rubber-lined grooves, leaving air space above and below the model.

Unless models are very sturdily constructed, they do not travel well. They should be made of wood, not cardboard, and should be in good condition before shipment. It is difficult for any but expert model-makers to make repairs and usually repairs take considerable time and are costly.

PANELS

The least expensive method of packing panels is to place them face to face and back to back with sheets of corrugated board between, then wrap in heavy paper and seal. This method can be used successfully provided there are no projecting items mounted on the panels. Panels containing photographs and labels only can be packed in this manner, but there should be a frame which projects slightly all around the edge of the panel to protect the surface of the mounts from being rubbed in transit. Sponge-rubber or excelsior pads should be placed between the wrapped panels and the walls of the packing case to cushion the edges in transit *(fig. 47, page 109)*.

The slotted box forms a better means of shipping panels. They may be slipped into felt or rubber-lined grooves built on to the sides of the packing

Diagram R. CROSS SECTION OF INTERLOCKING FRAMES.

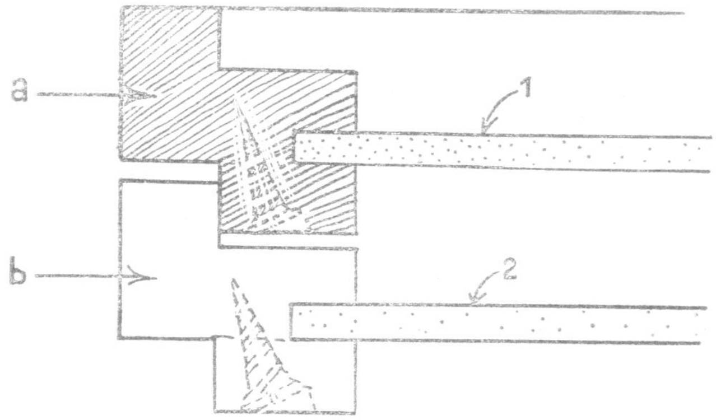

(a) Frame I, (1) panel.
(b) Frame II, (2) panel.

case. Enough space is left between grooves to make certain no object mounted on a panel will touch another object or panel during transit.

If fragile items are displayed on panels, it is wise to remove these and pack them separately in another container for shipment.

As an aid to packing, frames of panels are sometimes so moulded that they nest one within the other, protecting in this way shallow objects attached to the surface of the panels and forming a solid mass of six to eight framed panels which cannot shift nor move. The group of panels is then slipped as a single unit into a packing case. This method eliminates slots and grooves for individual panels and all but the simplest kind of padding in the cases that are to contain them. Excelsior or sponge-rubber pads cushion the group of panels in transit (*fig. 48, page 110, fig. 11, page 83,* and *diagram* R, *page 47*).

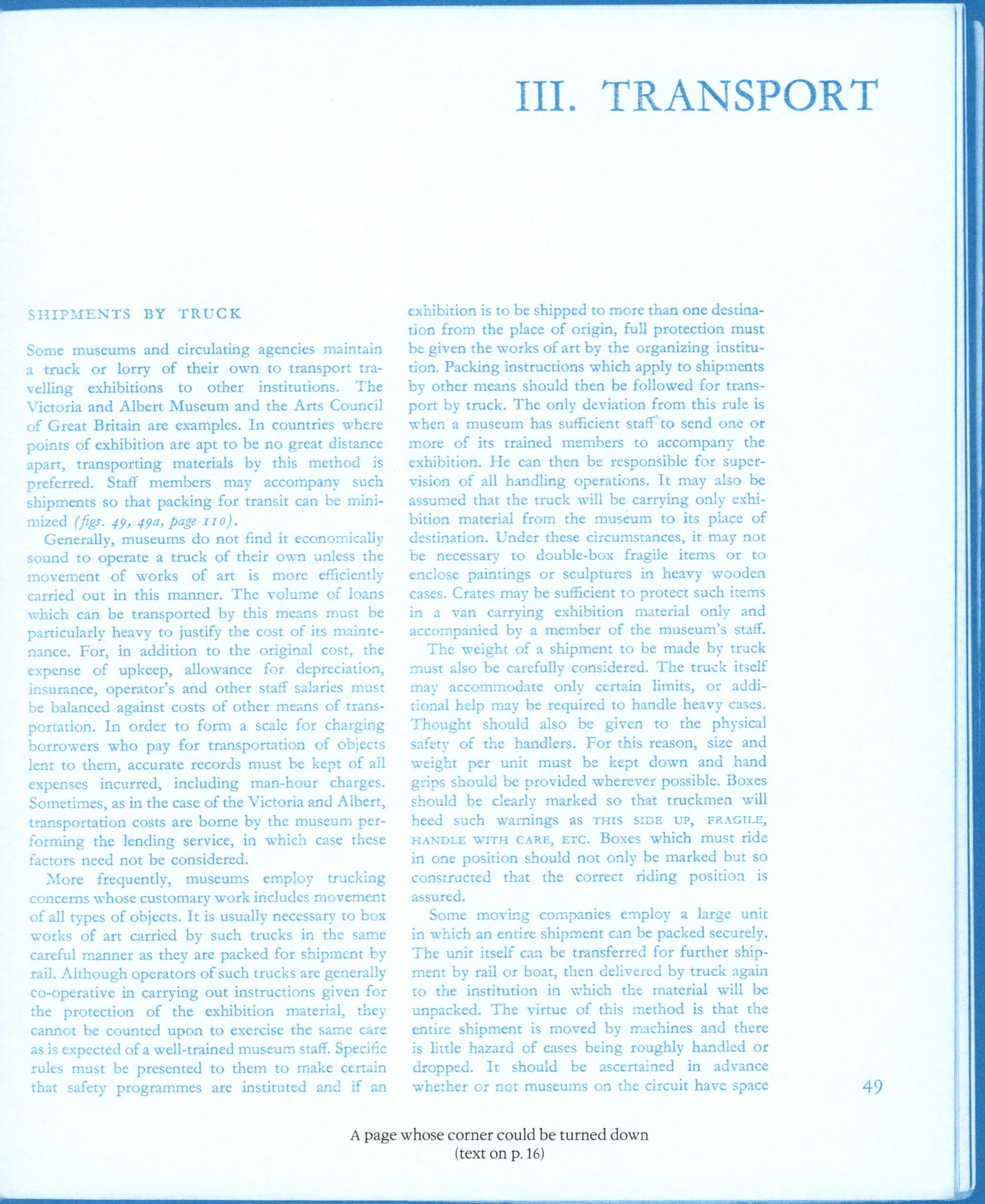

III. TRANSPORT

SHIPMENTS BY TRUCK

Some museums and circulating agencies maintain a truck or lorry of their own to transport travelling exhibitions to other institutions. The Victoria and Albert Museum and the Arts Council of Great Britain are examples. In countries where points of exhibition are apt to be no great distance apart, transporting materials by this method is preferred. Staff members may accompany such shipments so that packing for transit can be minimized *(figs. 49, 49a, page 110)*.

Generally, museums do not find it economically sound to operate a truck of their own unless the movement of works of art is more efficiently carried out in this manner. The volume of loans which can be transported by this means must be particularly heavy to justify the cost of its maintenance. For, in addition to the original cost, the expense of upkeep, allowance for depreciation, insurance, operator's and other staff salaries must be balanced against costs of other means of transportation. In order to form a scale for charging borrowers who pay for transportation of objects lent to them, accurate records must be kept of all expenses incurred, including man-hour charges. Sometimes, as in the case of the Victoria and Albert, transportation costs are borne by the museum performing the lending service, in which case these factors need not be considered.

More frequently, museums employ trucking concerns whose customary work includes movement of all types of objects. It is usually necessary to box works of art carried by such trucks in the same careful manner as they are packed for shipment by rail. Although operators of such trucks are generally co-operative in carrying out instructions given for the protection of the exhibition material, they cannot be counted upon to exercise the same care as is expected of a well-trained museum staff. Specific rules must be presented to them to make certain that safety programmes are instituted and if an exhibition is to be shipped to more than one destination from the place of origin, full protection must be given the works of art by the organizing institution. Packing instructions which apply to shipments by other means should then be followed for transport by truck. The only deviation from this rule is when a museum has sufficient staff to send one or more of its trained members to accompany the exhibition. He can then be responsible for supervision of all handling operations. It may also be assumed that the truck will be carrying only exhibition material from the museum to its place of destination. Under these circumstances, it may not be necessary to double-box fragile items or to enclose paintings or sculptures in heavy wooden cases. Crates may be sufficient to protect such items in a van carrying exhibition material only and accompanied by a member of the museum's staff.

The weight of a shipment to be made by truck must also be carefully considered. The truck itself may accommodate only certain limits, or additional help may be required to handle heavy cases. Thought should also be given to the physical safety of the handlers. For this reason, size and weight per unit must be kept down and hand grips should be provided wherever possible. Boxes should be clearly marked so that truckmen will heed such warnings as THIS SIDE UP, FRAGILE, HANDLE WITH CARE, ETC. Boxes which must ride in one position should not only be marked but so constructed that the correct riding position is assured.

Some moving companies employ a large unit in which an entire shipment can be packed securely. The unit itself can be transferred for further shipment by rail or boat, then delivered by truck again to the institution in which the material will be unpacked. The virtue of this method is that the entire shipment is moved by machines and there is little hazard of cases being roughly handled or dropped. It should be ascertained in advance whether or not museums on the circuit have space

49

A page whose corner could be turned down
(text on p. 16)

enough to receive such a unit so that unpacking can be done on the premises.

Because it is not general practice to ship a travelling exhibition which will move from one destination to another over a considerable period of time by truck, fuller instructions for handling unboxed works of art have been omitted. Museum practice should be followed for such movements, under the guidance of a member of the museum staff (for general handling instructions, see Appendix B, pages 63-66).

SHIPMENTS BY RAIL

Two methods of shipment by rail exist in many countries; an express or fast freight agency which is a special organization existing to expedite shipments by rail through their own salaried staff, members of which are stationed at all leading and many minor points of embarkation, and the ordinary rail freight which is carried by the railroad and handled by its staff only. If shipments are made by rail freight, arrangements must normally be made to pick up boxes left in freight offices at railway stations, transporting them by truck to their point of destination. Express companies often provide trucking services from station to point of destination as well as handling the shipment by rail.

It is generally agreed that rail-freight shipments are exposed to hazards of handling far greater than those to which express shipments are subjected. Though rail freight is slower and the rates much lower than those of express companies, it is preferable to ship works of art or other fragile or valuable materials by the less hazardous means of transport. Furthermore, travelling exhibitions which must meet specific dates will generally need to be carried as swiftly as possible.

On the North American continent, the Railway Express Company offers a Fine Arts Bill of Lading which implies a measure of special handling for the consignment. It is effected by what the Railway Express Company designates as its Uniform Special Contract for the "transportation of paintings, carvings, glassware, sculpture, etc., of a value over $550". When there are 10 or more cases in a shipment on special contract the company will usually provide direct transit from museum door to freight car, thereby eliminating unnecessary handling at intermediate collection depots. Arrangements for this service should be made in advance with the local express office.

The Railway Express Agency's basic shipping rate includes a minimum insurance of $50 per box or 50 cents per pound for shipments weighing more than 100 pounds, without additional charge. Above this minimum allowed, charges for additional coverage are computed according to a sliding scale on a weight-plus-valuation basis. If the shipper is already protected by insurance which covers the exhibition in transit as well as on exhibition, he will be paying double insurance to use the special contract with a valuation of $550 per case. It is therefore not warranted except when extremely valuable material is included and it is thought that the special handling guaranteed by the Railway Express Contract might minimize damages in transit.

The Railway Express Agency operates within the United States and has services to and from Alaska, Canada, Cuba and Hawaii. A similar company offering the same services operates in Canada. Beyond this area, shipping services, rules and documents vary considerably from country to country. The American Express Company, offering international service, can furnish information about rail service and rules in many countries, or act as an agent for the shipper in co-ordinating arrangements necessary with the various carriers to transport an exhibition to its ultimate destination. Offices exist in about 150 cities in 33 countries. Exhibitors can usually secure information through consulates as well.

OCEAN TRANSPORT

Hazards are perhaps greater across water than for shipments by rail and objects must be duly protected to withstand repeated handling at points of embarkation and arrival. Boxes must be strongly constructed to undergo the pressures to which containers are subjected in being loaded from dock to ship or during the voyage when a boat rolls and pitches. If storms are encountered these stresses may be very severe. If the interior packing does not hold the contents firmly in place, they will be thrown about inside the box. If proper precautions have not been taken to eliminate salt air and resist temperature changes, the contents may suffer serious damage. Exhibitors must pay particular attention to packing procedures to guarantee safe shipment overseas. *Unless special arrangements are made by the circulating agency to have a shipment examined by customs at the place of destination, boxes may be opened on the docks, repacked for delivery to the museum with less care than is customary in a museum.* Further handling by rail or truck is also usually involved after shipments are delivered at docks.

Import and export regulations frequently tend to obstruct instead of encourage the movement of cultural material from one country to another. At present difficulties arise not only from tariff barriers and restrictive interpretations of these laws but also from a general lack of information about customs regulations on the part of institutions and their agents. Under the leadership of Unesco, some progress is being made toward breaking down trade barriers and fostering the exchange of educational, scientific and cultural materials. In November 1948 the *Agreement for Facilitating the International Circulation of Visual and Auditory Materials of an Educational, Scientific and Cultural Character,*[1] designed to remove duties, quotas, licences and other obstacles to exchange, was introduced at the General Conference and is now open for acceptance by all countries which are members of Unesco or the United Nations. A second *Agreement on the Importation of Educational, Scientific and Cultural Materials*[2] is also in process of ratification by a considerable number of Member States. Thirteen countries[3] have already ratified this agreement which will grant duty-free entry to a wide range of commodities including works of art, visual and auditory materials entering their borders. (For present rules governing import and export regulations in different countries see index by country provided in the book *Trade Barriers to Knowledge,* published by Unesco, Paris, 1951).

Institutions shipping exhibitions for international tour must familiarize themselves with present import and export regulations so that they can issue proper instructions to their agents. Such papers as consular invoices, certificates of originality, proofs of antiquity and other essentials must be provided for many shipments entering various countries. When sending shipping instructions, the circulating agency should include a list of the documents required by foreign countries of exit and entry well in advance of shipping dates so that the exhibitor responsible for shipment outside the country will have time to obtain import and export licences if required. Shipments will not be accepted at certain ports if contents are packed with hay or straw instead of excelsior or shredded paper (see General Packing Instructions, pages 31-37).

Customs brokers or forwarding agents are usually familiar with the procedures necessary for clearing imports and exports through customs. The charge for their service is generally reasonable compared with the time required for importers and exporters to clear shipments through customs without professional help. These agents can work much more efficiently, however, if they receive specific instructions from importers as to how they wish to have their shipments handled and if they are authorized to sign bills of lading, affidavits, bonds and other customs documents when required. Museums, by issuing proper instructions to foreign and domestic agents, can also facilitate the work of the customs officials.

Documents required for ocean voyages usually include some or all of the following:

Bills of Lading—showing names and addresses of shippers and consignees, marks and/or numbers of cases being shipped, weights, size and general description of contents. Unless the carrier requires a full value declaration, a nominal value, or the value for which no additional charge is made (usually $500) is shown on the bill of lading.

Export Licence—declarations or licences as required by various countries for exports.

Dock Receipt—for carrier employed to deliver shipment to pier.

Delivery Order—for carrier employed to collect shipment from pier.

Import Licences—as required by countries of destination.

Other documents—consular or commercial invoices listing each item with its value and showing names and addresses of consignors and consignees, certificates of originality, authenticity, antiquity, etc., as required by countries of destination.

The shipper or circulating agency should always ascertain the latest regulations from the proper consulate, the United States Department of Commerce or other informed authority before making any shipments. Shipments sent without proper papers must often wait months for clearance at docks or other storage houses, sometimes subjected to hazards of handling or exposure which should be avoided.

---

1 As of January 1953, the Agreement had been ratified by the following eight countries: Cambodia, Canada, Iraq, Norway, Pakistan, Philippines, Syria, Yugoslavia.

2 Copies of these agreements may be obtained from United Nations Headquarters in New York, or from Unesco in Paris.

3 The 13 countries ratifying this agreement are: Cambodia, Ceylon, Cuba, Egypt, Israel, Laos, Monaco, Pakistan, Philippines, Sweden, Thailand, Viet-Nam and Yugoslavia.

Many of the large steamships are equipped with strong rooms where valuable merchandise may be stored and such stowage should always be requested for shipments of works of art. It is usually unnecessary to declare a valuation over $500 to obtain this stowage though certain steamship companies require it, charging an increased freight rate for this preferred placement.

AIR TRANSPORT

The most rapid method of transporting works of art often requires the least effort. It is reputed to be smoother than any surface shipping and therefore requires no additional precautions. Because the shipments are handled a number of times after arrival at points of destination, however, it is wise to pack materials according to the standards set for rail shipment. If it is known that a cargo will be carried directly from airport to museum by truck, lighter packing cases, built of plywood or rigid, tough composition board reinforced by heavy lumber cleats, might be used. Cardboard or corrugated board cartons are not safe because there is considerable risk of puncture during loading and unloading operations. In the new pressurized cabins, boxes are subject to little or no change of humidity or air pressure and therefore travel in relative safety while in the air. On long hauls overland, exhibitions would be less subject to handling if transported by air and consequently the risk of shock would be substantially reduced.

Exhibitors should check on whether or not delivery service is provided by an airline. It is often necessary to arrange in advance with a private trucking company to collect the shipment at the airport and deliver it to its destination.

The principal disadvantages in air shipment are:

1. Shipments weighing over 1,000 pounds are usually divided into several lots and shipped on succesive planes. If one or more planes are delayed at take-off, arrangements to clear shipments at ports of entry and to pick up for delivery have to be made several times. Unless papers are issued for each box in a shipment, delays occur until additional copies can be procured for the detained portion of the shipment. Separate sets of documents and waybills should be provided for each portion weighing up to 1,000 pounds.
2. Exhibitions are exposed to risk of total loss should any air accident occur, whereas with surface shipment some salvage is usually effected.

Although little has been done to date to create new means of transporting works of art by air, the development of light, but strong, metal, fibre or plastic containers scientifically designed for this purpose may eventually take place. Such containers might provide built-in shock absorption so that double boxing would be necessary only for the most fragile, delicate and valuable items. New means may also be developed for protecting objects against rapidly changing relative humidity. As boxes are moved from pressurized cabins to areas of different climate, extreme changes in temperature and humidity may take place. New means will probably be found to slow the penetration of heat and dampness to the packed object. It has been suggested that precise control may, eventually, be achieved by packing in with objects chemical compounds tending to produce the desired conditions, then tightly sealing exhibits which normally are not subject to air-tight enclosure. For instance, silica gel, a chemical which absorbs and holds moisture, is being used by many companies exporting materials overseas to dehydrate the air inside moisture-proof or reasonably moisture-proof containers and thus maintain humidity of this air at a point below that at which corrosive action or mildew can take place. Such practices may be tested to discover their application to shipments of works of art.

New materials have recently been made available which may prove of great value for ocean and air transport in preventing rust, corrosion or mildew in certain articles. Transparent sheetings made from rubber or latex derivatives are impervious to water and moisture vapour which penetrate ordinarily-used waterproof papers. It is even conceivable that liquid plastic sprays can be employed to seal containers for transit or for storage.

Most commercial airlines issue booklets containing rates, documentary requirements, rules and regulations applicable for shipments between international airports. As documentary requirements for various countries are subject to change, it is necessary to check all such information with the proper consular offices, the United States Department of Commerce or the Office of International Trade.

IV. INSURANCE

The preparation of travelling exhibitions, whether involving original works of art, reproductions or other materials, constitutes various risks which can usually be covered by insurance. The principal threat of damage to art objects occurs when a work is moved from its permanent resting place. As one curator has put it, "Insurance policies are taken out to cover every stage in the operations, which is an indication that accidents may occur from the moment a picture is taken down". For this reason, most policies written for exhibitions on tour cover all items included against all risks from "wall to wall" (meaning that an object is insured from the moment it leaves its owner until it is returned). Specific arrangements for insurance depend upon the nature of the material to be insured, the knowledge and reputation of the institution insuring the collection as well as the extent of responsibility it assumes, the method of shipment and finally, the underwriters. Consequently no set of rules or instructions can be listed to guide those organizing an exhibition for tour. Certain factors influencing all shipments can be mentioned, however, to assist those who must make the necessary decisions concerning insurance.

TYPE OF POLICY

The average museum carries insurance which covers the property of others while on loan in the same manner that its own collections are covered against loss or damage by theft, vandalism, carelessness in handling, accidents, etc., with certain exclusions listed by the insurers. When borrowing an object for tour, it is advisable to obtain instructions from the owner before an object is shipped as to the extent of coverage to be carried, the valuations listed and the method of shipping to be employed. Sometimes an owner wishes to extend his own policy to cover the article while it is away from his premises. In this case, the museum usually pays the premium to the owner for the period of the loan. It is generally easier to handle insurance for a large collection, however, if all items included are carried under one "all risk" policy. In this way, values may be listed monthly, reports of damages made at similar intervals and items returned to owners cancelled from the policy at the same time. The policy may be written so that all shipments involving the responsibility of the museum are automatically covered whether or not notice is given to the insurers at the time the shipment takes place. This type of policy is usually called a *Fine Arts Floater*. It is written under the so-called inland marine policy form which was devised to provide coverage for transport risks, not principally water-borne, and it has been expanded over the years to cover numerous types of exposure. Policies which will cover a collection during ocean transit are usually drawn up separately or coverage is added to the "floater" policy in an endorsement made at the time of shipment by boat.

Exhibitors of a travelling exhibition usually have little to do with arrangements for insurance. In making claims and settling them, it is usually more efficient for the sponsoring institution or circulating agency to handle all arrangements rather than divide the responsibility between the institutions exhibiting the loans. A portion of the rental fee paid by each exhibitor covers his share in the cost of the insurance. His responsibility to the institution circulating the exhibition and ultimately to the original lenders is none the less real. The acceptance of the exhibition for showing in his galleries carries with it an obligation to both sponsoring institution and lenders to exercise all care in handling the material included. Because a few institutions do not automatically assume this responsibility, clauses protecting the sponsoring institution or circulating agency must often be inserted in exhibition contracts, such as "exhibitors will be held responsible for losses or damages due to carelessness".

A similar responsibility must be assumed by all

THIS COULD BE ABOUT THE
MIDDLE PAGE OF THE BOOK
(text on p. 17)

organizations borrowing works of art for circulation. The circulating agency must exercise the same care for borrowed objects as it gives its own collection. It must guarantee the lender adequate protection for his loan by providing safe packing and instructions to those who will handle the objects; it must request that exhibitions be guarded at all times; that no repairs be made by exhibitors; that all damages or losses are reported at once. Such measures may effect a reduction in premiums for policies carried on travelling exhibitions if their exercise results in few losses or damages to objects on tour. Conversely, insurance may be voided if the institution circulating the collection is guilty of misrepresentation, negligence or carelessness or the borrowing institution fails to carry out instructions issued to exhibitors.

"BAILEE" LIABILITY INSURANCE

If an owner maintains his own insurance on a loan, the museum organizing the exhibition often takes out so-called "bailee" liability insurance to cover itself should the owner's insurers prosecute a claim against the museum or circulating agency borrowing the loan. Sometimes this type of coverage can be added to a museum's "floater" policy in an endorsement on an annual basis and often it limits any single claim by such phrases as "not liable for more than $100,000 for any one casualty".

ESTABLISHING VALUES AND SETTLEMENTS

When an object is borrowed for a travelling exhibition, the owner usually signs a form of agreement which states the type of coverage provided by the insurance policy and he is asked to give a valuation representing the extent of payment to be made should full loss occur. The insurance company depends upon the museum to see that these valuations are fairly drawn. Since it is extremely difficult to determine the market value of a work of art except by sale or auction, the means of arriving at the figure for insurance should be agreed upon by insurers, the borrowing institution and lender prior to issuing the insurance. Such agreements prevent any difficulty in settling claims should loss or damage occur. If disagreements take place, settlement is generally made by calling upon the decision of a third party, usually someone recognized as an "expert" in the marketing of works of art.

Similar difficulties may arise in settling the cost of repairs or depreciation to an object damaged on tour. Again, the insurers depend largely upon the museum staff to ascertain the fairness of an owner's claim. The cost of minor repairs, which can sometimes be made by a museum staff, are often assumed by the borrowing institution so that "nuisance" claims need not be reported to insurers. Avoidance of such claims often results in lower premium rates. But extreme caution must be exercised in making such repairs and no repairs whatsoever should be undertaken without the written permission of the lender. Any repair involving a technical skill should be undertaken only by experienced men. In fact, most standard "floater" policies specifically state: "Does not insure against loss or damage occasioned by: wear and tear, gradual deterioration, moths, vermin, inherent vice or damage sustained due to and resulting from any repairing, restoration or retouching process."

DECLARED VALUATIONS

In general practice, a collection is fully insured during a tour by a "floater" policy. During transit, the exhibitor must declare a nominal valuation on each case carried and the carrier is then liable up to this amount. The valuation declared is usually carried free of charge. Higher valuations may be permitted and sometimes such practices result in better handling (see Railway Express Company's Special Contract, page 50).

CARRIER INSURANCE

When an exhibition is in transit, the carrier assumes a certain amount of responsibility for its safety. His own insurance can only rarely be arranged to cover the full value of the exhibition and is usually limited to the value declared on each case, the bill of lading or the amount of coverage and insuring conditions permitted by his company. Such conditions usually limit his liability to a fraction of the value of works of art, even though additional charges may be paid for a higher valuation declared on a shipment. Consequently, the owner, or that organization responsible for the safety of the objects on tour rarely relies upon the carrier's insurance to cover the shipment in transit. To recover a loss in full, exhibitors must make specific arrangements with the carrier at the time shipment is made to provide full insurance during transit.

There are additional difficulties encountered in

using carrier insurance exclusively. Settlement of claims placed against a carrier usually requires more time than for similar claims placed against a shipper's own insurers. Moreover, such claims are unusual and the lack of familiarity with the kind of article insured means that the carrier will require more detailed proof of the cause and extent of the loss. Such settlements often cost more in time to achieve than their value warrants.

In general, the standard "floater" policy relieves the shipper of certain responsibilities in dealing with carriers. Providing that the exhibitor declares a proper valuation to the carrier to encourage careful handling, the insurers assume responsibility for collecting claims against the carrier for damages occurring during transit. Furthermore, the "floater" policies usually automatically cover shipments regardless of means of transport. The fullest protection is thus afforded when all risks of inland transport, whether by rail, truck or air are insured under a single policy.

REPORTS TO INSURERS

Most policies require the insured to report loss or damage within a limited period after its occurence in order to place a claim. When a collection is on tour, the claim is often deferred until an item has been returned to its owner at the end of the tour. It is nevertheless necessary to establish the cause and extent of a damage when it occurs and circulating agencies must depend upon exhibitors to report such conditions immediately. For this purpose exhibitors often provide condition sheets on which reports can be made easily. The sponsoring institution may indicate previous conditions on this sheet and ask exhibitors to check questionable items against this record and to make additional reports as necessary. The provision of these sheets serves not only as a convenience to exhibitors but as a forceful reminder of the necessity of making such reports. Moreover they form a file on damages, an important record for the circulating agency (see sample sheet furnished by the Museum of Modern Art, Appendix A, page 61).

AIR-FREIGHT INSURANCE

The standard "floater" policy usually covers air shipments unless such coverage is specifically excluded in the contract. In view of the growing importance of air-freight transport, it seems advisable to include such risks in any standard policy held to cover loans or shipments. Some contracts, while they do not entirely eliminate air coverage, limit it to 50 per cent of the top valuation insured for rail or truck shipments. Values of the limits specified in the policy can be covered by endorsement. Moreover, the usual breakage clause in insurance contracts is not affected by the difference in means of transport.

OCEAN-FREIGHT INSURANCE

Standard "floater" policies *do not* afford coverage during ocean transit unless specifically arranged. As in inland insurance, the "open cargo" or "floater" policy form is the most satisfactory because it covers shipments as soon as they are made, whether or not the shipping date is known to the exhibitor. Details must be reported as soon as they are known, but insurance is provided during the interim. Coverage usually attaches from the time the property leaves the point of shipment and remains in force until its delivery at the final point of destination. This is called "warehouse to warehouse" coverage.

Valuations must be placed on items prior to shipment and shipper as well as insurer must agree to third party arbitration if there should be any dispute over valuations. Often the valuation declared to the shipper and the type of stowage provided aboard have considerable bearing on the rate of premium charged by insurers. Most ocean bills of lading limit the carrier's liability to $500 per packing case unless a higher value is declared, for which an increased freight charge is made. Preferred stowage can usually be obtained for shipments of works of art without any increase in freight rate and many insurers insist that shippers request this preferred stowage and handling for such shipments. Shippers should ascertain in advance whether or not the steamship company will issue preferred stowage without the declaration of excess value. The saving in insurance premiums effected by obtaining this special handling and stowage may in any case offset the extra freight charges so incurred.

It is important nevertheless to avoid the inclusion of clauses specifying special stowage, special handling or that goods be packed and unpacked by competent packers in an insurance contract. If the shipper cannot guarantee such conditions his insurance may be voided.

Because the first insurance on property in transit was written to protect against loss through "perils of the sea", marine insurance has acquired considerable weight of precedent. Thus we find that ocean marine contracts are more restrictive as to assumption of risk and less amenable to change. It is wise, therefore, to consider carefully all clauses in a marine insurance contract to make certain that all coverage necessary is included and that no requirements are placed upon the policy-holder that he cannot fulfill. Such a policy can include coverage against many kinds of damages and the more hazards covered, the higher the premium rate. Limited coverages are used primarily to insure commodities of low value and those less susceptible to damage; works of art require the maximum protection gained in using an all-risk insurance. Because particular conditions pertain to each collection of material shipped overseas, many museums write specific policies for each exhibition so shipped rather than cover these risks in endorsements to their regular "floater" policy.

EXCLUSIONS FROM GENERAL "FLOATER" POLICY

The normal all-risk fine arts "floater" policy does not cover objects loaned to exhibitions on fairgrounds or expositions. Arrangements for insurance under these conditions must be made separately because the legal complications of suit against a government, state or municipality are such that special clauses must be inserted in standard policies.

Similar special arrangements must be made to cover objects against risk of "war, invasion, hostilities, rebellion, insurrection, seizure or destruction under quarantine or customs regulations, confiscation by order of any government or public authority, or risks of contraband or illegal transportation and/or trade". This is an excluding clause which forms part of standard inland marine policy forms. Insurance against strikes, riots and civil commotions can be effected under a separate endorsement or rider, but actual war risk can be obtained only during the time a shipment is water-borne. Such coverage is primarily against risks resulting from the presence of mines or submarines. War risk coverage on land cannot be obtained unless a government makes provision for it.

Since there is relatively little fine arts insurance, many agents, brokers, claim adjusters and insurance companies are not as familiar with the coverage as they should be. Therefore it is wise to select an agent or broker who is experienced in handling and placing fine arts coverage. By working with such an agent or broker over a period of time, coverage may be broadened and insurance costs materially reduced.

At the present time, a committee of the American Association of Art Museum Directors is making a thorough study of insurance problems, types of coverage, rates, conditions, etc., and when this report is available, it should contain much valuable information for those interested in placing fine arts insurance. Meanwhile a sample policy used by a group of museums in Canada and the United States exchanging exhibitions on tour in both countries may serve as a guide (see Appendix C, sample insurance policy for fine arts coverage).

APPENDIX A

SAMPLE FORMS

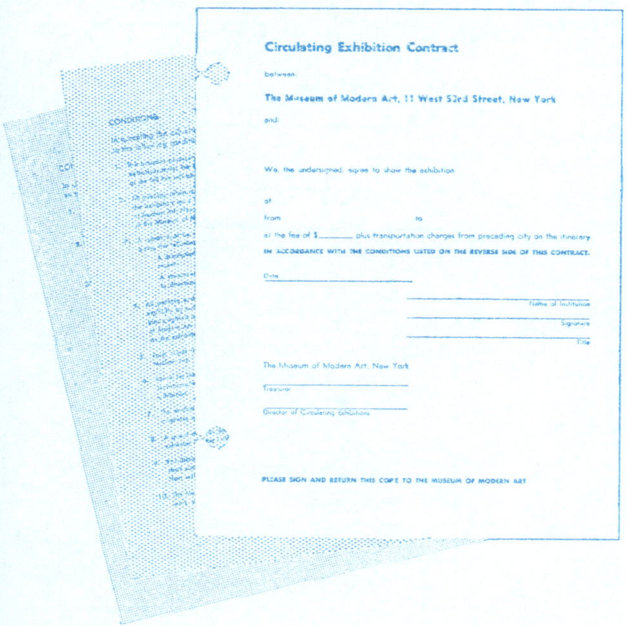

Circulating Exhibition Contract

between:

The Museum of Modern Art, 11 West 53rd Street, New York

and:

We, the undersigned, agree to show the exhibition

at

from to

at the fee of $______ plus transportation charges from preceding city on the itinerary

IN ACCORDANCE WITH THE CONDITIONS LISTED ON THE REVERSE SIDE OF THIS CONTRACT.

Date

Name of Institution

Signature

Title

The Museum of Modern Art, New York

Treasurer

Director of Circulating Exhibitions

PLEASE SIGN AND RETURN THIS COPY TO THE MUSEUM OF MODERN ART

1. Exhibition Contract.
Conditions are printed on reverse of contract.

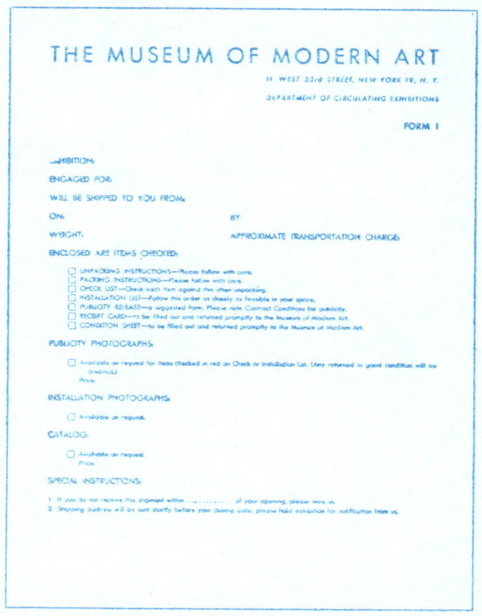

THE MUSEUM OF MODERN ART

11 WEST 53rd STREET, NEW YORK 19, N. Y.

DEPARTMENT OF CIRCULATING EXHIBITIONS

FORM I

EXHIBITION:

ENGAGED FOR:

WILL BE SHIPPED TO YOU FROM:

ON: BY:

WEIGHT: APPROXIMATE TRANSPORTATION CHARGE:

ENCLOSED ARE ITEMS CHECKED:

- ☐ UNPACKING INSTRUCTIONS—Please follow with care.
- ☐ PACKING INSTRUCTIONS—Please follow with care.
- ☐ CHECK LIST—Check each item against this when unpacking.
- ☐ INSTALLATION LIST—Follow this order as closely as feasible in your space.
- ☐ PUBLICITY RELEASE—a suggested form. Please note Contract Conditions for publicity.
- ☐ RECEIPT CARD—to be filled out and returned promptly to the Museum of Modern Art.
- ☐ CONDITION SHEET—to be filled out and returned promptly to the Museum of Modern Art.

PUBLICITY PHOTOGRAPHS:

- ☐ Available on request for items checked in red on Check or Installation List. (Any returned in good condition will be credited.)
  Price:

INSTALLATION PHOTOGRAPHS:

- ☐ Available on request.

CATALOG:

- ☐ Available on request.
  Price:

SPECIAL INSTRUCTIONS:

1. If you do not receive the shipment within .... of your opening, please wire us.
2. Shipping address will be sent shortly before your closing date; please hold exhibition for notification from us.

2. Form Letter I.
Announcement of the arrival of an exhibition. Various instructions may be enclosed with this letter form (see *3, 4, 5, 6, 7, 8, pages 58-61*).

READ AND CAREFULLY FOLLOW THE ATTACHED INSTRUCTIONS

An increasing amount of **damage** to the contents of exhibitions has resulted from the failure of exhibitors to observe handling instructions. These instructions have been developed through long experience to guarantee the best **protection** possible. They must be observed if the quality of the contents of circulating exhibitions is to be maintained & rental & insurance **costs** kept as low as possible.

3. Packing and Unpacking Instructions.

(a) Printed card enclosed with the instructions for unpacking. This is also printed on a gummed label in red ink and appears on the cover of each packing case to call attention to the packing and unpacking instructions.

(b) Special instructions regarding gummed tape are enclosed with all exhibitions including pictures with glass.

PLEASE NOTE....

IMPORTANT INSTRUCTIONS

REGARDING GUMMED TAPE ON PICTURES COVERED WITH GLASS

1. Every picture covered with glass should be taped with strips of gummed tape NOT MORE THAN ONE HALF INCH APART.

   When pictures start on tour from the Museum of Modern Art they are so taped - with the PARTICULAR KIND OF TAPE THAT DOES NOT REQUIRE WATER.

   The cooperation of all exhibitors is requested in seeing to it that TAPE REQUIRING WATER IS NEVER USED AS A SUBSTITUTE. This is to guard against any possible water damage to a picture.

2. In order to preserve tape for use in repacking - using a sheet of glass, or other slick surface (any other surface will adhere to the tape and make it unusable), pile strips of tape belonging to each picture on top of each other smoothly with the numbered piece on top.

   Wrap in paper so that tape will be kept clean and not dry out during the showing of the exhibition.

3. If tape is too dry for re-use, please request a fresh supply well in advance of packing date from:

Department of Circulating Exhibitions
Museum of Modern Art
11 West 53rd Street
New York 19, New York

DO NOT PUT TAPE OVER
LABEL OF FRAME

remimeo 4/17/50

(c) Unpacking instructions also appear on the cover of each case but a copy is sent to each exhibition with the first form letter so that any unusual caution will be understood by the person in charge of the exhibition and directions to those who will handle unpacking can be issued in advance.

Packing instructions are incorporated on the same page with unpacking instructions so that exhibitors will note how the material removed is to be replaced in the case. These instructions are also attached to the cover of each case.

Pages 1-7

CARVERS, MODELERS AND WELDERS — 1950-52

An exhibition circulated by The Museum of Modern Art, New York, N.Y.

UNPACKING INSTRUCTIONS - BOX #1: - 1 stone sculpture 50.921 Salerno: Horse & Clown
- Wood base for 50.921

1. Lift out package containing wood block base for sculpture.
2. Unbolt Brace #1 and Brace #2 from outside of box. Lift out braces. Replace short bolts in braces.
3. Lift wrapped sculpture from box.

   CAUTION: SCULPTURE WEIGHS 124 pounds. TWO MEN SHOULD HANDLE THE PIECE.

4. Replace - 2 corrugated boards and wrapping paper from package, 2 braces with bolts in ends, cloth - in box and put on lid making sure all bolts are sared.

PACKING INSTRUCTIONS - BOX #1: - 1 stone sculpture 50.921 Salerno: Horse & Clown
- Wood base for 50.921

CAUTION: SCULPTURE WEIGHS 124 pounds. HANDLE WITH CARE. TWO MEN SHOULD HANDLE PIECE

1. Wrap sculpture in cloth marked with same number. Tie securely.
2. Place curved short side of sculpture against wide pads at right side of box.
3. Set Brace #1 pad against sculpture in marked spot in box. Bolt in place from outside of box.
4. Set Brace #2 pad against sculpture in marked spot in box. Bolt in place from outside of box.
5. Wrap wood base for 50.921 between 2 sheets of corrugated board. Wrap in heavy paper and seal. Slide package into marked space at top of box.
6. Bolt lid on box SECURELY.

58

4. Check List.

(a) An itemized list of the contents of an exhibition gives the exhibitor a guide by which he can easily and swiftly assemble the collection in the order of presentation.

CHAIM SOUTINE 1951-52

An exhibition circulated by The Museum of Modern Art, New York, N.Y.

CHECK LIST:

- 1 title poster 18 x 25
-19 identification labels } Box #3
-19 paintings

Museum Number	Title and medium	Framed Size	Box Number
51.628	STILL LIFE WITH SOUP TUREEN, c.1916 Oil on c.	30 1/2 x 35 3/4x1	2
51.629	VILLAGE SQUARE, c.1920. Oil on canvas	36 1/2 x 40 1/2x1	1
51.630	GNARLED TREES, c.1921. Oil on canvas	45 x 32 x 1	1
51.631	WOMAN IN RED, c.1922. Oil on canvas	43 x 32 1/2x1	1
51.632	THE PASTRY COOK WITH RED HANDKERCHIEF, c.1922-23 Oil on canvas	35 5/8 x 28 1/4x1	2
51.633	SIDE OF BEEF, 1922-23. Oil on canvas	35 3/4 x 28 1/4x1	2
51.634	LANDSCAPE, c.1923. Oil on canvas	39 1/4 x 33 1/4x1	1
51.636	CHOIR BOY WITH SURPLICE, c.1928. Oil on c.	31 3/4 x 26 1/2x1	3
51.638	TREE OF VENCE, 1929. Oil on canvas	38 1/2 x 31 x 1	1
51.735	SERVANT GIRL IN BLUE, 1934-35. Oil on wood	31 x 31 1/2 x 2	3
51.640	PORTRAIT OF A YOUNG MAN, 1935. Oil on canvas	29 3/4 x 21 x 1	3
51.641	WOMAN IN PROFILE, 1937. Oil on canvas	25 1/4 x 17 7/8x1	3
51.644	HOUSE OF CAGNES, 1923. Oil on canvas	30 1/2 x 35 1/2x1	2
51.637	THE VALET, 1929. Oil on canvas	36 x 25 1/2x 2 1/2	2
27.51	RAY-FISH AND BREAD, c.1924. Oil on canvas	45 x 41 1/2 x1 3/4	1
51.835	GLADIOLAS. Oil on canvas	38 1/2x30 1/2 x1	2
51.836	LANDSCAPE AT CERET, c.1920. Oil on canvas	32 1/4x 43 x 1	1
51.837	STILL LIFE WITH CARNATIONS, c.1919. Oil on c.	28 3/4 x 25 1/4x1	3
51.639	PLUCKED GOOSE. Oil on wood	29 x 27 x 4 1/4	3

(b) Often the check list can be combined with the installation list so that the exhibitor has but one form to refer to in putting the exhibition together in his galleries.

SOUTH AMERICAN TEXTILES 1951-52

An exhibition circulated by The Museum of Modern Art, New York, New York

CHECK AND INSTALLATION LIST:

- Title Poster 24 x 20"
- 9 Panels 24 x 20"
- 6 Panels 20 x 30"
- 3 Panels 30 x 40"
- 3 Section labels 3 3/4 x 12"
- 20 unmounted textiles (6 of which are ponchos)
- 20 identification labels for the unmounted textiles
- 6 shoulder forms for the ponchos (hanging poles for remaining unmounted textiles NOT provided)
- 1 head form for mask

Install. Number	Museum Number	Object	Region	Size & type of install.
1.	-----	Title poster		24 x 20 panel
2.	-----	Introductory label		24 x 20 panel
3.	-----	Map of South America		24 x 20 panel
4.	-----	Photo panel		24 x 20 panel
5.	-----	Photo panel		24 x 20 panel
6.	-----	Section label AYMARA		3 3/4 x 12 panel
7.	51.516	Mask	Central Highland	Use head form provided
8.	51.518 51.522	Woman's belt Woman's undersash	Chucinto La Paz	30 x 40 panel
9.	51.520 51.519	Man's belt Knitted cap	Tequili Island Juliaca	30 x 20 panel
10.	51.517 51.521	Coca bag Beaded headband	Tequili Island Central Highland	30 x 20 panel
11	-----	Photo: Heirloom poncho, Aymara, La Paz, Bolivia		20 x 24 panel
12.	51.507	Boy's poncho	Juli, SE Titicaca	32½x24½ Use shoulder form
13.	51.505	Poncho	SE Titicaca	60x56½ Use shoulder form
14.	51.511	Child's poncho	La Paz	40½x17½ Use shoulder form
15.	51.515	Potato sack	Chucinto	38½x20 Tie & stuff with paper
16.	51.514	Potato sack	Chucinto	40½x21½ Tie & stuff with paper

31 MK It comes as a surprise that here, where the subject of proactive advertising for an exhibition is addressed, the impact of an appealing exhibition title is left unmentioned. All the titles that are presented in connection with the illustrations seem correct in their explanatory pragmatism, however they do everything but inspire or arouse curiosity: *Carvings from East and West; Yugoslav Folk Art; South American Textiles; Economic Life in Sweden; Useful Objects,* etc. An alternative can be seen in Martin Kippenberger's artistic manual *241 Bildtitel zum Ausleihen für Künstler* (241 Image Titles for Artists to Borrow) (1986). In this small publication, the artist took texts that he had seen on T-shirts in Rio de Janeiro and catalogued them with Roman numerals: from the romantic CXVII – *Trans Macao* to the cryptic CXXXIV – *Paradex,* from the explicit CLXXIII – *Donttouchmytuts* to the zeitgeisty LXXXIX – *American Cools.* More recent artists' books also offer inspiration for finding a title, such as Peter Downsbrough, *The List 6.2017,* which features an alphabetical directory of all 113 of his artist books (from *A CALAIS / ADJUST / AFTER / AND [...] to WITH) IN PLACE / WITHIN (TIME) / WORDS / WORD VOL. 2); Algunas títulos de exposiciones individuales* (Some titles of solo shows) by Xoán Anleo (2016), with a list of over 2.000 randomly assembled individual exhibition titles *(Interior Design for Bastards, Unisex love nest, A long time ago last night, etc.);* or *Art Titles 1969 – 2010* by Gilbert & George (2011), in which all 2.500 titles of their pictures, books, catalogues, sculptures, and films are meticulously listed both chronologically and alphabetically (from *Bacon 32,* 1968 to *Jack Freak Pictures,* 2011).

MODERN BUILDINGS FOR SCHOOLS AND COLLEGES I and II 1947-48

An exhibition circulated by The Museum of Modern Art, New York, N.Y.

CHECK and INSTALLATION LIST

- 24 photo panels 30 x 40"
- 3 photo panels 30 x 45"
- 16 label panels 30 x 13"

Installation No.	Title
PART I : SCHOOLS	
Panel #1	Title
Label #2	ACALANES UNION HIGH SCHOOL, Lafayette, California 1940-41
Panel #2	" " " Bird's-eye view
Label #3	RUGEN SCHOOL, Glenview, Illinois 1942
Panel #3	" " General exterior
Label #4	RAUL VIDAL ELEMENTARY SCHOOL, Niteroi, Rio de Janeiro, Brazil. 1942
Panel #4	" " " " Classrooms and courtyard
Label #5	EDISON TECHNICAL HIGH SCHOOL, Fresno, California 1942
Panel #5	" " " " Enclosed corridor
Label #6	BRUDERHOLZ SCHOOL, Basel, Switzerland. 1938-39
Panel #6	" " Open covered passageway
Label #7	BELL SCHOOL, Los Angeles, California. 1934-35
Panel #7	" " Indoor-outdoor classroom
Label #8	CROW ISLAND ELEMENTARY SCHOOL, Winnetka, Illinois. 1940 Plan
Panel #8	" " " " Schoolroom interior
Label #9	BRUDERHOLZ SCHOOL, Basel, Switzerland. 1938-39
Panel #9	" " Classroom interior
Label #10	BRUDERHOLZ SCHOOL, Basel, Switzerland 1938-39 Plan
Panel #10	" " Classroom wing
Label #11	ALBANY SCHOOL, Berkeley, California. 1944
Panel #11	" " Court view with covered passages
Label #12	SCHOOL-COMMUNITY CENTER, Center Line, Michigan. 1942
Panel #12	" " " Auditorium and classroom wing

(continued on page 2)

5. Installation List.
This guide is prepared for exhibitors so that the sequence of objects and labels is readily established as material is removed from packing boxes to galleries. Sometimes an installation list is mandatory. Hanging pictures or other items without following the sequence indicated may mean complete confusion to the gallery visitor. When such a list is given exhibitors are requested to study it carefully, making no changes in the intended order unless absolutely essential in order to accommodate the exhibition in a specific space.

THE MUSEUM OF MODERN ART
11 WEST 53 STREET, NEW YORK 19, N. Y.
TELEPHONE: CIRCLE 5-8900

FOR IMMEDIATE RELEASE

SOUTH AMERICAN TEXTILES

An exhibition of ponchos, knitted caps, masks, saddle-bags and belts selected from two outstanding collections in New York City, will be on view at __________ from __________ to __________.

Contemporary in that none have been produced more than two generations ago, these textiles have been woven by the Indians for their own use. They were secured from the Quechua and Aymara Indian as well as the Mestizo who is part white and part Indian. Nearly every article included is comparatively rare since the superstitious native is unwilling to part with personal belongings.

Dwelling mainly in the high mountains of the Andes, around Lake Titicaca in Peru and Bolivia, the Indians were able to retain much of their own tradition despite four centuries of Spanish rule. The Quechua is the modern descendant of the Inca people, while the Aymara, perhaps because of the harsh, high and cold environment in which he lives, is somewhat the more primitive even today. Except for difference of language, the Quechua and the Aymara share a similar way of life. Both farm, tend herd or work in mines, while the Mestizo occupies an important place in the political and industrial life of Bolivia and Peru. Composing the middle class, he makes up the great mass of voters.

Although certain changes in craftsmanship have occurred, everywhere weaving is still done in the old type of griddle-back and belt looms by each family, and the color schemes and patterning established by his ancestors, still characterize his textile Where the Quechua's are extremely rich and flamboyant, outstanding for spectacular color combinations and elaborate embroideries, the Aymara's decorative sense is extremely restrained. His sparse use of pattern and rather delicate colors may sometimes make his textiles appear like pale imitations of the Quechua's. The Mestizo clearly reveals his European heritage. His color combinations contrast sharply and although he makes use of the geometrical figures found in Indian weavings, his designs also often resemble European folk art.

After its showing at __________ the exhibition will continue its tour throughout this country.

6. Publicity Release.
A suggested form of newspaper story to be issued at the time the exhibition is opened. The exhibitor is not asked to follow the form completely but to use it as a guide. He may wish to divide the information so that it forms several newspaper stories to be released at different times during his showing, thereby increasing public interest in the exhibition on view. Stories may be amplified and facts which pertain to his particular showing incorporated with this information furnished by the circulating agency to relate the exhibition to local events or conditions All such information increases interest in an exhibition, but it is important to furnish exhibitors with a basic news release.

31 MK

60

THE MUSEUM OF MODERN ART · 11 WEST 53 STREET · NEW YORK 19

Exhibition..
(title)

No. of boxes received..................on..................
If unpacked and in good condition, check here..................
If damaged, please fill out detailed report on Condition Form provided for the purpose.

If to be unpacked later, give approximate date we may expect your report on condition..................

(RECEIPT) ....
(signature)

7. Receipt Card.

The prompt return of this card to the circulating agency informs it of the safe arrival of the exhibition at its intended destination. It is issued to allow the exhibitor a quick reply without the necessity of full correspondance.

8. Condition Report.

This form was arrived at after considerable experience. It was found that exhibitors, because of the pressure of their other duties, often delayed writing in detail about damages until it was too late to make repairs or claims to insurers before the next shipment had to be made. Such practice leads to further damage and an inability to trace conditions which have caused a damage to occur. The exhibition contract specifies that this form be filled out promptly and returned to the circulating agency. When this agency carries insurance on all items contained in an exhibition, this form permits an instant report to the insurers. Having one policy and a record of conditions when the exhibition starts on tour, it is a simple matter to check the condition of the material against this record at each stop and to ascertain when and how a damage may have occurred.

9. Form Letter II.

This is an advance notice of shipment. Information to guide the exhibitor in making arrangements for shipping is enclosed (see *10, 11, 12, page 62*).

THE MUSEUM OF MODERN ART, 11 West 53rd Street, New York, N.Y.

REPORT ON THE CONDITION OF THE CIRCULATING EXHIBITION ____________

UPON ITS RECEIPT IN ____________ FOR BOOKING ____________

Please check the material in the exhibition against the check list provided and list below all damages and omissions from the list.

Please note whether in your opinion damage occurred in transit or while in your possession. Describe condition of item in detail.

Museum Number	Artist	Title and Medium	Description of damage

Box condition. If necessary, please request new bolts and washers from the Museum of Modern Art.

____
Signature of person in charge

____
Institution

____
DATE received

6/11/51

THE MUSEUM OF MODERN ART

11 WEST 53rd STREET, NEW YORK 19, N. Y.

DEPARTMENT OF CIRCULATING EXHIBITIONS

FORM II

EXHIBITION:

CLOSING:

OPENS NEXT:

PLEASE SHIP ON:

BY

ADDRESSED TO:

DECLARE VALUATION:

ENCLOSED ARE:

- ☐ ADDRESS CARDS FOR   BOXES
- ☐ PACKING INSTRUCTIONS—Please follow with care. Check all items against this list.
- ☐ FORM FOR YOUR COMMENTS ON EXHIBITION—Please return to Museum of Modern Art promptly.
- ☐ TWO CARDS FOR NOTIFICATION OF SHIPMENT—One of these to be sent to us and the other to the next exhibitor.

SPECIAL INSTRUCTIONS:

61

from **The Museum of Modern Art**

WORKS OF ART to

HANDLE WITH CARE

10. Address Cards.
Address cards may be furnished by the circulating agency to clarify instructions to the transit agents and to identify the shipment in transit should any one case out of a group be misplaced. This particular form is issued principally for shipment by rail in the United States. It is better to use cards tacked to the cover of a case for successive shipments than to write such information on the box. The latter practice produces a confusion of addresses which the transport company may not properly decipher.

EXHIBITIONS CIRCULATED BY THE MUSEUM OF MODERN ART, NEW YORK, N.Y.

PUBLICITY REPORT

Title of Exhibition ____________________

Name of Sponsoring Organization ____________________

Address ____________________

Date of Showing ____________________

Attendance ____________________

Newspaper Space ____________________
(number of items in inches) (If extra copies of publicity are available, please attach & return)

Photographs in Newspapers ____________________
(number)

Radio Talks ____________________

School visits, special groups, etc. ____________________

Comments about the exhibition ____________________

4/10/51 remimeo

11. Publicity Report.
It is often helpful to circulating agencies in planning future programmes to have specific comments or criticisms of exhibitions from subscribers. Such information is more readily given if the circulating agency requests it along with other information for its records such as attendance figures, special groups who have visited the exhibition, etc.

THE MUSEUM OF MODERN ART · 11 WEST 53 STREET · NEW YORK 19

Exhibition ____________________
(title)

collected by ____________________
(name of company handling shipment)

on ____________________

Receipt number for shipment ____________________

Shipped to ____________________

(NOTIFICATION OF SHIPMENT) ____________________
(signature)

12. Notification of Shipment. ↑
Two cards are issued, one to be mailed to the circulating agency and the second to inform the next exhibitor that shipment has been made to him.

13. Labe s. →
This is a sample label typed on a so-called "bulletin" or poster-size typewriter.

CARVERS-MODELERS-WELDERS
A Selection of Recent American Sculpture

Within the variety of approaches in recent American sculpture a certain skeletal appearance recurs. The light and floating quality produced by this "open-work" technique has only recently been associated with sculpture. Instead of being built in the round these sculptures are drawings in space. In defying weight, the very material itself of which they are made becomes almost immaterial. Where formerly the surface was made to capture highlights to lead the eye around the form, a variety of metals such as copper, steel and bronze now are welded together into a knotty, nubbly surface often stretched into thin bands to silhouette the form, making light an incidental factor only. This airiness is retained even in sculpture of malleable materials such as plastic. Set against the light, the actual surface of the plastic shape becomes less important than the inner, loosely built structure of wire screening and plaster.

Only the carver in wood or stone still builds up his sculpture significantly in the round. His concept often is governed by the shape and nature of the material he works with, making for a much closer relationship between the artist and his medium. Where it is essential for the carver to keep within the range of the intrinsic possibilities of the particular material and to submit to the three-dimensionality of a piece of stone or wood - the modeler is relatively free to extend into space in any direction.

The carver's work in this exhibition derives from Brancusi's concentrated forms and expressive use of and pleasure in the material, Flannagan's sensitive and touching stone sculpture and Nadelman's mannered "folk art" carvings. While the modeler's and welder's lacy quality stems as much from Lipchitz' "Transparents" in which his object was to create sculpture "which can be seen through and affects us from all sides at once," as it does from Calder's individual experiments with movement in space as illustrated in his "Mobiles", with the difference that the welder has in common with Calder the use of industrial techniques for his artistic purpose.

62

THIS IS THE PAGE WITH NOTHING SPECIAL ABOUT IT
(text on p. 18)

APPENDIX B

GENERAL HANDLING RULES

These instructions were prepared by Robert P. Sugden, General Services Manager, the Metropolitan Museum of Art, for their publication *Care and Handling of Art Objects*. Permission has been granted by the author to reprint these instructions from the guidebook.

CARE AND HANDLING OF PAINTINGS

1. No one shall handle, move, or carry more than one painting at a time. Carry it with one hand beneath and the other at the side of the picture, both at points where the frame is solid. Never carry a painting by the top of the frame or by the stretcher.
2. Large paintings must be moved by no fewer than two men, one of whom is experienced in correct handling of paintings. (By "large" is meant large enough to be awkward for one man. It does not mean that it is all right for one man to move anything he happens to be strong enough to lift.)
3. Do not stack paintings—one leaning against another—unless it is absolutely unavoidable, and then only with permission of the curator or other responsible person in charge.
4. Separate paintings with composition sheets (corrugated cardboard, compo board, etc.), if stacking is absolutely necessary. Stack the largest painting first, followed by smaller ones in order, with no more than five paintings in any one stack. Each composition sheet must completely cover the larger of the two paintings it separates.
5. Paintings standing on the floor must rest on pads or padded wooden strips.
6. Separate paintings on side trucks with composition sheets. There must never be so many paintings on a truck that the outside painting or its frame, extends beyond the edge of the truck. Pad the floor of the truck to prevent damage to frames.
7. Do not move large, heavy paintings on side trucks unless the truck's supporting framework is high enough, that is, at least two-thirds the height of the picture. The weight must be borne by the frame resting against the truck support; it should never be borne by the stretcher alone.
8. Lash the paintings in place before the truck is moved. Two men must accompany each loaded, moving truck. At least one of them must be an experienced man.

Added Protection for Canvases and Frames

9. When dismantling an exhibition, remove screw eyes, wires, hooks, etc., from the frames as soon as they come from the walls so that neither pictures nor frames will be harmed in transit or in storage.
10. Avoid direct contact with painted surfaces at all times. Do not attempt to remove slight scratches, rubbed spots, or dirt marks with your hand, a cloth, or by any other means. Where varnish is in poor condition, even gentle pressure will leave a mark which may call for treatment of the entire surface.
11. Wear white cotton gloves to avoid damaging finger marks when working with light-coloured, matt finish, or gilded frames. Clean hands are not enough in this case, as perspiration spots so easily spoil the frames' appearance.

Report all Damages

12. Report any damage which appears to be of recent origin, no matter how slight it seems to be. Get in the habit of examining paintings to determine condition.

13. If paint flakes or frame parts become detached, save all the pieces. Repairs are much easier if all the parts are available.

CARE AND HANDLING OF SMALL OBJECTS

Ceramics, Enamels, Glass, etc.

1. Never handle any object unnecessarily. Work with proper supervision.
2. Move only one object at a time and carry it with one hand underneath. Unpack trays over padded tables so that detached parts will not be lost or damaged.
3. Do not lift small, fragile objects by handles, rims, or other projections; for these parts may have been broken and repaired. Hold the body of the piece gently but firmly. Check each object in and out of the tray when it is composed of more than one part. Pack each part separately within the tray.
4. Always use padded trays for moving small objects. Do not move them by hand except for placement in trays. Use sufficient cotton or padding within the tray to prevent contact with other objects. Whenever possible, objects should be so placed that they do not project above the top of the tray.
5. Make sure that hands are clean. Use gloves or tissue when handling objects with glazed, polished metal, or other highly finished surfaces. (All such material shows finger marks, which are difficult to remove.) Apply this rule to mat finishes and painted decoration as well. Smooth-surfaced objects are hard to handle with gloves or tissue; with them, extra care is necessary.
6. Do not move trays by hand from one part of the building to another. Use the trucks provided for the purpose. Speed and jarring in motion should be strictly avoided. Take time to do the job properly.

Small Sculptures

7. To avoid chipping and scratching in transit, small, heavy objects should always be set on pads and carefully supported so that the weight is evenly distributed.

Ivories and Wood Carvings

8. Ivories and small wood carvings are affected by sudden changes of atmosphere. Do not leave such pieces near open windows or doors particularly during the winter months.

Arms and Armour

9. Arms and elements of armour are subject to damage in many ways. Such material should not be handled by the inexperienced except under competent direction. Always handle with gloves as finger marks cause rust. Any exposure to dampness should be avoided.

Jewellery

10. Never place cotton in direct contact with jewellery. It will catch on delicate parts, may loosen settings, and thus cause loss of stones. Wrap jewellery in tissue first and then in cotton if added protection is needed. (Ivories, enamels, and old glass should be treated in the same way, that is, wrapped in tissue first, then in cotton.) Staff supervision is necessary when working with jewelled objects.

Examine objects to determine condition, then handle accordingly. Report every damage no matter how slight. Save all parts which become detached. Avoid haste in handling objects. Avoid speed with loaded trucks.

CARE AND HANDLING OF LARGE OBJECTS

Sculpture

1. Moving large sculpture is a technical problem. Do not attempt it with too little help or without competent direction. Haste in handling may result in injury to the handlers or damage to the objects.
2. Do not carry heavy sculpture by hand, even if you are able to lift it. It should always be moved on padded trucks, supported and, if necessary, tied to prevent harmful movement while the truck is in motion.
3. Examination of the object before handling is particularly recommended for sculptural material. Knowing the points of weakness in advance is important to the safe movement of the piece. When there is any doubt about whether or not it is strong enough to withstand the strain of transit, get the advice of the person in charge.

Woodwork and Furniture

4. Always move woodwork or furniture on trucks or trolleys (dollies). Never slide or push such objects along the floor, for legs and bases are usually in a weakened condition owing to age or previous damage.
5. Always lift chairs under the seat rail, never by the backs or arms. Carry tables and other furniture by the solid parts of their framework, not the ornamentation.
6. Cover upholstered furniture in transit, as delicate fabrics are difficult to clean. Do not touch the upholstery on the arms, seats, or backs of chairs or sofas.
7. Do not overload flat-bed trucks. Placing chairs, etc., on top of tables or other objects is a dangerous practice. Separate pieces of furniture with pads to prevent contact if more than one is placed on the truck at the same time. Do not allow objects to extend beyond the edge of the truck. Unlocked drawers and cabinet doors as well as folding table tops, movable parts, etc., must be held in place (tied if necessary) to prevent damage in transit.
8. Remove marble tops for transit and transport them in a vertical position on side trucks. Do not carry them horizontally as they may break of their own weight.
9. Wood panelling is seldom as strong as it looks. Movement of it should never be undertaken without sufficient help and proper supervision. As mouldings and trim are lightly attached, do not try to lift or move woodwork by projecting parts.

Report every damage which appears to be new. Preserve all fragments which may become detached.

CARE AND HANDLING OF TEXTILES

Tapestries and Rugs

1. Never lift mounted textiles so that all the weight is borne by the fabric alone. Use the supporting bar, roller, or stretcher for lifting and handling textiles.
2. Avoid stretching, tugging, and pulling. Textiles which seem to be sturdy are frequently old, worn, or repaired. They tear easily.
3. Remove screw eyes, wires, or other projections before rolling textiles on supporting bars. In storage such projections wear through and injure fabrics permanently. Roll tapestries and rugs evenly, avoiding wrinkling and creasing. Roll lined material face out.
4. Rugs and tapestries on rollers should not be picked up by one man or grasped at the middle of the bar. Use two men, one supporting each end, for greater protection of this type of material in transit.
5. Do not pile rolled or folded textiles one on top of another unless it is absolutely necessary. This practice results in broken threads which are virtually impossible to repair.
6. Observe safety rules when removing rugs and tapestries from exhibition. There should be a man at the foot of each ladder in use to steady it.

Costumes and Small Textiles

7. Handle mounted textiles by the stretcher or frame. Even slight pressure on tightly stretched fabrics causes serious damage.
8. Avoid folding textiles, laces, costumes, etc., wherever possible. If it is necessary to fold them, tissue paper should be placed in the folds to prevent creasing.
9. Clean hands are essential in working with textiles. Many fabrics are so fragile that cleaning is impossible.
10. Cover costumed manikins in transit and in temporary storage. They should be lifted by the framework when moved, to avoid soiling or tearing the costumes.
11. After removing textiles, costumes, etc., from exhibition, be sure that all pins are removed to prevent rust stains and blood stains from scratched fingers.

Work on textiles should be done under staff supervision. Report any damage which appears to be new.

CARE AND HANDLING OF WORKS ON PAPER

Works in this group are among the most fragile and easily damaged in the museum. Treat them with the consideration they deserve. They are not to be handled unless it is your job to do so and then only under proper supervision.

Drawings, Watercolours, Prints, Miniatures, etc.

1. Handle as little as possible and only with clean hands. Never touch material of this kind with wet, sticky, or dirty hands.

2. When moving unmounted material, lift each sheet by the upper corners so that it hangs free without buckling. Use great care to avoid bending, cracking, and tearing. Support such works on clean cardboard when carrying them by hand.
3. Never stack prints, drawings, etc., one on top of another unless they are matted or are separated by cellophane, glassine, or tissue paper. Do not allow newsprint, printed matter, or other paper of poor quality to come into direct contact with the objects. Cover works awaiting installation or transportation with tissue paper to exclude dust and dirt.
4. Do not permit works on paper to be shuffled or rubbed against each other. Difficult and expensive retouching is the only way in which damage done in this manner can be repaired.
5. Do not expose prints, drawings, watercolours, and illuminated manuscripts to direct sunlight whether on exhibition, awaiting installation, or in storage.

Rare Books

6. Many bindings which appear to be in good condition are extremely fragile. Leather bindings are easily stained. Do not handle rare books unless it is necessary for you to do so.
7. Turn the pages from the upper, outer corners when it is necessary to open books. Moistened fingers are extremely harmful to paper.
8. Open books gently so as not to crack the bindings—that is, never try to make an open book lie flat. Never stack open books one on top of another. Do not place open books face down. Do not stand books on their front edges, whether on tables, trucks, or shelves.

Report every new damage no matter how slight. Save all fragments which become detached.

APPENDIX C

SAMPLE INSURANCE POLICY FOR FINE ARTS COVERAGE

1. This Policy attaches on the 1st Day of November 1951, at noon Standard Time at place of issuance and is deemed to be continuous and expires when cancelled.
2. To cover on Paintings, Books, Manuscripts, Pictures, Prints, Etchings, Drawings (including frames and glass and brackets), Tapestries, Bronzes, Statuary, Potteries, Porcelains, Glassware, Marble and similar objects of Art held by the assured in trust or for which they may have assumed liability or which they may be instructed to insure, to attach at the time the property becomes at the risk of the Assured.
3. This Policy is to cover the property insured hereunder against all risks of loss or damage to such property (except hereinafter excluded):
   (a) while on EXHIBITION by members of the Western Association of Art Museum Directors or other exhibiting galleries while under the sponsorship of the Western Association of Art Museum Directors;
   (b) while in TRANSIT by railroad, express and/or Motor Truck and/or other form of LAND conveyance within the limits of the United States or Canada;
   (c) while in TRANSIT by AIR SERVICE OF THE RAILWAY EXPRESS AGENCY INC. and/or by APPROVED AIRCRAFT, meaning any Civil Aircraft of the United States (excluding Alaska) operated by any American Flag Scheduled Air Carrier holding a Certificate of Public Convenience and necessity issued by the Civil Aeronautics Board, or Scheduled Air Carriers (CIVILIAN) bearing a valued airworthiness certificate issued by the department of transportation of Canada.
4. It is understood and agreed that the same coverage as granted to shows sponsored by the Western Association of Art Museum Directors is available to active members and to associate members of the Association, to cover fine arts or other similar materials they own, loan or rent to others, or which they may borrow from others. To avail themselves of this coverage, active members or associate members must notify the Executive Secretary of the Association or the J. Glen Liston Insurance Agency, the Company's agent at Seattle, Washington, on or before the attachment of risk. The policy does not provide automatic coverage on permanent material owned by members, but coverage on such permanent material owned by members may be granted at rates to be arranged for each individual gallery or museum.
5. The amount of insurance provided for hereunder is provisional, it being the intent of this insurance to insure hereunder the value of the property described herein at the agreed net value between the owner and the assured.
6. It is understood and agreed that the limits of liability of this Company shall be as follows:

Location	*Limit of liability* $
Any Museum, Art Gallery or other location	100,000
Motor Vehicle	
On any one motor vehicle or trailer on shipments of 150 miles or less	50,000
On any one motor vehicle or trailer on shipments of over 150 miles	25,000
Aircraft	
On any one aircraft at any one time	25,000
Other Carriers	150,000

It is further understood and agreed that the limits of liability of this Company in any one loss, disaster or casualty, whether for partial or total loss or salvage charges or expenses or all combined shall not exceed SIX HUNDRED THOUSAND AND NO/100 DOLLARS ($600,000).

to be skipped perhaps
(text on p. 19)

7. The assured hereby agrees to report to this Company through its agent, ... , not later than twenty days (20) after the first day of each month following the date of inception of this policy the total daily average of such property insured hereunder during the preceding month.

8. The assured agrees to pay premiums monthly at rate of . . . . . per \$100 based on the monthly report as required hereunder. Shipments by aircraft are to be reported at the following rate:

At and From Points and/or Places within the Continental United States to Points and/or Places within the Continental United States 10 cents per \$100.

9. The named assured, ... , will make every effort to see that:
   (a) On shipments via railroad freight a valuation of not less than 50 cents (fifty cents) per pound shall be declared to the carrier.
   (b) On shipments via Railway Express Agency Inc. a lot value of \$550 or a value of \$550 per box shall be declared to the carrier on all express shipments.
   (c) Due diligence is used in packing and unpacking the property insured under this policy.

10. In the event of the discovery of concealed loss or damage following a transit risk of property insured hereunder, the time and place of said loss or damage not being determined whether it be prior or subsequent to the inception date or subsequent to cancellation date of this policy, the liability of this company shall be limited to that proportion of any such loss or damage that the number of days of this company's coverage of the risk in transit prior to the discovery of said loss or damage shall bear to the total number of days elapsed in transit.

11. This policy is extended to cover property on exhibition at fairgrounds up to an amount not exceeding Twenty-Five Thousand and No/100 dollars (\$25,000).

The assured agrees to report such values separately and to pay an additional premium of 4/1,000 dollars (\$.004) per \$100 per day in addition to usual premium required by paragraph eight of this rider form.

12. It is understood and agreed that in the event of the total loss of any article or articles which are a part of a set, this Company agrees to pay the Assured the full amount of the value of such set and the Assured agrees to surrender the remaining article or articles of the set to this Company.

13. This Policy does not insure against:
   (a) Loss or damage occasioned by wear and tear, gradual deterioration, moth vermin, inherent vice or damage sustained due to and resulting from any repairing, restoration or retouching process;
   (b) Loss or damage caused by or resulting from: (1) Hostile or warlike action in time of peace or war; including action in hindering, combating or defending against an actual, impending or expected attack; (*a*) by any government or sovereign power (*de jure* or *de facto*), or by any authority maintaining or using military, naval or air forces; or (*b*) by military, naval or air forces; or (*c*) by an agent of any such government, power, authority or forces; (2) any weapon of war, employing atomic fission or radioactive force whether in time of peace or war; (3) insurrection, rebellion, revolution, civil war, usurped power, or action taken by governmental authority in hindering, combating or defending against such an occurrence, seizure or destruction under quarantine or customs regulations, confiscation by order of any government or public authority, or risks of contraband or illegal transportation or trade.

14. Other terms and conditions remaining unchanged. Attached to and forming part of Policy No. . . . . of the . . . . Company of . . . .
Insured: . . . .
Agent

Note

Clause in basic policy reading:

"It is agreed by the Assured that the property insured hereunder will be packed and unpacked by competent packers."

has been deleted as superseded.

Clause in basic policy reading:

"In consideration of the agreement by the Assured to report additional items of a nature usually covered under a Fine Arts policy, acquired subsequent to attachment date of this policy, within ninety (90) days from the date acquired and to pay full premium thereon from the date acquired at *pro rata* of the policy rate, this policy also covers such additional items but shall cease to cover such additional items if they are not reported to this Company within the said ninety

(90) day period. This Company shall be liable under this provision in respect to any one loss, disaster or casualty, for not exceeding the actual cash value of such additional items, but in no event for more than 25 per cent of the total amount of the policy exclusive of this provision".
has been deleted as superseded.

Clause in basic policy reading:
"If the Assured cancels, earned premiums shall be computed in accordance with the customary short rate table and procedure. If the Company cancels, earned premiums shall be computed *pro rata*. Premium adjustment may be made at the time cancellation is effected and, if not then made, shall be made as soon as practicable after cancellation becomes effective. The Company's check or the check of its representative mailed or delivered as aforesaid shall be a sufficient tender of any refund of premium due to the Assured."
has been deleted as superseded.

Clause (c) in basic policy reading:
"Loss or damage occasioned by breakage of statuary, marbles, glassware, bric-a-brac porcelains, and similar fragile articles, unless caused by fire, lightning, aircraft, theft and/or attempted theft, cyclone, tornado, windstorm, earthquake, flood, explosion, malicious damage or collision, derailment or overturn of conveyance, unless endorsed hereon."
has been deleted.

INLAND MARINE DAILY REPORT

ZONE 4

Transmittal No.	Class	Index Card	Entered	Comm. %	Prem. State	App'v'd
					WASH.	

Agency No.
Agent J. GLEN LISTON INS. AGCY, 1411 FOURTH AVE. BLDG., SEATTLE, WASHINGTON
Broker or Sub Agent
Comm. %

COPY

Amount $ 600,000.00 Rate SEE RIDER ATTACHED Premium $ TO BE REPORTED
in consideration of the stipulations herein named
and of TO BE REPORTED * Dollars, Premium,
does insure THE WESTERN ASSOCIATION OF ART MUSEUM DIRECTORS hereinafter called
the Assured, whose address is SEATTLE, WASHINGTON
from the 1st day of NOVEMBER 1951, at noon, CONTINUOUS UNTIL CANCELLED
standard time at place of issuance, for the
sum of SIX HUNDRED THOUSAND AND NO/100 * * * * * * * * ** * * * * ** Dollars,

On property, as per schedule attached or listed below, against all risks of loss of or damage to such property except as hereinafter excluded.

Schedule of Items Insured

Give method of determining valuations SEE DMP 33073

IF COVERAGE AT LOCATION IS REQUIRED ANSWER THE FOLLOWING:
Location and Nature of Occupancy .... Construction of Building .... Contents Fire Rate ....
Precautions to safeguard property during exhibition ....
Date to be placed on exhibition .... Date to be removed ....

IF COVERAGE DURING TRANSIT IS REQUIRED ANSWER THE FOLLOWING:
From .... (Name and Address) To .... (Name and Address) Via .... (Mode of Transportation)
Number of Shipments .... Amount per Shipment ....
Are all articles to be packed by expert packers? .... Valuation to be declared to carriers ....

LOSS EXPERIENCE

Policy Dates	Premium	Losses

Countersigned by ....

(51-372) Printed in U. S. A.

32AM From the 16 books mentioned, 9 were published in the United States, one was published by the Arts Council in London, one in Paris, four by the UNESCO in Paris, and one was unattributed.

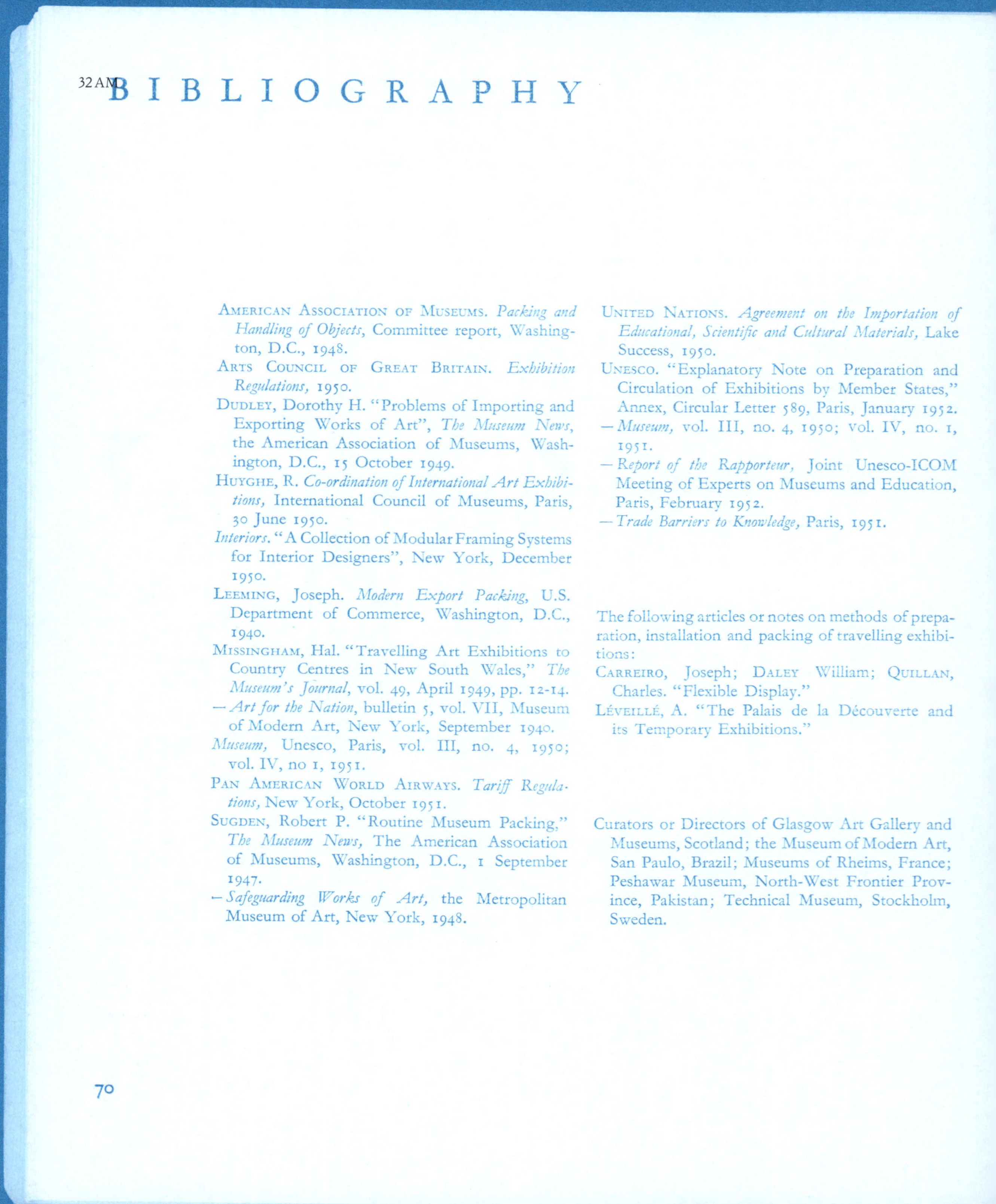

32AM

BIBLIOGRAPHY

AMERICAN ASSOCIATION OF MUSEUMS. *Packing and Handling of Objects*, Committee report, Washington, D.C., 1948.

ARTS COUNCIL OF GREAT BRITAIN. *Exhibition Regulations*, 1950.

DUDLEY, Dorothy H. "Problems of Importing and Exporting Works of Art", *The Museum News*, the American Association of Museums, Washington, D.C., 15 October 1949.

HUYGHE, R. *Co-ordination of International Art Exhibitions*, International Council of Museums, Paris, 30 June 1950.

Interiors. "A Collection of Modular Framing Systems for Interior Designers", New York, December 1950.

LEEMING, Joseph. *Modern Export Packing*, U.S. Department of Commerce, Washington, D.C., 1940.

MISSINGHAM, Hal. "Travelling Art Exhibitions to Country Centres in New South Wales," *The Museum's Journal*, vol. 49, April 1949, pp. 12-14.

— *Art for the Nation*, bulletin 5, vol. VII, Museum of Modern Art, New York, September 1940.

Museum, Unesco, Paris, vol. III, no. 4, 1950; vol. IV, no 1, 1951.

PAN AMERICAN WORLD AIRWAYS. *Tariff Regulations*, New York, October 1951.

SUGDEN, Robert P. "Routine Museum Packing," *The Museum News*, The American Association of Museums, Washington, D.C., 1 September 1947.

— *Safeguarding Works of Art*, the Metropolitan Museum of Art, New York, 1948.

UNITED NATIONS. *Agreement on the Importation of Educational, Scientific and Cultural Materials*, Lake Success, 1950.

UNESCO. "Explanatory Note on Preparation and Circulation of Exhibitions by Member States," Annex, Circular Letter 589, Paris, January 1952.

— *Museum*, vol. III, no. 4, 1950; vol. IV, no. 1, 1951.

— *Report of the Rapporteur*, Joint Unesco-ICOM Meeting of Experts on Museums and Education, Paris, February 1952.

— *Trade Barriers to Knowledge*, Paris, 1951.

The following articles or notes on methods of preparation, installation and packing of travelling exhibitions:

CARREIRO, Joseph; DALEY William; QUILLAN, Charles. "Flexible Display."

LÉVEILLÉ, A. "The Palais de la Découverte and its Temporary Exhibitions."

Curators or Directors of Glasgow Art Gallery and Museums, Scotland; the Museum of Modern Art, San Paulo, Brazil; Museums of Rheims, France; Peshawar Museum, North-West Frontier Province, Pakistan; Technical Museum, Stockholm, Sweden.

70

33 KE Anecdotal evidence. In contrast to the diversified structure of the first section of the *Manual,* the *Illustrations* section strings together image after image like a pearl necklace. The contents page only leaves a single line – the last line – to indicate the existence of this section, a pictorial survey of over four dozen different locations. The series of images displays its diversity in a kind of revue. It covers a huge scope without mentioning any dates (with one exception): it takes place in a purported present. The sequence sets a prelude with a cultically laden central perspective, with its iconographic echoes of da Vinci's *The Last Supper.* It then describes a movement from the candlelit *Men in Steel* to men at work – the exhibition installers at the Victoria and Albert Museum – touching on the audiovisual equipment of an educational programme: loudspeakers, records and a projector that appear to have strayed from a film set. They find themselves juxtaposed with George Nelson's lightweight Struc-Tube, Alvin Lustig's three-dimensional cage system, and appeared contemporaneously with Buckminster Fuller's geodesic domes. With the depictions of cases ↪ 109, the sequence increases in its photographic and didactical vehemence, and in doing so traces an arc back to the chapter *Packing Works of Art for Tour* ↪ 039.

Despite the diversity of the selected images, their numbering ensures an administrative coherence, and this has the advantage of enabling connections with the various descriptions in the text section. Over the pages, related objects are grouped into sequences, but dissimilar items also appear side-by-side. The elements are presented in considered amounts in spacious settings. The rules of the layout – the combination of three image widths, the constant nature of the annotations, a limited variability of positions, a predilection for space and lightness – produce spreads with a rigorous system.

33 KE
34 KE
35 KE
36 MK

34 KE The 38 pages that comprise the Illustrations section have an area of 1,4 m² and would fit onto the surface of a desk. Its units of information pull in different directions: a) images, b) titles, c) themes, d) places, e) exhibitors, and f) modes of exhibition – the core elements of the *Manual.*

The peephole-like rectangles and the who-where-what-how nature of the texts do many things at once: they fly over the geometric displays in the hall of the *Yugoslav Folk Art* exhibition, they take you on a North American *tour d'horizon* to a Swedish exhibition bus, they come across Van Gogh with a bandaged ear among diagrams of spectral analyses, or they stop in front of a panel displaying three-dimensional atomic models under the title *Discontinuité de la Matière.*

An exemplary result can't be attained without convolution: the use of metal eyelets in the corners of the mats of the *World of Illusion* by the Department of Education at the MoMA.

If we view this series of images as a presentation of presentational techniques, then we end up in the realm of self-similarity.

35 KE The sequence of annotated images spans a broad horizon of typologies in over 49 locations and 70 photographs. It aims for the exemplary and adheres to the business of exhibiting: showing and telling. It renounces magazine-like rallying cries. With its small to postcard-size formats, it maintains a low volume and places trust in the clarity of the exhibits. It is assembled with a feel for the graphical: a Wunderkammer of interiors, exhibition views, panels, modular systems, boxes, and nesting objects. Constant motives are images within images and successions of different frames.

But there is, however, a noticeable difference between the imagery and the typography. The illustrations are bound to the principle of specificity. They present their subject in the best possible light, they are atmospheric platforms, their soberness deliberately staged. The typography, on the other hand, is governed by the principle of generality. It is understated, traditionalistic, and suitable for other purposes. Seen in this way, its expressive spectrum tends to the universal.

36 MK The subsequent pages highlight around 30 views of exhibitions, which show diverse exhibits like animal skins, Chinese dolls, medieval weapons, household products, or urban projects using suitable display solutions like wall panels, display case arrangements, specifically made vitrines, folding tables, grid and pole structures, and pavilions.

continued on the next page

This universal spectrum could also be infinitely expanded with dog exhibitions, car expos, and trade fair booths. Personally I am ambivalent, if not skeptic, towards this architecture of display, and tend towards completely avoiding it where possible. In my opinion, exhibits should not be placed in the right light—something exhibition architects often do—but in the true light of the given space—; a mode of display should not be invented but instead the existing qualities of a space should be recognised, analysed, responded to, and, if necessary, gently optimised. As a curator, I am primarily interested in what you come across at a particular location—the genius loci—which then often informs the theme of the exhibition. Consequently, I understand the specified space as a display. Each exhibition space—which is still neutral—is rough around the edges in a proverbial sense, which ultimately influences and shapes the perception of the exhibited object. This starting point often results in a symbiosis between location and work, which could be labeled as a revertive construction where the original space and the temporary exhibit overlay and merge into one another. The more self-evident and harmonious this symbiosis is, the more the notion of display vanishes (to the point of unrecognisability). It becomes then interesting when the boundaries between exhibit and display actually disperse—when the exhibit itself has display character, or when the display is elevated to the status of art. This ambivalence is for example exemplified by Piero Manzoni's 1961 work *Socle du Monde:* on the one hand a sculptural cube in a park in Herning, Denmark, on the other a display pedestal bearing the world as a work of art.

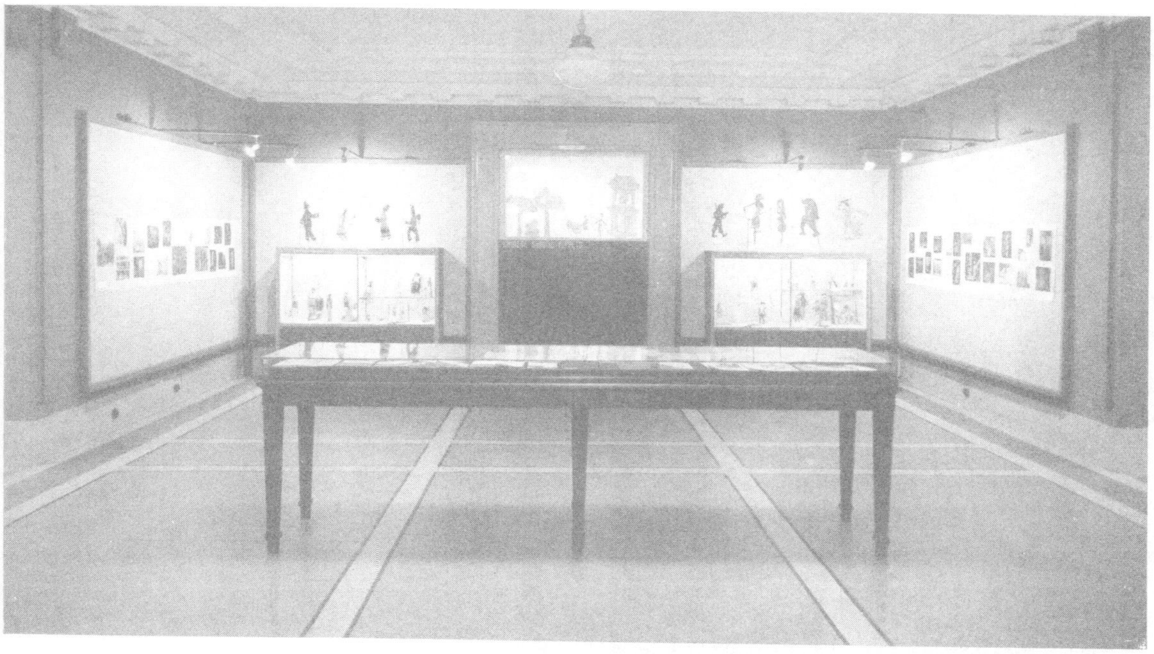

1. Chinese Shadow Puppets, a temporary exhibition at the Detroit Institute of Arts, Detroit, Michigan. Special lighting and arrangement of puppets point up characteristics of these works of art more forcefully than the usual permanent installation of such objects with other materials of the same culture.

1. Ombres chinoises. Exposition temporaire au Detroit Institute of Arts, Detroit, Michigan. Grâce à un éclairage spécial et à la façon dont sont disposées ces figures, leur caractère particulier est mis en valeur de façon plus frappante que dans les présentations habituelles où on les expose avec d'autres collections appartenant à la même culture.

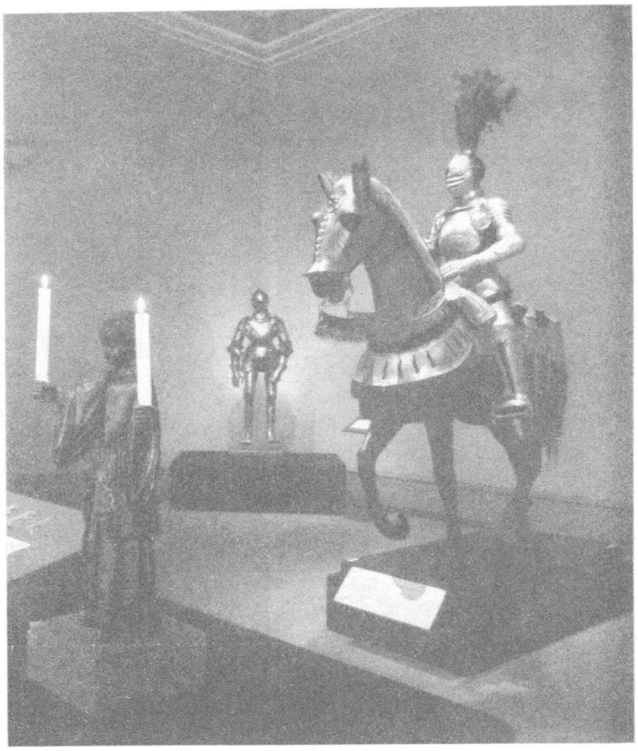

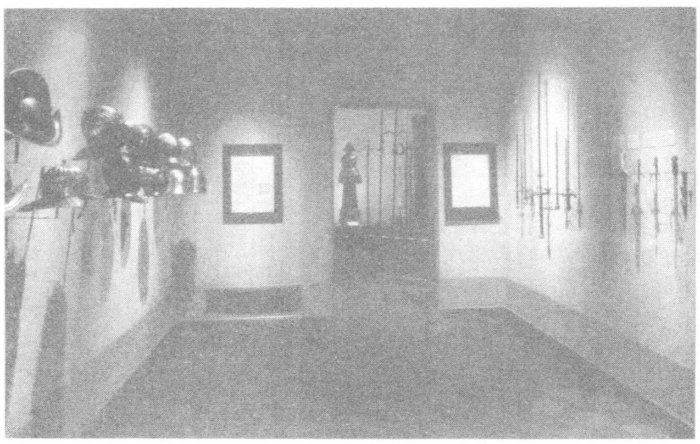

2, 2a. Men in Steel, an exhibition of armour at the Virginia Museum of Fine Arts, Richmond, Virginia. Even the title of the exhibition introduces a surprise approach to mediæval armour. Few permanent installations of armour give the visitor as keen a sense of the pageantry, the splendour or the elegance of the mediæval battle dress suggested within these two rooms.

2, 2a. Hommes d'acier. Exposition d'armures au Virginia Museum of Fine Arts, Richmond, Virginia. Ce titre, à lui seul, traduit le sentiment de surprise causé par cette exposition d'armures médiévales. Peu de collections permanentes procurent au visiteur une impression aussi réelle de ce qu'était la tenue de combat au moyen âge, merveilleux déploiement de splendeur et d'élégance évoquées par ces deux salles

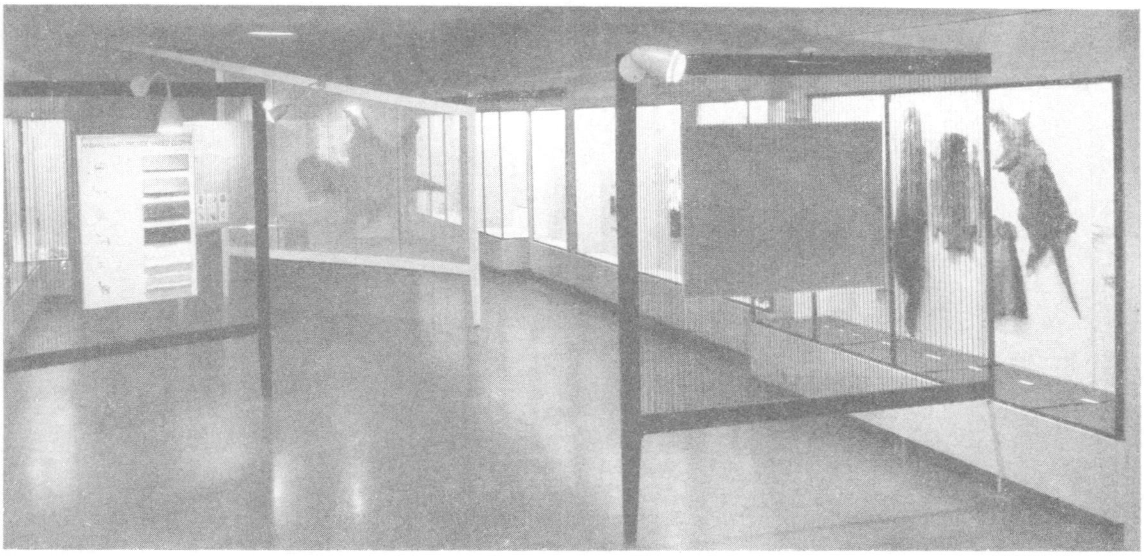

3. Stories in Hair and Fur, a temporary exhibition at the Cranbrook Institute of Science, Bloomfield Hills, Michigan. One of the few science museums with regular programmes of temporary exhibitions, some of which have been circulated.

3. Cheveux, pelages et fourrures. Exposition temporaire au Cranbrook Institute of Science, Blomfiels Hills, Michigan. Un des rares musées scientifiques qui possèdent un programme régulier d'expositions temporaires; certaines d'entre elles ont été mises en circulation.

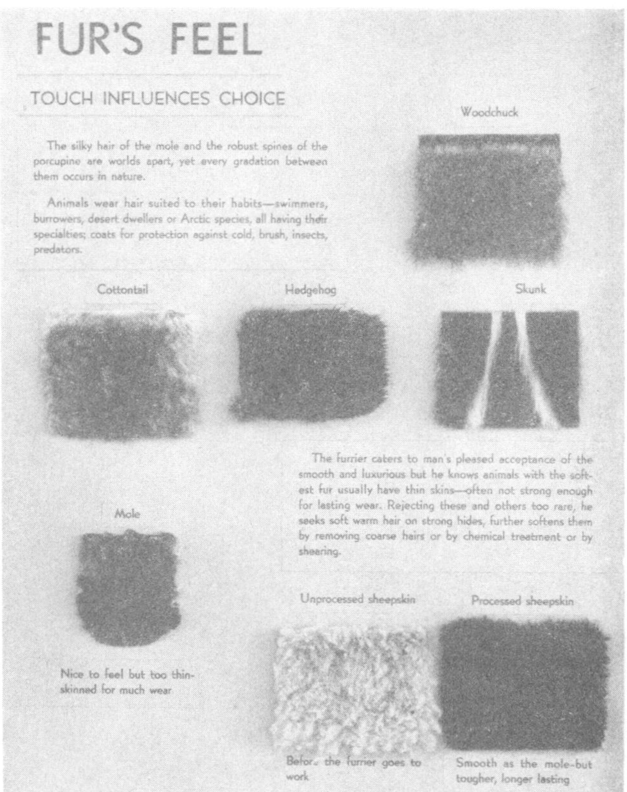

3a. Fur's Feel, one of the panels from the exhibition shown in the installation photograph above.

3a. La fourrure au toucher. Un des panneaux de l'exposition que l'on voit ci-dessus.

37KE The specific characteristics of photographic reproductions, with their (at times) uneven, cloudy tonal values, alludes to both an achievement and a challenge of relief printing: by using halftone blocks to print images.

At this point, a little technical history is needed on the epoch of relief printing before it (via various technological refinements) was supplanted by the offset technique. For centuries, the images used in the relief printing process relied on the artisanship of woodcutters. This manual reproduction reached its heyday with the evolution of xylography—book and newspaper printers employed legions of wood engravers. They already had the technical equipment: photographic methods for transferring the templates to wooden blocks, mechanical apparatus for carving parallel lines.

The method for producing halftone blocks can be traced to an invention by Georg Meisenbach and his Chemigraphic Art Institute in Munich (c. 1880). Using photochemical processes—exposure, hardening, and etching of light-sensitive zinc plates—he succeeded in creating printing plates for the accurate reproduction of photographs. A breakthrough moment was the resolution of halftones into grid points, which was made possible by the optical refractions of a line grid engraved onto glass.[10]

37KE

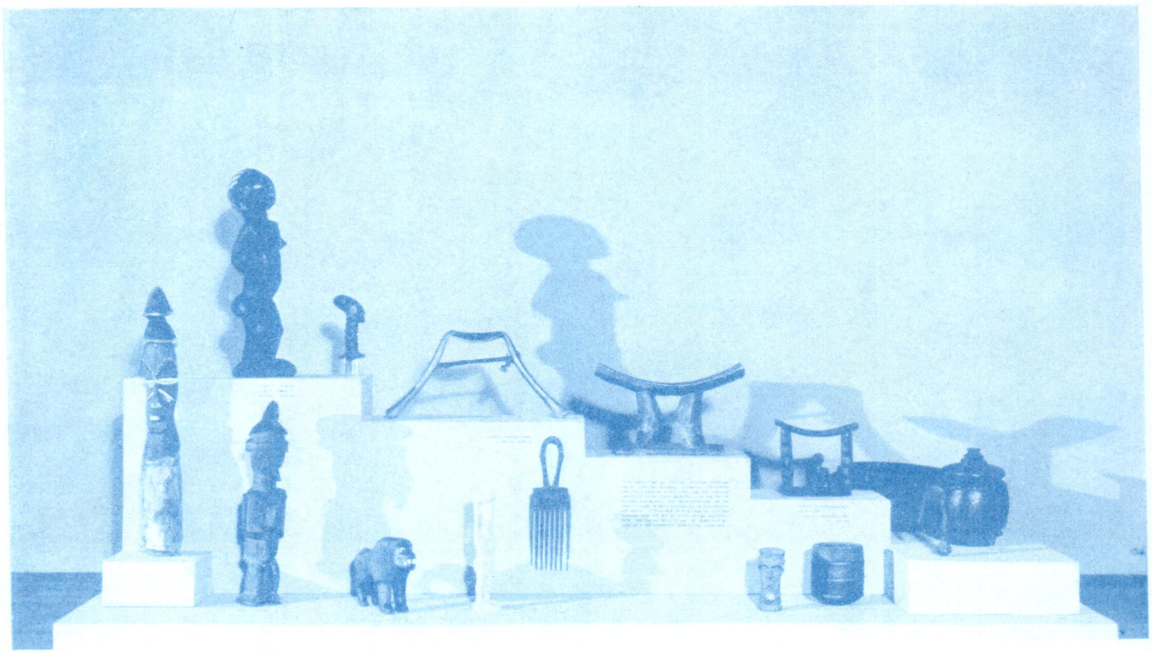

4. *Carvings from East and West*, an exhibition for schools assembled by the American Museum of Natural History, New York, from its collections. While not an art museum, the institution has held many important temporary exhibitions and a series of circulating exhibitions is prepared annually for the city's schools. Permanent cases in the schools house the loans which are planned and installed by the museum's staff.

4. *Objets sculptés de l'Est et de l'Ouest*. Exposition organisée pour les écoles avec les collections de l'American Museum of Natural History, New York. Bien que cette institution ne soit pas un musée d'art, plusieurs expositions temporaires importantes y ont eu lieu et, chaque année, elle met sur pied une série d'expositions circulantes, destinées aux établissements d'enseignement de la ville. Ceux-ci possèdent des vitrines permanentes dans lesquelles le personnel du musée se charge de mettre en place les collections prêtées.

76

↩179 PAGE SEVENTY-SIX

38AM The Gallery of Art Interpretation at the Art Institute of Chicago was an attempt of education through art. Between 1944 and 1952 the museum's first curator of modern painting and sculpture, Katherine Kuh, ran this space as an interpretive laboratory where she showed thematic exhibitions accompanying the exhibitions in the main gallery. The architect Ludwig Mies van der Rohe, who had just emigrated and settled in Chicago to become the head of the architecture school at Chicago's Illinois Institute of Technology, redesigned the Gallery of Art Interpretation into a spare, flexible, modern exhibition space. In 1950, in conjunction with a major retrospective of the art of Vincent van Gogh staged by the Art Institute, Katherine Kuh devoted the Gallery of Art Interpretation to explain the painter's use of colour, line, and brushstroke. The exhibition drew upon the artist's journals, photographs of art that had influenced him and of places in which he had lived and worked, including also colour and black-and-white reproductions of his drawings and paintings. True to her modernist approach, she divided the gallery according to formal themes: colour, texture, space, and drawing. Five panels tracing Van Gogh's artistic development were interrelated by colour charts, to indicate the shifts in his palette over time from dark to brilliant colour. Other exhibitions in the Gallery of Art Interpretation were thematic *(Explaining Abstract Art; From Nature to Art; How Real Is Realism?)*, monographic *(Who Is Posada?; Close-Up of Tintoretto)*, or related to a major exhibition *(Constable and Turner: The Road to Impressionism)*.[11]

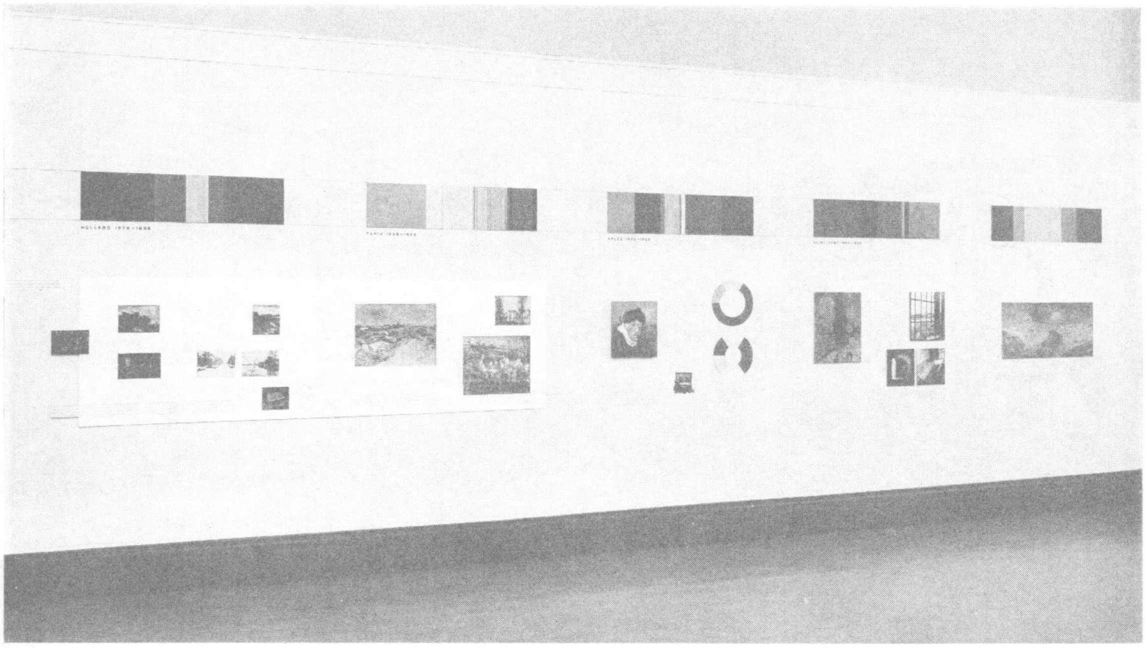

5. Exhibition of the work of Vincent van Gogh held at the Art Institute of Chicago. The photograph shows the Institute's Gallery of Art Interpretation's explanatory exhibition chiefly concerned with the painter's use of colour. It was planned as a circulating exhibition to be used with or without the collection of original paintings with which it was associated at the institute. It was circulated in the United States by the American Federation of Arts.

5. Photographie montrant l'exposition didactique organisée par la Gallery of Art Interpretation de l'Art Institute, Chicago; exposition destinée principalement à révéler la manière dont Van Gogh employait les couleurs. Il s'agissait, dans l'esprit des organisateurs, d'une exposition itinérante qu'on enverrait à d'autres musées, accompagnée ou non des œuvres originales qui figuraient dans sa présentation primitive. C'est l'American Federation of Arts qui en a organisé le circuit aux États-Unis.

38AM

77

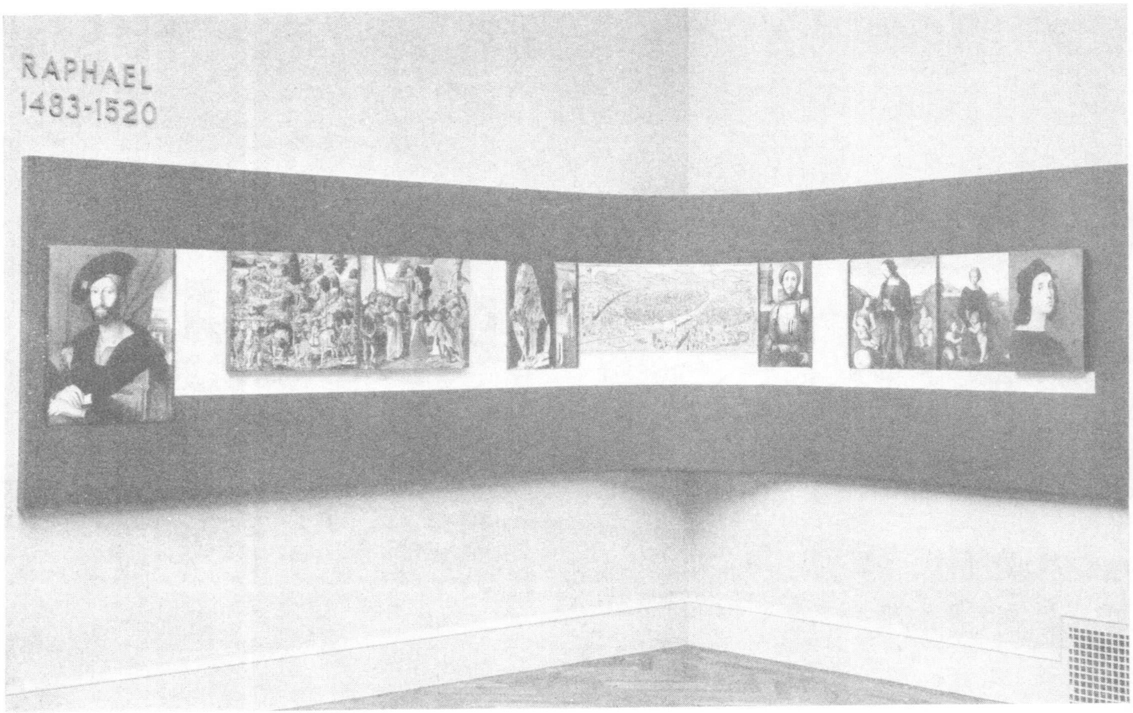

5a. A special exhibition at the Metropolitan Museum of Art, New York, entitled *Silent Gallery Talk on the Bache Collection.* Photographs and photostats of material related to paintings in the Bache collection are shown with labels which tell the visitor about the pictures, the artists and the period in which they lived.

5a. Exposition au Metropolitan Museum of Art, New York, intitulée: *Visite-conférence en images sur la collection Bache.* Présentation de photographies et de photostats relatifs aux peintures de la collection Bache, accompagnés d'étiquettes donnant au visiteur des renseignements sur les tableaux, leurs auteurs, et l'époque à laquelle ceux-ci vécurent.

39 AM	MoMA Teaching Portfolios
No. 1	*Modern Sculpture,* edited by Elodie Courter Osborn, 1949
No. 2	*Texture and Pattern,* edited by Elodie Courter Osborn, 1949
No. 3	*Modern Art Old and New,* edited by Rene d'Harnoncourt, 1950
No. 4	*Useful Objects Today,* edited by Greta Daniel, 1954

MoMA Publications

The MoMA Department of Education, headed by Victor D'Amico, operated a school for children and adult amateurs in the arts for many years. From these classes came material for several books, including *How To Make Modern Jewelry, How To Make Objects of Wood* and *How To Make Pottery and Ceramic Sculpture.*

39 AM

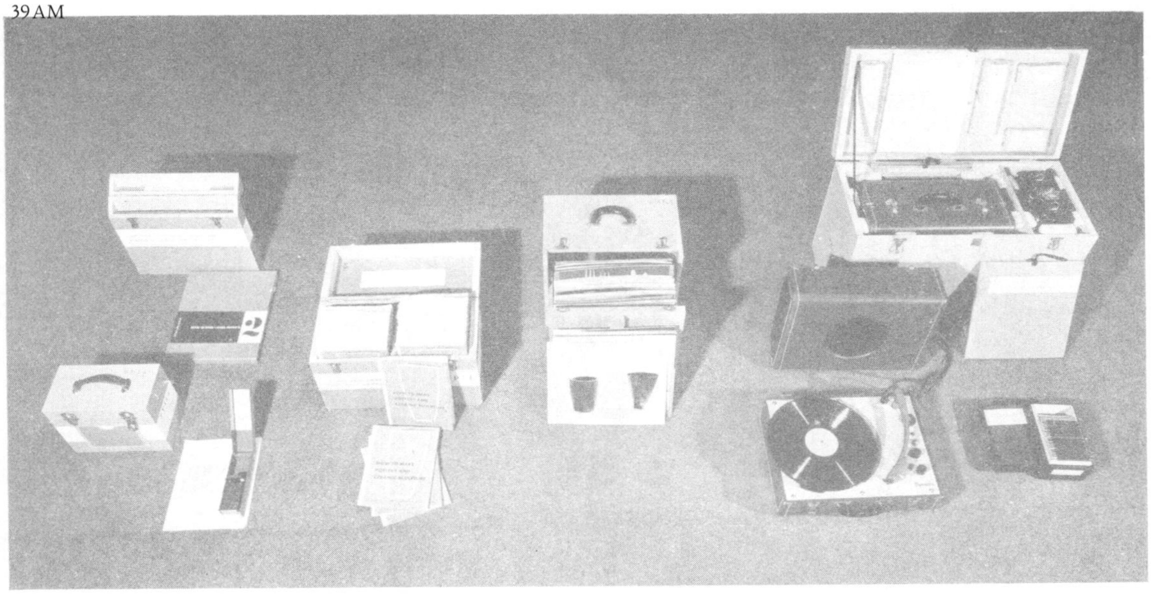

6. Types of educational material prepared and circulated by the Museum of Modern Art's Educational Programme to schools, clubs and other educational institutions. Slide projector, set of slides and printed talks; portfolio of enlarged photographs and texts; classroom booklet of instruction *How to Make Pottery and Ceramic Sculpture*; exhibition of enlarged photographs of pottery forms; set containing slides, lecture on a record together with record player and loudspeaker.

6. Exemple de matériel éducatif préparé et mis en circulation par l'Educational Programme du Museum of Modern Art, à l'usage des écoles, des clubs et de toutes autres institutions à caractère éducatif: appareil à projections, collection de diapositifs et de conférences imprimées; enveloppe contenant des agrandissements photographiques avec les textes explicatifs; notices à l'usage des classes *Comment exécuter des poteries et des sculptures en céramique ;* collection d'agrandissements photographiques de modèles de poterie; caissette contenant des diapositifs, une conférence sur disque ainsi qu'un gramophone et un haut-parleur.

79

40 MK

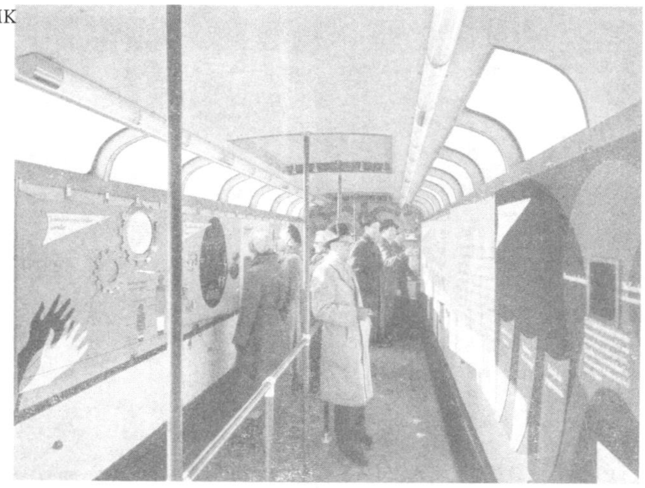

7. Economic Life in Sweden, an exhibition jointly organized by the Tekniska Museum at Stockholm and a Swedish society for economic information shown in the "exhibition bus" which has visited about 200 places in Sweden.

7. La vie économique en Suède. Exposition organisée par le Tekniska Museum, de Stockholm, en collaboration avec une société suédoise d'information économique; vue de l'intérieur de l' « exposition-bus » qui a parcouru près de deux cents localités suédoises.

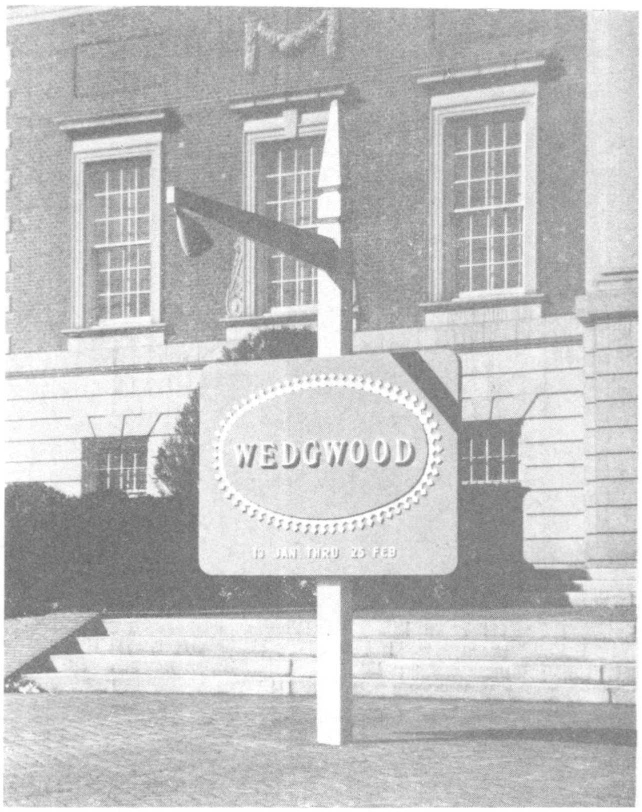

8. Painted wood placard or poster advertising an exhibition of Wedgwood china at the Virginia Museum of Fine Arts, Richmond, Virginia, facing the street at the entrance to the museum.

8. Panneau publicitaire de bois peint annonçant l'exposition de porcelaine de Wedgwood au Virginia Museum of Fine Arts, Richmond, Virginia, et placé dans la rue, face à la porte d'entrée du musée.

80

9, 9a, 9b. Exhibition of *Ancient Sardinian civilization and Nuraghi bronzes* organized by the Centro per la funzione educativa dei musei (Centre for the Educational Function through Museums), in Rome. These photographs show the series of exhibition walls, detachable showcases and lighting fixtures suitable for exhibitions of painting, sculpture, goldsmith's work and art reproductions which can be moved from one city to another. This exhibition of bronzes was shown at the National Gallery of Modern Art, headquarters for the centre in Rome and at the Palazzo Strozzi in Florence

9, 9a, 9b. Exposition organisée par le Centro per la funzione educativa dei musei, Rome (Centre de l'éducation par les musées) et consacrée à l'*Ancienne civilisation sarde et bronzes nuraghes*. Les photographies montrent la série de panneaux, de vitrines démontables et d'appareillage électrique portatif utilisables pour des expositions de peintures, de sculpture, d'orfèvrerie et de reproductions d'art, et pouvant être transportées d'une ville à l'autre. Cette exposition fut présentée à la Galleria Nazionale d'arte moderna, à Rome et au palais Strozzi à Florence.

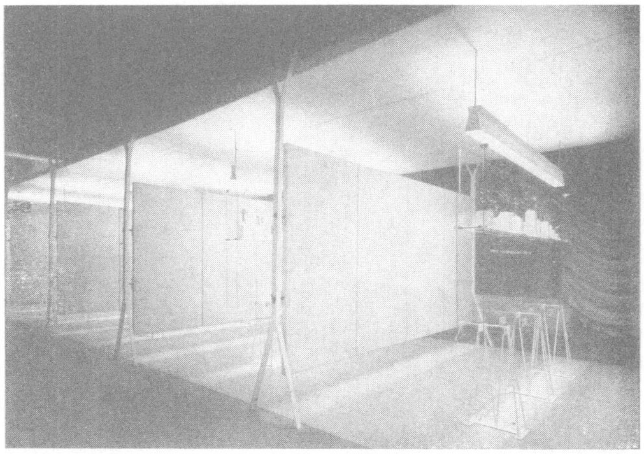

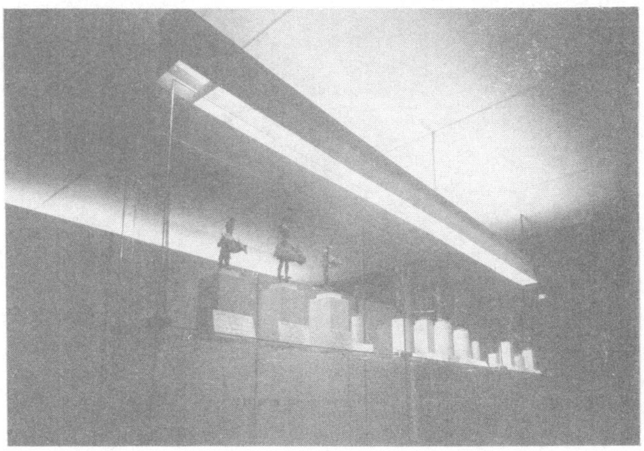

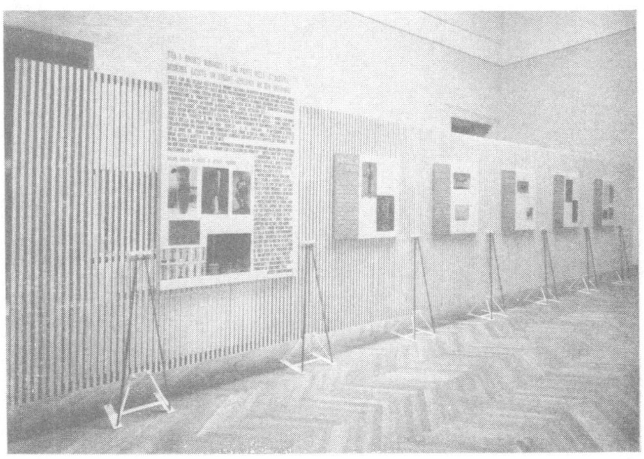

41 AM “The most recent and the most important step, however, is the establishment of a Centre for the Educational Function of Museums in Rome. Its headquarters are at the National Gallery of Modern Art in the Valle Giulia, and consist of a few exhibition rooms and a lecture-hall. It has a series of exhibition-walls and detachable showcases designed by the architect Franco Minissi and suitable for exhibitions of painting, sculpture, goldsmith’s work and art reproductions. Regard must be paid to the fact that the problem of educating the masses in visual art is a very delicate one in Italy, where all or nearly all museums and schools of art are either State institutions or public bodies controlled by the State; and thus every effort to move the public’s taste in a given direction risks incurring the accusation that it amounts to undue influence by the State on public opinion. But the activities undertaken by the State to educate the public in visual art through museums are inspired by no planning motive; they are merely designed to re-establish contact between museums and the main trends in criticism, between museums and schools, between museums and artists, and between museums and the general public. It is only by making use of the lessons of history, fully and in their application to the present day, that complete creative freedom can be attained which it is the duty of every democratic State to guarantee.”[12]

41 AM

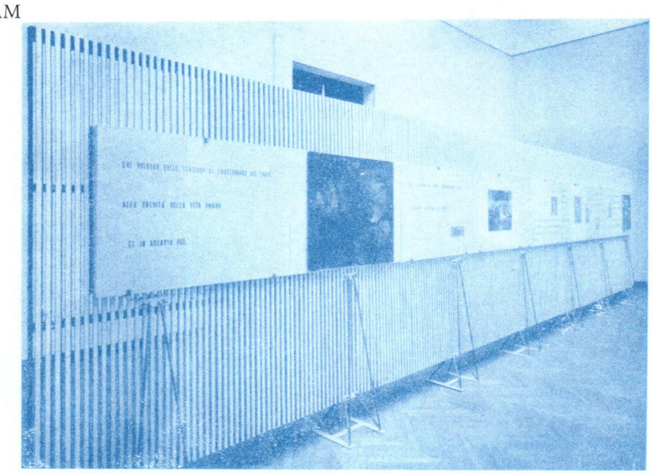

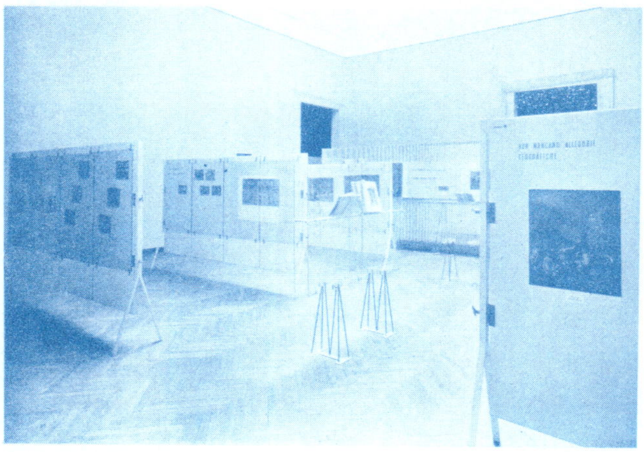

10, 10a. The same equipment used for an exhibition of colour reproductions *(figs. 9, 9a, 9b).*

10, 10a. Le même matériel, employé pour une exposition de reproductions en couleurs *(fig. 9, 9a, 9b).*

82

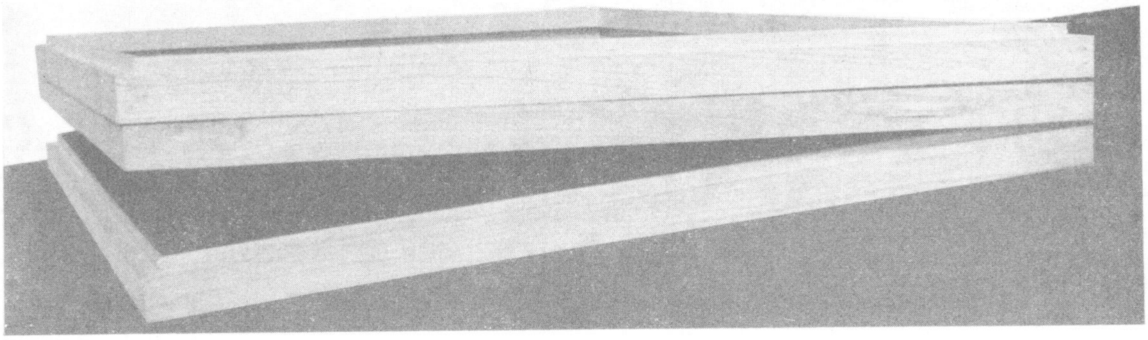

11. Circulating exhibition organized by the Palais de la découverte, Paris. The nesting frames.

11. Exposition itinérante organisée par le Palais de la découverte, Paris. Cadres s'emboitant les uns dans les autres.

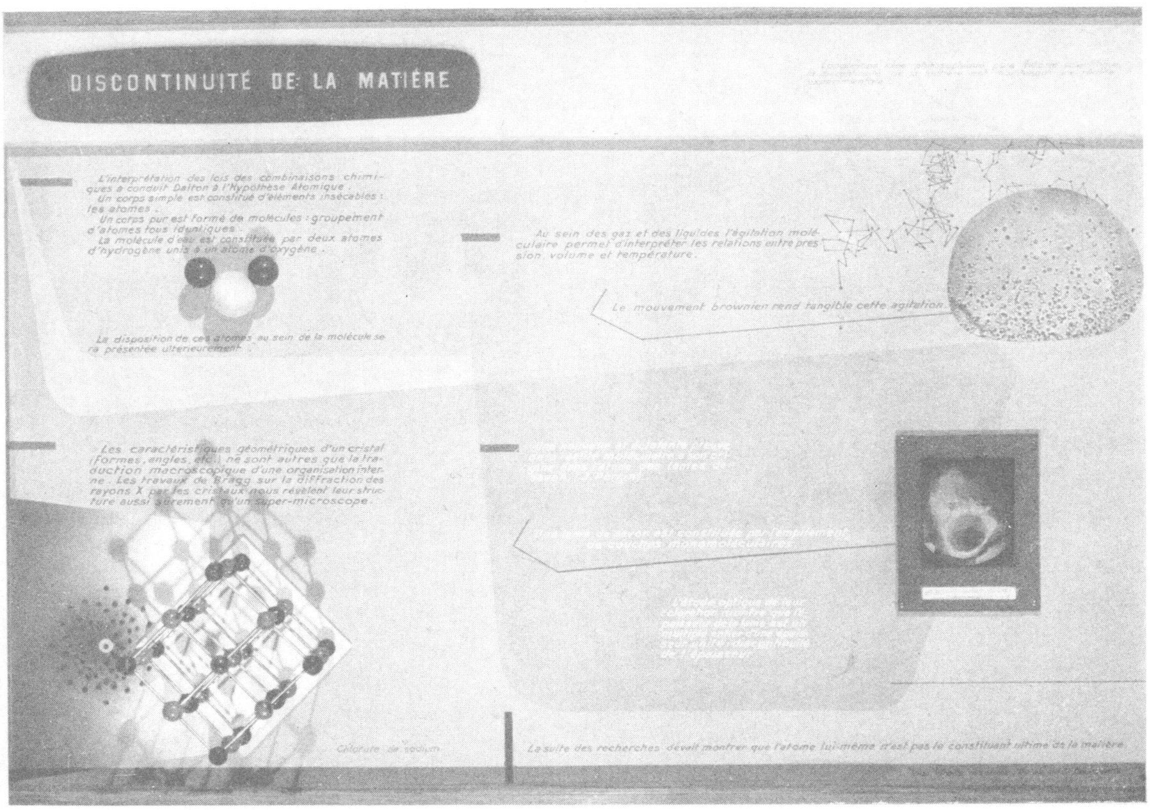

11a. Panel with three dimensional objects attached. Palais de la découverte, Paris.

11a. Palais de la découverte, Paris. Panneau portant des objets à trois dimensions.

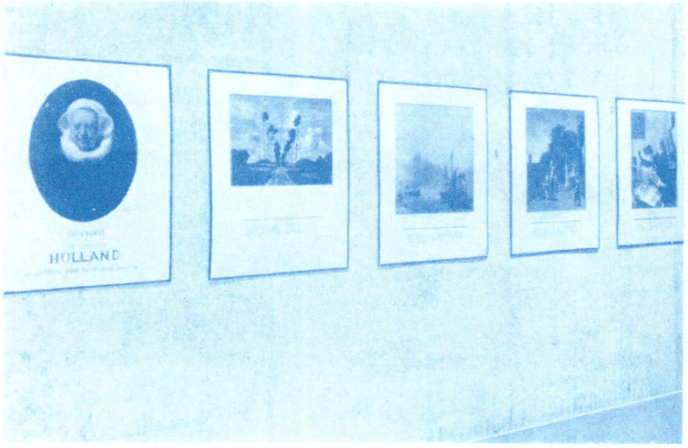

12. Scenes of Holland, a travelling exhibition showing colour reproductions matted with celluloid covers taped at edges. The mats are cut away to reveal pictures mounted on the backing board beneath. Virginia Museum of Fine Arts, Richmond, Virginia.

12. Scènes hollandaises. Exposition itinérante organisée par le Virginia Museum of Fine Arts, Richmond, Virginia, et présentant des reproductions en couleurs montées en passe-partout sous celluloïd, les bords maintenus par des bandes adhésives. Les passe-partout sont découpés afin de laisser voir les tableaux, qui sont montés sur un carton de soutien.

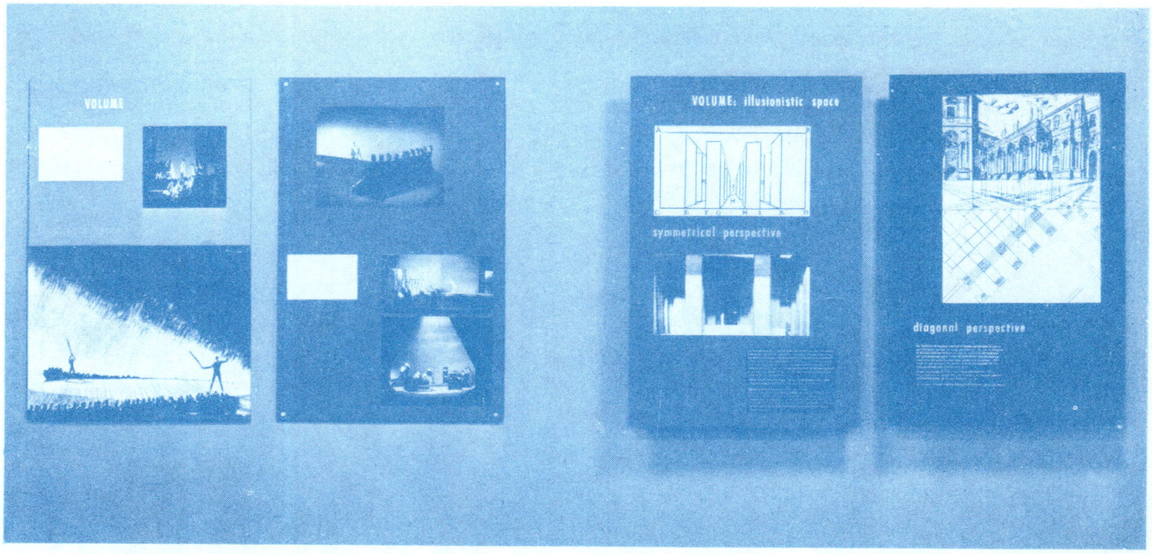

13. World of Illusion, an exhibition of stage design prepared by the Educational Programme of the Museum of Modern Art, New York. Photographs, drawings, prints and labels are mounted on coloured mats to enliven the display of monochromatic materials. The use of cut-out paper letters makes clear the organization of the exhibition. Note the use of metal eyelets in the corners of the mats.

13. Le monde de l'illusion. Exposition de projets et de dessins se rapportant au théâtre, organisée par l'Educational Programme du Museum of Modern Art, New York. Les photographies, les dessins, les estampes et les étiquettes explicatives sont montés sur des passe-partout de couleur afin de mettre une note plus vive dans cette présentation de pièces monochromes. Les lettres de papier découpé sont très nettes et mettent en évidence le plan de l'exposition. Remarquer l'emploi d'œillets de métal aux coins des passe-partout.

84

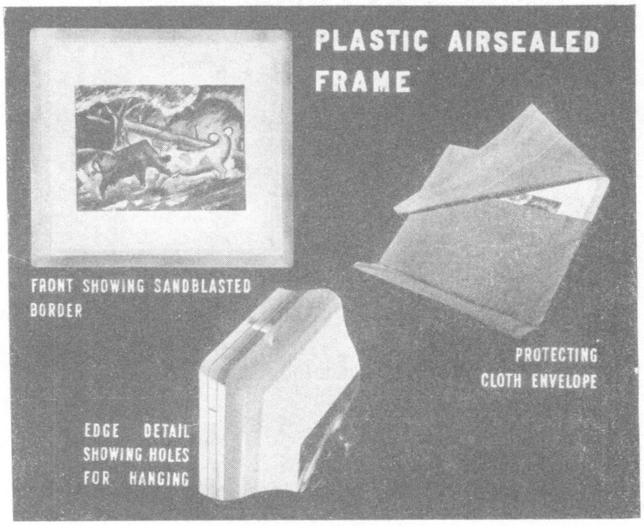

14. A moulded plastic frame designed at the Walker Art Centre, Minneapolis, Minnesota, to enclose watercolours in an airsealed envelope for a travelling exhibition to South America.

14. Cadre en matière plastique moulée, réalisée par le Walker Art Center, Minneapolis, Minnesota, afin de constituer une enveloppe absolument hermétique pour les aquarelles destinées à une exposition itinérante en Amérique du Sud.

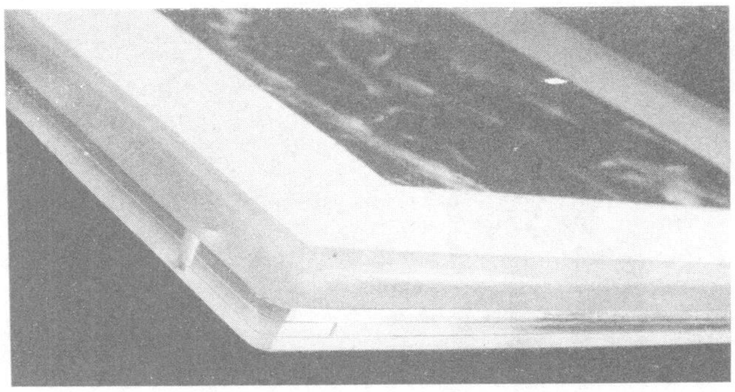

14a. Detail of this frame showing holes driven through plastic "sandwich" to provide means of hanging.

14a. Détail de cadre montrant les trous percés dans le « sandwich » de matière plastique pour l'accrochage.

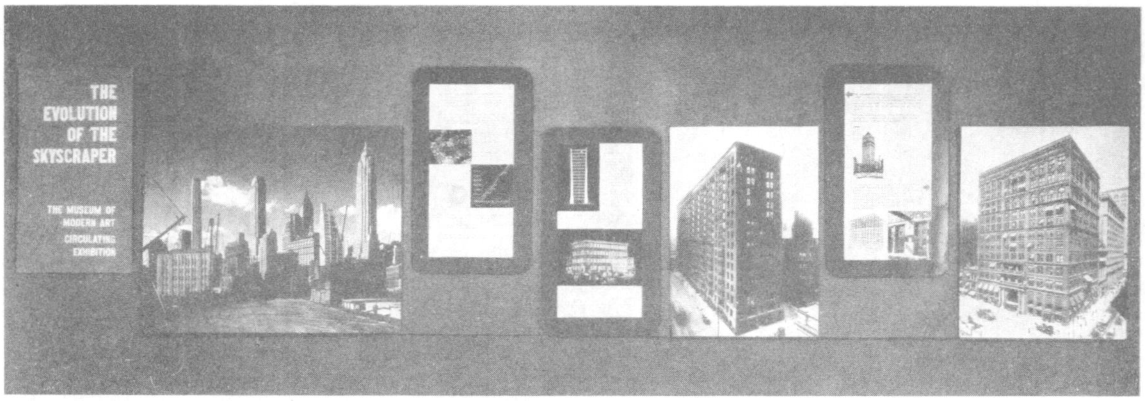

15. Evolution of a Skyscraper, a travelling exhibition from the Museum of Modern Art, New York, which toured many schools, universities, museums and galleries. The rounded corners of panels eliminated wear and tear on this material and photographs were later removed, the panels being used again for another exhibition.

15. L'évolution d'un gratte-ciel. Exposition itinérante, organisée par le Museum of Modern Art, New York, qui a fait le tour de nombreuses écoles, universités et musées. Les coins arrondis des panneaux évitent les détériorations qu'ils subissent à la longue. Par la suite, les photographies furent retirées et les panneaux furent utilisés pour une nouvelle exposition.

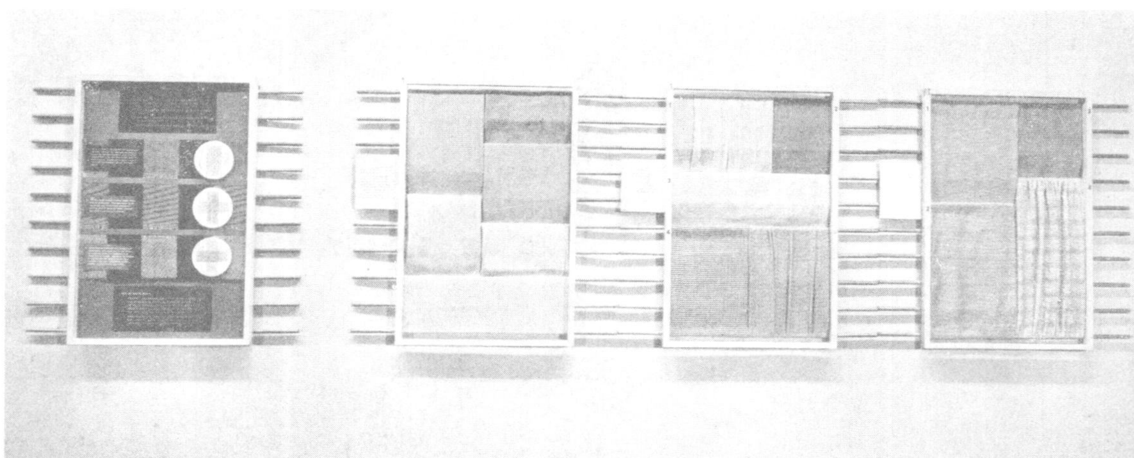

16. Modern Textile Design, circulated by the Museum of Modern Art, New York. Samples of textiles are looped over dowels and sewn together on the reverse side.

16. L'art textile contemporain. Exposition itinérante organisée par le Museum of Modern Art, New York. Des échantillons de textiles sont enfilés sur les tringles et cousus ensemble à l'envers.

17. Textiles by Anni Albers, a travelling exhibition prepared by the Museum of Modern Art, New York. This photograph shows clearly the method of attaching textiles to dowels or poles which can be hung from ceiling or wall by using picture-wire affixed to the ends of the wood strips. Valuable and rare pieces are framed like paintings.

17. Textiles d'Anni Albers. Exposition circulante organisée par le Museum of Modern Art, New York. La photographie montre clairement la manière d'attacher des textiles à des tringles ou à des baguettes de bois qui peuvent être suspendues au plafond ou au mur avec du cordon à tableaux métallique fixé à celles-ci à chaque extrémité.

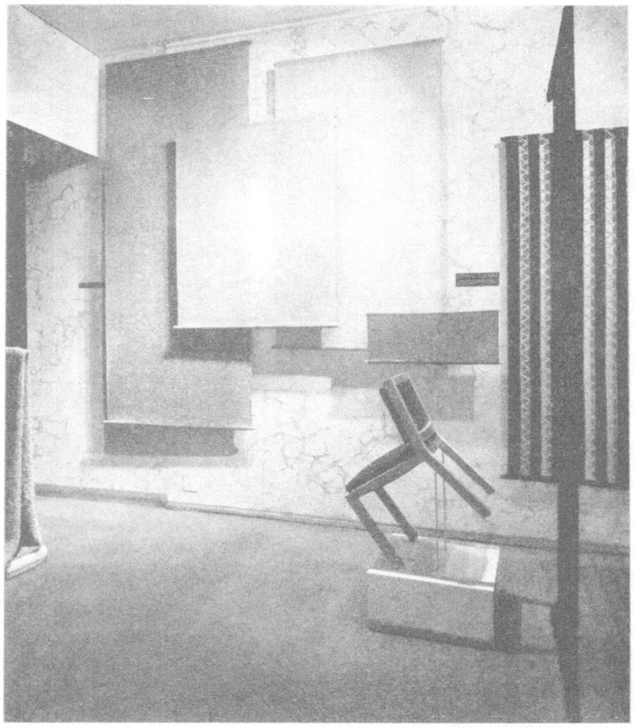

17a. Small items are mounted, matted and covered with celluloid, taped at the edges.

17a. Les fragments rares ou de très grande valeur sont encadrés comme des peintures. Les petits échantillons sont montés en passe-partout, et recouverts de celluloïd maintenu sur le pourtour par des bandes adhésives.

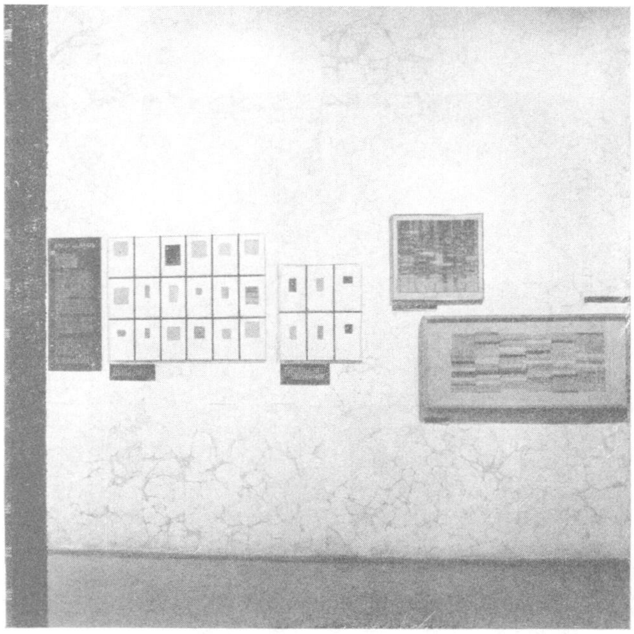

87

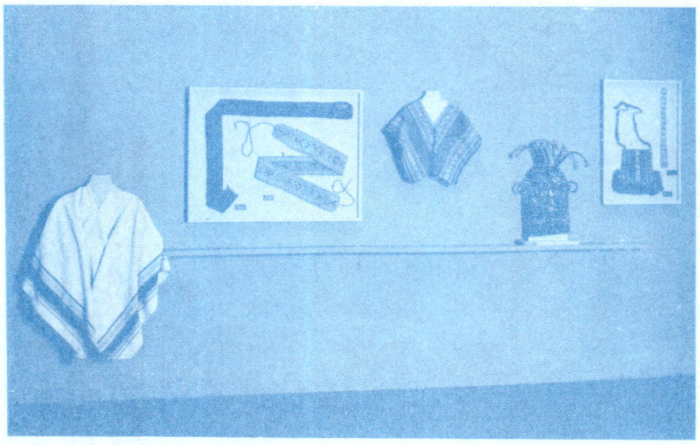

18. South American Textiles, a travelling exhibition, the Museum of Modern Art, New York. Panels help to unify the display of a variety of small objects. Small cut-out forms suggest figures or heads.

18. Textiles sud-américains. Exposition itinérante organisée par le Museum of Modern Art, New York. Les panneaux donnent de l'unité à la présentation de petits objets très divers. Des corps ou des têtes sont figurés par des silhouettes découpées.

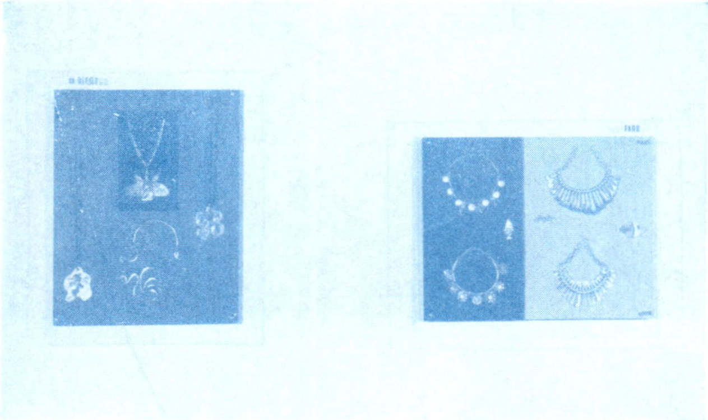

19. Modern Jewellery Design, a travelling exhibition, the Museum of Modern Art, New York, Painted and cloth-covered panels set off the jewellery; heavy plastic sheets protect the surfaces.

19. Bijoux modernes. Exposition itinérante organisée par le Museum of Modern Art, New York. Des panneaux peints ou recouverts d'étoffe mettent en valeur les bijoux; des feuilles épaisses de matière plastique en protègent la surface.

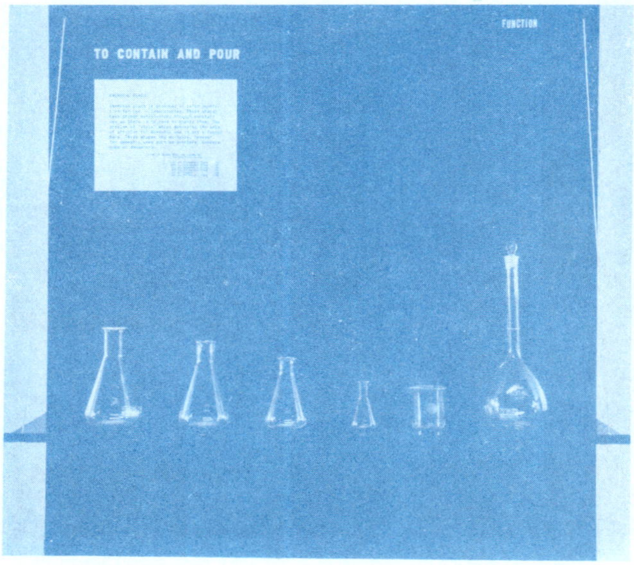

20. What is Good Design? A travelling exhibition on the principles of good design, the Museum of Modern Art, New York. Shelf is held in place by hinges and cord which allows it to drop to necessary level to support three-dimensional objects. Such panels can be used again for other exhibitions.

20. Art fonctionnel. Exposition itinérante, organisée par le Museum of Modern Art, New York, démontrant les principes de bonnes conceptions d'art fonctionnel. L'étagère est maintenue en place par des charnières et par un cordon qui lui donne l'aplomb nécessaire pour pouvoir y poser des objets à trois dimensions. Ce genre de panneau peut être utilisé à nouveau pour une autre exposition.

42KE A scene of effortlessness. This interlude shows a puppeteer with her four-legged friend. The delicate, shadowy exhibits are barely recognisable under the Plexiglas. The viewer would like to know what the halftone dots are, rather hiding than revealing. A light-coloured ellipse seems to resemble a plate, one object clearly has the form of a microscope. On the wall, in line with the display cases, hang tableaus with two columns of images—also UFOs?

43KE Information with much higher resolutions can be found in the depths of the MoMA archives. *Machine Art,* keyword and exhibition title with paradigmatic overtones, provides access to almost inexhaustible volumes of data. The comparison between the purported original and the halftone miniature in the *Manual* is striking: the brilliance of the digital reproduction, n-times the size of the printed version, lends tactility to even the images on the wall. The graceful assistant exudes an air of style while collapsing the folding table. A second archive image documents the full extent of the exhibition: a row of six display tables set against a wall, with nine corresponding panels containing written and visual descriptions. The administrative background can also be found there: a two-page typescript, the first few lines of which read "Young People's Rotating Exhibition No. 24/Arranged by The Museum of Modern Art/MACHINE ART/Check List & Installation", lists a total of 61 objects divided into thematic sections. Thus, a suspicion is confirmed: in the young woman's field of vision, among the delicate devices, is a brass plumb bob. The checklist for this table also counts three outside firm joint calipers, a bevel protractor, a Vernier depth gauge, and a celluloid protractor. In the case of this exhibition, the website section *Artists* takes on industrial dimensions: next to the names from a few designers, ten industrial companies are listed. This enables attributions. The self-aligning ball bearing, in front of the laboratory microscope, connects S.K.F. Industries, Inc., Hartford, CT, with the leading people of the *Rotating Exhibition* and their target audience. The abbreviation S.K.F. stands for Svenska Kullagerfabriken, a company founded in 1907.[13]

44KE The conceptual background to *Machine Art* brought about a publication of the same name. It accompanied the large-scale MoMA show from 1934 featuring 400 machine-made objects: machines, machine parts, scientific instruments, and useful everyday objects. Head curator Philip Johnson reflects on the conflict between the "craft spirit" and the machine-driven 19th century, and draws historical lines joining the engineering sciences to specific technical achievements and aesthetic refinements in America—from *The Great Exhibition* at Crystal Palace in London through the Arts and Crafts Movement to postulates of the Weimar Bauhaus under Gropius.

21. Useful Objects, a travelling exhibition of household objects, the Museum of Modern Art, New York. Demountable tables and frames used as supports are the same dimensions to facilitate packing of installation units.

21. Objets utiles. Exposition itin rante organisée par le Museum of Modern Art, New York. Présentation d'objets usuels. Les tables démontables et les cadres leur servant de supports sont de même dimensions, afin de faciliter l'emballage du matériel d'exposition.

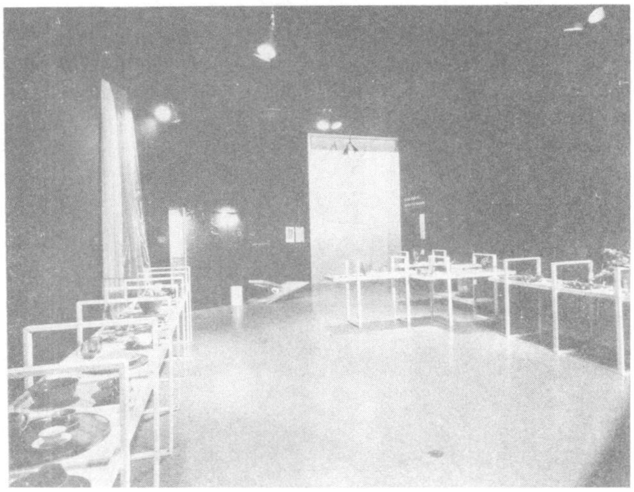

22. Machine Art, an exhibition for schools, prepared by The Educational Programme, the Museum of Modern Art, New York. Some objects are fixed to background panel, others may be removed for shipping. Tables fold flat for packing. The transparent covering is a sheet of heavy plastic called "plexiglas" which can be slipped out between grooves formed at the side of the case.

22. L'art dans la mécanique. Exposition organisée par l'Educational Programme du Museum of Modern Art, New York. Certains objets sont fixés aux panneaux de fond, les autres peuvent être enlevés pour le transport. Les tables se plient à plat pour l'emballage. Les vitrines sont formées par des feuilles de matière plastique épaisse, nommée « plexiglas » qui peuvent être glissées hors des rainures ménagées sur les côtés.

43KE
44KE

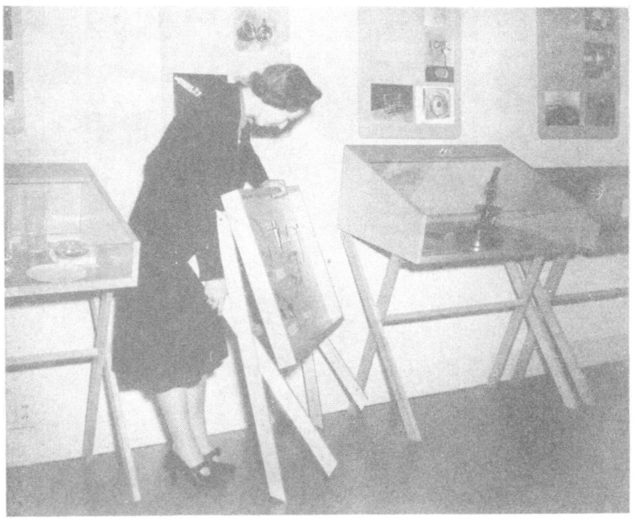

42KE

89

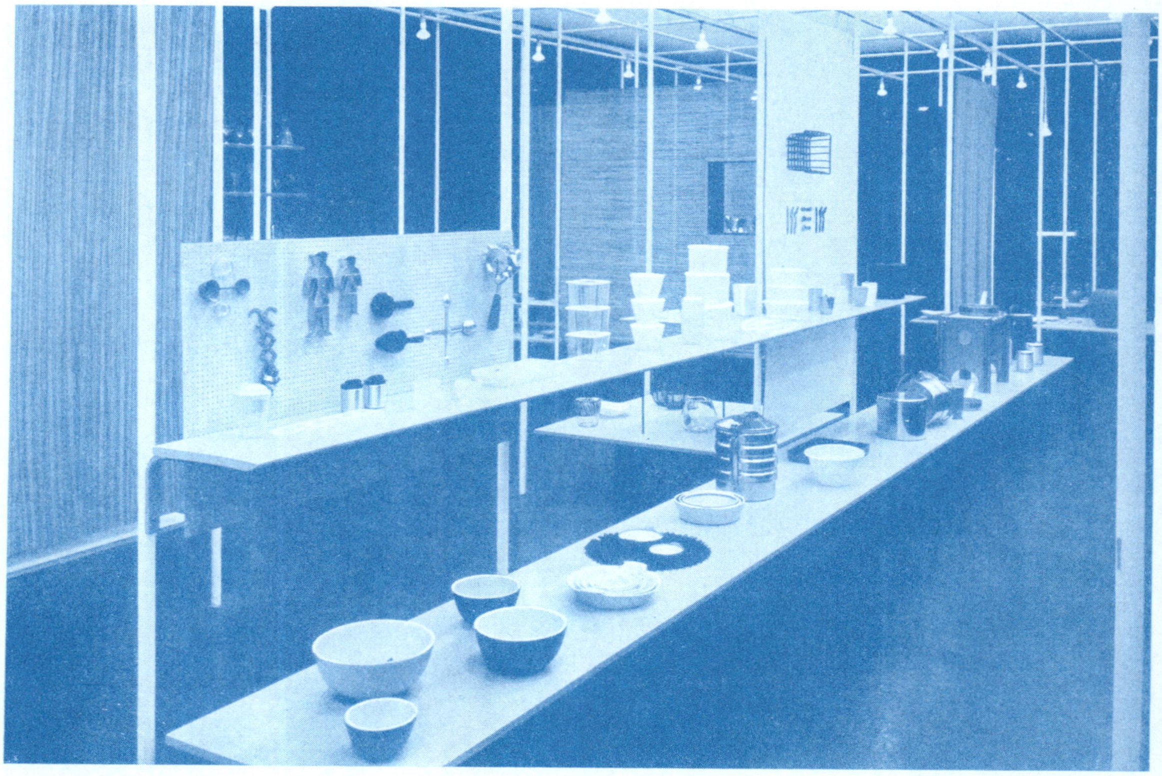

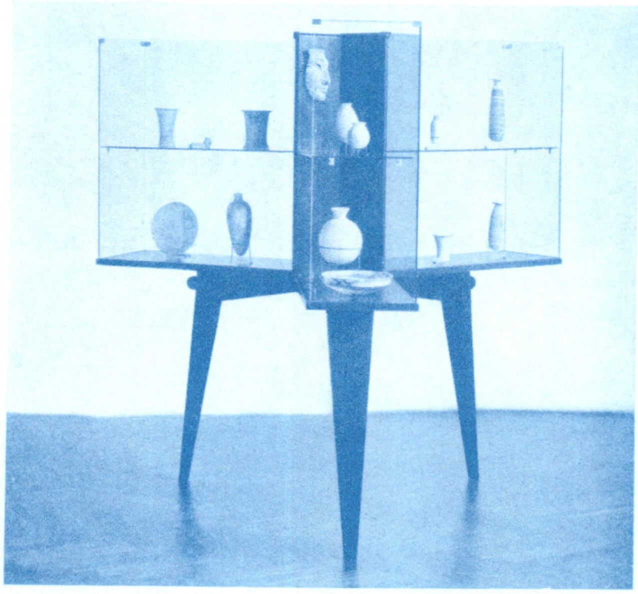

23. For Modern Living, an exhibition of contemporary housewares and furniture held at the Detroit Institute of Arts, Detroit, Michigan.

23. Intérieurs modernes. Exposition organisée par le Detroit Institute of Arts, Detroit, Michigan. Meubles et objets ménagers d'aujourd'hui.

24. Central three-winged case for exhibitions of pottery, sculpture or other small three-dimensional objects circulated in Poland built by the Muzeum Narodowe Warsaw. Lighting fixtures are set into the top of each section.

24. Vitrine centrale à trois éléments, construite par le Muzeum Narodowe de Varsovie pour les expositions circulantes, afin de présenter en Pologne des poteries, sculptures ou autres petits objets à trois dimensions. L'extérieur est éclairé par des ampoules fixées au sommet des trois éléments.

25. Yugoslav Folk Art, a travelling exhibition shown at the Royal Scottish Museum, Edinburgh, which includes numerous demountable installation units. Note cross form of case for pottery, table cases, free-standing wall panels devised to display many small articles.

25. Art populaire yougoslave. Exposition itinérante présentée par le Royal Scottish Museum, Edimbourg, montrant de nombreux exemples de matériel démontable. Remarquer la vitrine en forme de croix pour la céramique, les vitrines-tables et les panneaux muraux de centre, prévus pour la présentation de nombreux objets de petites dimensions.

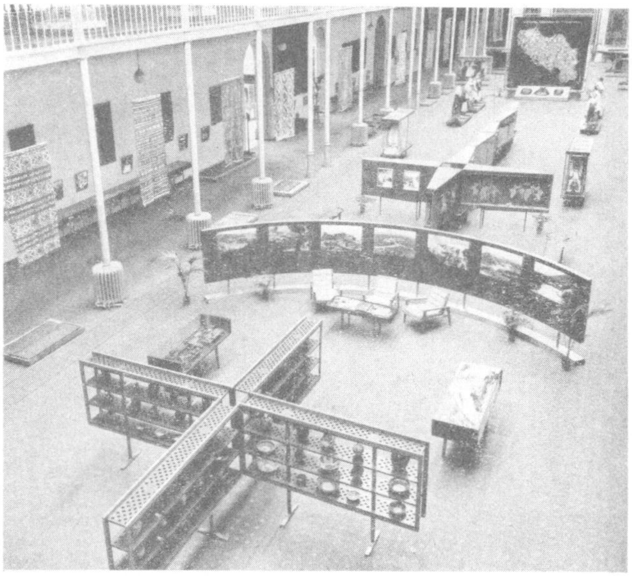

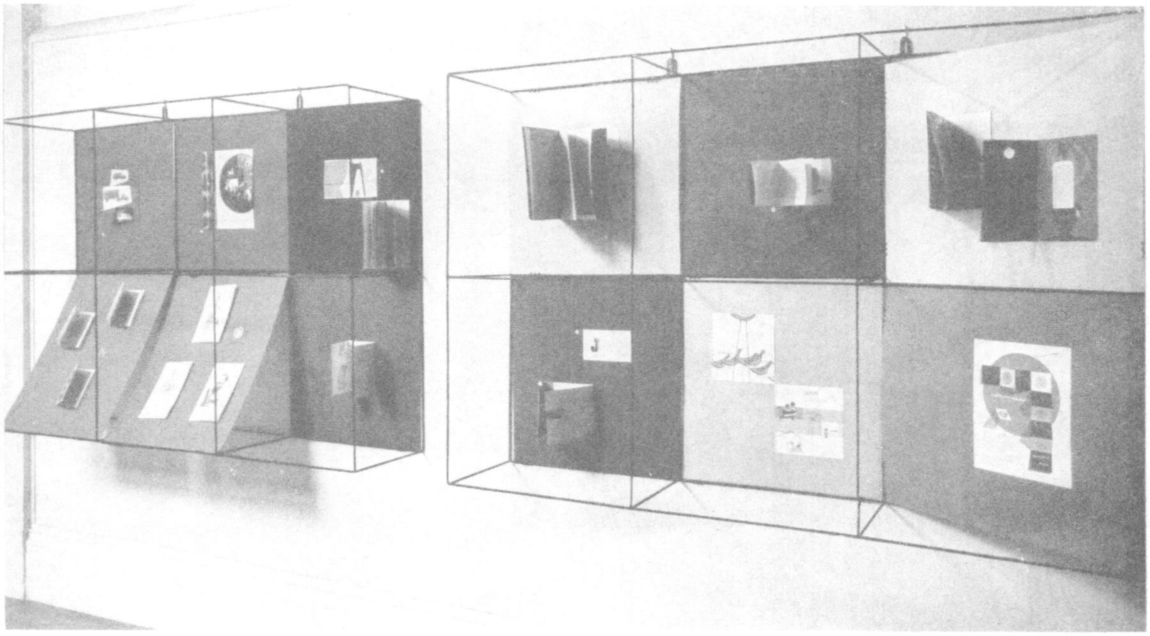

26. Wall case made of narrow gauge wire to display books, pages and various objects of the typographer's art, Container Corporation of America, Chicago, Illinois.

26. Vitrines murales faites de fil de fer pour l'exposition de livres, de pages tirées de livres, et de divers spécimens de l'art typographique. Container Corporation of America, Chicago, Illinois.

45KE Empty spaces are as much a part of page assembly as are the constructive, printed elements. The typesetter's shelves are full of spacing material: leadings, clumps, reglets, slugs, and larger space fillers. The print forms – lead that was precisely placed by the setter, bound by the solidity of perpendicularity, and enclosed in frames by the printer – had to withstand the mechanical forces of the cylinder printing machines.[13]

46KE The format of the booklet (176 × 213 mm) is a hair's breadth from the ratio 5:6 – opened up, the double page corresponds to 5:3. The graphical page construction follows traditional division in its type area and paper margins: outside and inside 12 mm, top 13 and bottom 18 mm. The proportions of the outer measurements are also found in the type area. In defining this domain, a typographical framework beyond the millimetre comes into play. The type area is 33 ciceros wide and 40 ciceros high. Its horizontal structure is based on a division into seven units – not including the space between the text columns (1 cicero). The column width corresponds to three units, or 14 ciceros. The margin column (one unit) allows for a variety of image sizes, determines an axis for title and page number, and, together with the outer margins, is a stabilising influence on the text columns. It creates a definite proportion between outer and inner. This succinct system also enables the structural composition of the Illustrations section. Its dynamic is not least attributable to the ratio 3:4:7.

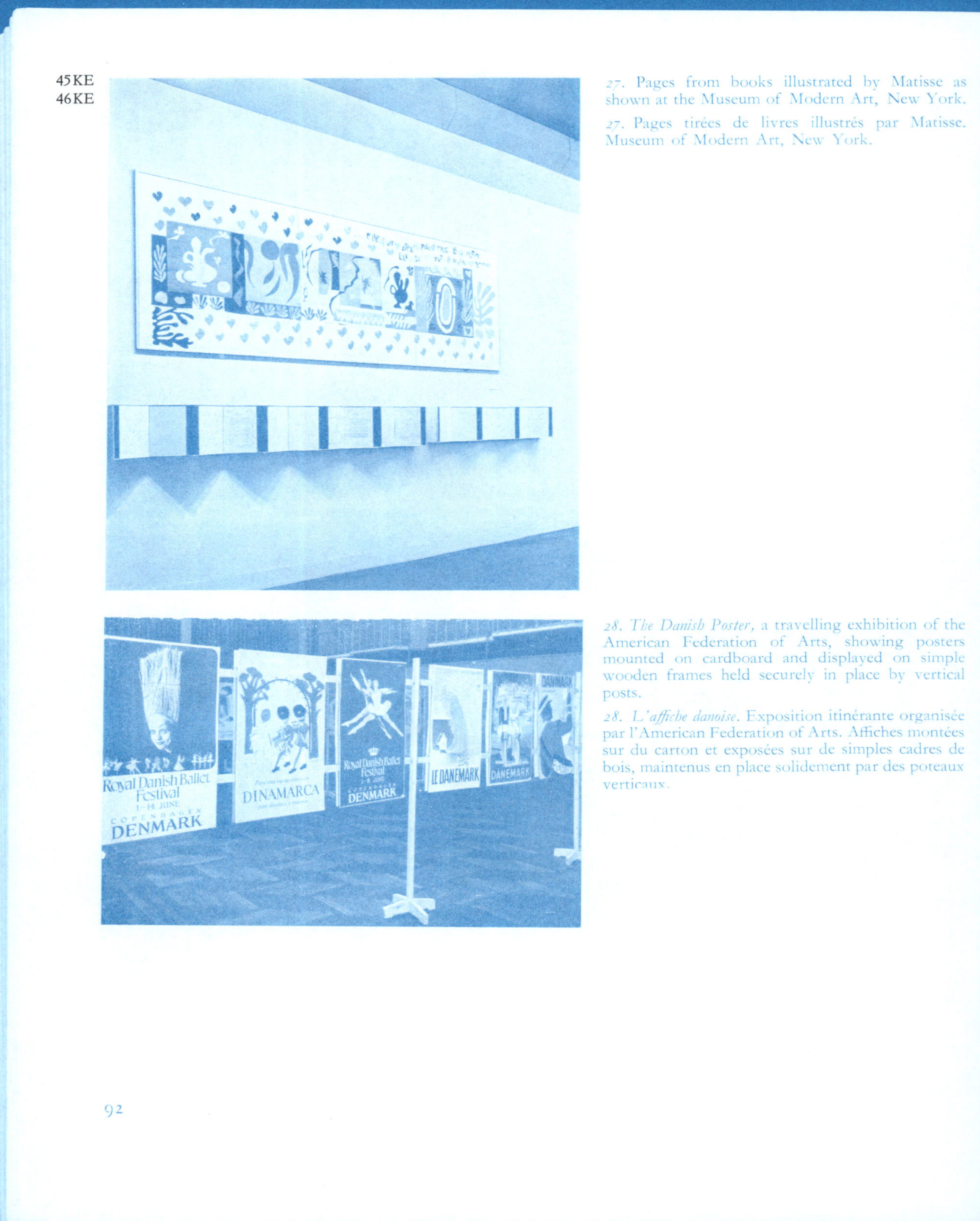

45KE
46KE

27. Pages from books illustrated by Matisse as shown at the Museum of Modern Art, New York.

27. Pages tirées de livres illustrés par Matisse. Museum of Modern Art, New York.

28. The Danish Poster, a travelling exhibition of the American Federation of Arts, showing posters mounted on cardboard and displayed on simple wooden frames held securely in place by vertical posts.

28. L'affiche danoise. Exposition itinérante organisée par l'American Federation of Arts. Affiches montées sur du carton et exposées sur de simples cadres de bois, maintenus en place solidement par des poteaux verticaux.

92

47 AM *Built in USA* was a chapter of the larger exhibition *America Builds* that was held at MoMA in 1944, which became a separate travelling exhibition accompanied by a catalogue, in 1945. Its curator, Elizabeth Mock, was highly critical of the *Modern Architecture: International Exhibition* of 1932, which she called an example of "badly assimilated European modernism", pointing out the highly biased selection of architects as well as the elimination of structural innovations, the social democratic programme, urban planning, and regionalism. In 947, Philip Johnson, curator of the *Modern Architecture: International Exhibition,* reclaimed his position at MoMA, eliminating Mock's regionalist approach.

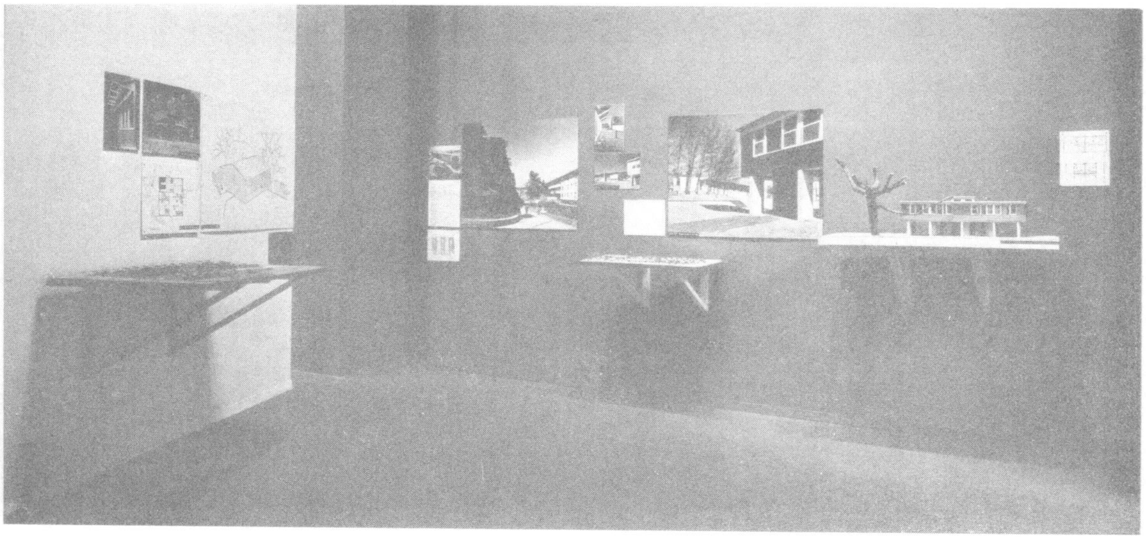

29. Built in U.S.A. An architectural exhibition held at the Museum of Modern Art, New York. Note triangular braces which support models at proper levels. These are nailed directly to the walls.

29. Construit aux États-Unis. Exposition d'architecture organisée par le Museum of Modern Art, New York. Remarquer les consoles triangulaires qui soutiennent les modèles et les mettent au niveau voulu. Celles-ci sont directement clouées au mur.

47 AM

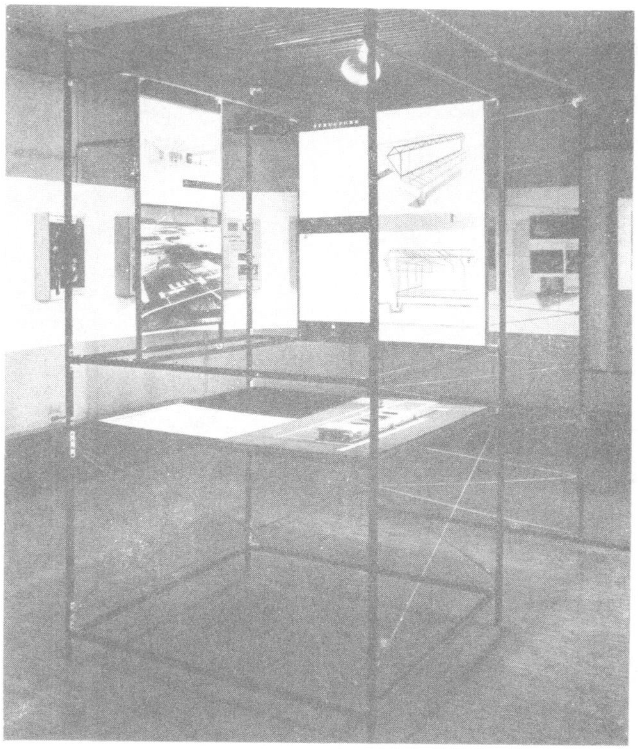

29a. Prefabricated units of square sectioned steel frames made by Unistrut Corporation, Wayne, Michigan, showing assembly which permits installation of architectural models.

29a. Éléments préfabriqués composés de cadres d'acier à section carrée, construits par l'Unistrut Corporation, Wayne, Michigan. On voit ici ces éléments montés de façon à permettre la présentation de maquettes d'architecture.

93

48AM The exhibition *Planning the Modern House,* about John Funk and the San Francisco based Bay Region School, organised in 1942, was a shift away from the International Style of architecture, which MoMA propagated 10 years earlier. The Bay Region Style combined the openness and clarity of the International Style with the regional traditions of using local materials and a sensitivity to the landscape. A number of successive architecture exhibitions at MoMA showcased regionalist tendencies in architecture, among them *Look at your Neighborhood,* held in 1944 on regionalist neighbourhood planning, and *America Builds* with a special section on regional planning.[14]

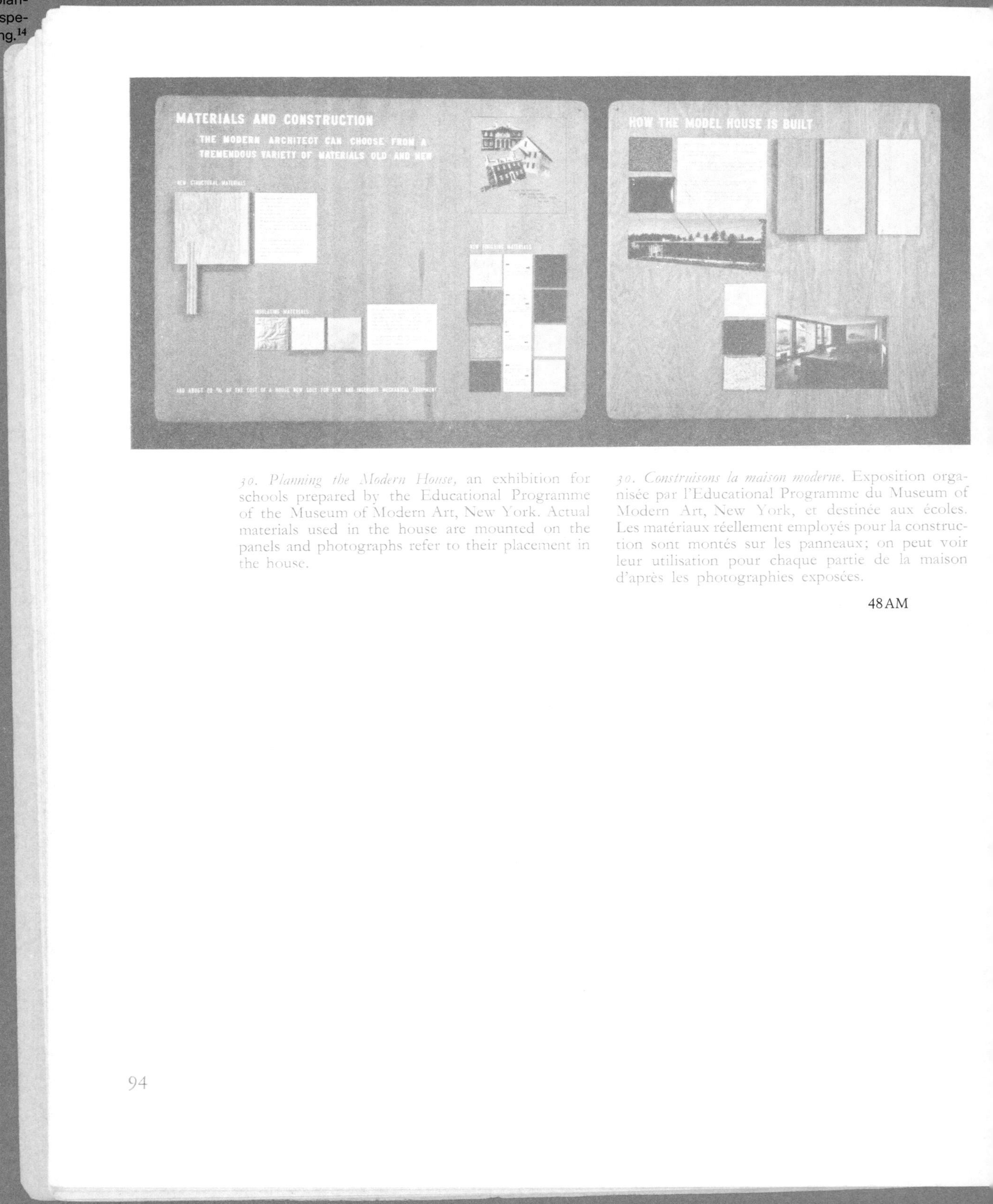

30. Planning the Modern House, an exhibition for schools prepared by the Educational Programme of the Museum of Modern Art, New York. Actual materials used in the house are mounted on the panels and photographs refer to their placement in the house.

30. Construisons la maison moderne. Exposition organisée par l'Educational Programme du Museum of Modern Art, New York, et destinée aux écoles. Les matériaux réellement employés pour la construction sont montés sur les panneaux; on peut voir leur utilisation pour chaque partie de la maison d'après les photographies exposées.

48AM

94

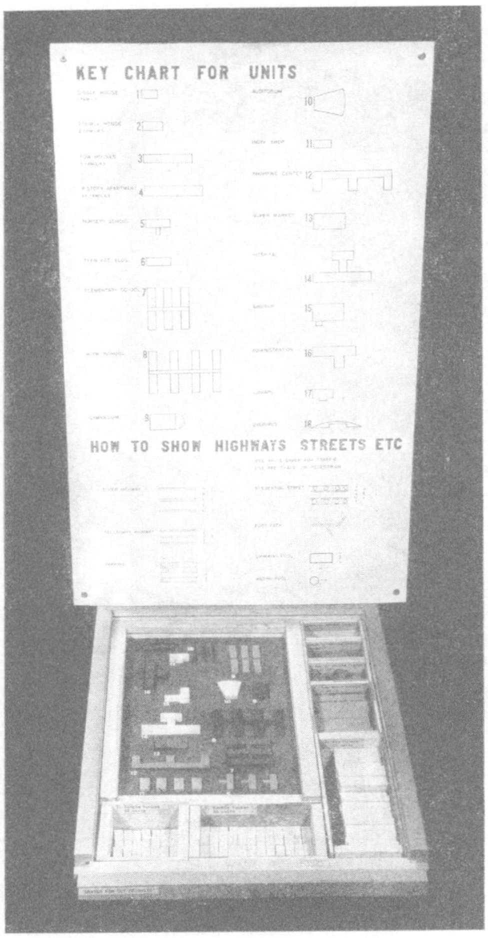

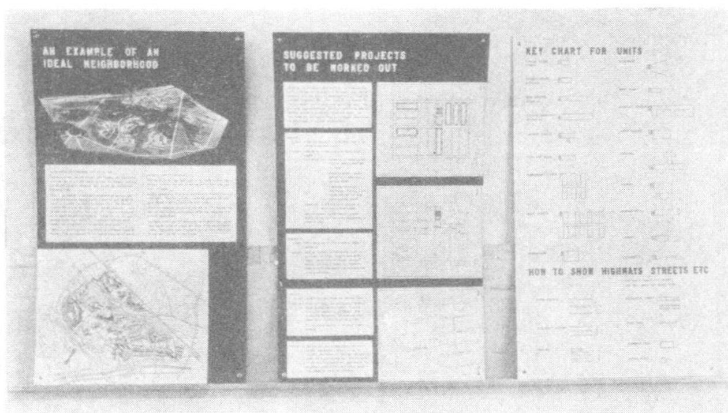

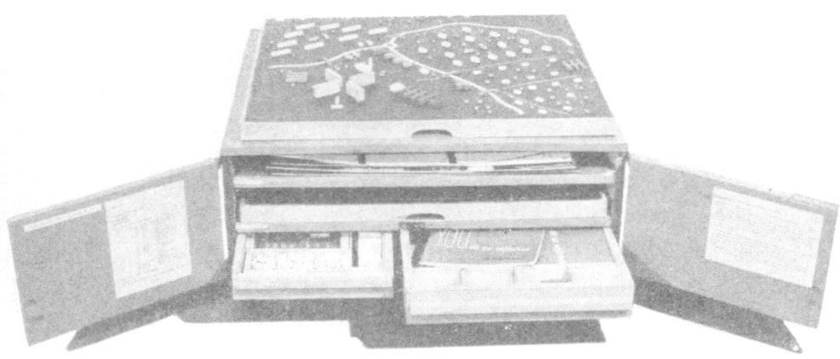

31, 31a, 31b. You and Your Neighbourhood, an exhibition for use in schools designed by the Educational Programme, the Museum of Modern Art, New York, containing charts, panels of photographs and labels as well as a model composed of units which are packed in a tray cut to hold each form. The packing case is fitted with shelves which hold the various parts of the exhibition neatly in place.

31, 31a, 31b. Votre voisinage et vous. Exposition organisée par l'Educational Programme du Museum of Modern Art, New York, et destinée à être utilisée dans les écoles. Elle se compose de plans, de panneaux, de photographies et d'étiquettes; elle comprend également une maquette composée de différentes pièces à assembler, emballées dans un casier divisé en autant de compartiments qu'il y a de séries de pièces. La caisse d'expédition est garnie d'étagères sur lesquelles se rangent, dans un ordre précis, les différents éléments qui composent l'exposition.

95

49 MK The display typology of the pavilion was especially evident at the large-scale exhibition *Von hier aus,* curated by Kasper König. The exhibition space—a 14.000 m², rectangular, trade fair hall in Cologne—was contextless. The Austrian architect Hermann Czech was commissioned to create a memorable genius loci, and responded to the challenge by constructing "houses within a house" (Czech). This resulted in an agglomeration of around 20 pavilions and so-called "memory spaces" (for Broodthaers, Hesse, Köpcke, and Palermo) with corresponding square and street settings, as well as different surfaces (from wallpaper to formworks for concrete) and light settings (from intimate lightbulbs to pallid hall lighting). As a result, each artist received an optimal, tailored environment for their work, but on the other hand the city-like display structure asserted an autonomous quality. For an exhibition, the basic question is always how much display, anti-display, and art a given space calls for, needs, or allows. This makes a manual obsolete, because the exhibition will ideally be site-specific and in this sense also unique.

50 AM *Planning your Town* was organised by the head of Yale University's Department of Architecture and Planning, Christopher Tunnard, to support his position that planning should be taught under the guise of design and should remain within the School of Architecture and Design, accordingly. The centrepiece was a model measuring 2,50 m by 4,00 m that depicted the appearance of a successful Virginia town in 1999, if proper planning procedures were instituted.[15]

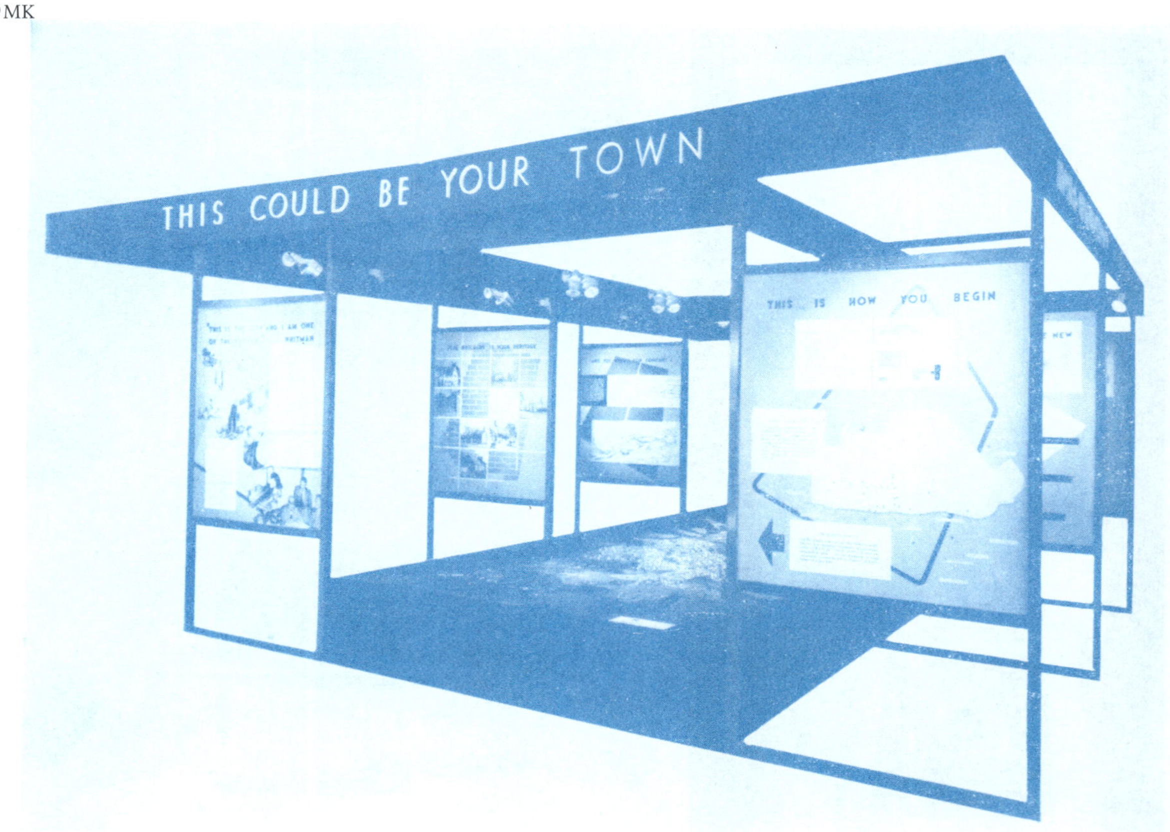

32. Planning Your Town, a travelling exhibition prepared by the Virginia Museum of Fine Arts, Richmond, Virginia, showing a model of a large area of land made in sections for shipping. Lighting fixtures, panels of photographs and labels fit into the structural scheme of installation which can be easily assembled and displayed in any open space.

32. Le plan de notre ville. Exposition circulante organisée par le Virginia Museum of Fine Arts, Richmond, Virginia. Maquette d'une vaste zone urbaine faite en plusieurs sections, en vue de son transport. On a compris dans la structure de l'installation le matériel d'éclairage, les panneaux portant des photographies et les étiquettes. Le tout est facilement mis en place et peut être présenté dans n'importe quel espace libre.

50 AM

96

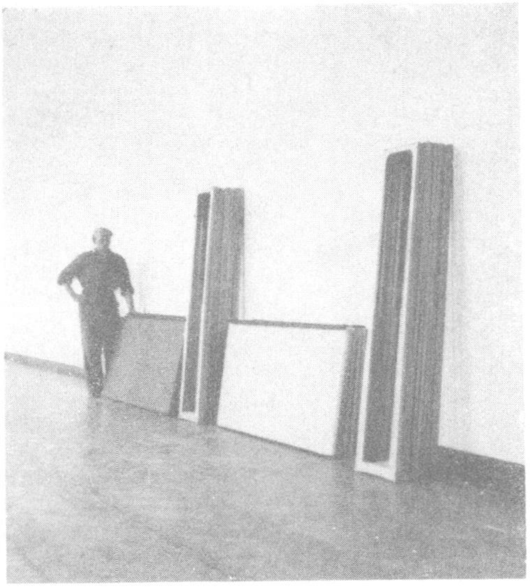

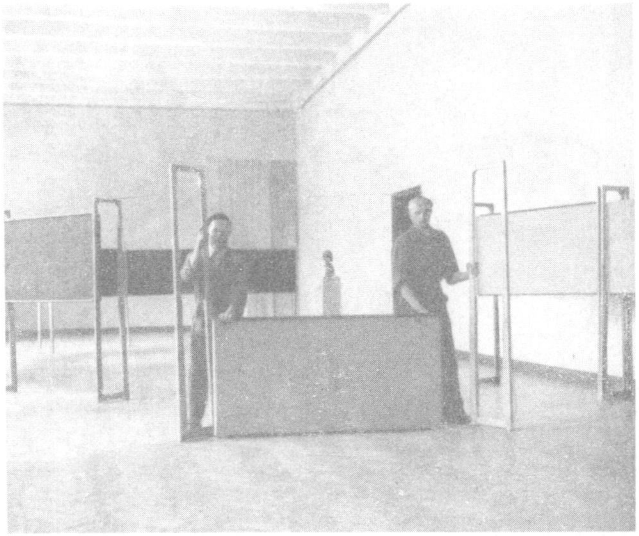

33, 33a, 33b. Series of pictures showing ease of assembling lightweight screens designed for travelling exhibitions in Poland. They are composed of cloth-covered plywood panels supported by two rectangular frames.

33, 33a, 33b. Séries de photographies montrant la facilité du montage d'écrans légers fabriqués pour les expositions itinérantes en Pologne. Ils se composent d'un panneau en contre-plaqué recouvert de toile et soutenu par deux cadres rectangulaires.

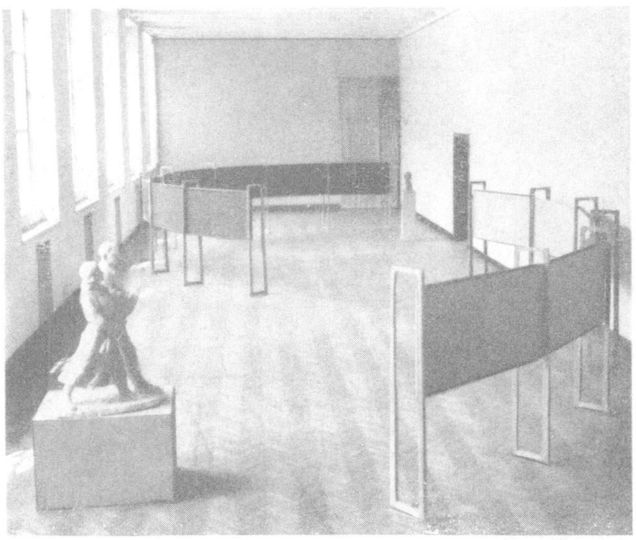

97

51KE *New Design in Exhibitions* was the name of an anthology published by Richard P. Lohse in the same year as the *Manual.* Despite their different objectives, the coincidence is quite remarkable. The same can't be claimed about the first performance of Samuel Beckett's *Waiting for Godot* in 1953 and the first demo recording of *That's When Your Heartaches Begin* by Elvis Presley. With their appearance in both publications, however, George Nelson's Struc-Tubes and the exhibition *For Modern Living* ↪098 opened up loopholes.

Lohse appeared as publisher, author, exhibition planner, and book designer. His introductory reflections are written in the style of a manifesto: "Every year, millions of individuals visit exhibitions. Millions of eyes absorb impressions of an agglomeration of vast energies – a cataract of themes and forms. Depending on the psyche of the visitors, greater or lesser fragments will be retained in the memory and later be re-embodied as active factors in everyday life after the manner of chain reactions. [...] The history of exhibitions is a history of politics and, no less, of the changes which have taken place in the foundations of our social structure."

The publication, an object of editorial spaciousness, modular construction, and artistic arrangement, is punctuated by elements of ingenious structural frameworks. The intensity of the layout is derived from its decentralised and dispersed image fields. It begins with a prologue of historical milestones, from *The Great Exhibition* in London in 1851 to an exhibition of the Dammerstock Siedlung in Karlsruhe in 1929. The subsequent 75 examples, demonstrated with texts, plans, and photographic sequences, fulfill programmatic requirements: they are characterised by "their culturally progressive approach [...] the high artistic quality of the exhibition style (and) the recognition that construction and form must be understood as a unit in the working process".[16]

51KE

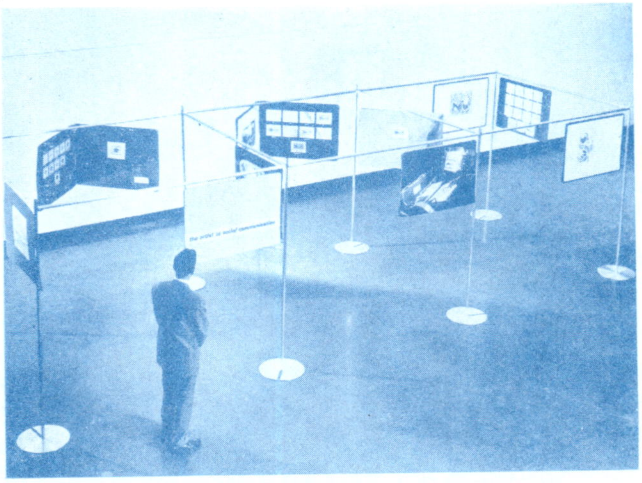

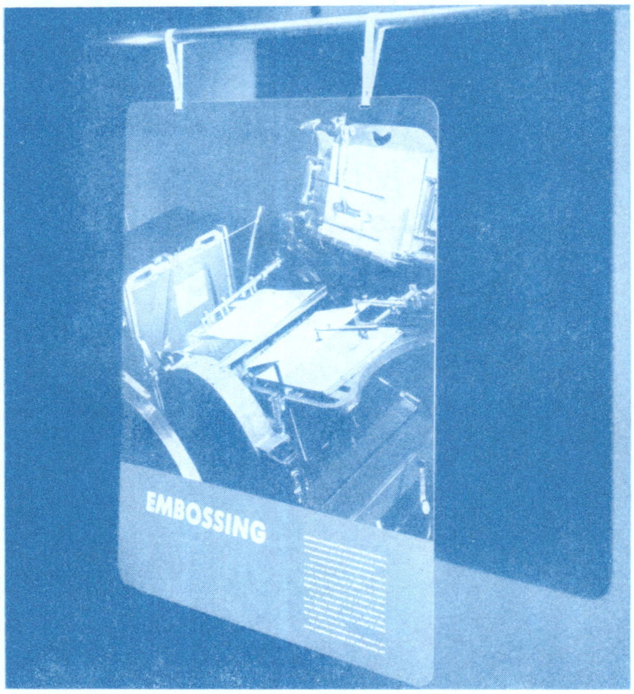

34, 34 a. "Struc-tube" designed by architect George Nelson. This versatile structural framework can be set up without tools and re-used indefinitely. It can be assembled and taken down quickly, is easily transportable and lightweight. Composed of aluminium bases, vertical tube supports that slide on to the base post and horizontal tubes which lock into the vertical members by means of plugs and keyholes (see *diagram G, page 30*). The placards are also aluminium and can be hung on tubes by plastic straps fitted with snap fasteners. Slots in the bases make it possible to stack them in the packing case.

34, 34a. Struc-tube réalisé d'après le projet de l'architecte George Nelson. Cette armature à combinaisons multiples peut être montée sans outils et indéfiniment réutilisée. Elle s'assemble et se démonte très rapidement; elle est facilement transportable et très légère. Elle est composée de pieds d'aluminium, de supports verticaux qui s'insèrent dans ces pieds, et de tubes horizontaux qu'on fixe par des clavettes entrant dans des trous (voir le croquis G). Les panneaux sont également en aluminium et se suspendent aux tubes par des attaches en matière plastique munies de boutons-pression. Des fentes ménagées dans les pieds d'aluminium permettent de les emboîter pour les mettre en caisse.

98

52AM Alvin Lustig (1915–1955) was an American book designer, graphic designer and typeface designer. Lustig studied design at Los Angeles City College, Art Center College of Design, and independently with architect Frank Lloyd Wright at his Taliesin studio. He began his career in 1937 designing book jackets in Los Angeles. In 1944 he became director of Visual Research for *Look Magazine*. In addition to his many contributions to graphic design, Lustig was an accomplished interior and architectural designer. In 1949, he designed what has become known as the "Lustig Chair" for Paramount Furniture in Beverly Hills, California. Josef Albers invited him to teach at Black Mountain College in 1945, and at Yale in 1951.

52AM

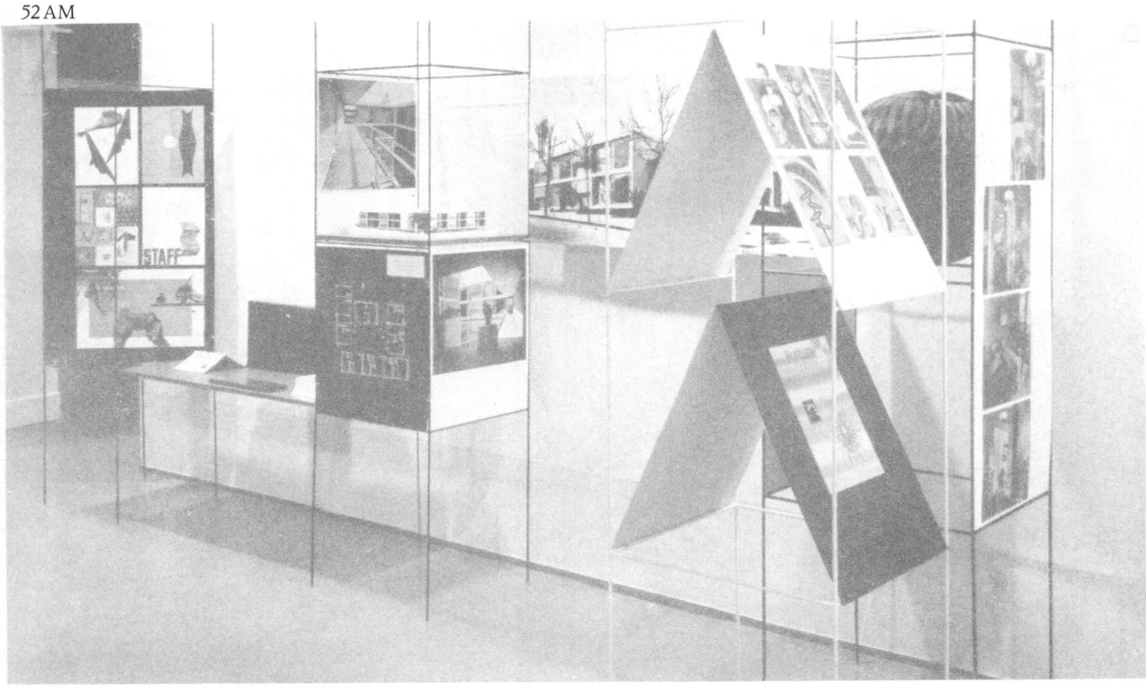

35. A system of cages which can be stacked for shipping and used either as three-dimensional frames to be hung from the ceiling or cubical stands on the floor. Made of 5/16-inch cold-rolled steel, welded together, painted. Panels are made of masonite (a pressed wood product), lacquered in bright colours. Panels are held in place with small aluminium airplane clips which bend around the steel frames and are held with a small screw through holes in the panels. Designed by Alvin Lustig, New York.

35. Système de cages qui peuvent s'emboiter les unes dans les autres pour le transport. Elles peuvent servir indifféremment de cadres à trois dimensions que l'on suspend au plafond, ou de supports en forme de tubes reposant sur le sol. Elles sont composées de tubes d'acier de 8 mm soudés et peints. Les panneaux sont faits de « masonite » (sorte de bois aggloméré), laqué de couleurs vives. Ils sont fixés par de petites pinces, du modèle de celles employées dans l'aviation, en aluminium, qui s'adaptent à la courbure du cadre et sont maintenus par une petite vis enfoncée dans des trous percés dans les panneaux. Modèle d'Alvin Lustig, New York.

99

53 AM The 1950 *Good Design* exhibition, a project sponsored jointly by the Museum of Modern Art, New York and the Chicago based interior design wholesale market Merchandise Mart, was the first of a series of annual home furnishing shows to be exhibited at the Mart throughout the year and at the Museum each November. These exhibitions of new products with the best designs opened in Chicago during the January market. At the time of the June market, additions were made, chosen from items produced after January. The exhibitions were designed by prominent architects and designers, e.g. Ray and Charles Eames (1950), Finn Juhl (1951), Paul Rudolph (1952), Alexander Girard (1953), and Franco Albini (1954).

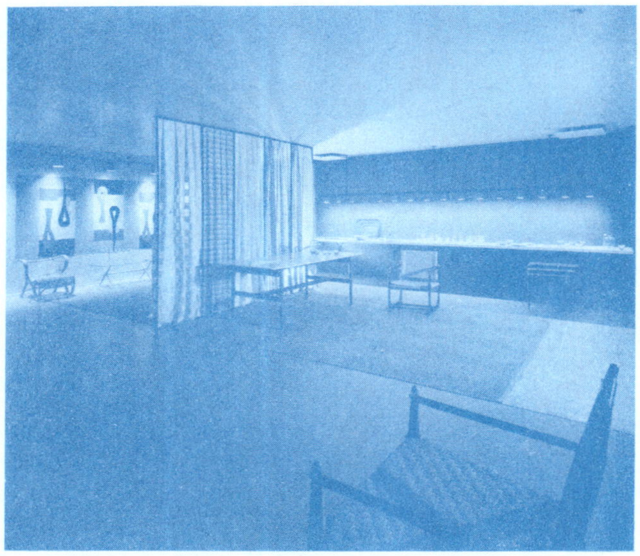

36. Good Design Exhibition, 1952, The Merchandise Mart, Chicago. This is the same unit system as that shown in illustration *29a* made by the Unistrut Corporation. The Unistrut channels come in various forms—single, double, triple, back to back, T, Greek key, swastika and other shapes—so that the most versatile arrangements are possible. Here fabrics are shown hung from channels attached to the ceiling, while shelves and lighting fixtures are attached to others against the walls.

36. Art industriel. Exposition 1952 organisée par The Merchandise Mart., Chicago. Même système d'éléments démontables que l'on peut voir photo *29a,* fait par la Unistrut Corporation. Les tubes Unistrut se présentent sous des formes très diverses : ils sont simples, doubles, triples, accolés; ils dessinent des croix grecques, des swastikas, etc. ; si bien qu'ils permettent des arrangements extrêmement variés. On voit ici des étoffes pendues à des tubes fixés au plafond alors que d'autres éléments, contre le mur, supportent des étagères et un dispositif d'éclairage.

53 AM

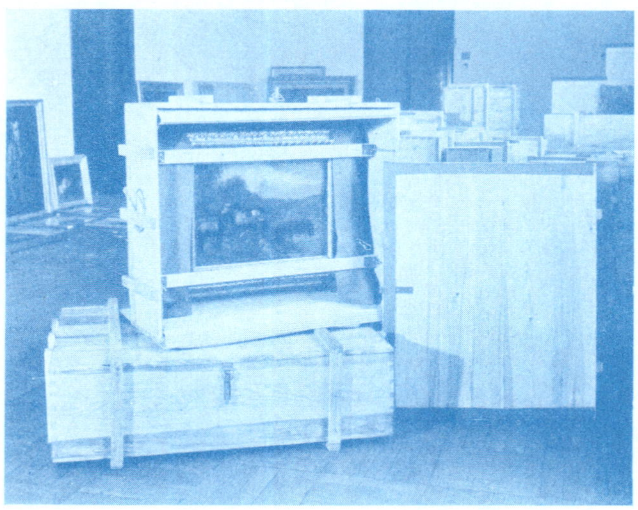

37. Box designed for travelling exhibition of paintings in Poland. Pictures are arranged horizontally and held in place by battens separated from paintings by layer of felt. Boxes are made of specially treated, damp-proof deal.

37. Caisse construite pour des expositions itinérantes de peintures en Pologne. Les tableaux sont disposés horizontalement et fixés par des barres; une couche de feutre est placée entre la barre et le tableau. Les caisses sont faites de bois de pin spécialement traité pour résister à l'humidité.

100

54KE An equilibrial construct. Balance is maintained by the artistry of the static measures and their photographic rendering. The motif of leaning seems familiar from Laurel & Hardy. Letters materialise from the braces and wedged partitions: an H adorned with nails, an A like that of Dürer's monogram. The shrouded body with a Virgin Mary-like form presents a further enigma, although the inscription on the fabric offers a clue: 50 stands for the middle of the century.[17]

55KE Jump cut. The spotlight is focused on the photographer. The *Manual's* credits attribute 25 photographs to Soichi Sunami. Searching his name initially yields iconic images from the pioneer era of modern dance. They were predominantly produced during his long-term collaboration with Martha Graham, a shining light in the field of movement.

Latency of movement could be the key phrase to discovering the continuum of Sunami's work. The visual arrangement of *Case containing sculpture* transports the viewer to an imaginary juxtaposition of silver prints in his darkroom. A comparative inspection casts light on the photograph of a mobile by Alexander Calder, with whom Soichi studied art (*Man-Eater with Pennants,* c. 1950). Both an epoch and a world war separate Sunami's photographs from the production rooms of the MoMA's Department of Circulating Exhibitions and the stage stills of Graham's ballet *Heretic* (1929). *Tableaux vivants* describes the expressionistic, somber prints and the choreographic style of the 12 dancers who repetitively revolt against restraints to the point of exhaustion to create these portrayals. The almost sculptural representation of Martha Graham's solo piece *Ekstasis* (1933) shows the dancer in a balancing act; already off balance, her limbs sweep in a turn, about to leave the frame at any moment.

56KE In his blog *The Pop Culture Philosopher,* Christopher Sunami, grandson of Soichi Sunami, describes the beginnings of the MoMA from the perspective of its co-founder Abby Rockefeller: "So when she conceived of the idea of building a museum devoted to modern art in New York City, he (husband John D. Rockefeller, jr.) strenuously resisted bankrolling it. When Soichi, a respected artist, joined the project, it gained some hard won credibility and legitimacy, and helped get the ball rolling for funding outside the family. Rockefeller returned the favour by offering Soichi a job on the museum's staff as the official documentary photographer, a position he went on to hold for nearly forty years."

Soichi Sunami was born in 1885 in Okayama, Japan, and emigrated to the US in 1905. In 1957 he became an American citizen. He died in 1971 in New York City. He produced over 20.000 large-format negatives for MoMA.

54KE
55KE
56KE

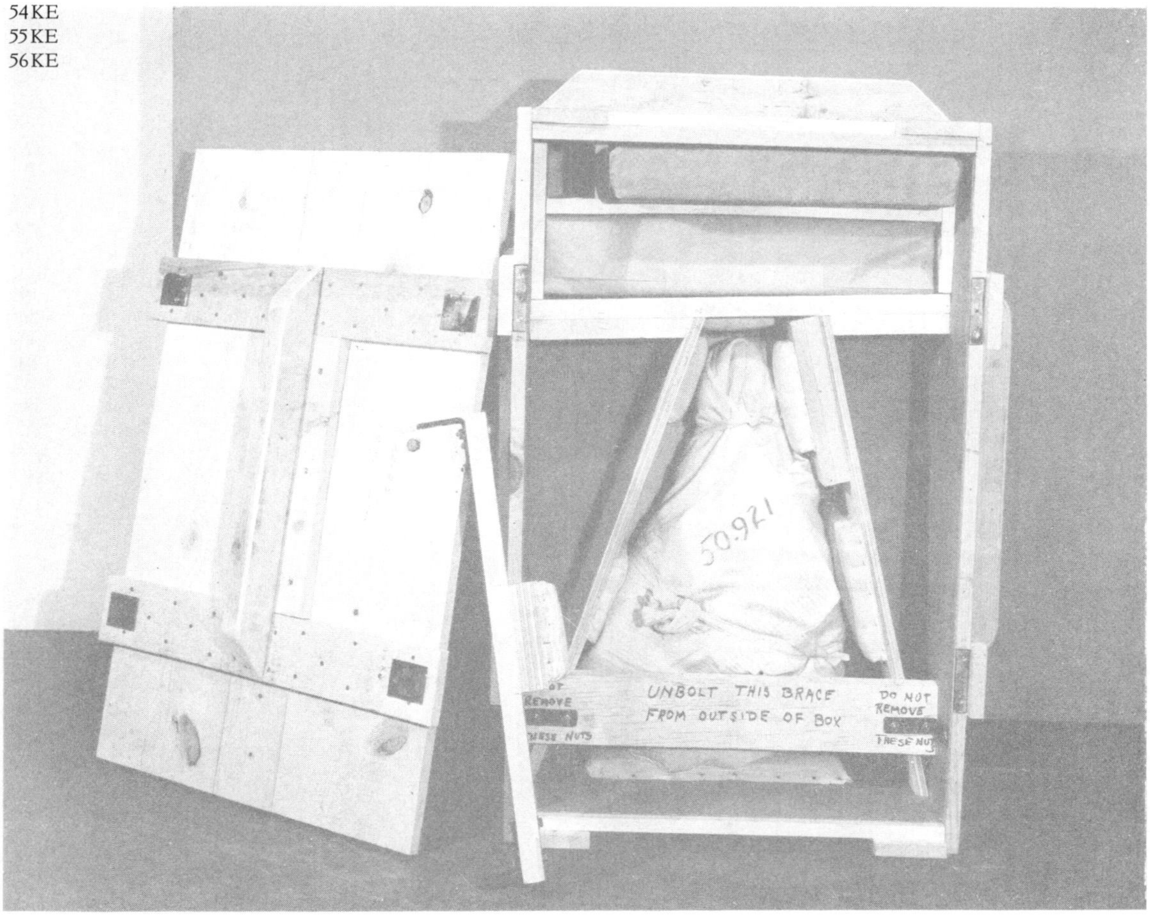

38. Case containing sculpture. Note "fin" on cover and at side to keep sculpture in upright position. Photograph also shows metal plates to receive bolts when closed for shipping. Box designed by the Museum of Modern Art, New York.

38. Caisse contenant une sculpture. Remarquer la « quille » placée sur le couvercle et sur la paroi latérale, afin que la caisse soit maintenue en position verticale. Les plaques métalliques destinées à recevoir les boulons sont également visibles sur la photographie. (Caisse conçue par le Museum of Modern Art, New York.)

101

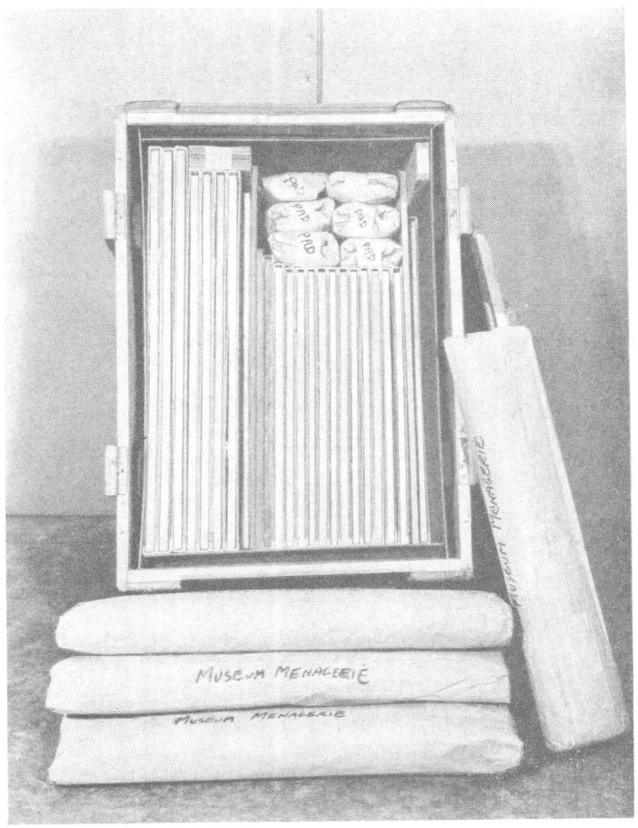

39. Case for framed watercolours uniformly matted, framed and slip-cased. Frames, cases and boxes can often be re-used for other exhibitions similarly prepared for tour. Pictures are fitted into case by filling in sections with excelsior wrapped pads. Large excelsior pads, shown at the bottom, are placed on top of open-ended inner cases to protect them from shifting during transit. Box designed by the Museum of Modern Art, New York.

39. Caisse destinée au transport d'aquarelles, toutes montées en passe-partout, encadrées et mises dans des étuis individuels. Les cadres, les enveloppes intérieures et les boites peuvent souvent être réutilisés pour d'autres expéditions circulantes. On maintient ces tableaux dans la caisse en remplissant les intervalles avec des tampons d'excelsior. Les grands boudins d'excelsior que l'on voit à la partie inférieure de la photographie sont placés à l'extrémité découverte des enveloppes intérieures pour les empêcher de bouger pendant le transport. (Caisse conçue par le Museum of Modern Art, New York.)

57KE Francis Bacon? The doorway ramp serves as a presentation platform for a collection of rectangles. In the daylight of the transitional zone, the pieces wait to be assigned their positions. The lines of the slatted frames converge in the hand of the sole protagonist, the painting he holds rests on a compartment of the custom-made transport box. The scene demonstrates the structure of the container with the clarity of an exploded-view drawing. The cases leaning in the shadows indicate the serial character of the packaging process. It is in no way incidental that the image is activated by eye contact with four eyes. A silent employee as an extra in a model situation of instructive nature? The protagonist of a cinematic choreography, an arm's length from the pole of disquiet – the swirling brush-strokes of an unspecified piece of cargo?

40. This photograph illustrates the method of packing shown in the diagram Q, page 42. Box designed by the Museum of Modern Art, New York.

40. Cette photographie montre la méthode d'emballage décrite sur le croquis Q. (Caisse conçue par le Museum of Modern Art, New York.)

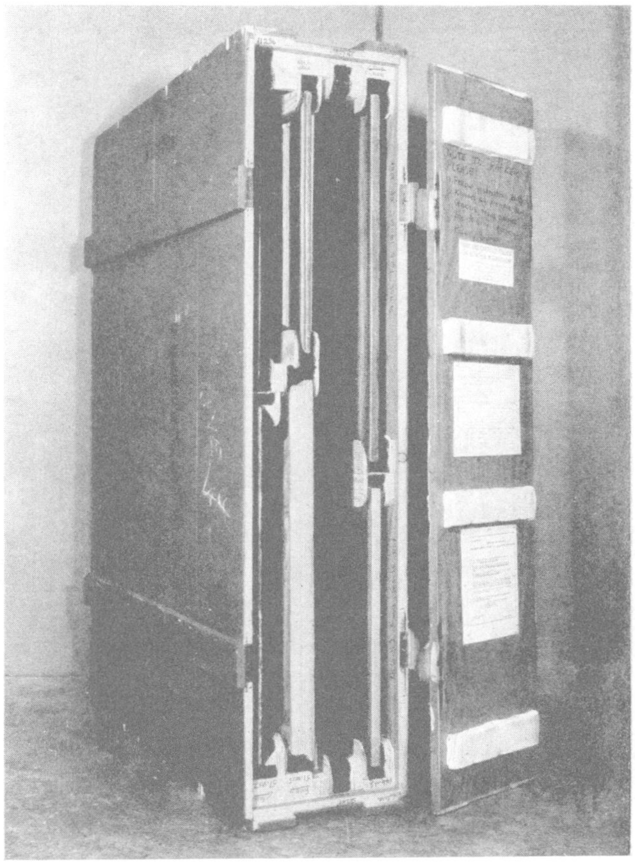

41. Packing box designed by the Addison Gallery of American Art, Andover, Massachusetts, for paintings. No removable packing materials are included. Paintings fit into individually constructed trays padded with felt to prevent pictures from rubbing against wood frames.

41. Caisse conçue et employée par l'Addison Gallery of American Art, Andover, Massachusetts, pour le transport des peintures. Aucun matériel d'emballage amovible n'est utilisé. Des tiroirs individuels, garnis de feutre afin d'empêcher tout frottement contre les cadres de bois, reçoivent les peintures.

57KE

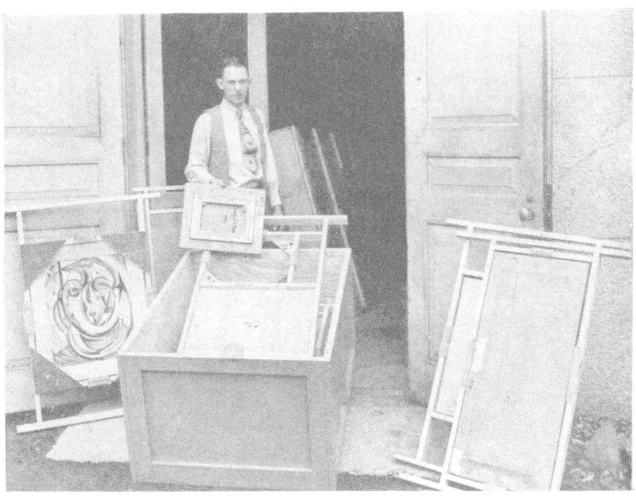

103

58KE If the congruence of the depicted objects and the annotated descriptions left nothing to be desired, there wouldn't be the instructive underside of the lid. Besides the particularly inaccessible sculptures it contained a friendly request: "NOTE TO PACKER PLEASE": The rest can be read with the aid of a magnifying glass:

1. Follow instructions carefully
2. Remove all previous shipping stickers from outside of box to avoid confusing Railway Express.

The exterior world of these excelsior-packed shipments was exposed to the circumstances of the North American transport system. American Railway Express, Inc., a consolidation of the four main parcel express companies of the 19th century, became a national monopoly during World War I. At the end of the 1920s it mutated into the Railway Express Agency, an organisation of 86 rail companies, and focused on refrigerated transport, and with its Air Express Division had an exclusive agreement for air freight. The company didn't make it into the era of tractor trailers and container logistics—it terminated operations in 1975 (see also →075).[18]

59KE A role reversal. The sculptures function as placeholders, while the excelsior thematically sets the image diagonals in motion. Excelsior is a balm for noses and ears. It appears as the motto on the coat of arms of New York, sail- and steamboats bear it as a name, the Süddeutsche Zeitung uses *Excelsior* as its body type (with a slight modification). A trail of sawdust leads us back to the year 1842: A US patent document describes a machine for manufacturing wood shavings as a substitute for curled hair in stuffing beds. The first printed mention of the neologism excelsior mattress wasn't long in coming—it became a trademark.[19]

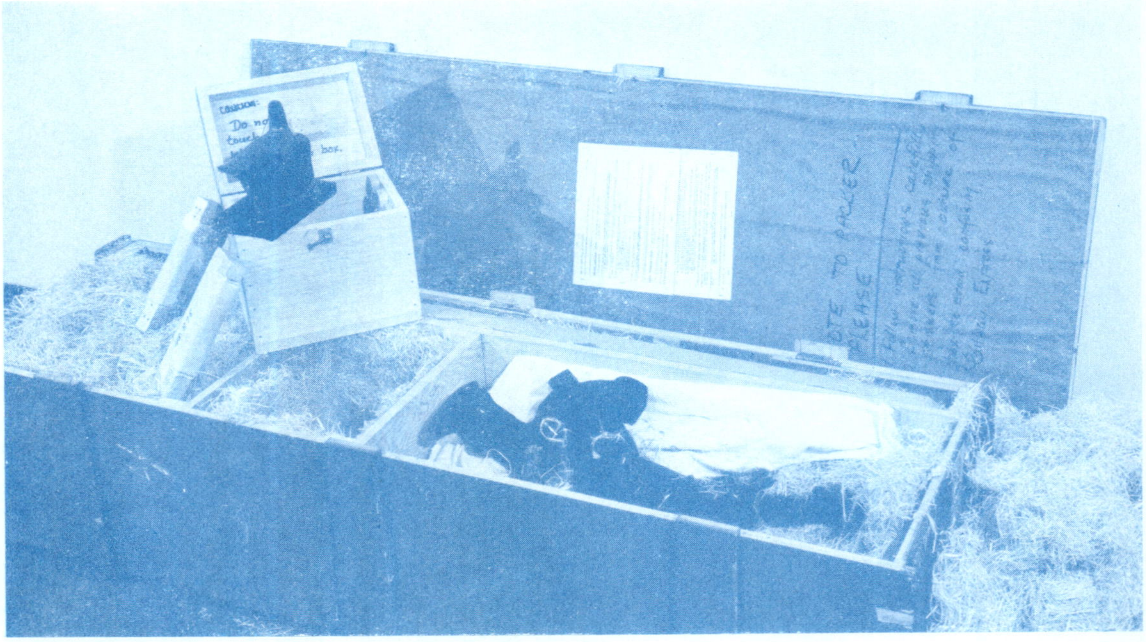

42. The small piece of sculpture shown at the left is to be placed in the inner wooden box, held in place by two padded braces, then placed in its own excelsior-filled compartment. The sculpture at the right is shown in its bed of excelsior. When packed for shipping it would be wrapped in the cloth case prior to being placed in the excelsior. Box designed by the Museum of Modern Art, New York.

42. La petite sculpture que l'on voit à gauche va être mise dans la boite intérieure où deux barres capitonnées la maintiendront en place; le tout sera placé dans le compartiment correspondant, préalablement garni d'excelsior. On voit à droite une autre sculpture sur son matelas d'excelsior. Pour l'emballer, on l'enveloppe dans son sac d'étoffe avant de la placer dans l'excelsior. (Caisse conçue par le Museum of Modern Art, New York.)

58KE
59KE

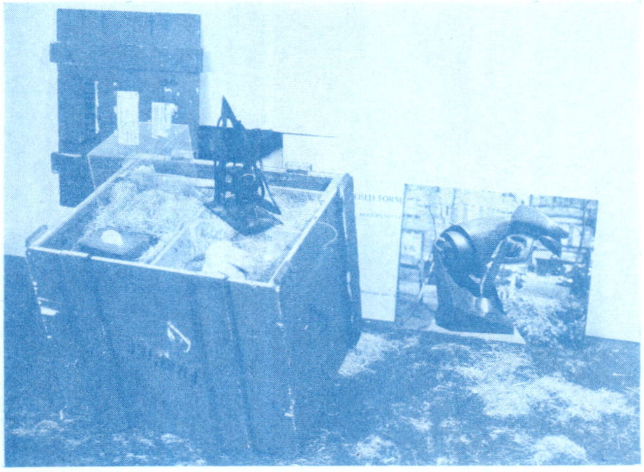

43. Photograph shows sculpture exhibition which contains a plastic vitrine to protect fragile pieces from damage during showings.

43. Photographie montrant une exposition de sculpture où figure une vitrine en matière plastique destinée à protéger les pièces fragiles contre les détériorations possibles au cours de leur présentation.

104

60KE Claustrophilia at base camp. A self-explanatory cabinet of interiors of the first, second, and third order, and so on. A variation on the Russian doll, a completed puzzle of figure–ground relationships–if it weren't for the ambiguous image-like neither-nor: excelsior. The camera is fixed, the photographic lamps are set, the frame motif continues in this sparsely lit locality. A block-like base elevates the box, the lids are arranged accordingly, and even the vestiges of excelsior have a part to play in the performance.

61MK I particularly like this illustration as it evokes an image that often confronts me when I'm devising an exhibition: a nested assemblage reminiscent of matryoshka dolls. I love devising exhibitions in such a way that the first glance confuses and the second reveals further conceptual layers. Like in the exhibition *Schöner Wohnen* (2004), where for example two identical wall clocks were shown, which–if they were even recognised as artworks–weren't *Untitled (Perfect Lovers)* by Félix González-Torres (which did appear with a curtain made of plastic beads and a blueish mirror), but *Two Clocks* by Dieter Kiessling, which references Félix González-Torres's work and in which both clocks also run synchronously, yet which no longer appear synchronised due to their transposed hands. For the catalogue, Johannes Schwartz took 19 photographs of the exhibition. These photographs were then presented as artworks in 2016 in the spin-off exhibition *Schöner Wöhnen* (sic) as part of an installation by Heimo Zobernig at the international furniture fair Interieur in Kortrijk.

60KE

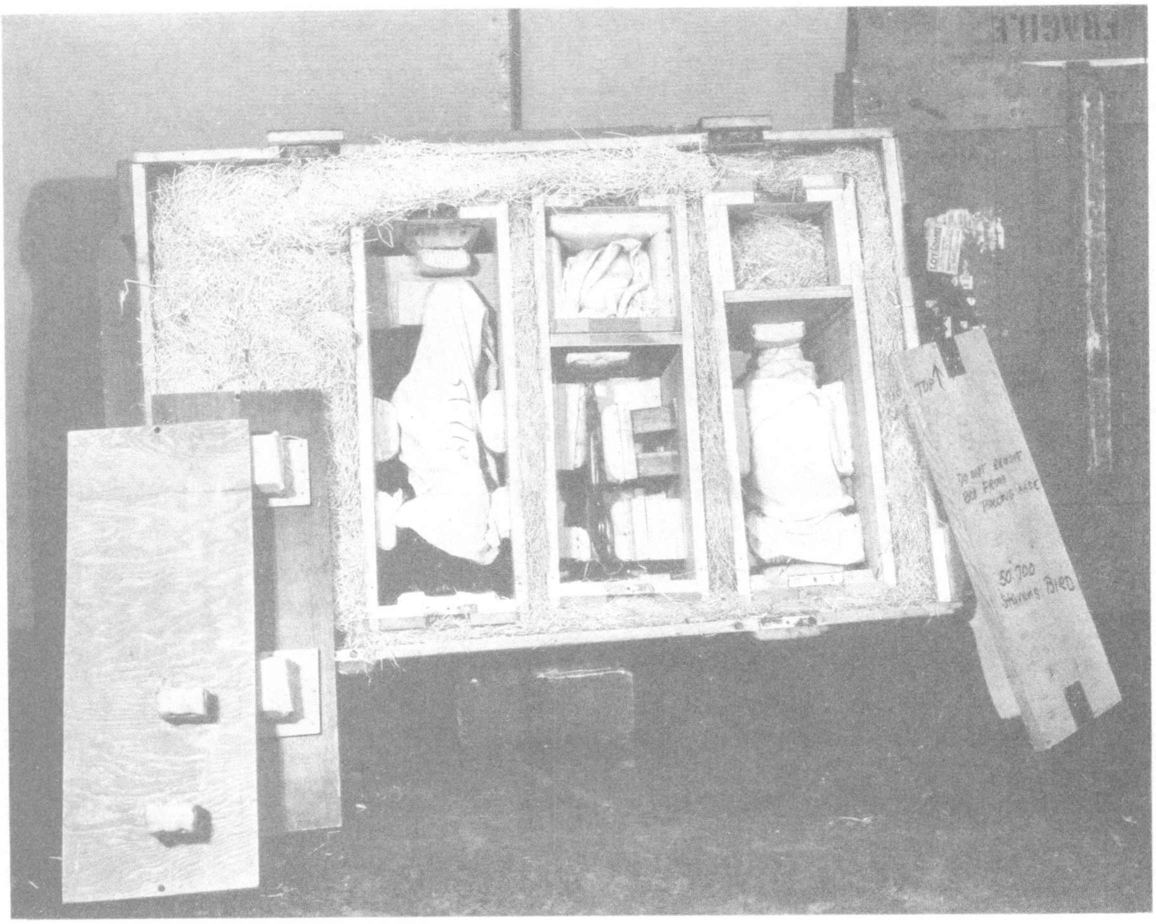

44. This photograph shows a box containing several inner boxes of wood, lined with sponge-rubber pads and braces fitted to hold sculpture in place. The inner boxes are then "floated" in tightly packed-in excelsior. Exhibitors are requested not to remove the inner cases from the packing box. Box designed by the Museum of Modern Art, New York.

44. Contre-caisse contenant plusieurs caissettes intérieures en bois, tapissées de coussinets en caoutchouc mousse et munies de supports qui maintiennent les sculptures en place. Ces caissettes intérieures sont ensuite « suspendues » dans une couche compacte d'excelsior. Les destinataires sont priés de ne pas les retirer de la contre-caisse. (Caisse conçue par le Museum of Modern Art, New York.)

61MK

105

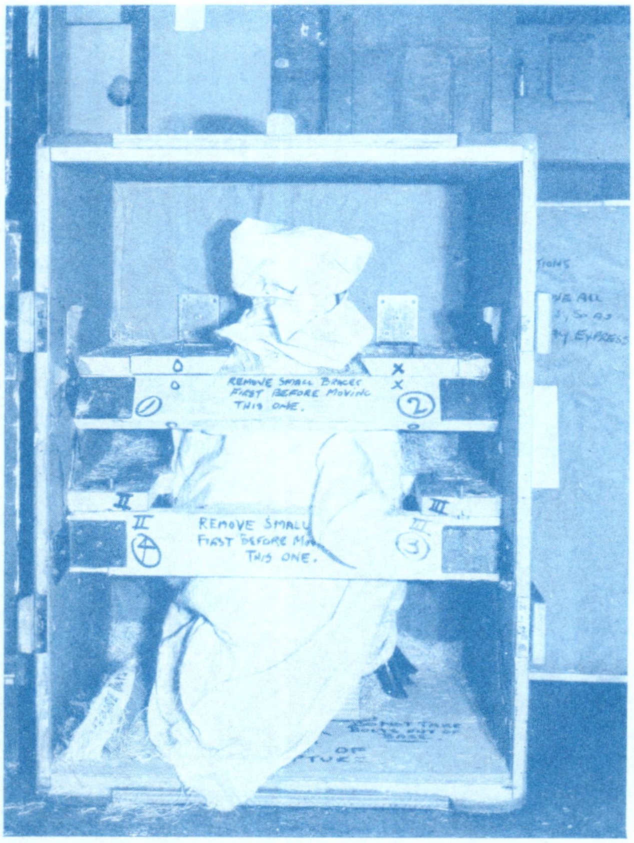

45. Note how wooden braces fit around sculpture. These are attached to the walls of the packing case by screws through right-angle metal plates. Directions to packers are written directly on braces with indelible ink. Box designed by the Museum of Modern Art, New York.

45. Remarquer la façon dont les supports de bois épousent la forme de la sculpture. Ils sont vissés à la paroi de la caisse à travers des plaques de métal. Des instructions à l'usage des emballeurs sont écrites, sur les supports eux-mêmes, à l'encre indélébile. (Caisse conçue par le Museum of Modern Art, New York.)

62 KE The precision of the box around the black figure is repeated in the tight framing of the image. The zigzag fold of the layers seems to conform to a typographical left-top-to-right-bottom syntax. The conspicuous instructions reach an end at the "Fragile Sculpture", which evokes the image of a woman sawn in half. Artist and title, noted on the lid, invite further research. Thus, not much separates the *Standing Woman* by Wilhelm Lehmbruck and Duchamp's *Nude Descending a Staircase (No. 2)*. Both belonged to the exhibits of the Armory Show in 1913, the *First International Exhibition of Modern Art* in New York. Signatures engraved on the pedestal bear witness to the initial stations of the *Standing Woman:* W. Lehmbruck, Paris, 1910 and Bronzegiesserei Düsseldorf.[20]

63 MK In contrast to the illustration on page ↩113, this somewhat sinister illustration evokes associations with the *Art of the Container,* and reminds me of the following works: a) Robert Morris, *Untitled (box for standing)* (1961), a coffin-like, standing sculpture based on the artist's physical dimensions; b) Richard Artschwager, *Crate Sculptures* (1995), whose enclosed, irregular cubature only hints at its content; c) Heimo Zobernig, *Untitled (HZ2006–064)* (2006), in which a male mannequin on a rolling platform is enclosed by a cage-like structure.

45a. Container for very large bronze figure. Felt pads line all braces wherever they come in contact with the sculpture and are placed at top and at base. Note marking on box to guide shippers and packers. The bolts encircled in ink at the sides are those which release the braces holding the figure in place. Box designed by the Museum of Modern Art, New York.

45a. Grande caisse pour le transport d'une statue de bronze de grandes dimensions. Des tampons amortisseurs en feutre sont placés à tous les points de contact entre le bronze et les supports ainsi qu'aux deux extrémités. Noter les indications à l'usage des commissionnaires et des emballeurs. Les boulons à dévisser pour détacher les supports qui maintiennent la statue sont entourés d'un cercle à l'encre. (Caisse conçue par le Museum of Modern Art, New York.)

62 KE
63 MK

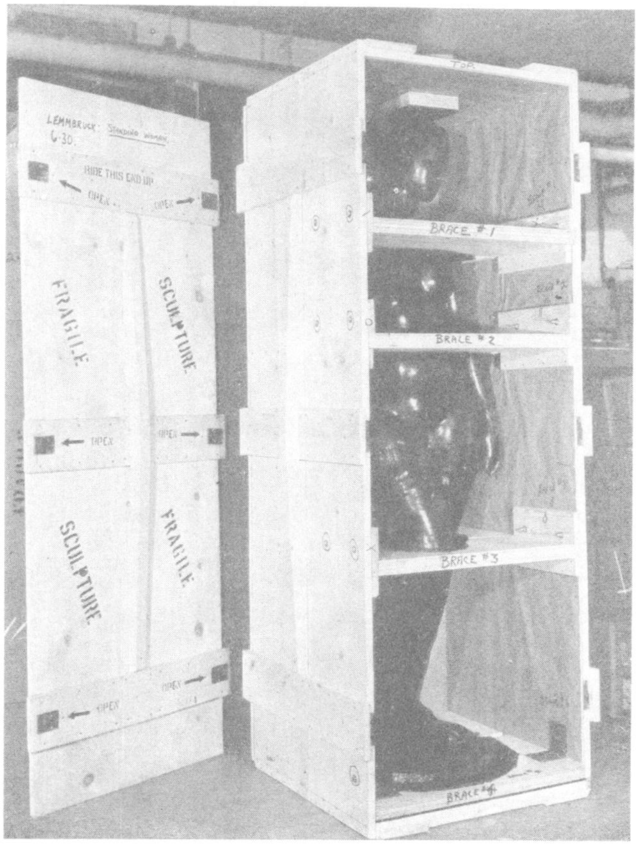

107

64AM In 1946, the Museum of Modern Art, New York, in collaboration with the Art Institute of Chicago and the San Francisco Museum of Art organised a large exhibition of works by Henry Moore. The *Reclining Figure* shown in the series of photographs was a predecessor of the large marble sculpture Moore was commissioned in 1955 to create for the piazza in front of UNESCO's new headquarters in Paris.

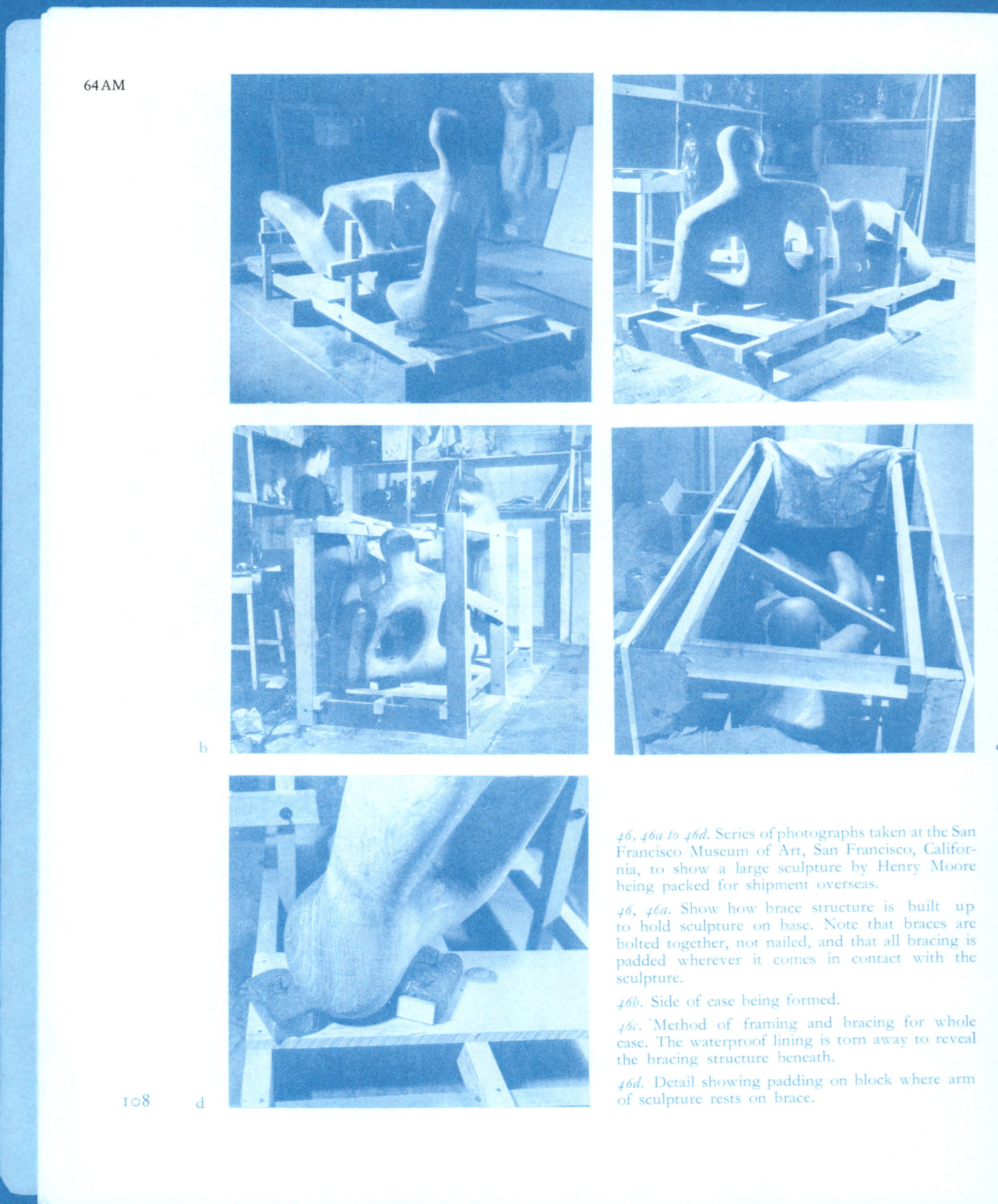

64AM

a

b

c

d

46, 46a to 46d. Series of photographs taken at the San Francisco Museum of Art, San Francisco, California, to show a large sculpture by Henry Moore being packed for shipment overseas.

46, 46a. Show how brace structure is built up to hold sculpture on base. Note that braces are bolted together, not nailed, and that all bracing is padded wherever it comes in contact with the sculpture.

46b. Side of case being formed.

46c. 'Method of framing and bracing for whole case. The waterproof lining is torn away to reveal the bracing structure beneath.

46d. Detail showing padding on block where arm of sculpture rests on brace.

108

47. Package of panels of enlarged photographs wrapped together and sealed with gummed tape. Blocks shown at intervals around package are cloth-covered sponge-rubber pads which cushion the package in transit. Box designed by the Museum of Modern Art, New York.

47. Ce paquet contient plusieurs panneaux portant des agrandissements photographiques, enveloppés ensemble. Il est fermé par des bandes gommées. Les blocs que l'on voit disposés à intervalles réguliers sur le pourtour sont des tampons de caoutchouc mousse recouvert d'étoffe, destinés à amortir les chocs durant le parcours. (Caisse conçue par le Museum of Modern Art, New York.)

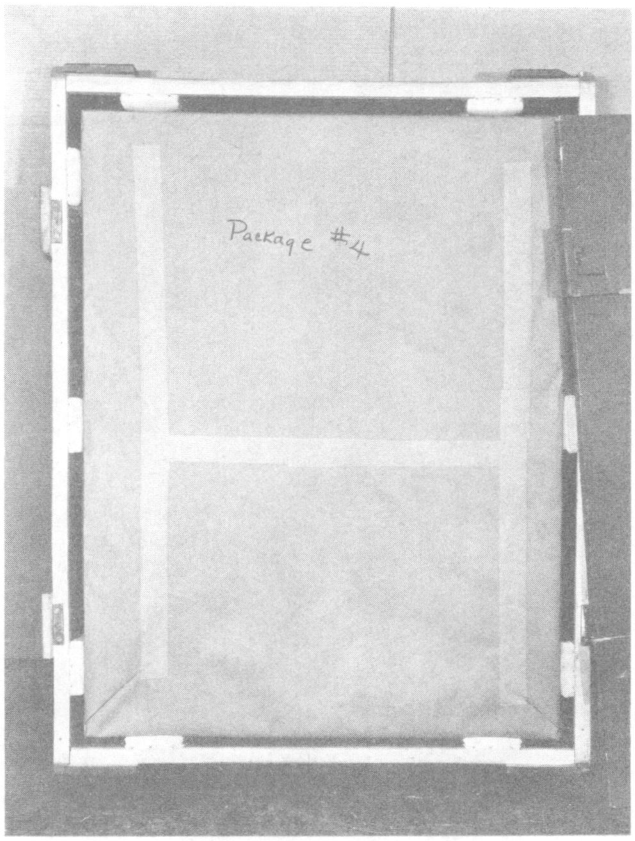

46, 46a à *46d.* Série de photographies prises au San Francisco Museum of Art, San Francisco, Californie. Elles montrent les opérations d'emballage, pour son envoi outre-mer, d'une grande sculpture d'Henry Moore :

46, 46a. On voit ici l'agencement des barres destinées à assujettir la statue à sa base. Remarquer que les barres sont fixées les unes aux autres par des boulons et non par des clous et qu'elles sont garnies à chaque point de contact avec la sculpture.

46b. Construction d'un des côtés du cadre.

46c. Le cadre achevé. Manière dont sont disposées la charpente et les barres de soutien. On a arraché l'enveloppe imperméable extérieure afin de laisser voir l'agencement des barres de soutien.

46d. Détail montrant les blocs de bois rembourrés sur lesquels vient s'appuyer le bras de la statue.

This is the last page of the book.
(text on p. 20)

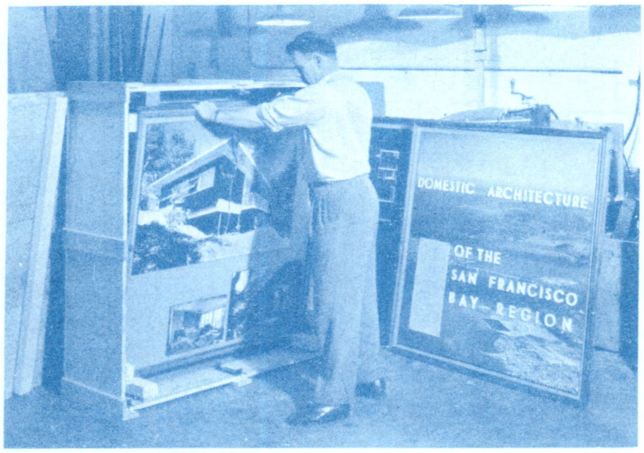

48. Frames of panels interlock so that they form a rigid structure in the packing-case during transit. The frames are supported on sponge-rubber covered braces attached to the box on all four sides to cushion the unit from shock. Designed by the San Francisco Museum of Art, San Francisco, California.

48. Les cadres des panneaux s'emboîtent de façon à composer un ensemble rigide dans la caisse pendant le transport. Les cadres reposent sur des barres de soutien garnies de caoutchouc mousse, fixées aux parois latérales de la caisse et qui amortiront les chocs subis. Modèle et réalisation du San Francisco Museum of Art, San Francisco, Californie.

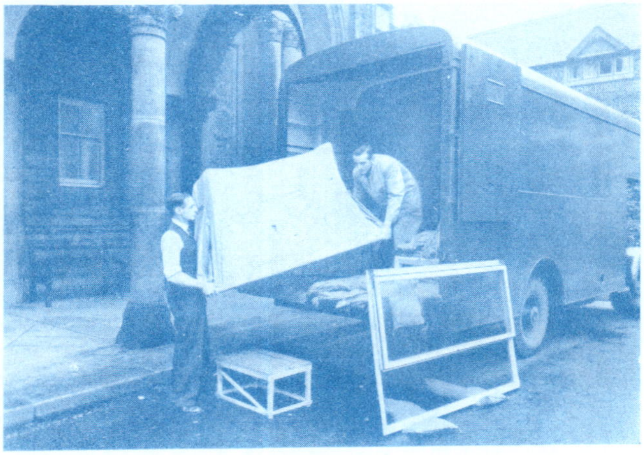

49. Collapsible glass showcase being removed from Victoria and Albert Museum lorry.

49. Déchargement d'une vitrine démontable du camion du service de prêt du Victoria and Albert Museum.

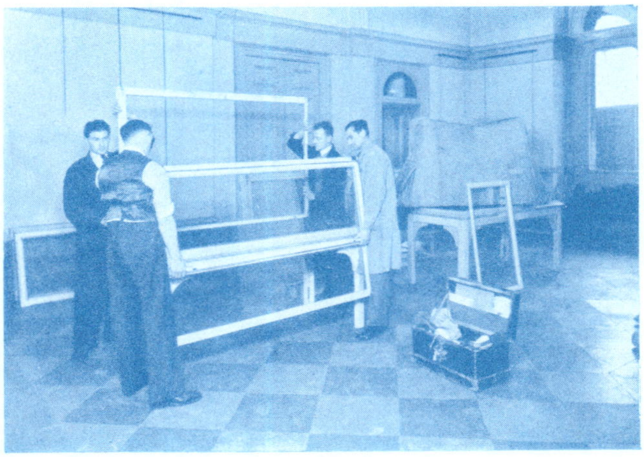

49a. Installation in exhibition gallery by men accompanying the exhibition with two members of the host museum staff.

49a. Montage de la vitrine arrivée à destination par les hommes accompagnant l'exposition et en présence de deux fonctionnaires du musée récipiendaire.

110

This is the page after the last page of the book.
(text on p. 21)

Unless otherwise noted, all diagrams have been drawn by the author / Sauf indication contraire, tous les croquis ont été dessinés par l'auteur: *B*—E. Courter, Museum of Modern Art, New York, N.Y.; *D, R*—San Francisco Museum of Art, San Francisco, California; *E*—Victor E. D'Amico, Museum of Modern Art, New York, N.Y.; *H, I, J, K*—*Modern Export Packing*, Joseph Leeming, U.S. Department of Commerce; *L (a), (b), M, N, O, P*—*Safeguarding Works of Art*, Robert P. Sugden, Metropolitan Museum of Art, New York, N.Y.; *L (c)*—Fogg Art Museum, Harvard University, Cambridge, Massachusetts; *Q*—William Miller, Museum of Modern Art, New York, N.Y., Museum's Department of Circulating Exhibitions.

1, 23. Detroit Institute of Arts (*23* Elmer L. Astleford), Detroit, Michigan.

2, 2a, 8, 12, 32. Virginia Museum of Fine Arts (Whitaker Studio), Richmond, Virginia.

3, 3a. Cranbrook Institute of Science (Croze), Cranbrook, Bloomfield Hills, Michigan.

4. American Museum of Natural History, New York, N.Y.

5. Art Institute of Chicago, Chicago, Illinois (American Federation of Arts, Washington, D.C.).

5a. Metropolitan Museum of Art, New York.

6, 13, 15, 16, 17, 17a, 19, 20, 21, 22, 27, 29, 30, 31, 31a, 31b, 36, 38, 39, 40, 42, 43, 44, 45, 45a, 47. Museum of Modern Art, New York, N.Y. (*6, 13, 15, 16, 17, 17a, 18, 19, 20, 21, 22, 27, 29, 31, 31a, 31b, 38, 39, 40, 42, 43, 44, 45, 45a, 47*, Soichi Sunami, New York, N.Y.; *18*. Oliver Baker, New York, N.Y.; *36*. The Merchandise Mart, Chicago, Ill., Phot. Carl Ullrich, Inc., Chicago, Ill.).

7. Tekniska Museet (Holmquist Foto), Stockholm.

9, 9a, 9b, 10, 10a. Ministero della Pubblica Istruzione, Gabinetto Fotografico Nazionale, Roma.

11, 11a. Palais de la découverte, Paris.

14, 14a. Walker Art Center, Minneapolis, Minnesota.

24, 33, 33a, 33b, 37. Muzeum Narodowe w Warszawie (*33, 33a, 33b* Tadeusz Pawluć, Stanislaw Zamecznik, Archit.).

29a. Unistrut Corporation, Wayne, Michigan.

34, 34a. George Nelson, New York, N.Y. (*34* Phot. Stephen Michael; *34a* Phot. Hedrich-Blessing, Chicago, Ill.).

35. Alvin Lustig, New York, N.Y.

41. Addison Gallery of American Art (Phot. F. Cookson, Andover Art Studio), Andover, Massachusetts.

46, 46a, 46b, 46c, 46d, 48. San Francisco Museum of Art, San Francisco, California.

49, 49a. Victoria and Albert Museum, London (Pickard of Leeds Ltd., Leeds).

TABLE OF CONTENTS
(unless there is one earlier)
(text on p. 23)

65 KE The global distribution of the *Manual* justifies a look at the parallel systems of typographic measurement, which are calculated using different values. The deviations can all be traced back to the divergent historical determinations of the foot as a unit of length. The French Didot point, used in Europe, and the American-English pica point, are not equivalent and therefore incompatible.

Today, the situation is different again: The DTP (desk top publishing) point, used in software programs and thus even more intangible, is based on the international foot as defined in 1959: it is equivalent to 1/72 of an inch or 1/864 of a foot (12 point = 1 pica = 1/6 inch, 1 point = 0,3527 mm).

Type gauges, halftone screen finders and type specimens from the time allow an approximation of the material's visual organisation. Without a detective's incentive, re-measuring and reckoning would be unappealing. Guesswork belongs to the anonymous practices of the Imprimerie Union. Are the rules of the game revealed, or does a hidden message come to light?

65 KE

UNESCO PUBLICATIONS: NATIONAL DISTRIBUTORS

ARGENTINA: Editorial Sudamericana, S.A. Alsina 500, Buenos Aires; ASSOCIATED STATES OF CAMBODIA, LAOS AND VIET-NAM: Librairie Nouvelle Albert Portail, Boite Postale 283, Saigon. *Sub-depot:* K. Chantarith, C.C.R., 38 rue Van Vollenhoven, Phnom-Penh; AUSTRALIA: Oxford University Press, 346 Little Collins St., Melbourne; AUSTRIA: Wilhelm Frick Verlag, 27 Graben, Vienna I; BELGIUM: Librairie Encyclopédique, 7 rue du Luxembourg, Brussels IV; BOLIVIA: Libreria Selecciones, Av. 16 de Julio 216, La Paz; BRAZIL: Livraria Agir Editora, rua México 98-B, Caixa postal 3291, Rio de Janeiro; CANADA: University of Toronto; Press, Toronto. Periodica Inc., Centre de Publications Internationales, 4234 rue de la Roche, Montreal 34. CEYLON: Lake House Bookshop, The Associated Newspapers of Ceylon Ltd., Colombo I; CHILE: Libreria Lope de Vega, Calle Estado 54, Santiago de Chile; COLOMBIA: Emilio Royo Martin, Carrera 9a, No. 1791, Bogota; COSTA RICA: Trejos Hermanos, Apartado 1313, San Jose; CUBA: Unesco Centro Regional en el Hemisfero Occidental, Calle 5 No. 306 Vedado, Apartado 1358, Havana; CYPRUS: M. E. Constantinides, P.O. Box 473, Nicosia; CZECHOSLOVAKIA: Artia Ltd., 30 Ve smečkách, Prague 2; DENMARK: Ejnar Munksgaard Ltd., 6 Nørregade, Copenhagen K.; ECUADOR: Casa de la Cultura Ecuatoriana, ave. 6 de Diciembre, 332, Quito; EGYPT: La Renaissance d'Égypte, 9 Adly Pasha Street, Cairo; FINLAND: Akateeminen Kirjakauppa, 2 Keskuskatu, Helsinki; FORMOSA: The World Book Co, Ltd., 99 Chung King Rd., Section I, Taipeh; FRANCE: Unesco Bookshop, 19 avenue Kléber, Paris 16e; GERMANY: Unesco Vertrieb für Deutschland, R. Oldenbourg, Munich; GREECE: Eleftheroudakis, Librairie internationale, Athens; HAITI: Librairie "A la Caravelle", 36 rue Roux, Boite postale III-B, Port-au-Prince; HUNGARY: Kultura, P.O.B. 149, Budapest 62; INDIA: Orient Longmans Ltd., Indian Mercantile Chamber, Nicol Road, Bombay; 17 Chittaranjan Ave. Calcutta; 36-A Mount Road, Madras; *Sub-depots:* Oxford Book and Stationery Co., Scindia House, New Delhi; Rajkamal Publications Ltd., Himalaya House, Hornby Road, Bombay I; INDONESIA: G.C.T. van Dorp & Co., Djalan Nusantara 22, Jakarta; IRAQ: McKenzie's Bookshop, Baghdad; ISRAEL: Blumstein's Bookstores Ltd., 35 Allenby Road, Tel Aviv; ITALY: Libreria Commissionaria G.C. Sansoni, via Gino Capponi 26, Casella postale 552, Florence; JAMAICA: Sangster's Book Room, 99 Harbour Street, Kingston; Knox Educational Services, Spaldings; JAPAN: Maruzen Co, Inc., 6 Tori-Nichome, Nihonbashi, Tokyo; JORDAN: Joseph I. Bahous & Co., Dar-ul-Kutub, Salt Road, Amman; LEBANON: Librairie Universelle, Avenue des Français, Beirut; LUXEMBOURG: Librairie Paul Bruck, 50 Grand-Rue; MADAGASCAR: La Librairie de Madagascar, Tananarive; MALAYAN FEDERATION AND SINGAPORE: Peter Chong & Co., P.O. Box 135, Singapore; MALTA: Sapienza's Library 26 Kingsway, Valletta; MEXICO: Difusora de las publicaciones de la Unesco, 127 Avenida Ejido, Esc. 401, Mexico, D.F.; NETHERLANDS: N.V. Martinus Nijhoff, Lange Voorhout 9, The Hague; NEW ZEALAND: Unesco Publications Centre, 7 De Lacy Street, Dunedin, N.E.2; NIGERIA: C.M.S. Bookshop, P.O. Box 174, Lagos; NORWAY: A/S Bokjornet, Stortingplass 7, Oslo; PAKISTAN: Ferozsons, 60 The Mall, Lahore; McLeod Road, Karachi; 35 The Mall, Peshawar; PANAMA: Agencia Internacional de Publicaciones, Apartado 2052, Plaza de Arango No. 3, Panama, R.P.; PERU: Librería Internacional del Perú, S.A., Apartado 1417, Lima; PHILIPPINES: Philippine Education Co., 1104 Castillejos, Quiapo, Manila; PORTUGAL: Publicações Európa-América, Ltda., 4 Rua da Barroca, Lisbon; PUERTO RICO: Pan-American Book Co., San Juan 12; SENEGAL: Librairie "Tous les Livres", 30 rue de Thiong, Dakar; SPAIN: Aguilar, S.A. de Ediciones, Juan Bravo 38, Madrid; SURINAM: Radhakishun & Co, Ltd. (Book Dept.), Watermolenstraat 36, Paramaribo; SWEDEN: A/B C.E. Fritzes Kungl., Hovbokhandel, Fredsgatan 2, Stockholm 16; SWITZERLAND: Librairie de l'Université, S.A., Case postale 72, Fribourg; Europa Verlag, 5 Rämistrasse, Zürich; SYRIA: Librairie Universelle, Damascus; TANGIER: Centre international, 54 rue du Statut; THAILAND: Suksapan Panit, Arkarn 9, Rajdamnern Ave., Bangkok; TUNISIA: Agence Aghlébite, 20 Grande-Rue, Postal address, B.P. 2, Kairouan; TURKEY: Librairie Hachette, 469 Istiklal Caddesi, Beyoglu, Istambul; UNION OF BURMA: Burma Educational Bookshop, 551-3 Merchant Street, P.O. Box 222, Rangoon; UNION OF SOUTH AFRICA: Van Schaik's Bookstore (Pty) Ltd., P.O. Box 724, Pretoria; UNITED KINGDOM AND N. IRELAND: H.M. Stationery Office, P.O. Box 569, London, S.E.1.; UNITED STATES OF AMERICA: Columbia University Press, 2960 Broadway, New York 27, N.Y.; URUGUAY: Unesco, Centro de Cooperación Científica para América Latina, Bulevar Artigas 1320, Montevideo; VENEZUELA: Libreria Villegas Venezolana, Madrices a Marrón, 28, Caracas; YUGOSLAVIA: Jugoslovenska Knjiga, Terazije 27/II, Belgrade.

UNESCO BOOK COUPONS

Unesco Book Coupons can be used to purchase all books and periodicals of an educational, scientific or cultural character. For full information please write to:

UNESCO COUPON OFFICE, 19 avenue Kléber, Paris 16e, France.

THESE ARE THE END PAPERS OF THE BOOK
(text on p. 28 and inside back cover)

227 GLOBAL DISTRIBUTION
231 A WORD OF WARNING IS NEEDED. THE MANUAL AND THE UNIVERSAL

66 KE A flea circus. 99 percent of the *Manual* is set in 8-point Garamond Roman – a font size for the sharp-sighted, and one that is normally reserved for small print. This allows inferences to be made about the format of the *Manual:* it was created as a medium for consultation.

A breakdown of the different types of font

- Body text: 8/9-point (1-point spaced, with italic markups)
- Legends, footnotes: 8/8-point
- Subheading 1: 10-point, capitals
- Subheading 2: 7-point, capitals
- Subheading 3: 10-point italics
- Diagram headings: 10-point, part italics, part capitals
- Image commentaries in the Illustrations section: 8/8-point italics
- Proper nouns, city names (in special cases): 8-point small caps
- Chapter title 1: 24-point, capitals
- Chapter title 2: 18-point, capitals, widely spaced

The rule of unity is broken once in the cover title. Monotype Garamond (*Manual of Travelling Exhibitions,* 48-point) is joined by capitals of the French typeface Garamont, a product of the Parisian type foundry Deberny et Peignot.

67 MK The back cover, with the price listed in the bottom corner, immediately calls to mind Lawrence Weiner's first artist's book, *Statements* (New York: The Louis Kellner Foundation/Seth Siegelaub, 1968), which prominently displays the price – $1.95 – on its cover, something quite unusual at the time. An interesting aspect of Weiner's book, which had a print run of 1.000, was that it was intended as both an independent work of art and a mass product accessible to everyone, even available at train station kiosks (according to Siegelaub in his conversation with Monk). In reality, his book was rarely sold and instead given away, because at the time there were no specialised bookstores or dedicated collectors of such works (one of the first critical essays on artists' books was "Book as Artwork 1960/1970" written by Germano Celant and only published in 1971; one year later one of the first artists' book exhibitions took place at the gallery of Nigel Greenwood in London that was based on Celant's text; or Printed Matter, Inc. and the Franklin Furnace Archive, who both specialise in artists' books, were each founded in New York only in 1976). *Statements* and the *Manual of Travelling Exhibitions* can both be bought on the secondary book market, the latter is now 40 times more expensive than when it was originally published, selling for at least €69, the one by Weiner for €900 upwards. For all those interested, the following is a list of all the artists' books I have mentioned and their current prices (as of 2017).

- Xoán Anleo, *Algunas títulos de exposiciones individuales* (2016): €15
- Michael Asher, *Writings 1973 – 1983 On Works 1969 – 1979* (1984): €825
- George Brecht, *Book* (1972): €6.500
- George Brecht, *Book* (Facsimile 2017): €15
- Daniel Buren, *Mot á mot* (2002): from €100
- Peter Downsbrough, *The List 6.2017* (2017): €12
- Gilbert & George, *Art Titles 1969 – 2010* (2011): €9,90 to €1.067 (signed)
- Martin Kippenberger, *241 Bildtitel zum Ausleihen* (1986): €128 to €519
- Uwe Koch, *Kommentiertes Werkverzeichnis der Bücher von Martin Kippenberger 1977 – 1997* (2002): €19 and €45
- Moritz Küng, *Schöner Wohnen* (2004): €100
- Jonathan Monk, *Cover Version* (2004): €60 to €150
- Lynda Morris, Germano Celant. *Book as Artwork 1960/1972* ((1972) Reprint 2010): €150 to €900
- Philippe Parreno et al., *All Hawaii Entrées/Lunar Reggae* (2006): €5 to €85
- Harald Szeemann, *Live in Your Head: When Attitudes Become Form* (1969): €220 to €540
- Lawrence Weiner, *Statements* (1968): €900
- Heimo Zobernig, *Books & Posters: Catalogue raisonné 1980 – 2015* (2016): €10 to €80

66 KE

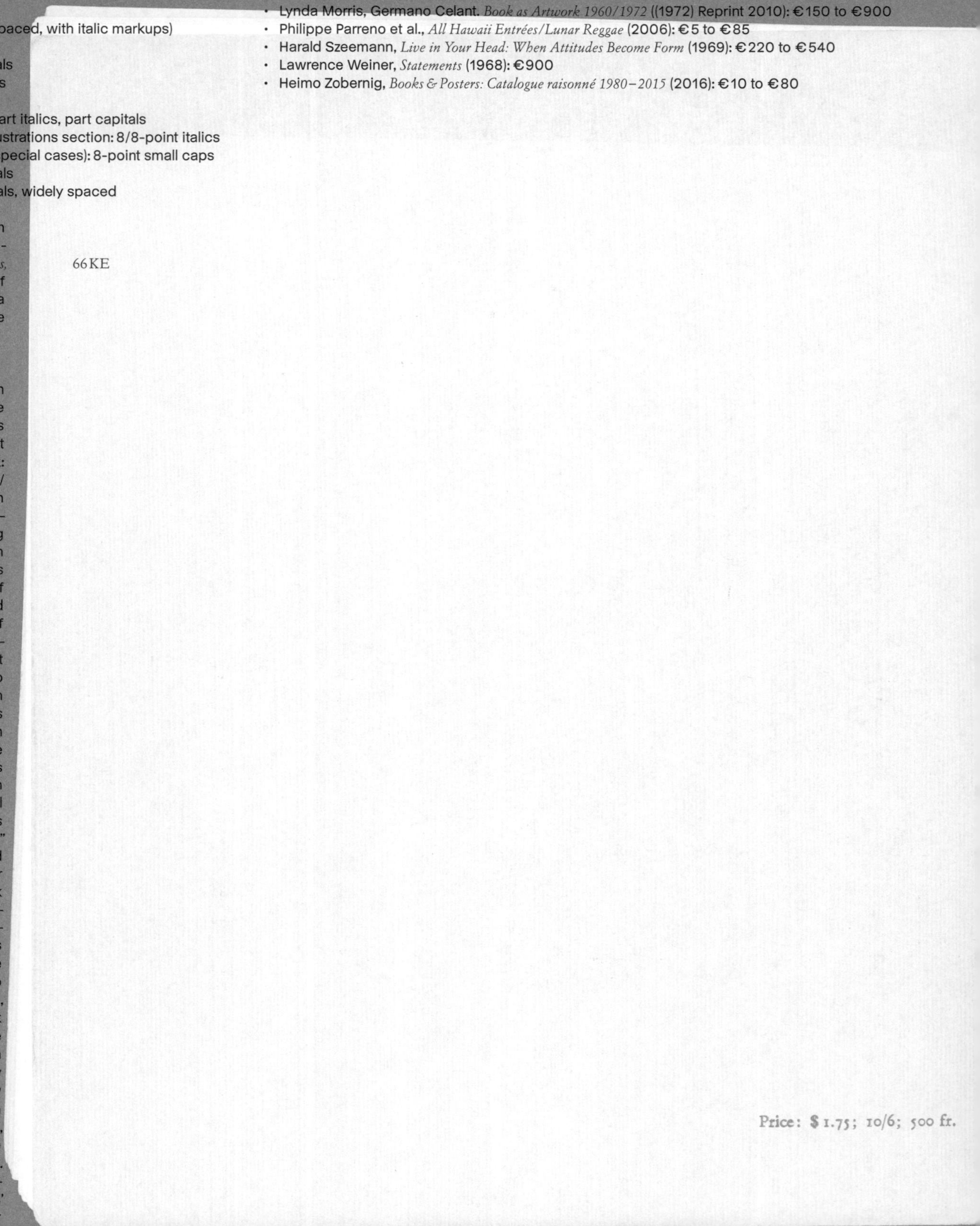

67 MK

PREFACE

The *Manual of Travelling Exhibitions* is a handbook that addressed museums working with travelling exhibitions, both as recipients and as lenders of exhibits. The book presents the practical issues of travelling exhibitions in four chapters. The first chapter—*Travelling Exhibitions*—is about the design of transportable displays for various exhibits. Three further chapters present instructions for the packing of objects, their transport, and insurance. A large image section shows examples for each of the four topics, including exhibition displays and specific presentation formats, as well as display systems, teaching materials, transport cases, and even insurance forms.

While the *Manual of Travelling Exhibitions* was initially published as a guidebook for museum practitioners, it can be read as a document of its time, containing more than just pragmatic instructions. A critical re-reading of the *Manual* provides an understanding of the role of the museum, the purpose of exhibitions or the potential of art as an educational tool in the immediate post-war years. In the same way that the popular DIY manuals of the 1970s show us the broader implications of self-building and participatory architecture, new to their time, the *Manual of Travelling Exhibitions* tells us a lot about the developments that took place in the 1950s and the attempts for worldwide emancipation through education, in which exhibitions and their design played a pivotal role. By re-reading the *Manual of Travelling Exhibitions,* we retrace the historical situation in which it was possible to charge the medium of the exhibition with enormous importance, up to the point where world peace was thought to be achievable through exhibiting. A strikingly close relation runs through the publication—that of the highest humanist goals on the one hand and seemingly minor details of the pragmatic organisation of exhibitions, on the other. The distance between world peace and a joinery detail used for a transport crate is only a couple of pages.

The world into which the *Manual of Travelling Exhibitions* was published in 1953 was still recovering from the catastrophe of the Second World War. A new world organisation, the United Nations (UN), was set up as a replacement for the ineffective League of Nations in order to prevent another such conflict. In 1945, representatives of 51 member states signed the UN Charter at a conference in San Francisco. The extensive conference that lasted for two months took place at the San Francisco Museum of Modern Art, whose director at the time was Grace McCann Morley, the author of the *Manual's* foreword. This close relationship between the establishment of a new world organisation and the cultural space of a museum might be symptomatic of the universalist approach to culture of the time and the shared optimism regarding the goals of human kind.

UNESCO was founded in 1946 with the purpose to foster, and in many ways construct the notion of global peaceful coexistence through the promotion of education, science and culture. The preamble of its constitution states: "Since wars begin in the minds of men, it is in the minds of men that the defences of peace must be constructed." It was thought that this *construction work* should be the joint agenda of educational, scientific and cultural programmes and institutions around the globe. In the first few years of UNESCO, an inventory of cultural and educational institutions that had been destroyed in the war was drawn up. Subsequently, international aid measures to restore the damaged school systems were set up, as well as programmes for the restoration of research and teaching centres, libraries, archives, and museums.

Exhibitions as a form played a crucial role in the concept of UNESCO, as they were considered a mass medium: a globally understandable communication tool and a comprehensive educative instrument that was comparable to the two other mass media of the era: newspapers and radio. Two new technological concepts that were explored by designers at the time supported the idea of the travelling exhibition as a mass medium: information theory and visual communication. Information theory had developed the idea that information was the substance through which communication works, that it could be analysed into *elementary particles,* and therefore synthesised, processed, and sent to a receiver. This idea of information can be found in the publication where there is no differentiation made between art exhibitions and exhibitions of archaeological or ethnographic objects, findings of natural science, government information, consumer products and even trade fairs. Every one of these exhibitions transmitted information, serving to educate the visitors.

With sources in the classic avant-garde practices, visual communication explored the conveyance of ideas and information through visual means. Pioneered by Otto Neurath in the 1930s and imported to the US by Bauhaus émigrés such as Herbert Bayer, László Moholy-Nagy and György Kepes, the term visual communication evoked an idea of communication that is not limited by conventional language barriers. Visual communication therefore had the potential to become a universal *language* accessible to every human being, a concept that seemed ideal for the universalist approach of UNESCO.

In 1950, UNESCO created its own Division of Museums and Monuments, in order to "deal on an inter-governmental level with questions in museography and the protection, preservation and restoration of monuments and archaeological and historic sites". Importantly the Division of Museums and Monuments developed and carried out the exchange of information concerning museum work, the exchange of museum professionals through grants, as well as the exchange of travelling exhibitions between member states. It also maintained a museographical documentation centre in the Paris headquarters, where museums were asked to place their publications, catalogues, guides and photographic documentation of their exhibitions. Today's UNESCO World Heritage Programme is the most prominent offshoot of the early Division of Museums and Monuments. The Division's work was published in a quarterly periodical called *Museum* edited by Raymonde Frin, who is also listed as an advisor to the *Manual of Travelling Exhibitions.* The titles of its first issues represented UNESCO's understanding of museum work as a form of education: "Museums and education", "Children and the museum", "Museums in the service of all". The issue no. 3/1950, titled "Museums and circulating exhibitions", can be seen as a blueprint for the *Manual of Travelling Exhibitions.* Many of its authors appear in the acknowledgments page in the *Manual*, almost all of the non-American case studies in the *Manual,* including the images, are taken from this issue of *Museum.*

However, there is a noticeable difference between the 1950 publication of *Museum* and the *Manual* which was published three years later. The issue of *Museum* was edited in Paris and shows mainly European case studies, whereas the *Manual* was made in New York, edited by the director of the Museum of Modern Art's Department of Circulating Exhibitions, with the majority of its case studies taken from American museums. This might be due to the availability of high quality image material at the MoMA and an advanced experience with the subject of travelling exhibitions, but it might also indicate a shift away from the universalist ethos of UNESCO, and towards an emerging US American ambition for cultural hegemony.

1953 was a decisive year in postwar history. The euphoria of a global peaceful universal culture, which shaped the first years of UNESCO, was dampened by geopolitical conflicts that ultimately turned into the Cold War. The arms race and economic competition between the two blocks was complemented by a range of cultural competitions to extend their successive spheres of influence. American cultural policy used UNESCO as a platform to promote specifically Western concepts of culture. Government agencies such as the United States Information Agency were established in order to formulate and spread propagandistic information about the benefits of the American system. The travelling exhibition was again one of their favourite formats.

This book consists of two parts: The first part comprises the original *Manual of Travelling Exhibitions* as a reprint, accompanied by a series of comments from the perspectives of graphic design and book making by Kurt Eckert, and on curating and exhibition making by Moritz Küng, and an additional layer of comments was added by Andreas Müller, building on the research of the editorial team. The comments make visible the act of re-reading, an intellectual appropriation, transformation, and co-production of the historic book. The intentions of the comments can be very different: they can interpret a given idea by following it up or specifying it in more detail, they can actualise it by comparing it with the present situation, they can contextualise it by describing the historical situation, they can create associations with similar or contrary thoughts, they can criticise it from varying positions. This method of re-reading allows us to approach the historic publication and to explore its potential for today's many discourses about exhibition design. The second part of the publication consists of contributions by various authors based on specific passages in the original book. Different forms of text are combined with artistic works, photographs and archival materials to contextualise specific aspects of the *Manual.* Nader Vossoughian and Florian Walzel each write on concepts of universal knowledge. Vossoughian explores the ideas of a universal visual language and a world museum, as they were developed in the work of Otto Neurath, Paul Otlet, and Le Corbusier. Walzel speculates about the *Manual's* implicit universalist positions lying underneath the pragmatic instructions for the handling of objects for transport.

Two essays explore the establishment of specific departments of circulating exhibitions at important museums: Jennifer Tobias, librarian at MoMA, describes Elodie Courter Osborn's role in establishing the Department of Circulating Exhibitions at MoMA, and especially her popularisation of modernism through educational exhibitions. Design historian Joanna Weddell explores the redevelopment of the Victoria & Albert Museum's Circulation Department after the Second World War, departing from an interview that its director, Peter Floud, gave at the time. Both Jochen Eisenbrand and Martin Beck use the work of the American exhibition designer George Nelson as a starting point for their contributions. Nelson was an important figure in postwar American design, influential both in the educational approach to exhibition design and in its use for propaganda. Beck writes on Nelson's well-known demountable display system for travelling exhibitions while Eisenbrand describes how Nelson was involved in the United States Information Agency's policy of travelling exhibitions as an instrument of both information and propaganda.

Several contributions elaborate on details of the *Manual's* instructions: Vanessa Joan Müller writes about the varying roles and functions of display pedestals starting from a drawing of a demountable pedestal. Gitte Villesen expands on the idea of vitrine displays by showing a complex vitrine work of her own. Maxim Weirich, in conversation with Tina Köhler, compares the *Manual's* instructions on the logistics of transport with the conditions and processes of today's art logistics industry. Specific images in the *Manual* serve as starting points for several contributions: Rike Frank and Grant Watson's glossary relates to the installation photograph of Anni Albers' MoMA textile exhibition. Clémentine Deliss speculates about an image depicting a display of carved objects and unfolds a number of questions concerning the display of ethnographic exhibits at the time of the *Manual* and today. Both Sophie Lichtenberg's series of photographs of interior details of camper vans and Andreas Müller's collection of images of museum mobiles comment on the idea of the travelling of entire exhibition spaces. Lydia Kähny explores the format of the boxed exhibition using the example of the German Werkbund's educational boxes and Marcel Duchamp's work *La Boîte-en-valise.* Aaron Werbick and Jonathan Maho write on the work of the Polish exhibition designer Stanisław Zamecznik, one of the few non-American designers represented in the case studies in the *Manual.*

There is a strange contradiction between the grandiose, ideologically backed claims that the editors of the *Manual* assign to the media of exhibitions and the pragmatic, hands-on information of a manual. In our re-reading of the *Manual* we assume that these two strains should be read together as two sides of the same phenomenon. Both the pragmatic information and the political intentions formulated between the lines are characteristic for the modernist idea of exhibiting as a form of educating, which informed the *Manual* in the first place and runs through every page of it, its content and structure, its selection of images, its graphic design, and its production as a material object.

The reconstruction of a situation where exhibitions belonged to the realm of education is interesting for exhibition making practices in our current age, where it is often that exhibitions are considered simply as plain entertainment or as individual artistic expressions. Within the complex terrain of radical changes in mass communication that have taken place since the advent of the internet, the idea of an exhibition as a mass medium might be an interesting anachronism. Yet, we find the seriousness in which the *Manual* claims exhibitions as communication devices, awkwardly compelling.

THE DEVELOPMENT OF THE UNESCO-LOGO

01

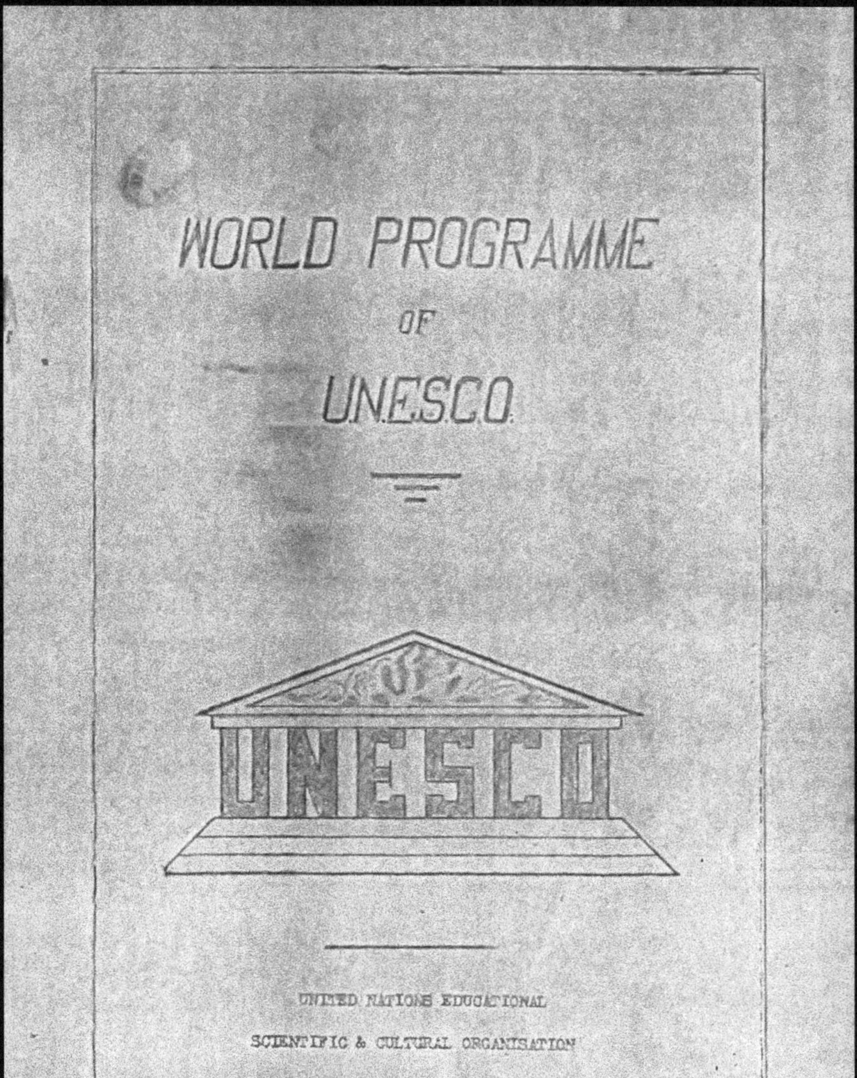

02

03

After viewing the historical material, finding the origins of the UNESCO logo appears to be no straightforward task, not least because attentive secretaries seem to recall the creators of many different designs. In 1949, the search had already begun for the story of the UNESCO logo, and in the same year the answer was found: at the request of the then Director-General Julian Huxley, a member of the secretariat designed the first logo in late 1946 or early 1947. The first draft of the logo, printed on the UNESCO newsletter *Reconstruction and Rehabilitation* from June 1947, bears much more of a resemblance to the logo of the United Nations. Just two months later, however, in a newsletter from August 1947, another UNESCO logo appears, one that clearly seems to serve as a prototype for the logo still in use today.

As not all UNESCO member states were part of the 1883 Paris Convention for the Protection of Industrial Property, a resolution at the 1954 General Conference prompted all members to introduce patent and design laws to grant protection to the logo. During this 8th General Conference in Montevideo, the hitherto provisional UNESCO logo was chosen as the official symbol of the organisation. It was subsequently printed on all UNESCO publications and continues to appear in the organisation's letterhead.

Fig. 01 First UNESCO logo, mid-1947
Fig. 02 Preliminary cover draft of the World Programme of UNESCO
Fig. 03 Current UNESCO logo

READ CAREFULLY AND FOLLOW THE ATTACHED INSTRUCTIONS: ELODIE COURTER OSBORN AND THE DISSEMINATION OF 20TH-CENTURY MODERNISM

JENNIFER TOBIAS

When Elodie Courter Osborn (1911–1994) authored the *Manual of Travelling Exhibitions* for the United Nations Educational, Scientific, and Cultural Organisation (UNESCO) in 1953,[1] she drew from over a decade of experience with the Museum of Modern Art's Circulating Exhibitions programme (CE, 1933–1947) and subsequent efforts with the American Federation of Arts (AFA, 1940s–1950s). This essay discusses Osborn's work at MoMA, its influence upon the *Manual,* and in particular how methods of persuasion and pedagogy based upon modernist principles were mobilised in the service of popularisation.

The study begins with Osborn's background and her involvement with the CE programme, as well as a brief summary of MoMA's involvement with UNESCO at the time. An early MoMA CE and a later teaching portfolio are then discussed as precursors to the *Manual.* Confluences between MoMA techniques and the *Manual* conclude the essay, underscoring Osborn's role in developing communication techniques consistent with the modernist message.

MOMA'S CIRCULATING EXHIBITIONS PROGRAMME, 1933–1952

MoMA's Department of Circulating Exhibitions was a vital but virtually unexamined element of the museum's promotional mission.[2] The innovative department was established in 1933 but MoMA's first efforts date to 1931 with a portfolio of reproductions, organised by founding Director Alfred H. Barr Jr., titled *A Brief Survey of Modern Painting in Colour Reproductions* (BSMP, 1931–39, 86 venues), along with a travelling version of the influential International Style show, circulated as *International Exhibition of Modern Architecture* (1932–33, 14 venues) and *Photographic Exhibition of Modern Architecture* (1932–33, approximately 10 venues).[3]

Between 1931 and the apex of the programme in 1954, MoMA circulated 461 exhibitions among 3.700 venues including K–12 schools, technical colleges, clubs, military installations, and department stores, mostly in the US.[4] As evidence of the programme's early, domestic success, an internal report noted:

> "Apart from the major exhibitions and the series of catalogues which are published in connection with them, the most valuable educational service now being provided by the Museum [...] is unquestionably the circulating exhibition programme [...] [These] exhibitions are considered in many quarters to represent a standard of excellence for such services."[5]

OSBORN AT MOMA AND AFTER

In her 12-year tenure at MoMA, most of it as CE director, Elodie Courter Osborn was crucial to establishing and shaping the programme.[6] Immediately after graduating from Wellesley with a degree in art history, she sought work at the museum "in spite of the advice of the

1 Elodie Courter Osborn, *Manual of Travelling Exhibitions,* UNESCO, Paris 1953.

2 For a more detailed history of the programme see the Historical Note in NY MoMA Archives, "Department of Circulating Exhibitions Records Finding Aid", 1992, www.moma.org/learn/resources/archives/EAD/CEf.

3 These have been thoroughly analysed in Terence Riley and Stephen Perrella, *The International Style: Exhibition 15 and the Museum of Modern Art,* Rizzoli, New York 1992.

4 "Circulating Exhibitions 1931–1954", Bulletin of the Museum of Modern Art 21, no. 3–4, 1954.

5 Artemas Packard, "Report on the Development of The Museum of Modern Art: Introduction and General Considerations, 1935–36", 1936, pp. 40–41.

6 Roberta Smith, "Elodie Osborn, 82, First Director Of the Modern's Travelling Shows", *New York Times,* 1994.

Placement Bureau [...] that there simply were no jobs there. She turned up at the door [...]".[7] She began as a volunteer in 1933, then becoming the programme secretary in 1935 and director two years later.[8] She almost single-handedly developed the programme's domestic agenda and was involved in all its aspects, from overall direction to budget to curatorial negotiations to copyediting. According to one author, Osborn "became in a few years the museum's most influential instrument of tastemaking"[9] by "introducing audiences far from Manhattan to works from the Modern's collection, and to the museum's taste and historical viewpoint".[10]

Indeed, records show a consistently proactive, efficient, and innovative director who gave voice, design, and reach to a broad, mostly US audience. As the *Manual* itself states:

> "Under her direction, exhibitions of every type, size and complexity were assembled, boxed skillfully for ease and safety of frequent unpacking and repacking, circulated back and forth across the continent for one or several years at a time, and even sent outside the country [...] [She] met and solved in her work almost every conceivable problem."[11]

Barr said that "Elodie was the kind who when she left the museum it took four people to replace her."[12] That moment came in 1947 when she departed to start a family, although she continued working on several teaching portfolios. After Osborn's departure, the CE programme was reoriented towards international destinations and actual artworks,[13] leaving domestic and reproduction shows behind.

After leaving the Museum, Osborn became involved with the American Federation of Arts (AFA), which recommended her for authorship of the *Manual.*[14] Founded in 1909, the coalition of US arts institutions has continuously promoted American arts abroad through exhibitions, publications, and related media. During this period Osborn served as an adviser to the group's Exhibition Committee and as the vice chairman of its International Exhibitions Committee. She was also involved in an AFA-sponsored film series.[15]

At the time of the *Manual's* publication, the AFA was characteristically (if uncritically) active in its efforts to promote American art internationally. For example, the group organised the first official US presence at the Venice Biennale in 1952 and during this period the AFA also organised a State Department funded "reorientation programme" of educational exhibitions in German museums.[16]

UNESCO AND MOMA AT MID-CENTURY

UNESCO was founded in 1945 with the mission to promote education, science, culture, international understanding, especially in response to the destruction of World War II. The UK, France, US, Czechoslovakia, and Poland were prominent among the 37 original member states.[17] Anticipating the *Manual,* in 1951 UNESCO adopted several resolutions encouraging cultivation of travelling exhibitions and related activities, in particular Resolution 4.4232:

> "To encourage Member States to prepare and to circulate, in co-operation with the appropriate professional organisations, including the International Council of Museums and international organisation of artists, exhibitions to travel from country to country, especially exhibitions of original works by contemporary artists, folk art, and exhibitions having an international appeal on account of their subject and character."[18]

In 1953, the year the *Manual* was published, UNESCO had 64 member states with Spain, Nepal, Libya, and Chile joining that year and Soviet Russia, Belarus, and Ukraine joining the following year. Cold War tensions made participation fraught, however, with the membership of Czechoslovakia, Poland, and Hungary.[19] That year UNESCO published over 600 books, with five concerning art.[20] The following year, UNESCO adopted one of its most notable policies, the Hague Convention for the Protection of Cultural Property in the Event of Armed Conflict. Revised in 1999, the Hague Convention strongly reflects UNESCO's wartime origins and the values of cultural preservation espoused by the *Manual.*[21]

MOMA AND UNESCO

MoMA was involved with UNESCO before and after Osborn's tenure, but no evidence of her direct participation has yet surfaced at the MoMA or UNESCO archives. MoMA's strongest connections to UNESCO were forged

7 Russell Lynes, *Good Old Modern: An Intimate Portrait of the Museum of Modern Art,* Atheneum, New York 1973, p. 117. Barr taught at Wellesley but prior to Osborn's arrival.

8 Ibid.

9 Ibid., p. 107.

10 Smith, "Elodie Osborn, 82, First Director Of the Modern's Travelling Shows".

11 Osborn, *Manual of Travelling Exhibitions,* UNESCO, Paris 1953, p. 5.

12 Lynes, 1973, pp. 260–1.

13 Alfred H. Barr Jr. Papers, I.A.243; mf 2178:1291. The Museum of Modern Art Archives, New York. Hereafter "AHB". Jane Sabersky to Barr and others, 14.01.1954. Sabersky's detailed memo arguing for reconception of CE anticipated the turning point. For an in-depth study of this initiative see Franc, Helen. "Early Years of the International Program and Council". In Museum of Modern Art at Mid-Century: At Home and Abroad, edited by John Elderfield. MoMA, New York 1994.

14 Osborn, *Manual of Travelling Exhibitions,* UNESCO, Paris 1953, p. 5. René d'Harnoncourt was an AFA Trustee in the 1950s and 1960s.

15 Smith, "Elodie Osborn, 82, First Director Of the Modern's Travelling Shows".

16 American Federation of Arts, "AFA History", n.d., www.amfedarts.org/about-the-afa/afa-history/.

17 UNESCO, "The Organisation's History", n.d., www.unesco.org/new/en/unesco/about-us/who-we-are/history/.

18 UNESCO. Records of the General Conference, 6th Session, Resolutions, 1951, p. 26. www.unesdoc.unesco.org/images/0011/001145/114588E.pdf

19 UNESCO, "List of the 195 Members [...] of UNESCO and the date on which they became members", n.d., www.unesco.org/new/en/member-states/countries/.

20 Search of print books published by UNESCO in 1953 and then limited to the subject keyword "art" in www.worldcat.org. 02.04.2017.

21 UNESCO, "Convention for the Protection of Cultural Property in the Event of Armed Conflict", 1954, www.unesco.org/new/en/culture/themes armed-conflict-and-heritage/convention-and-protocols/1954-hague-convention/.

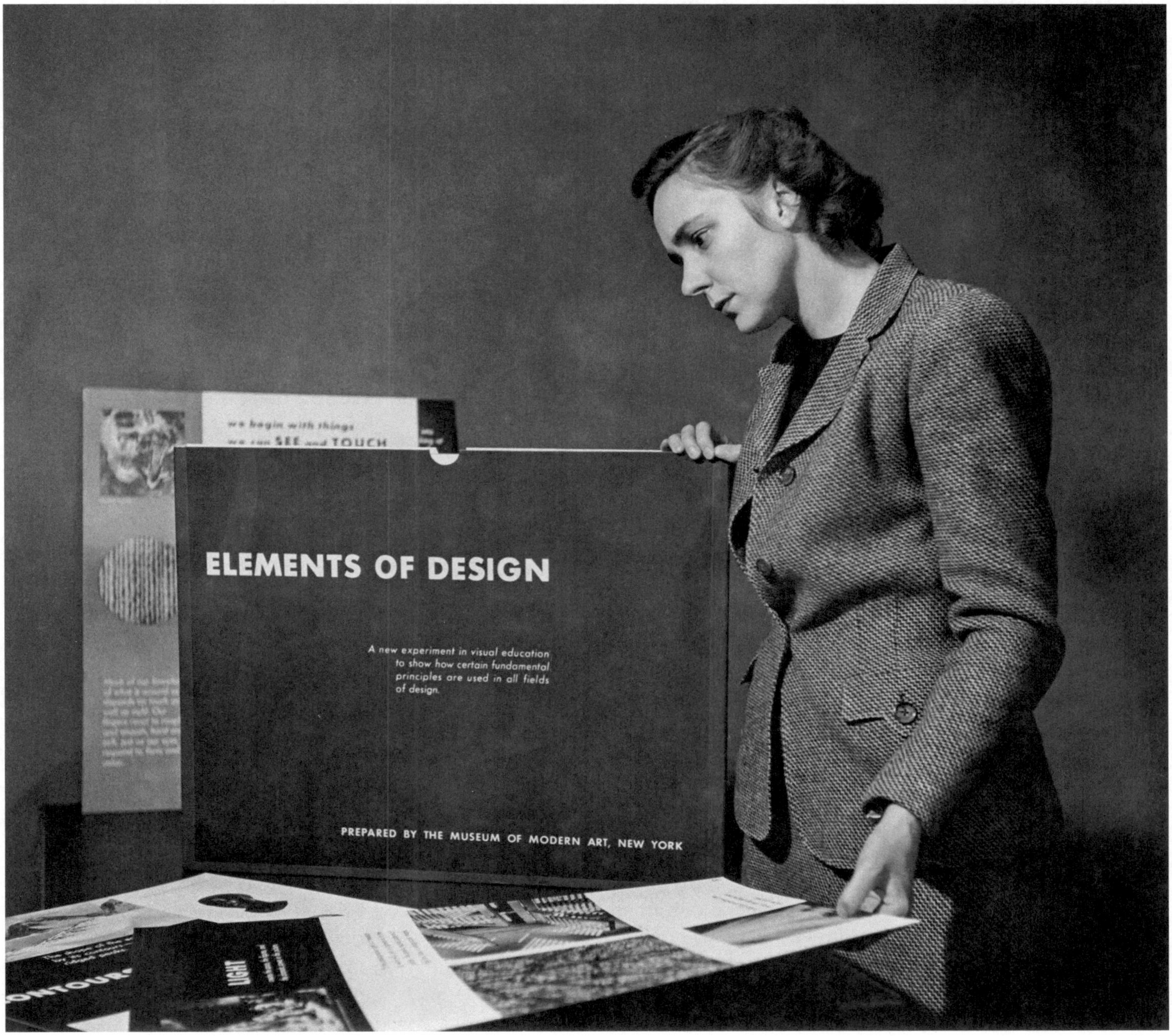

04

Fig. 04 Elodie Courter Osborn, Director of the Department of Circulating Exhibitions, Museum of Modern Art, New York 1945

through the International Program (IP, founded 1952) and its advisory International Council (IC, founded 1953).[22] The best-known and most critically examined IC and IP activities in Europe at mid-century concern travelling exhibitions, with most attention directed to Dorothy Miller's *Americans* exhibitions and Edward Steichen's *Family of Man.*[23] The IC also facilitated architect and MoMA figure Philip Johnson's 1958 design of the executive board committee room at UNESCO's Paris headquarters.[24]

At the time that the *Manual* was written, three MoMA figures were most directly involved with UNESCO: Barr, Director René d'Harnoncourt, and post-Osborn Circulating Exhibitions Director Porter McCray. In 1946 Barr was asked to advise about UNESCO by the US State Department,[25] and he attended the 1947 conference.[26] In 1950 he served (reluctantly) as honorary advisor for an unrealised journal initiative.[27] In this period McCray served on the US delegation, and d'Harnoncourt advised about several UNESCO conferences. Both d'Harnoncourt and McCray spoke at conferences and participated in nominating delegates for international events.

UNESCO's consistent advocacy for travelling exhibitions is found in d'Harnoncourt's files from this period. An example of a report from a 1952 seminar on the role of museums in education presages Osborn's *Manual:*

> "Consideration was [...] given to the urgent need for a well prepared handbook dealing with the major aspects of museum administrative developments and practices and covering the wide variety of educational activities which can be undertaken to the benefit of their clientele [...] There is a real need for a comprehensive handbook, which can be bought cheaply and circulating readily among museum and teaching personnel. The aim is not to standardise ideas, aims or methods, for there can be no universally applicable, cut and dried formulae."[28]

MoMA's International Program coordinated the American delegation to UNESCO's 1954 First International Congress of Plastic Arts in Venice, sponsoring David Smith and another American artist.[29] (Smith's opinion of US UNESCO was frank: "you need only ask any artist what UNESCO has done for art or artists. The answer is usually, nothing [...] UNESCO has been involved with questionnaires, art history, philosophy, language, etc. but in the US nothing related to art.")[30]

Barr and d'Harnoncourt also stayed abreast of UNESCO's efforts to disseminate colour reproductions of artworks, a longstanding practice integral to MoMA's Publications and CE programmes.[31]

While there is a tendency to think of MoMA's mid-century efforts as a unilateral American statement about modernism, it's worth noting that the movement was and remains contested in the States. During the Cold War period in particular, Barr persistently resisted reactionary criticism through public statements and popular press articles such as "Is Modern Art Communistic?"[32] Characteristically, his papers include a note about "UNESCO trouble" – referring to a screed by one-term Idaho Congressman John Wood[33] declaring the organisation to be "the greatest subversive plot in history" to establish "world government" through a "scheme to pervert public education"[34] – and a pro-modern agenda organised in response by Grace McCann Morley, San Francisco Museum of Modern Art founding director – and author of the UNESCO manual introduction.[35]

MOMA PRECURSORS, 1931 AND 1945

Design and writing methods developed or used by Osborn to amplify the modernist message are examined here in an early MoMA CE and a late teaching portfolio. Techniques manifested in these shows will be seen to resonate in the *Manual* decades later.

Within two years of opening in 1929, MoMA organised its first travelling show of reproductions, titled *A Brief Survey of Modern Painting in Colour Reproductions* (BSMP, 1931–39, 86 venues). The widely distributed, long-lived show reflects Barr's earliest efforts to disseminate modernism through reproductions, an early attempt at a practice that would become established at both MoMA and UNESCO. Though Osborn arrived at MoMA two years into BSMP's eight-year run, the show established a narrative and method upon which she would build.

The show's tour of over 80 US venues included department stores (Wanamaker's, May's, Kresge's), public galleries (Vancouver Art Gallery, Louisiana Museum of Art) commercial galleries (Addison Gallery, Sarachek Fine Arts in Kansas City), a library, women's clubs, Howard

22 For an overview, see the Historical Note in Museum of Modern Art, "International Council and International Program Records", 2014, www.moma.org/learn/resources/archives/EAD/ICIP_SeriesIB_VIf.html?page=ICIP_SeriesIB_VIb.html#subseries1. Hereafter"IC/IP".

23 See Kimmelman, Szarkowski, and Zelavansky in *The Museum of Modern Art at Mid-Century: At Home and Abroad,* New York: Museum of Modern Art, New York 1994. Also Eric J. Sandeen, *Picturing an Exhibition: The Family of Man and 1950s America,* University of New Mexico, Albuquerque 1995. The Museum of American Art, Berlin is an especially creative approach. For a survey of the ongoing project, packaged to resemble Alfred H. Barr's popularisation *What is Modern Painting?,* 1943, see Künstlerhaus Bethanien and Museum of American Art Berlin, *What Is Modern Art?,* Revolver, Frankfurt 2006, www.whatismodernart.de.

24 Executive Board Room of UNESCO Headquarters Building, Paris, 1958. IC/IP, I.B. 268–287. The Museum of Modern Art Archives, New York.

25 AHB I.A. 287; mf 2181: 521, 529, 532. MoMA Archives, NY.

26 AHB I.A. 287; mf 2181: 512. MoMA Archives, NY.

27 AHB I.A. 287; mf 2181: 499. MoMA Archives, NY.

28 UNESCO, "International Seminar on the Role of Museums in Education", 1954. René d'Harnoncourt Papers, VII. 234. The Museum of Modern Art Archives, New York. Hereafter "RDH".

29 IC/IP. IV.A. 38. MoMA Archives, NY.

30 IC/IP. IV.B. 9. MoMA Archives, NY.

31 UNESCO, "Catalogue of Colour Reproductions of Painting Prior to 1860 (new edition): Expert's Working Party", 1952. RDH: VII. 235. MoMA Archives, NY.

32 Alfred H. Barr Jr., Defining Modern Art: Selected Writings of Alfred H. Barr Jr., Abrams, New York 1986 pp. 214–219.

33 "John Travers Wood", Biographical Directory of the United States Congress, n.d., www.bioguide.congress.gov/scripts/biodisplay.pl?index=W000700.

34 John Wood, "The Greatest Subversive Plot in History", self-published excerpt from Congresssional Record of 18.10.1951. RDH. VII. 235. MoMA Archives, NY.

35 AHB. I.A. 287; mf 2181:466. MoMA Archives, NY.

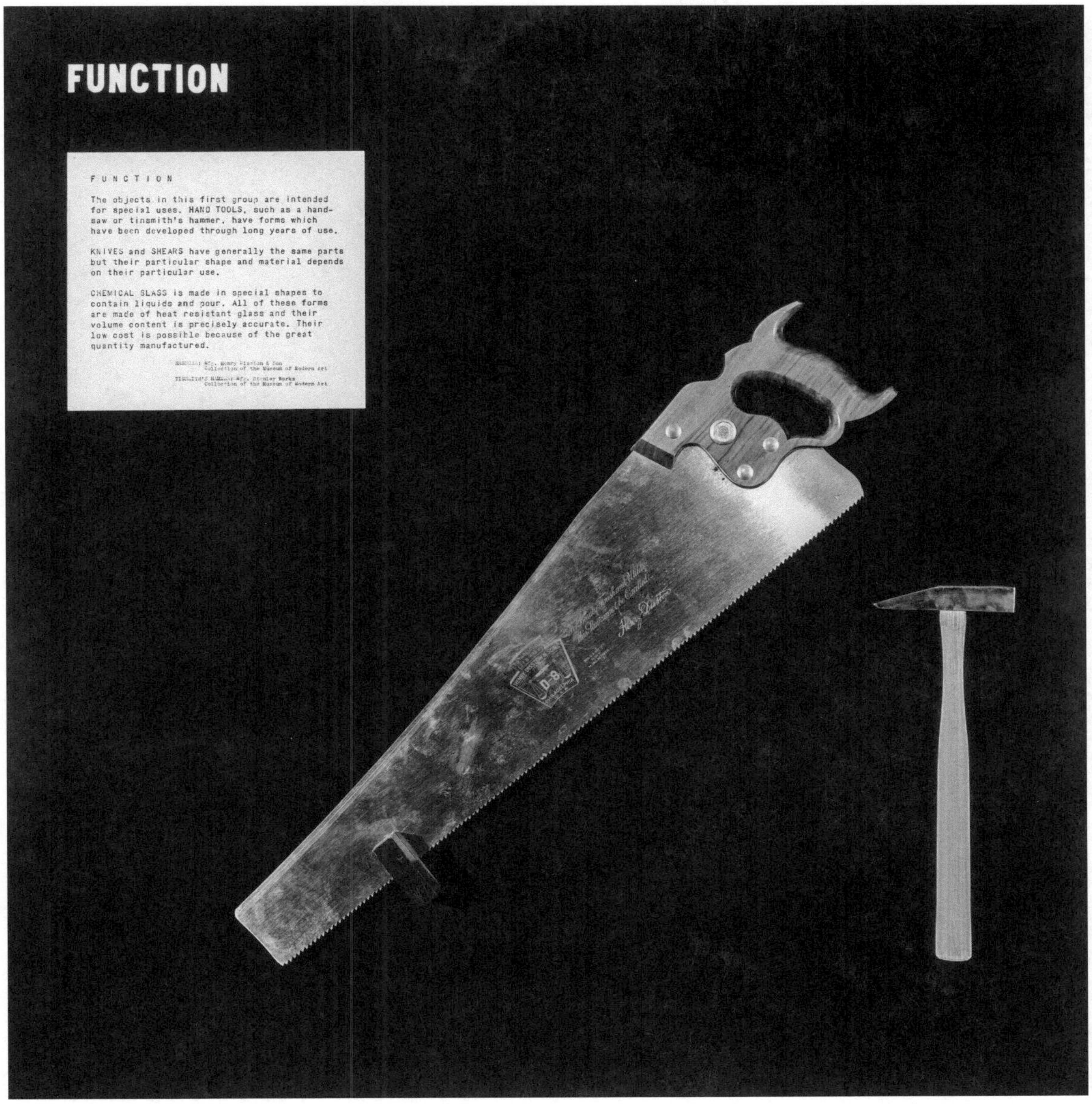

05

Fig. 05 Panel 2 of the master set of installation photographs for The Museum of Modern Art circulating exhibition *What is Good Design?* (1942–1945)

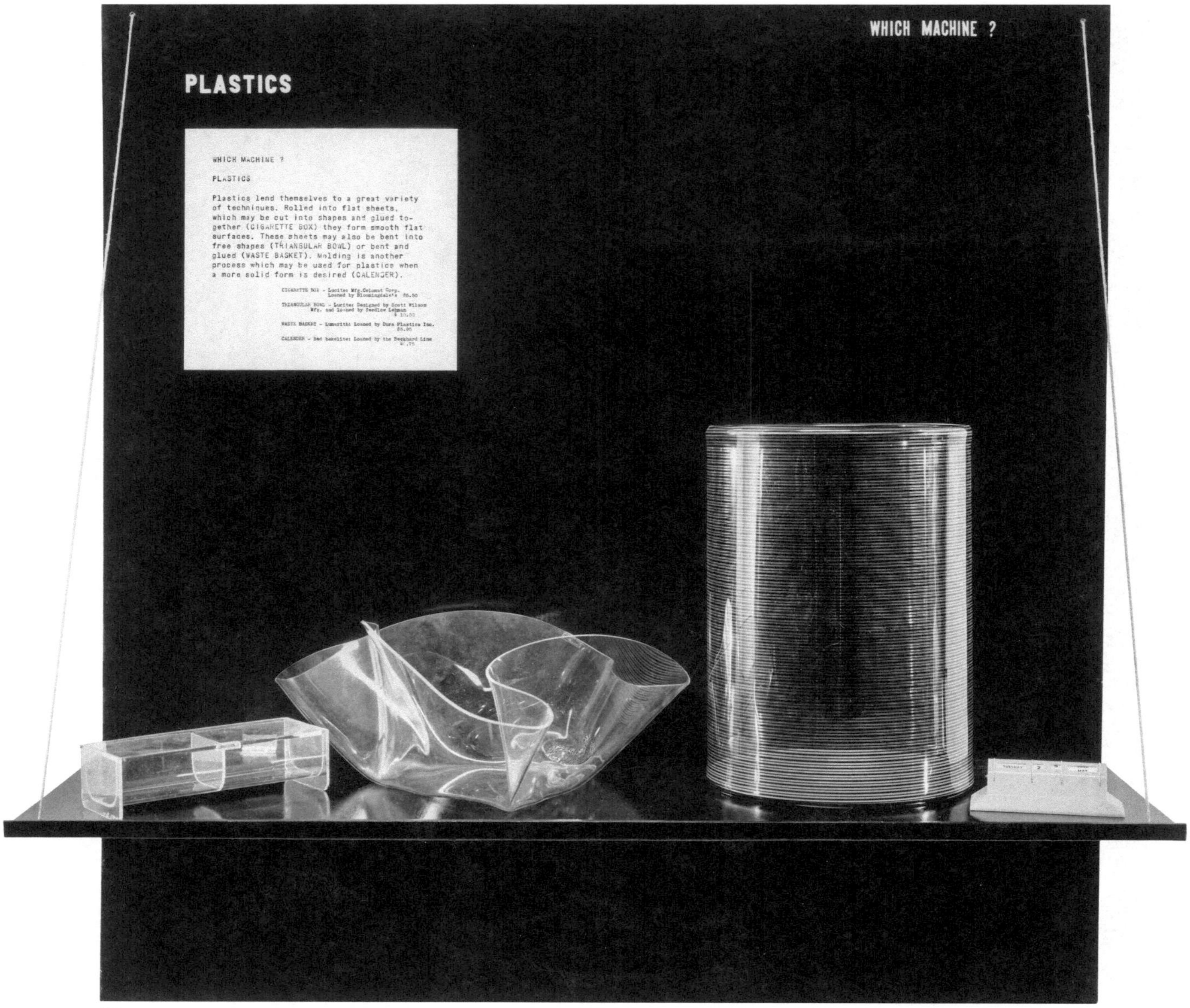

06

Fig. 06 Panel 15 of the master set of installation photographs for The Museum of Modern Art circulating exhibition *What is Good Design?* (1942–1945)

University, and many colleges. In 1936, three years after the closure of the Bauhaus, the show travelled to Yale and Black Mountain College, where several former faculty members taught.

Consistent with basic techniques described in the UNESCO manual, BSMP was comprised of reproductions in slim frames (with and without mats) accompanied by "wall labels and placards". On the one hand, this enabled venues to shape an independent narrative; on the other, the presentation results in a secular, decorative effect, suggesting a commercial or domestic setting and effectively removing the works from the "ritual space" posited by Duncan.[36]

The circulating version of approximately sixty images was organised into two sections: nineteenth and twentieth-century painting. These in turn were subdivided into four individually rentable parts, a model common to several CEs. Drafts show that while Barr thought in a scholarly, continuous narrative, an editor (possibly Osborn) thought about packaging the subdivisions, noting at one point: "Revise arrangement so that sections do not depend on each other."[37] This enabled sections to be marketed to different audiences and gave a degree of flexibility to venues. Unlike fully curated exhibitions, venues now had a kit of parts with which to make independent statements, choosing which segments to rent as well as the installation setting and sequencing.

The rhetorical methods of BSMP are consistent with Barr's drive to popularise modernism, with emphasis on celebration of free expression in the face of oppressive forces. We find anticipation of audience disbelief, a tonal mix of low-key discursion, and blatant appeals for open-mindedness. All are found in the conclusion to the 1932 on-site version of the catalogue:

> "Modern painting may seem confusing [...] [The artist] picks and chooses whatever he wishes in the attempt to work out a synthesis of expression. Side by side today are artists who paint exactly what they see in nature and artists who paint story pictures of romantic [...] landscapes, sociological and political problem pictures, sentimental portraits, dreams [...] To enjoy the work of these artists it is well to forget prejudice, both modern and old-fashioned, to give the picture itself a chance to live!" [38]

Over a decade later, two years before her departure, and the year of UNESCO's founding, in 1945 Osborn organised *Elements of Design,* a striking set of 24 poster-sized panels described as "a new experiment in visual education to show how certain fundamental principles are used in all fields of design (Fig. 04)".[39] Fabricated to travel through the mail for installation virtually anywhere, *Elements* was intended for "colleges, art schools, and the educational departments of museums". It is discussed here as a distillation of modernist art, design, and didactic principles espoused by the CE and Education Departments at the time, for the residual effects of wartime communications methods, and as a precursor of the UNESCO manual.

Osborn developed *Elements* with Victor D'Amico, MoMA's innovative founding Education Director from (1937–1969)[40] and Robert Wolff, previously Dean and director of the Painting and Sculpture programme at the Illinois Institute of Design in Chicago (Wolff was recruited by László Moholy-Nagy to the post-Bauhaus outpost).[41]

The *Elements* argument for a universal formal language is clear at the outset: "the fundamental promise of the exhibition is that design does not exist as a separate concept, but is intrinsic in all objects of the natural as well as the man-made world". Thus, "Whatever the designer's tools and materials, he works with the same basic elements: line, form, space, light, colour."

The *Elements* narrative appeals through its simplicity and wonder, reflected in the aphoristic, Futura-rendered text and Wolff's spacious, dynamic layouts. Modernist art and design masterpieces predominate, including works by Mondrian, Calder, Aalto, and Moholy-Nagy, among many others. The attempt to universalise modernism is subtle, conveyed through numerous references to nature and selective inclusion of works from ostensibly timeless cultures.

The rhetoric of nature is found throughout *Elements,* and is clearest in the *Measured Line panel,* positioning modern design as a rational complement to the unruly jags of nature and a reassuring tool of civic planning. This is argued by juxtaposing images of a beautiful but gnarled tree and Mies van der Rohe's 1931 Berlin exhibition house, along with the caption:

36 Carol Duncan, "The Modern Art Museum: It's a Man's World", in *Civilizing Rituals: Inside Public Art Museums,* Routledge, London 1995, pp. 102–32.

37 Department of Circulating Exhibitions Records, II.1.42.1. The Museum of Modern Art Archives, New York. Herafter "CE".

38 Alfred H. Barr Jr., *Brief Survey of Modern Painting: Notes on the Museum's Circulating Exhibition of Colour Reproductions of Modern Paintings,* MoMA, New York 1934, p. 18.

39 *Elements of Design: A New Experiment in Visual Education to Show How Certain Fundamental Principles Are Used in All Fields of Design.* MoMA, New York 1945.

40 Child Welfare Foundation of Japan. Victor D'Amico, *Art as a Human Necessity,* Kodomo no Shiro, Tokyo 1995. See also the Biographical Note in the Victor D'Amico Papers, The Museum of Modern Art Archives, New York, www.moma.org/learn/resources/archives/EAD/damicof.

41 Farnsworth Fowle, "Robert J. Wolff, 72, Abstract Artist". *The New York Times,* 02.01.1978. www.nytimes.com/1978/01/02/archives/robert-j-wolff-72-abstract-artist.html.

> "The measured line is man's invention; it does not exist in nature [...] Both are wonders of design. The tree grows that way. The house must be planned and engineered. The beauty of the measured line is implicit in its precision and logic."

The selective use of timeless artworks is also striking, such as an unattributed Indian bowl illustrating two-dimensional space or the images of a Mayan temple and Egyptian statue illustrating the panel on mass (Fig. 06), "simple, massive forms [that] are among man's greatest monuments to human dignity and power".

The final panel makes the most overt humanist appeal. Proclaiming, "The images of design vary with each civilisation [but] the elements of design never change", the panel shows figurative art from diverse cultures and time periods superimposed on an unattributed background photograph of modern, urban humanity. The examples of ostensibly timeless art include an Easter Island figure, a T'ang Dynasty Bodhisattva, ancient Cypriot and Roman busts—and Wilhelm Lehmbruck's *Head of a Young Woman* (1911). A note in a draft manuscript from the authors of *Elements* indicates there may have been a struggle with this ending: "Conclusion. Integration—God knows how."[42]

With VE day mere months before the debut of *Elements* in October, 1945, it's no surprise that a wartime mindset subtly infuses *Elements*. This is clear in the project's press release, which attributes the set's "seeing is learning" approach not to modernist design principles but to "the visual method of teaching used so extensively in World War II [...] adapted to civilian use". This would have made sense to readers, but it's also an indirect reference to Wolff. During World War II, Wolff headed the non-engineering graphics section of the Naval Training Aids Development Center in New York, a remarkable laboratory focused on diverse communication techniques. A margin note on an *Elements* draft mentions the centre specifically.[43]

INTERPRETING THE UNESCO MANUAL

This background is helpful for recognising how design principles developed by Osborn at MoMA for CEs was codified into the UNESCO manual, intended as a "thoroughly practical guide" in service of "the necessity and the moral obligation to extend educational opportunities and to make cultural values more readily accessible to all, without regard to social distinction or geographic isolation."[44]

To that end, Osborn's introduction asserts that "Visual presentation offers an international means of communication in which language barriers begin to disappear", bringing with it the hope that "Information can be exchanged, problems and subjects common to several nations can be studied and through such exhibitions gain wide public attention."[45] This message is consistent with principles espoused by the influential modern artists, designers, and curators acknowledged in the introduction, including Herbert Bayer, Alvin Lustig, George Nelson, Grace McCann Morley, and Edgar Kaufmann.

Echoing the wartime context of *Elements of Design*, Osborn's introduction notes the peacetime increase in international travelling exhibitions and astutely reflects upon their wartime instrumentalisation: "It is somewhat ironic that the war years produced the most vigorous exchange of cultural materials between countries", and offers hope for a future in which "Presentation of the visual arts, the handicrafts, architecture, civic planning, scientific discoveries and achievements, [and] the history of different countries offers a means of better understanding the aspirations, customs and character of different peoples."[46]

Modernist design and communication principles described in the *Manual* are the clearest link to Osborn's time at MoMA, especially reproduction or panel shows such as *World of Illusion* (2 versions, 1947–53, 39 venues, ↪ 092) and *Evolution of a Skyscraper* (1939–44, 17 venues, ↪ 094). The blending of images and text into modular panels with dynamic, often asymmetrical layouts is typical.[47] The CE programme made use of the large-scale typewriter described in the *Manual*, most likely a Swissa machine with Bulletin font or a Smith-Corona Speech-Riter. The use of reproductions is also striking—and contradictory. In exhibitions by the CE and in the *Manual*, photographs and art reproductions are invariably treated as illustrations and not artworks (even compared to prints) yet they were also considered uninflected substitutes for artworks. This attitude is notable in the *Manual*, as in the pronouncement that "it is better to substitute a photographic reproduction of a first-rate work of art than to assemble collections of second class material for tour".[48]

42 CE 54(1). "Design Exhibition", n.d. MoMA Archives, New York.
43 CE 54(1). MoMA Archives, New York.
44 Osborn, *Manual of Travelling Exhibitions*, p. 12.
45 Ibid., p. 11.
46 Ibid.
47 Curator Edward Steichen was notorious for photographic interventions, as discussed by Christopher Phillips in *The Contest of Meaning: Critical Histories of Photography*, MIT, Cambridge 1989.

Osborn also organised shows involving actual objects, usually replaceable design objects. The example in the *Manual,* from *What is Good Design?* (1942–1945, 17 venues, ↻096), is typical. The related schematic drawing (Diagram D, ↻034) suggests a protected apparatus for more valuable objects, but its viability is questionable. Not noted in the *Manual* is the occasional acquisition of objects by the public documented in CE records.

Fixture design in the *Manual* also reflects the influence of Victor D'Amico, who worked closely with Osborn on *Elements of Design.* Design was integral to D'Amico's approach, and he was especially adept at child-centred projects. The folding display case of the *Manual* is characteristic ↻097. The hands-on, desk-like structure was designed for a version of Philip Johnson's famed 1934 *Machine Art* exhibition that travelled to schools (1941–44, 6 venues) and is a remarkable departure from the Museum installation of the show. At mid-century, D'Amico developed similar furnishings for the well-known Children's Art Carnival, a popular, self-contained MoMA environment that was adapted for travel to Delhi, Milan, Barcelona, and Brussels. D'Amico even retrofitted a boat for art making; the Art Barge is active to this day.[49]

CONCLUSION

This opportunity to *carefully read* into the historical and rhetorical context of the *Manual* leads us ultimately back to Osborn, a formative yet under-recognised figure at MoMA whose experience continued at the AFA and was then institutionalised into the *Manual.* The record shows a pragmatic if uncritical administrator who mobilised contemporary communication techniques consistent with modernist principles of universalism, rationalism, and form, for purposes of global cultural exchange.

48 Osborn, *Manual of Travelling Exhibitions,* p. 18.
49 "The Barge History". The Art Barge, 12.04.2012. www.theartbarge.org/barge/the-barge-history/.

MUSEUMS AND MONUMENTS

The Museums and Monuments Division combined museological and archeological projects. Its publication series of the same name started with reprints from the UNESCO journal *Museum,* mostly on museological topics, and later on included books specifically developed for the series. The Museums and Monuments Division was the predecessor of the current Division of Cultural Heritage, which administers the World Heritage Program.

I
Sites and Monuments: Problems of Today Conditions
100 pages, 115 illustrations, plans, index, 2nd ed., 1953 (bilingual English and French).

II
The Care of Paintings
164 pages, 87 illustrations, diagrams, index, 2nd ed., 1952 (bilingual English and French).

III
Cuzco: Reconstruction of the Town and Restoration of its Monuments
56 pages, 64 illustrations and maps, 1952 (also in French and Spanish).

IV
Saint Sophia of Ochrida: Preservation and Restoration of the Building and its Frescoes
28 pages, 37 illustrations and maps, 1953 (also in French).

V
Manual of Travelling Exhibitions
112 pages, 18 diagrams, 70 illustrations, 1953 (also in French).

VI
Lebanon: Suggestions for the Plan of Tripoli and for the Surroundings of the Baalbeck Acropolis
48 pages, 1 map, 7 diagrams, 44 illustrations, 1954 (also in French).

VII
Syria: Problems of Preservation and Presentation of Sites and Monuments
52 pages, 61 illustrations, 3 maps, 1954 (also in French and Arabic).

VIII
Protection of Cultural Property in the Event of armed Conflict
346 pages, 124 figures, 137 illustrations, 1958 (also in French).

IX
The Organisation of Museums: Practical Advice
188 pages, 18 figures, 8 tables, 91 illustrations, 1959 (also in French).

X
Temporary and Travelling Exhibitions
123 pages, 23 figures, 88 illustrations, 1963 (also in French).

XI
The Conservation of Cultural roperty, with Special Reference to Tropical Conditions
Prepared in cooperation with the International Center for the Study of the Preservation and Restoration of Cultural Property, Rome, 341 pages, 60 figures, 43 illustrations, 1967 (also in French and Spanish).

XII
Field Manual for Museums
176 pages, 44 figures, 35 plates (also in French).

XIII
Underwater Archaeology: A nascent Discipline
308 pages, 97 figures, 67 plates, 1972 (also in French).

XIV
Preserving and Restoring Monuments and Historic Buildings
267 pages, 36 figures, 37 plates, 1972 (also in French).

XV
Museums, Imagination and Education
148 pages, 70 plates, 1973 (also in French).

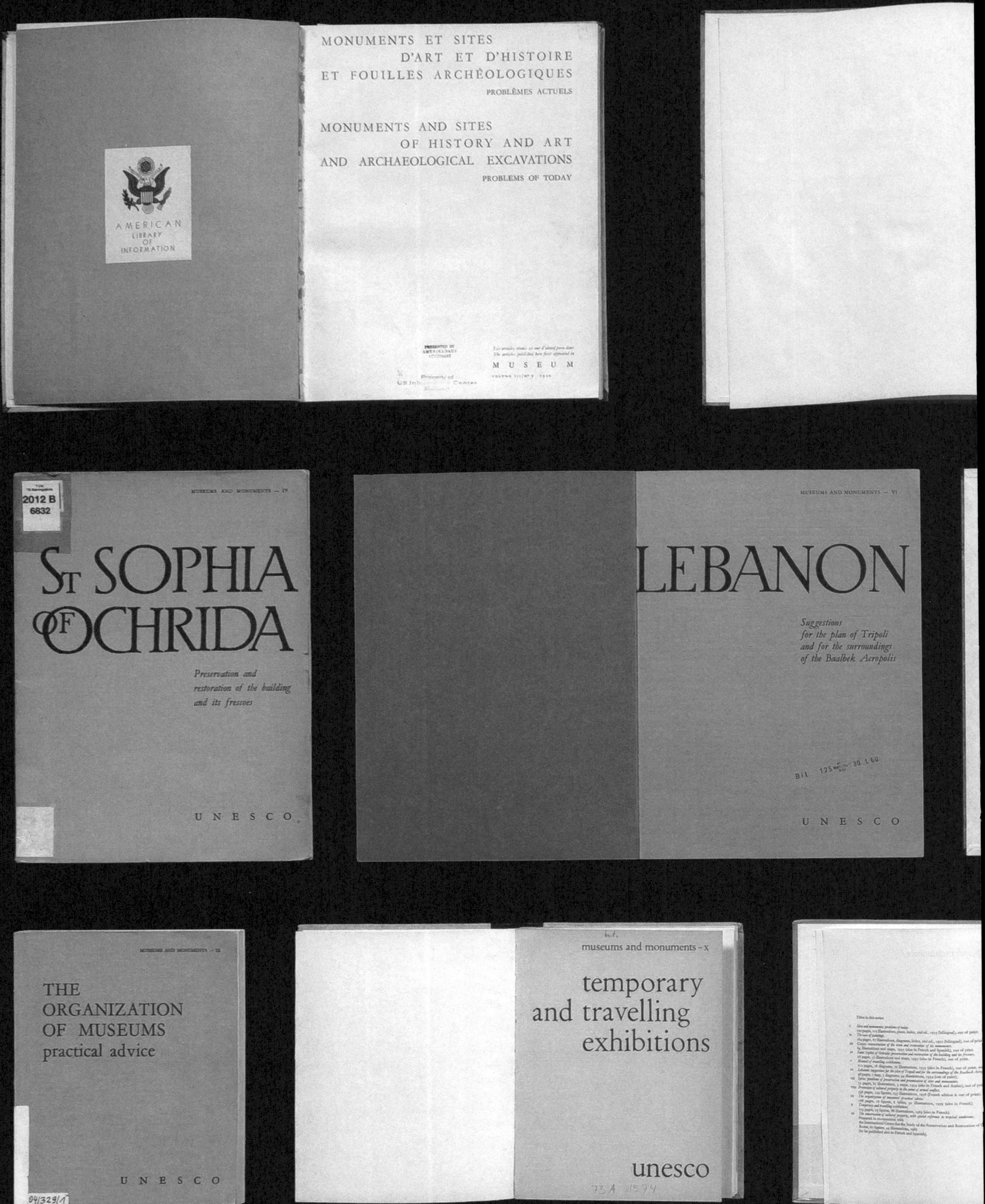

Fig. 07 I, II, III IV, VI, VII, VIII VIII, IX, X, XI, XII, XIII, XV

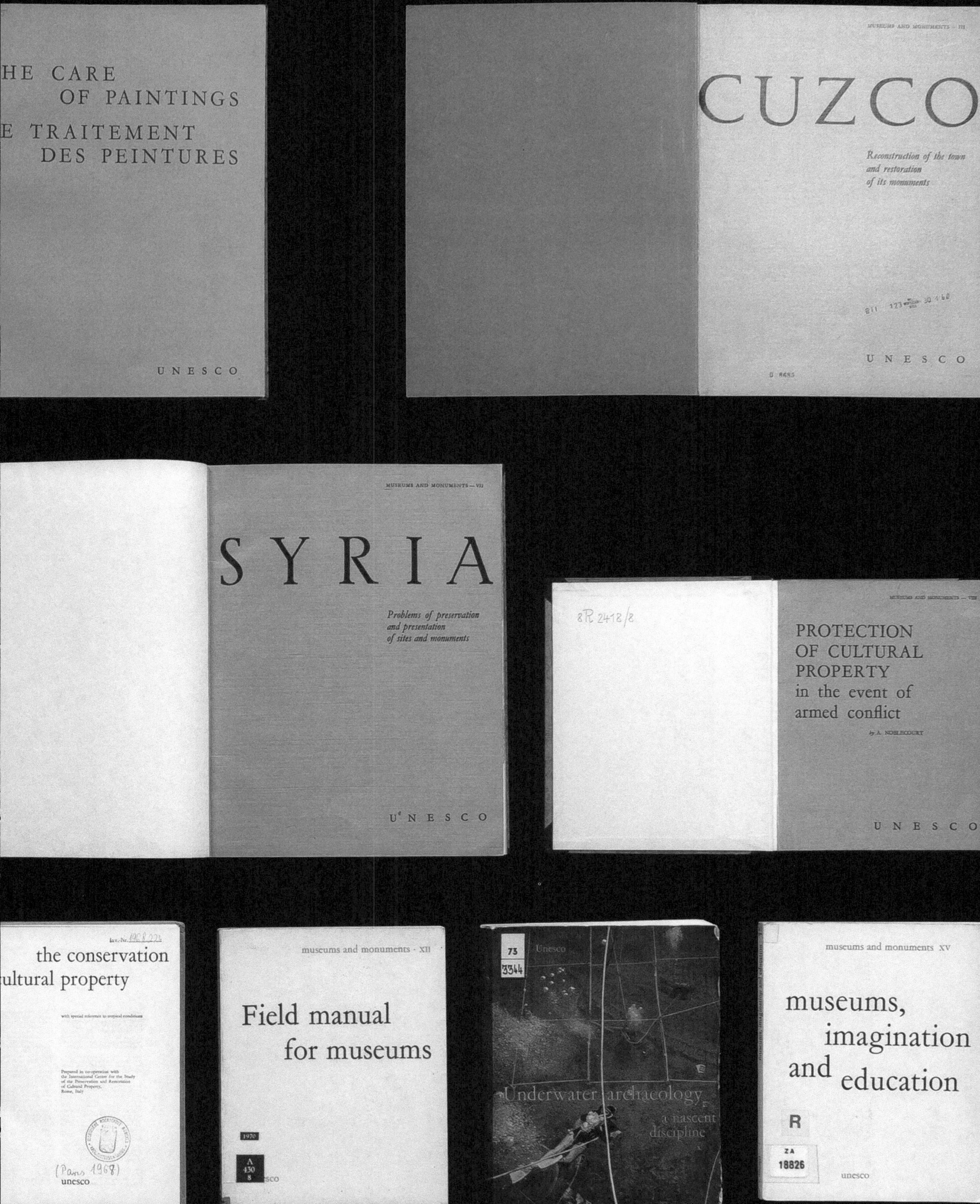
HE CARE
OF PAINTINGS
E TRAITEMENT
DES PEINTURES
UNESCO
MUSEUMS AND MONUMENTS — III
CUZCO
Reconstruction of the town
and restoration
of its monuments
UNESCO
MUSEUMS AND MONUMENTS — VII
SYRIA
Problems of preservation
and presentation
of sites and monuments
UNESCO
MUSEUMS AND MONUMENTS — VIII
PROTECTION
OF CULTURAL
PROPERTY
in the event of
armed conflict
by A. NOBLECOURT
UNESCO
the conservation
ultural property
unesco
museums and monuments · XII
Field manual
for museums
1970
Unesco
Underwater archaeology
a nascent
discipline
museums and monuments XV
museums,
imagination
and education
unesco

THE PROTOTYPE: THE V&A DEPARTMENT OF CIRCULATION

JOANNA WEDDELL

Elodie Courter Osborn (1911–1994) acknowledged the assistance of Peter Floud (1911–1960), Keeper of Circulation at the Victoria and Albert Museum (V&A), London, amongst the many specialist professionals consulted. In her introduction Osborn described the V&A Circulation Department, known in-house as Circ, as the "originator" and "prototype" for travelling exhibitions with "the most comprehensive facilities for this purpose". Osborn believed that "Such an example on the part of one of the principal museums of the world is an inspiration to other institutions to create educational programmes of similar merit".[1] Originally a Victorian government intervention to improve manufacturing and exports, Circ's 1947 incarnation harmonised with the post-war political mood as the Attlee government actively pursued state-control and reconstruction.

Floud started at the V&A as Circ's assistant keeper in 1935 and was a member of the Communist Party of Great Britain.[2] Floud, a dynamic and visionary Keeper from 1947 to 1960, developed a strong ethos of public service in the exhibitions programme and innovations in both display and acquisitions.[3] As Floud's *Times* obituary noted: "In building up the Department of Circulation after the war he had almost to begin anew, transforming the character of the department and bringing it in closer touch with the needs of the post-war world".[4] Floud introduced shorter loans and a range of exhibitions that responded to the very different needs of the host institutions which ranged from large city art galleries to working men's clubs. Floud's scholarly understanding of British industrial design was linked to his role as an arm of the Civil Service in the Department of Education and Science.

In 1951 a joint UNESCO and ICOM meeting of experts on museums and education emphasised the need to extend the educational influence of museums across the whole population.[5] The meeting agreed that museums should aim to connect exhibitions with everyday contemporary life, adapt opening hours to improve accessibility for all, promote free admission, and make exhibition labels didactic so that costly catalogues were unnecessary. This last point was one pursued by Floud in Circ displays.

From early in 1947 Circ produced self-contained travelling exhibitions for loan to regional museums and art galleries that were accompanied by posters and press handouts for publicity, descriptive notes mounted on a lectern, and individual object labels. At this stage only a minority of Circ's shows were accompanied by additional illustrated booklets and introductory leaflets, though information was provided for those galleries wishing to issue their own catalogues. The lectern can be seen as metonymic, standing for Circ's ethos of access for all.

Floud made it clear that "The labelling of the exhibitions tends to be rather fuller than in the Victoria and Albert Museum itself, and in some cases the whole method

1 Elodie Courter Osborn, *Manual of Travelling Exhibitions,* UNESCO, Paris 1953, p. 11.

2 Linda Sandino, "Art School Trained Staff and Communists in the V&A Circulation Department, c. 1947–1958", Artists Work in Museums: Histories, Interventions, Subjectivities, ed. Matilda Pye and Linda Sandino, Wunderkammer Press, Bath 2013.

3 Joanna Weddell, "The Ethos of the Victoria & Albert Museum Circulation Department 1947–1960", Design Objects and the Museum, ed. Liz Farrelly and Joanna Weddell, Bloomsbury, London 2016, pp. 15–25.

4 "Peter Floud Obituary", *The Times,* 25.01.1960.

5 Grace L. McCann Morley, Report of the Rapporteur, Joint UNESCO and ICOM Meeting of Experts on Museums and Education, 13.02.1952, Para 5.

6 Peter Floud, V&A Museum Circulation Department: Its History and Scope, V&A Museum, HMSO, London [n.d.] post-1949, p. 5.

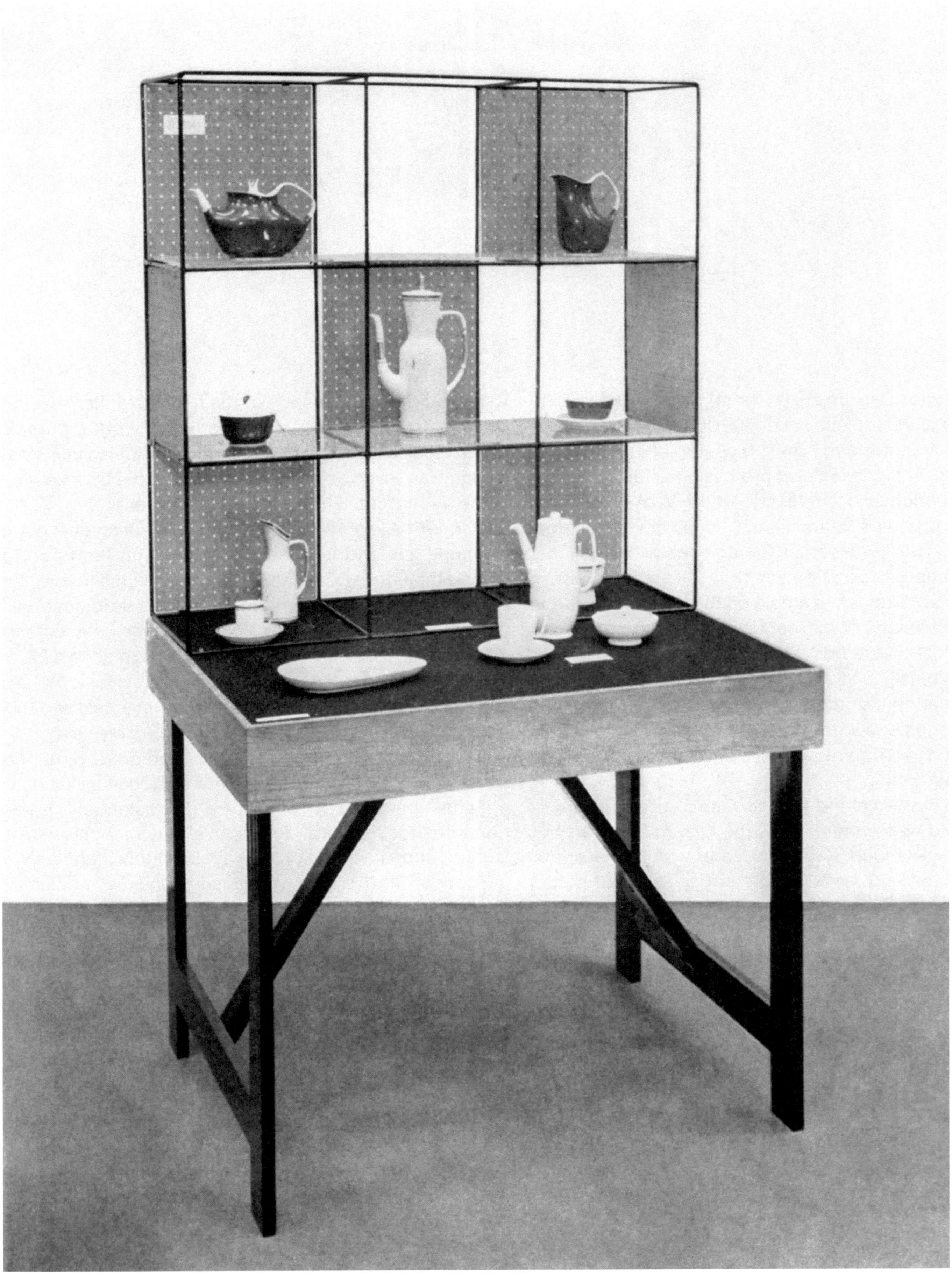

08

Fig. 08 Open display for pottery, designed by Elizabeth Aslin for the Victoria and Albert Museum, London

of presentation is frankly didactic".[6] In Floud's view "all museums can be of use to intelligent teachers" and museums are "anxious to be of use", offering not merely the chance to "accumulate new information" but "an extra breadth and reality that is unattainable in the classroom". Circ's travelling exhibitions were designed as complete entities; venues did not need to add their own material, and indeed should not without prior consultation. Floud stressed the importance of established channels of distribution without which circulating exhibitions would "moulder in the storage vaults of the bureaucratic organisations".[7] Bennett notes that the earlier, Victorian, South Kensington Museum "[...] marked a significant turning-point in the development of British museum policy in clearly enunciating the principles of the modern museum conceived as an instrument of public education. It provided the axis around which London's museum complex was to develop throughout the rest of the century and exerted a strong influence on the development of museums in the provincial cities and towns".[8]

As part of the Ministry of Education & Science in the post-war period, Circ can be read as a clear continuation of Bennett's model in its approach.

In spite of Floud's reference to loans to secondary schools in the *Draft Script,* these were gradually phased out as the education sector expanded with the rise in school leaving age and demand increased beyond Circ's ability to provide such a service. Circ's collection did "not in any way represent a collection of throw-outs, discarded as being unworthy of exhibition at South Kensington, or even of second-class examples of lesser monetary value",[9] as Floud is also keen to emphasise in the *Draft Script.* Some travelling exhibitions did tour abroad but Floud's ambition to send shows to "the Dominions and Colonies" was largely unrealised. Circ exhibitions with a broadly national identity were toured either under the auspices of the British Council, for example *English Silver* 1660–1830 travelling to Amsterdam, Rome, Geneva, and Copenhagen in 1957, or by trade organisations promoting exports, such as a version of *English Chintz,* 1960, sent to South Africa and Australia by the Manchester Cotton Board.

In the earlier UNESCO publication, *Museums and Circulating Exhibitions* (1950) Circ's work is extensively illustrated, and shows a curatorial selection of objects and arrangement of displays, displays in London and the regions, the work of packers and drivers, and the wide range of material toured and display methods used. In the early 1950s Circ did begin to experiment with open display units of a similar size to the older enclosed floor cases that could be placed in the middle of a gallery or against a wall. This display method accompanied more innovative design exhibitions of contemporary tableware, new to the public as it was for export or import from abroad and, crucially, was of low monetary value.

In the 1953 UNESCO *Manual of Travelling Exhibitions* just two illustrations show the work of V&A packers and drivers in regional installation, while there is a wealth of images of modern displays from MoMA. In contrast, the V&A illustrations show traditional collapsible display cases dating from 1909 which, even if updated by bleaching the wood lighter, did not begin to be replaced with more modern metal-framed showcases by the Ministry of Works until 1959. Some older cases were still in use in 1963.

Floud reorganised the display categories in 1954, introducing larger and more valuable exhibitions displayed either wholly or partly on newer display units. Circ created displays in the V&A restaurant, next to its own offices, and from 1954 began showing contemporary furnishing fabrics and wallpapers selected by the Department directly from foreign manufacturers. These shows were surveys of "the most significant work" of foreign designers, much of which had not been seen in Britain before, and which were then circulated to museums and art galleries, with the V&A imprimatur. The display was flexible with regional curators able to show loose fabrics hanging against walls or screens in long lengths hung from wires and rods; labels were sewn on at eye level and the use of spotlights encouraged.[10]

Continuing this more tactile approach, in 1956 Circ exhibited the first of a planned series of contemporary ceramics – "the most interesting of the industrial wares which have been recently designed in a modern spirit" – again in the V&A restaurant for later regional circulation.[11] Ceramics were displayed on newly produced open display units, bringing them closer to a contemporary department store display, a contrast to the heavy, glazed and locked Edwardian vitrines. The restaurant displays had been used as a trial and "Many people showed a

7 Peter Floud, "Commentary on a Projected International Circulating Exhibition: The Museum, an Educational Center", typescript memorandum, International Council of Museums (ICOM), United Nations Educational, Scientific and Cultural Organisation (UNESCO), WS/101.108, Paris, 30.10.1951.

8 Tony Bennett, *The Birth of the Museum,* Routledge, London 1995, pp. 70–72, p. 81.

9 Peter Floud, "The Circulation Department of the Victoria & Albert Museum", *Museum: Museums and Circulating Exhibitions,* Paris: UNESCO, III. 4: 852 (1950): pp. 296–303. 16 illustrations, pp. 39–55.

10 *The Victoria and Albert Museum Circulation Department Exhibitions 1956: Exhibitions for Loan to Museums, Art Galleries and Libraries,* HMSO, London 1955, p. 16, MA/17/3/2 Circ Exhibition and Loan Collection Prospectuses, V&A. T13 Contemporary American Furnishing Fabrics, T14 Contemporary German Furnishing Fabrics, T15 Contemporary Scandinavian Furnishing Fabrics, T16 Contemporary Italian, Swiss and French Furnishing Fabrics, each valued at £300.

great desire to touch the pottery, and this was not entirely discouraged."[12] The advantage of an open display in drawing public attention and interest was felt to outweigh the disadvantages, even though few regional museums would be able to provide continuous warding.

The expectation was that visitors would touch and handle the objects, in spite of the caveat that the shows would need careful supervision. The experimental nature of these open displays had prompted the acquisition of the easily replaceable tableware. These new displays had been specially designed in-house by Elizabeth Aslin with a wooden table base covered in black felt with black painted legs folding in underneath for transport (Fig. 08). The base supported black enamelled iron grids with clear Perspex shelves, the grid squares alternately backed by perforated boards. The backing boards were for hanging flat objects and painted in five bright colours to contrast with the paler china. In an approach adopted from American museums, objects were secured with adhesive tape both to prevent accidents and to deter theft, although it was recognised that this was not a "satisfactory deterrent to pilfering".[13]

Here both the nature of the objects and the method of display create "an exhibition which introduces, exceptionally, the atmosphere of the department store, the poor man's museum".[14] As in Bourdieu, Darbel & Schnapper, these "objects which could have been supplied to the public by a large department store, its location and even the publicity which preceded it made it a cultural event and it was therefore more directly addressed to a cultivated public. The mere fact that they should be consecrated by their presentation in a consecrated place is sufficient in itself to profoundly change the meaning (and more precisely the level of supply) of works which would be more accessible if exhibited in a familiar place."[15]

In spite of the reluctance of the main Museum to exhibit contemporary objects, Circ may have hoped or "assumed that a museum will have a more diverse public, the greater the diversity of the works it exhibits", in pursuit of access for all, though Bourdieu, Darbel & Schnapper found no such causal effect.[16] Circ's display and motive appear similar to the Museum of Modern Art's popular *Useful Objects* shows that toured in the US, promoting *good design* choices to the consumer.[17] Similar initiatives include the Walker Art Center's Everyday Art Gallery,[18] perhaps more overtly didactic, and in the UK, the Council of Industrial Design's *good design* exhibitions, some also staged in department stores.[19] The background of some Circ staff in department store display and the Department's preference for using external, rather than in-house, designers should be noted.

The appropriation of the department store display for the touring exhibition may represent an attempt by curatorial authority to aestheticise the production of commodities, or may show that cultural production has itself submitted to commodification.[20] The ability to act as a distanced but authoritative locus for a meeting between (low) industrial design and (high) art may be seen as a distinctive feature of Circ's contemporary displays, allowing them to elide categorisation as a straightforward agent of commodification or aestheticisation.

11 *The Victoria and Albert Museum Circulation Department Exhibitions 1957: Exhibitions for Loan to Museums, Art Galleries and Libraries,* HMSO, London 1956, pp. 1–4, MA/17/3/3 Circ Exhibition and Loan Collection Prospectuses, V&A. C15 Modern Tablewares, from Germany, Holland and Italy; C16 Modern Scandinavian Tablewares.
12 Hugh Wakefield, "Open Display", *Museums Journal,* 1957, p. 243.
13 Ibid.
14 Pierre Bourdieu and Alain Darbel with Dominique Schnapper, *The Love of Art: European Art Museums and Their Public,* trans. Caroline Beattie and Nick Merriman, Polity Press, Cambridge [1969] 1991, p. 50.
15 Ibid., p. 90.
16 16 Ibid., p. 86.
17 Mary Anne Staniszewski, *The Power of Display, a History of Exhibition Installations at the Museum of Modern Art,* MIT Press, Massachusetts 1999, pp. 160–190.
18 Arthur J. Pulos, *The American Design Adventure,* MIT Press, Massachusetts 1988, pp. 68–77.
19 Ness Wood, "'I Would Suggest That You Should Not think of the Design Center as a Museum; It is a Live, Active, Moving Thing': *Designs of the Year,* 1957", *Design Objects and the Museum,* ed. Liz Farrelly and Joanna Weddell, Bloomsbury, London 2016, pp. 27–40.
20 Paul Wood, "Commodity", *Critical Terms for Art History,* ed. Robert Nelson and Richard Shiff, University of Chicago Press, Chicago 1996, pp. 382–406.

DRAFT SCRIPT OF A RADIO INTERVIEW WITH PETER FLOUD

[MA/15/14]

Draft Script.

B. Now I want to introduce Peter Floud, who is in charge of the Circulation Department at the Victoria and Albert Museum. Tell me, what is this Circulation Department. I'm afraid I've never heard of it.

F. Well; its a special Department of the Museum which sends round exhibitions - circulates them in fact - to all parts of the British Islés, and sometimes to the Empire too. It has very large special collections which are used entirely for this purpose.

B. That sounds an excellent scheme. You've recently started it have you ?

F. Good Heavens, no. It has a very long history. In fact we're celebrating our centenary this year.

B. Really. How's that ? Surely the Victoria and Albert Museum isnt loo years old yet ?

F. Its not far short of it, but, you see, this business of circulating exhibitions round the country goes back before the foundation of the Museum. As far as I know, what happened was this. In the 1830's people began to get worried about the low standard of British industrial design. They were apprehensive that if the

09

Fig. 09 – Fig. 13 Draft Script of a radio Interview with Peter Floud, Keeper of the Circulation Department at the Victoria & Albert Museum, London, UK (n.d. 1948), MA/15/14, V&A Archive.

general level of design wasnt improved, British production - porcelain, glass, silks, and so on - would be unable to compete with the high-class French and Italian goods. One of the main steps that they took, was to set up a chain of Art Schools - Schools of Design, they were called, - all over the country, where industrial workers could be trained. It soon occured to someone that these Schools would do better work if the students could see fine examples of applied art such as Sevres porcelain or Venetian glass, so, in 1848 a Mr. Gruner was given £100 and sent off to Italy to buy a collection of such things. Some of them were kept in London, but the others were circulated round the provincial schools. That was really the start of the whole scheme, for this little collection was later taken over by the ~~Museum of Ornamental Art~~ South Kensington Museum, which subsequently became the Victoria and Albert Museum. Throughout all this 100 years the principle of sending special collections circulating round the country has always continued.

B. I suppose the collection bought with this £100 has grown enormously during the course of these 100 years.

F. Oh yes, out of all proportion. I dont know what

the value of the circulation collections now is, but they include about 60,000 different items. XX I suppose they must be worth about ¼ million pounds. Of course it hasnt grown only in numbers, the whole scope of the scheme is much wider now than it was originally. The original idea was that the standard of industrial design could quickly be improved by making sure that the artisans actually working in the cotton mills or the potteries could sit down and copy beautiful historic exmaples. Of course it later became obvious that this wasnt enough, and that the consumer must be helped to improve his taste as well. They therefore decided that these special collections should be sent round not only to the Art Schools, but also to provincial Museums where they could be seen by the general public, and, at the end of the first world war, they made an even more important change and decided to send round special exhibitions to Secondary Schools and Teachers Training Colleges as well. That was a clear recognition that standards of taste are most easily influenced while the future consumer is still at school.

B. One thing puzzles me. You spoke about having 60,000 different objects. Surely that must mean that the standard is rather low. Isnt it inevitable that all the best things remain in the Museum in South Kensington, and that its only the second-rate material that is sent round to the provinces.

F. Of course we have to guard against that. But its not too difficult. You see, in some fields the V. and A. is so rich that it can easily lend out wonderful examples without noticeably depleting the London collections at all; for example, English embroideries, or Chinese porcelain. Only this morning I was looking through the loan collection of English water-colours, and came across some beautiful Turners and Constables. The standard's really very high on the whole.

B. When you're dealing with so much valuable material, isnt the question of transport rather a headache. Dont you have a lot of breakages ?

F. No. Its amazing how few we have. The Museum has a team of skilled packers, who've really developed their work to a fine art. I've seen them pack up a collection of delicate wine-glasses so skilfully that they arrive absolutely safe after having been thrown about on the railways helf across England. For instance, a collection of English pottery and porcelain which we sent to South Africa arrived absolutely intact.

B. That reminds me. I was wanting to ask you about lending things to the Empire.

F. We're hoping to do this on a much bigger scale in the next few years. Up till now we havent been able to include the Empire in any organised system of loans, but we have sent quite a number of exhibits around at various times. As far as I can remember at this moment we have collections of pottery in South Africa, some costumes in Tasmania, and some small collections of .... in Australia. Of course we realise that this is only a drop in the ocean compared to the tremendous demand that there is in all the Dominions and Colonies. Obviously its going to be a big job to organise anything really satisfactory, but we're determined to do so. After all, the national museum collections in London really belong to the whole Empire, and we must do our best to see that at least a part of their enormous riches are made available to the colonies and dominions.

THE LANGUAGE OF THE WORLD MUSEUM

NADER VOSSOUGHIAN

By 1933, the Austrian Otto Neurath's Museum of Society and Economy had opened satellite branches in Amsterdam, The Hague, London, Berlin, and Moscow. By 1933, Neurath had published his *Society and Economy* (1930), *The Colourful World* (1929), *Technology and Humanity* (1932), and *Pictorial Statistics according to the Vienna Method for Schools* (1933). By 1933, Neurath was receiving visitors from all over the world and travelling throughout all of Europe and Asia. During the same period of time, Neurath was one year shy of leaving Vienna for good. National Socialism was gaining sway in Austria and the Museum of Society and Economy in Vienna would become one of its earliest casualties. This is not to say that all was lost, as in 1934 Neurath would be able to re-establish himself in The Hague, where he had only recently opened his International Foundation for Visual Education. Moreover, he was also taking his ideas about museums in new directions. In 1933, Neurath published a seminal statement in the progressive American social welfare journal *Survey Graphic,* in which he made the bold and somewhat grandiose claim that the serial reproduction of modern museums could promote the democratisation of culture in economic and cultural terms.[1] It could do so economically, Neurath reasoned, because Fordist assembly line production methods could help reduce costs incurred through the purchasing and displaying of exhibits, and culturally, he contended, because standardising museums could foster a common sense of history and tradition worldwide. As Neurath remarked in the pages of *Survey Graphic,* "to speak of the museum of the future is like speaking of the automobile of the future. Automobiles are manufactured in series and not produced one by one in a smithy".[2]

According to Neurath, just as he had perfected the standardisation of museum displays during the 1920s—developing uniform standards for graphic representation, layout, and production—so too had he now reached a point where he was prepared to produce copies of his museum that he could disseminate all throughout the world. For him, the museum had become an increasingly ephemeral medium whose identity was no longer site-specific. Accordingly, he began to view the modern museum as a form of communication whose boundaries were no longer constrained by physical matter: "Just as in Vienna the Department of Transformation has succeeded in securing complete unity of method", he wrote, referring to what would later be known as the Isotype (or International System of Typographic Picture Education), "so our effort should be to create a similarly uniform method for all the museums of a country—yes, of the whole world. Only through a unified, planned, central control of all museums and educational institutions is it possible to lead the public from one museum to another with the greatest benefit to its education, and thereby to

1 An excellent background source on the history of survey graphics is Cara Finnegan, *Social Welfare and Visual Politics: The Story of Survey Graphic.* Available from www.newdeal.feri.org/sg/essay.htm.

2 Otto Neurath, "Museums of the Future", in *Empiricism and Sociology,* ed. Marie Neurath and Robert Stohne Cohen, Reidel, Dordrecht 1973, p. 218.

make the individual more and more familiar with the world in which he lives. Museums, exhibitions and periodicals might be regarded as three different means of education with the identical purpose of making him less afraid of the world in which he lives."[3]

In order to realise his dream of a mechanically reproducible museum, Neurath began to work out, conceptually, "universal spaces", that is, exhibition halls that could be adapted to any geographical or cultural circumstance.[4] He began developing them in conjunction with the artist Gerd Arntz, whom he had met in 1926 and had been working with since 1928. On account of his contact with the German avant-garde, Arntz, like Neurath, wanted to merge what objects *say,* semiotically speaking, with how they *appear,* in ontological terms. Arntz was a socialist concerned with making social reality accessible to the masses, and he sought accordingly to develop a visual idiom that could cast the plight of the working class in a dialectical light, that is to say, in relation to the larger economic *superstructure* of modern society. At the same time, Arntz wanted his work to be accessible and not overly abstract. His and Neurath's was thus a search for the primal beginnings of language, where "groups of people are truly represented by groups of people",[5] as Arntz once put it, much as rationalist philosopher Leibniz had sought to achieve in his own work on the scientific origins of language. Arntz and Neurath sought to create *meta-Isotypes,* that is, three-dimensional axonometric and two-dimensional elevation drawings that illustrated how, ideally, the graphic displays of the Museum of Society and Economy could be standardised in space and time.

In trying to account for Neurath's preoccupation with standardisation and museums, a more compelling answer, I would argue, is to look at Neurath's relationship with the Belgian bibliographer and museum director Paul Otlet, whose efforts to consolidate the knowledge of the world into a single, common database paralleled Neurath's concern for democratising the dissemination of culture and information. Otlet had founded his *World Palace* in 1910 with the intention of creating an international museum of world culture. In 1928, he initiated talks to create a great "World City" in Geneva, with assistance from Le Corbusier and his cousin Pierre Jeanneret. Neurath was inspired by the ambition and scope of Otlet's World City endeavor, and it undoubtedly exercised an indelible influence on him in terms of helping him elaborate further his thoughts on modern museums. Neurath wanted to bring knowledge and rationality to the masses, and he recognised in Otlet's vision of a World Museum a means of achieving this ideal in the realm of cultural production. "In our own day Paul Otlet (Palais Mondial, Brussels) is taking a step further", Neurath wrote in 1936. "His idea is the building of a *Cite Mondiale* for the organisation of museums and the distribution of printed materials and pictures. He made a start to get together picture material from all countries. He has the desire to get museums of a new sort started in all countries: MUNDANEUMs, that is, museums of man's development."[6] In hindsight, Neurath probably mischaracterised Otlet's goals—the idea of standardising museums throughout the world was more his dream than Otlet's—but Otlet nevertheless helped Neurath adapt his ideas about museums to the global arena, to consider how his philosophy about museums and visual communication could be executed on an international scale.

Otlet began the World Palace with exhibits drawn from the 1910 Brussels World's Fair *(Exposition Universelle et Internationale).* He started it with help from Henri La Fontaine, with whom he collaborated on the creation of a mammoth card catalogue from 1895 onwards (the catalogue boasted 1.5 million entries in 1897 and over 9 million by 1912).[7] The creation of the World Palace drew inspiration, if partially, from the Scottish naturalist and town planner Patrick Geddes, a figure who played a significant role in the World's Fairs of 1900 in Paris and 1910 in Brussels. Geddes had himself dreamed of creating a universal "index museum to the world" during the last decade of the nineteenth century.[8] Otlet, like Geddes, believed that museums and exhibitions were forums for showcasing the unity of human knowledge, and he sought to create a microcosm of the world that he could nurture and cultivate in a single enclosed space. As Otlet wrote in 1914, the museum "tends to become a world in miniature, a cosmoscope that permits the viewing and understanding of man, society, the universe".[9] At the World Palace, Otlet stressed uniformity and coherence. "It must be a museum of average types and standards",[10] he wrote, and in the curating of displays he was partial to innovations in transportation and communication (e.g., the creation of canals, the postal

3 Otto Neurath, "Museums of the Future", *in Empiricism and Sociology,* ed. Marie Neurath and Robert Stohne Cohen, Reidel, Dordrecht 1973, p. 222.

4 There is great debate as to when Neurath and Arntz actually began experimenting with the design of standardised museums. The Otto and Marie Neurath Isotype Collection in Reading dates these studies to Neurath's latter years in Holland (approximately 1938–1940). I however, would probably date their inception sooner (to as soon as 1933), given that Neurath had already published an elevation rendering of a 'universal' museum space in his International Picture Language of 1936. See Otto Neurath, *International Picture Language,* Reading University of Reading Department of Typography & Graphic Communication, Reading 1980, p. 43.

5 Gerd Arntz, "Zur Methode des Gesellschafts- und Wirtschaftsmuseum in Wien", in *Arbeiterbildung in der Zwischenkriegszeit: Otto Neurath — Gerd Arntz.* ed., Friedrich Stadler, Locker Verlag, Vienna and Munich 1982, Originally published in A–Z (1930).

6 Otto Neurath, *International Picture Language,* p. 64.

7 For a more in-depth treatment of Otlet's life and career, see W Boyd Rayward, "The Origins of Information Science and the International Institute of Bibliography/International Federation for Information and Documentation (FID)", *Journal of the American Society of Information Science 48,* 1997; W Boyd Rayward, "The Case of Paul Otlet, Pioneer of Information Science, Internationalist, Visionary: Reflections on Biography", 1991; W Boyd Rayward, "Introduction", *International Organisation and Dissemination of Knowledge: Selected Essays of Paul Otlet,* ed., W Boyd Rayward, Elsevier, Amsterdam 1990.

8 For a treatment of Geddes' contribution to the Paris Worlds Fair, see Philip Boardman, *The Worlds of Patrick Geddes: Biologist, Town Planner, Re-Educator, Peace-Warrior,* Routledge & Kegan Paul, London 1978, 178–184; Pieter van Wesemael, *Architecture of Instruction and Delight: A Socio–Historical Analysis of World Exhibitions as a Didactic Phenomenon* (1798–1851–1970), 010 Publishers, Rotterdam 2001), p. 433.

9 "Par leurs moyen, il tend à devenir un Monde en miniature, un Cosmoscope, permettant de voir et de comprendre l'Homme, la Société, l'Univers". Paul Otlet, *Le Musee International: Notice-Catalogue,* Office Central des Associations Internationals, Brussels 1914, p. 7.

10 "Ça doit être un Musée des meilleurs types et des standards". Paul Otlet, Ibid.

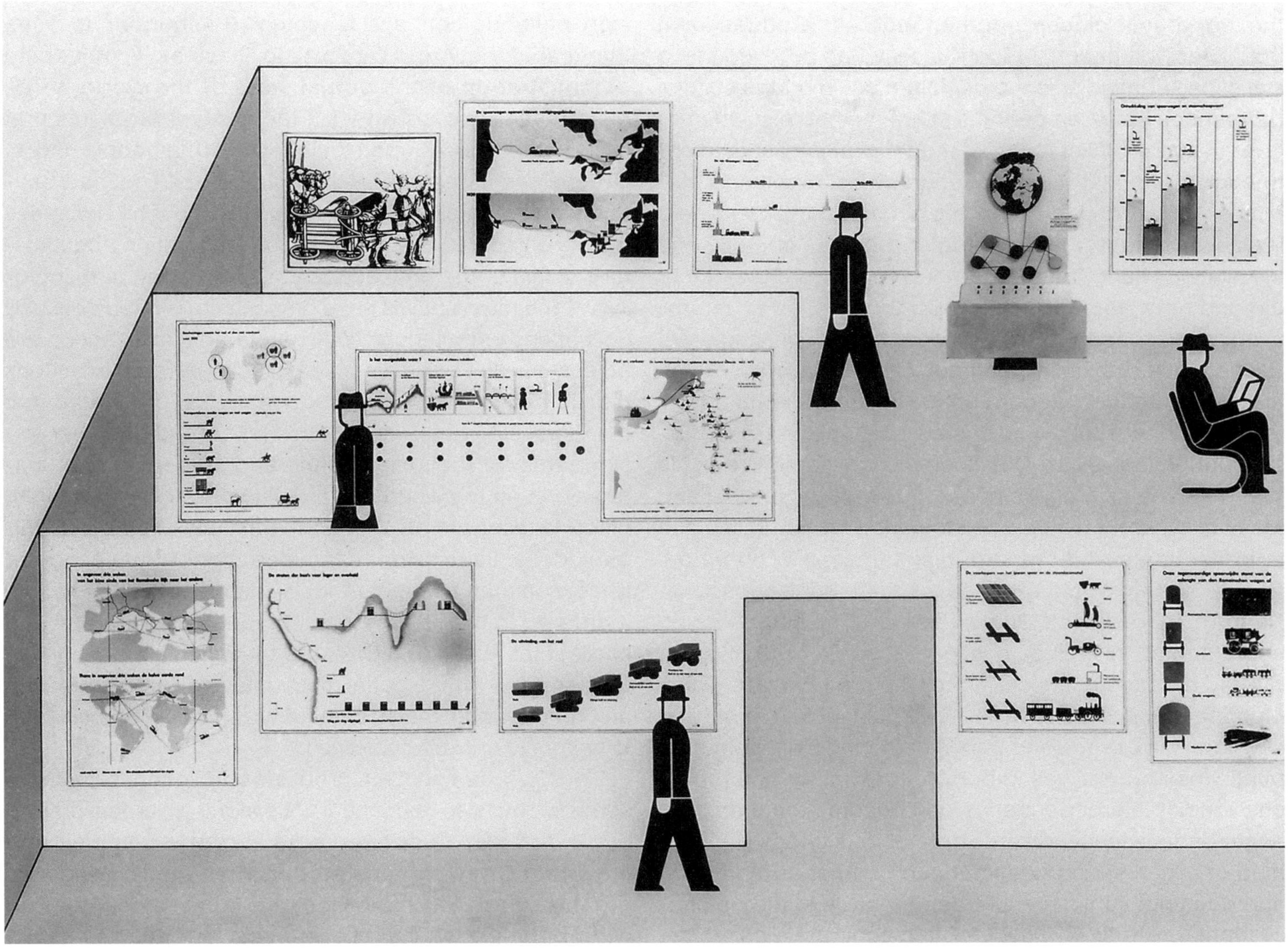

14

Fig. 14 *Museum without boundaries.* Design for a travelling exhibit (1936–1938). Collaboration between Neurath's International Foundation for Visual Education and the National Tuberculosis Association.

service, the telegraph, the telephone, etc.). For Otlet, the world of communication represented the glue that brought the world ever closer together, much as Geddes' own intellectual forebearer, Frédéric le Play, had believed that a statistically-based science of culture could bridge cultural differences between peoples in France and elsewhere.[11] Over the years, Otlet featured model airplanes and scientific tools and instruments, geographical maps and diagrams representing the earth and all its nations. There were vitrines laid out for the viewing of precious objects, and installations hung from all corners. There were projectors old and new, and gadgets drawn from the ages: microscopes, telescopes, navigation devices, and printing tools. Otlet organised exhibits geographically by nation or region and comparatively according to research methodology (e.g., historical, biological, or statistical analysis).

During the 1920s, Otlet increasingly came to see his World Palace as a public space that brought people and ideas of different nationalities together, as well as a place to consolidate and manage disinterested information. Post 1930, this would exercise a significant influence on Neurath, who shared Otlet's view that museums could serve social, as well as intellectual ends. In 1924, Otlet drafted his statements calling for the creation of a global Mundaneum, which he believed should include a university, library, museum, and public gathering hall. Promoting public intercourse was important for him, as "the repercussions of interdependence can become too cramped, engenders violence, disorder, disastrous chaos [...] if the idea of organisation does not carry with it coordination and does not sublimate interdependency to the point of solidarity".[12] In 1928, Otlet solicited concrete architectural proposals for the World City from Le Corbusier and from his partner and cousin Pierre Jeanneret. Although Otlet would have had reason to select the Belgian Garden City designer Louis Van der Swaelmen instead, who had created a prototype World City outside Brussels, he decided upon Le Corbusier because of his international prestige and his previous involvement in the 1927 League of Nations competition.[13]

In their joint publication *Mundaneum* (1928), Otlet and Le Corbusier outlined their plans for the World City. Otlet stated that the project was to be built on the shores of Lake Geneva, consisting of "a scientific association, museum, library, university, and institute. Together, they assume the functions of research, documentation, discussion, collaboration, and teaching."[14] According to Otlet, the goal of the World City was to "have as its object the demonstration of the actual state of the world, of its mechanisms, complexity [...] the general problems that impose themselves upon the attention of a people and its citizens and its leaders".[15] Otlet did not spell out how anyone would actually *live* in the world city, but he did stress that its core buildings would house information about history, science, the arts, education, geography, and sociology: "The museum will have presentations of objects and collections of materials", Otlet wrote, "but its intention will be essentially to visualise ideas, feelings, [and] intentions that lie behind. It will be an 'Idearium'".[16] Otlet stated that the World City would set bibliographical and documentary standards for the maintenance and preservation of cultures around the world and that it would act as a meeting place to discuss and exchange political, social, and cultural ideas. Its mission resembled that of the League of Nations in that it sought to foster peace and security, but it differed in that its role was primarily to be cultural and intellectual. The World City was to maintain a network of relationships with regional museums and institutions from around the world, the majority of which would be beholden to uniformly applied guidelines.

In their design, Le Corbusier and Jeanneret sited a series of low-rise residential units along a garden-draped boulevard, which opened onto a sports complex and the World City's campus proper. Their public buildings, organised around the proposal's minor axis, featured wide-open plazas that allowed each structure to assert its distinct identity. They made provisions for docking and railway stations, an airport, highway, and extensive system of footpaths. Although in his conceptual schemas, Otlet intended that the World City be conceived on a global scale in relation to other intellectual centres worldwide, as well as on an architectural and regional level, Le Corbusier focused almost exclusively on the project's relationship to its immediate physical location. He made extensive provisions for automobile facilities and transportation infrastructure, but he entirely ignored larger-scale telecommunications issues, many of which were already being discussed by architects and planners

11 See Paul Otlet, *Le Musee International: Notice-Catalogue,* Office Central des Assiciations Internationals, Brussels 1914, p. 9.

12 "Les répercussions de cette interdépendence devenue plus étroite, engendreront désormais violence, désordre, chaos plus désastreux encore si l'idée d'organisation n'y vient apporter coordination et sublime l'interdépendance elle-même jusqu'à la solidarité". Paul Otlet, *Mundaneum,* L'Union des Associations Internationales, Brussels 1928, p. 3.

13 See Paul Otlet, *Le Musee International: Notice-Catalogue,* Office Central des Associations Internationals, Brussels 1914; Kenneth Frampton, "The Humanitarian v. the Utilitarian Ideal", *Architectural Design 38:* 3, 1968.

14 "Cést l'Association scientifique, le Musée, la Bibliothèque, l'Université, l'Institut. Ensemble ils assument les fonctions de recherche, de documentation, de discussion, de collaboration, d'enseignement". Paul Otlet, *Mundaneum,* L'Union des Associations Internationales, Brussels 1928, p. 6.

15 [His goal was to] "avoir pour objet une démonstration de l'état actuel du monde, de son mécanisme complexe [...] des problemes generaux qui s'imposent d'une manière permanente a l'attention des peuples et à leurs dirigeants". Paul Otlet, *Mundaneum.*

16 "[Il y aura au musée présentation d'objets et un ensembles de matériaux,] mais le but essentiel sera de visualiser les idées, les sentiments, les intentions à la places a l'arrière [...] Ce sera un 'Idearium'". Paul Otlet, *Mundaneum.*

during the 1920s. Instead, Le Corbusier and Jeanneret focused primarily on the planning of the World City campus itself, many of its buildings looked more inward than outward. Indeed, the focal point of their design was the ziggurat-shaped World Museum whose profile dominated the World City's skyline. "The terrain has its culminating point at the place of the World Museum", Le Corbusier wrote.[17] Seemingly withdrawn from the world, unfolding, as Le Corbusier describes it, like a film in slow motion, the World Museum was to narrate the history of mankind from its primal beginnings. As Le Corbusier commented, "this form is a triple nave that unrolls along a spiral. At the start of the spiral: on top, pre-historic times [...] then the first historical epoch. And descending the spiral, the following [historical epoch] and the next, the entirety of world civilisation. History and archeology accumulate more and more documents. We learn more and more how man maintained himself through different periods of cultural organisation. The diorama becomes more and more vast and more and more precise. The spiral enlarges its spiral, the space is augmented. The exhibition of objects in space and time provoke [one] like a clamour getting stronger and stronger. Everything is linked together; every act, crazy, egotistical, reckless, or disinterested, has its consequence. The map of the world gets larger, modifies, pounds like a [...] prize in a slow-motion cinema. What a lesson!"[18]

Le Corbusier's World Museum symbolised both the end and the beginning of history, bringing a new *globalised* order to fruition, as Otlet would have termed it, and inaugurating (symbolically speaking) a period of harmony and cooperation between the countries of the world. It was to contain – as Le Corbusier reports – "statistics and iconographies, graphics situated throughout", as well as "images, scientific reconstructions [...] products natural and artificial, etc.".[19] It was to be a testament to the emergence of a new *global* consciousness, one that transcended the nationalisms that defined the nineteenth century. For Le Corbusier, the World Museum was a gathering point for the world's citizens and that brought together all aspects of culture and society into a single place, and allowed for the democratic exchange of ideas and beliefs at a neutral site. Above all, its helicoidal shape evoked the Biblical Tower of Babel.[20] In other words, Otlet and Le Corbusier sought to evoke the primal *origins* of culture, much like Neurath and Arntz later on in the 1930s. Faced with the fallout from the First World War – the antagonisms, the buried enmity, the fear of further conflict – Le Corbusier wanted to give nations a means by which to develop a common sense of history and tradition, and he and Jeanneret seized on the ziggurat form as a means of representing global unity. This was in the spirit of Le Corbusier's *purist* works, a stage in his career that ran concurrently with his work on the World City. For Le Corbusier, as well as for the painter Amédée Ozenfant with whom he started the purist movement, purism was an aesthetic that restored unity to art and architecture, reviving platonic geometries and ideal proportional systems. For Le Corbusier, the World City and its ziggurat-shaped World Museum were but further iterations of the desire for absolute clarity and proportion, derived as they were from the Pythagorean Golden Section.

Inspired by the same spirit of pacifism and global peace, Neurath shared Le Corbusier's longing for peace and cooperation between nations. Like Le Corbusier, he also believed that appealing to *universal* systems of representation – whether pictorial graphics or Golden Sections – could help mend the world's differences on a cultural and social level. More than simply internationalists, however, the triumvirate Neurath, Otlet and Le Corbusier viewed human beings as *biological* animals whose faculties of perception were identical for everyone, regardless of ethnicity or belief. Indeed, increasingly over the course of the 1930s, Neurath would characterise his pictorial graphics as signs whose grammar and syntax were naturally suited to the *in-born* proclivities of the optic nerves. Similarly, from his early writings on purism onwards, Le Corbusier spoke of his abstract geometries in terms of them being projections of "primary sensations" native to human experience. As for Otlet, he considered himself an apologist of the empiricist philosophy of Herbert Spencer, Auguste Comte, and the rationalist legal scholar Edmond Picard, and he believed passionately that the ordering of human knowledge could be conducted as rationally as the ordering of nature herself.[21]

Yet differences would also emerge in their work. Neurath, for one, was deeply inspired by the grandeur of Le Corbusier's World City design, but in his own collaborations with Otlet he began to emphasise the decentralising

17 Paul Otlet, *Mundaneum,* p. 33.

18 "Cette forme est une triple nef se deroulant au long d'une spirale: en haut, les temps préhistoriques et la représentation succincte – d'ailleurs saissante – que nous en avons. Puis les premières époques dites historiques. Et descendant la spirale, à la suite les unes les autres, toutes les civilisations mondiales. L'histoire et l'archéologie accumulant de plus en plus les documents. Nous savons de plus en plus comment l'homme s'est maintenu à travers les formes differentes de l'organisation et de la culture. Le diorama devient de plus en plus vaste et de plus en plus précis. La spirale agrandit son déroulement, la place augment. L'éxposition des objets dans le lieu et le temps provoque comme une clameur de plus en plus forte. Tout s'enchaîne; tous les actes fous, égoïstes, téméraires ou désintéressés ont leur conséquence[...] La carte du monde grandit, se modifie, palpite comme une floraison prise au ralenti du cinema. Quel enseignement!" Ibid., pp. 36–37.

19 "[...] les statistiques, l'iconographie, les graphiques situent tout;" "[...] les graphiques, les images transmises, les reconstitutions scientifiques, etc. [...] [d]es produits naturels ou artificiels, etc." Ibid.

20 For a treatment of the symbolic and cosmological significance of the World Museum, see Alfred Willis, "The Exoteric and Esoteric Functions of Le Corbusier's Mundaneum", *Modulus,* 1980–1981.

21 Dario Matteoni and Giuliano Gresleri, *La Cittd Mondiale,* Marsilio Editori, Venice 1982, p. 65.

and decentering tendencies exhibited by mass forms of communication, as well as by modern museums. In other words, while Le Corbusier conceived of the World Museum as a hermetically sealed facility, Neurath interpreted Otlet's vision on a much more comprehensive scale. He wanted to dispense as much information as possible to as many people as possible. Le Corbusier picked up on the monasticism latent to Otlet's thinking, while Neurath spun out a more public interpretation of his work that made the undifferentiated masses its focal point, rather than the contemplative museum connoisseur. This effort to forge a museum for the masses was not new to Neurath. In Vienna, he was known to entice herds of strangers out of streetcars and into his Museum of Society and Economy for a late-night tour (no doubt much public pleading was involved). He boasted, in addition, that two thousand visitors saw his museum daily, usually during quick coffee breaks from work. Nevertheless, Neurath gained a great deal from his exchanges with Otlet, particular with regard to standardisation. In the World City, "one will collect and conserve objects", Otlet wrote, "but they will never have to be rare or precious, copies and reproductions will suffice in backing up ideas".[22] In many regards, Neurath picked up on just this sentiment and put it to the furthest extreme. If you can reproduce an entire collection, why can't you copy entire museums, buildings included? As I hope to show, Neurath was to stress this vein of thinking in his own work, but only after engaging Otlet's ideas for an extensive period of time.

Neurath first visited Otlet at the World Palace in the summer of 1929. Neither of them spoke the other's language fluently (Neurath wrote in his native German, while Otlet, in French), yet they felt an immediate affinity that smoothed over any communications barriers. "I would like to repeat again", Neurath wrote in a letter dated July 6th, immediately after his return from Brussels, "that the incredible set-up of your museum, [your] tough chase after all-encompassing international plans made a deep impression on me. I would happily guess, provided we orient our workshops and scientific partnership toward doing quality work in the service of the future Mundaneum, that we would be able to give your plans a technically complete shape and complement our own work."[23] A week later, Neurath forwarded Otlet the mission statement of his Museum of Society and Economy, which he had published in Vienna's *Österreichische Gemeinde-Zeitung* in 1925.[24] In that document, Neurath asserted that there was an unspoken demand for social museums in contemporary culture, that is to say, institutions that could relate the importance of macrosocial forces – the balance of trade between nations, for example – to the everyday life of the average worker. He lamented the then-prevalent tendency of equating museums with "curiosity cabinets" (i.e., places for housing strange and exotic objects), and he called upon like-minded socialists to embrace the use of mass media technologies, e.g., "models, films, slide shows, also illustrations, lectures, publications and all other appropriate means" in a museological context.[25]

Towards the end of July 1929, Neurath travelled to Geneva to hear Otlet speak at the annual meeting of the Union of International Associations, an organisation Otlet started in 1910 with the aim of providing an "international framework for intellectual relations" for museums, universities, libraries, and intergovernmental organisations all throughout the world.[26] This two-day summit, which took place from the 2nd to the 3rd of August, ran in conjunction with the third biennial conference of the World Federation of Education Associations, where Otlet and his World Palace presented an exhibit entitled *Atlas of Civilization* between July 25 and August 5, 1929.[27] That Neurath was eager to engage Otlet's ideas is attested to by the fact that he was among the first to enter his name among those who attended Otlet's World City presentation. Moreover, during the World Federation of Education Associations meeting, Neurath and Otlet publicly announced plans to begin to work on a series of book and exhibition projects.

In October of 1929, Otlet and Neurath formalised this announcement by signing a joint protocol agreement, which pledged extensive cooperation between their respective institutions. The agreement, tenable for a period of two years, was known as the "Novus Orbis Pictus (N.O.P), Brussels, Geneva, Vienna Protocol". The acronym N.O.P, was a reference both to the initials of Otlet and Neurath and to an early encyclopedic picture book by Johann Amos Comenius known as *Orbis Sensualium Pictus* (1658). It called for the creation of an autonomous entity that would oversee relations between the Museum of Society and Economy and the World Palace. The N.O.P. was to be

22 "On collectionnera et on conserva des objets", he writes, "mais ils ne devront pas nécessairement être rares ou précieux, des copies et des reproductions étant suffisantes pour venir l'appui des idees". Paul Otlet, *Mundaneum*, p. 10.

23 "Ich möchte aber nochmals wiederholen", reported an emphatic Neurath in a July 6th letter, "daß mir die gewaltige Anlage Ihres Museums, die zähe Verfolgung umfassender internationaler Pläne tiefen Eindruck auf mich gemacht hat. Ich würde mich glücklich schätzen, wenn wir unsere auf Qualitätsarbeit eingestellten Ausstellungswerkstätten und die wissenschaftliche Arbeitsgemeinschaft dauernd in den Dienst des zukünftigen Mundaneums stellen dürfen, um Ihren Plänen technisch jeweils eine möglichst vollkommene Gestalt zu geben und um manches aus unserer Arbeit heraus zu ergänzen. Ich glaube, daß unser Archiv für pictographische Erziehung und unser Archiv für Sozialstatistik manches enthalten wird, was Ihnen und Ihren Mitarbeitern zusagt". Letter from Otto Neurath to Paul Otlet, 06.07.1929, *Paul Otlet Papers*, Mundaneum.

24 Ibid.

25 Otto Neurath, "Gesellschafts- und Wirtschaftsmuseum in Wien", Gesammelte Bildpädagogische Schriften. vol. 3. eds. Rudolf Haller and Robin Kinross, Holder-Pichler-Tempsky, Vienna 1991, 2. Originally published in *Österreichische Gemeinde-Zeitung*, 2:16, 1925, pp. 1–12.

26 W Boyd Rayward, 'Introduction', *International Organisation and Dissemination of Knowledge: Selected Essays of Paul Otlet*, ed. W Boyd Rayward, Elsevier, Amsterdam 1990, p. 5.

27 World Federation of Education Associations: Third Biennial Conference, Geneva, Switzerland, 25.07.–04.08.1929, *Paul Otlet Papers*, Mundaneum, 1929.

overseen by Anna Oderfeld and Lothian Small of the World Association of People's Federations, who were based in Geneva, but the core parties were still Otlet and Neurath themselves.

In effect, the mission of the N.O.P. was to campaign for the creation of a network of museums dispersed throughout the world and to publish a series of books on a range of subjects; specifically, a universal atlas containing geographical, climactic, social, and economic maps about all regions of the world and their histories, a specialist atlas for individual professions and targeted age groups, a world encyclopedia, with images and accompanying text, a children's book series, a children's newspaper, and an adult newspaper. The museums, on the other hand, known as Mundaneums, were to be standardised according to specifications drafted jointly by the Museum of Society and Economy and Otlet's World Palace. As stated in the statutes of the protocol agreement (which Neurath drafted, but with Otlet's blessings), "the Institute Novus Orbis Pictus, hereinafter called N.O.P., seeks to promote enlightenment through pictures, in particular books and exhibitions".[28] The document adds, "the Atlas of World Culture Novus Orbis Pictus should be disseminated throughout the world, the material of the World Museum (Mundaneum) copied in as many regional museums as possible. Thus the World Museum will consist primarily of reproducible pieces stuck together. The Institute will seek to collaborate with associations and learned organisations from all countries, in particular international organisations. Both creations of the N.O.P. have been established with the interest of consolidating scientific research, as well as spreading and democratising knowledge and its instruments to disseminate social education throughout the world".[29]

Neurath and Otlet divided their responsibilities as follows: while the Museum of Society and Economy was to look after resolving design issues – the construction and maintenance of exhibits, as well as overseeing publication of the *Atlas of Civilization* – the World Palace was to assume control of assembling, classifying, and organising each project on a macro level.[30] "What we from the Mu-So-Ec (Museum of Society and Economy) will contribute would be the method of pictoral statistics and the systematic cartographic execution [of projects], as well as the intensive wish to illustrate all chrono[grams], topo [grams], and quanto[grams] through copies, texts, etc.", Neurath wrote. "What the World Palace would be contributing would be a striving toward comprehensiveness and systematicity in the early stages of work, the abundance of objects, pictures, contemporary artistic expressions of all kinds, distinguishing text, and the wish to be as exacting as possible".[31] Neurath added that the World Palace would be expected to continue its work with Le Corbusier and Jeanneret on the World City in Geneva, and that this city, if built, would anchor and administer the dissemination of knowledge to individual Mundaneum institutes.

The impact that Otlet had for Neurath's own career was dramatic, particularly in terms of how he helped Neurath reinvent his Museum of Society and Economy as an international body, both in theory as well as in practice. To speak first of Neurath's concrete endeavors, in 1931 Neurath began the Vienna Mundaneum, an institute whose mission was to oversee international travelling exhibits and exhibitions commissioned to the Museum of Society and Economy. It received little assistance from Otlet, but he used the name nonetheless with Otlet's blessings. That year, Neurath also established the Izostat Institute in Moscow, which gave him a foothold in Soviet Russia. In 1932, the Museum of Society and Economy was donated permanent exhibition space by Amsterdam's Museum van den Arbeid and London's Association for Adult Education, and the following year Neurath opened the Hague Mundaneum (also known as the International Foundation for the Promotion of Visual Education by the Vienna Method).[32] In 1934, the Russell Sage Foundation helped Neurath open and coordinate Pictoral Statistics, Inc., which was based in New York.

In a theoretical sense, Otlet influenced the image and structure of the Museum of Society and Economy. He gave Neurath a new conceptual framework within which to think about his museum endeavors. The decentralised model that Neurath adopted during the 1930s – creating museums throughout the world, but with a central institution as their anchor – was a strategy he borrowed from Otlet. Moreover, Otlet helped Neurath shift the priorities of the Museum of Society and Economy away from class-based concerns to communication- and linguistic-based issues. While during the 1920s the

28 "Das Institut *Novus orbis pictus,* im folgenden immer N.O.P genannt, ist dazu bestimmt, bildhafte Aufklärung auf jede Weise, insbesondere durch Veröffentlichlichungen und Ausstellungen zu unterstützen". Otto Neurath and Paul Otlet, Statuten des "Novus Orbis Pictus" NOP, Brüssel-Genf-Wien, 1929, *Paul Otlet Papers,* Mundaneum.

29 "Der Weltkultur-Atlas *Novus orbis pictus* soll in möglichst vielen Ländern verbreitet werden, das Material des Weltmuseums (Mundaneum) in möglichst vielen Landesmuseen kopiert werden. Daher wird das Weltmuseum vorwiegend aus reproduzierbaren Stücken zusammengesetzt werden. Das Institut wird die Mitarbeit von Vereinen und Gelehrten aller Lander, insbesondere die der internationalen Organisationen zu gewinnen suchen. Beide Schöpfungen des N.O.P. sind Einrichtungen im Interesse der Verbindung wissenschaftlicher Forschung, sowie der Verbreitung und Demokratisierung des Wissens und Instrumente zur planmäßigen Ausbreitung sozialer Bildung auf der ganzen Erde". Otto Neurath and Paul Otlet, Statuten des "Novus Orbis Pictits" NOP, Brüssel-Genf-Wien, 1929, Ibid.

30 Otto Neurath, Paul Otlet, Anna Oderfeld, and Lothian Small, "Novus Orbis Pictus" (NOP), Brüssel-Genf-Wien Protokoll, 1929, Ibid.

31 "Was wir vom Ge-Wi-Mu [Gesellschafts- und Wirtschaftsmuseum] beisteuern, wäre die Methode der Bildstatistik und die systematische kartographische Durcharbeitung, sowie der intensive Wunsch, alle Crono-, Topo-, und Quantogramme durch Abbildungen, Texte usw. zu illustrieren. Vom Palais Mondial hingegen wäre beizusteuern ein Streben nach umfassender Systematik in die Anfangsstadien der Arbeit, die Fülle von Objekten, Bildern, zeitgenössischen Kunstäußerungen aller Art, kennzeichnenden Text und der Wunsch, daß dies alles aufs exakteste ausgeführt wird". Letter from Otto Neurath to Paul Otlet, 06.07.1929, *Paul Otlet Papers,* Mundaneum.

32 Friedrich Stadler (ed.), *Arbeiterbildung in der Zwischenkriegszeit: Otto Neurath – Gerd Arntz,* Locker Verlag, Vienna and Munich 1982, pp. 246–249.

Museum was primarily concerned with the plight of the worker – with the gap, that is, that separated the haves from the have-nots, both intellectually and economically – during the 1930s Neurath came to see his mission increasingly as a linguistic struggle, not an economic one. He was concerned more and more about the flow of information between nations rather than between classes. The most visible expression of this shift occurred in 1935, when Neurath began to refer to his graphic methods collectively as the International System of Typographic Picture Education or Isotype, and as he became more enamored of the project of creating an International Encyclopedia of Unified Science.[33] That is to say, rather than using the more provincial-sounding "Vienna Method of Pictoral Statistics", which aligned Neurath's graphic techniques with a specific geographical location (namely Vienna), in 1935 Neurath began to redefine the image of his museum philosophy in a more global light. At the same time, he became more acutely aware of the need to forge a common scientific language that reversed the trend of intellectual specialisation, and which made knowledge more accessible across national boundaries. As Neurath remarked in his *International Picture Language,* "reading a picture is like making observations with the eye in everyday experience: what we may say about a language picture is very like what we may say about other things seen by the eye. For example: the man has two legs; the picture-sign has two legs; but the word-sign *man* has not two legs".[34] The concept that Isotypes were natural, that is to say, intelligible to everyone regardless of nationality, was a conviction he first began to articulate in one of his many exchanges with Otlet, even though he first began to publicise this view during the mid-1930s. As Neurath wrote to Otlet in 1929, "we must have an international word for every mass of pictures! Quantogram works also with Teleki-Diagrams! Pictogram? Also pictocartogram, pictochrono-gram, pictoquantogram. Although I do not find these creations terribly charming. But chemical formulas are also just as boring!"[35]

For Neurath, museums had to offer a transnational means of communicating, an Esperanto-like language as universal as the laws of nature. This view was something he only cultivated, as I have already noted, after coming into contact with Otlet, who introduced him to the concept of the World City. Although the two eventually parted ways, their mutual influence upon one another was undeniable. Architecturally speaking, Otlet's World City, the designs for which were prepared by Le Corbusier and Jeanneret, motivated Neurath to engage problems of communication posed by international bodies and institutions. Otlet also brought to Neurath's attention the need to formulate a strategy of information sharing that linked centres of cultural production to the outer-most edge of a society. While Le Corbusier identified an architectural solution to the problem, Neurath's subsequent work led him to explore graphic- and information-intensive solutions that relied heavily on mass reproduction. While Le Corbusier and Jeanneret were ultimately to propose a mammoth, seven-story helicoidal structure that honoured the unity of all cultures, Neurath, through his graphic studies with Arntz, sought to celebrate the *interchangeability* of cultures, the fact that abstract types could substitute particular cultural traditions. Neurath's efforts to theorise universal spaces in the late 1930s were influenced by his exposure to Le Corbusier's work, which sought to forge a universal temple of culture. This quest for the Tower of Babel, for the origins of language, was an aspiration that the architect Le Corbusier shared with Neurath, but which would be mediated by Neurath's spirited (if short-lived) relationship with Paul Otlet.

33 For a discussion of the Ernst Mach Society and its relationship to the International Encyclopedia of the Unity of Science, see Friedrich Stadler, *The Vienna Circle: Studies in the Origins, Development and Influence of Logical Empiricism,* Springer, Vienna and New York 2001, pp. 356–371.

34 Otto Neurath, *International Picture Language,* p. 20.

35 "Wir müssen für Mengenbilder usw. Ein besonderes internationales Wort finden! Quantogramm gilt auch von Teleki-Tafeln! Piktogramm? Also Pictokartogramm, Pictochronogramm, Pictoquantogramm. Obgleich ich diese Bildungen nicht übermaßig entzückend finde. Aber chemische Formeln sind ja auch langweilig!" Letter from Otto Neurath to Paul Otlet, 22.10.1929, *Paul Otlet Papers,* Mundaneum.

THE SELFLESS PEDESTAL

VANESSA JOAN MÜLLER

The pedestal is one of those classical artifices of display that exists in order to place works of art in an optimal light. The fact that it has been attracting increased attention for some time, on both the theoretical and the artistic level, is closely linked to its own implicit reflection on its development as a presentation device within modern art, in areas like autonomy and contextualisation, spatial analysis and viewer interaction—making it an object of interest to contemporary artists. Viewed historically, the pedestal has repeatedly come into focus at different points in time; when installation-based work began to redefine the exhibition space, and when sculpture produced work that managed without it or vehemently rejected it in the idea of dehierarchisation. Although this didn't necessarily signify the disappearance of the pedestal, as art history evinces, it did lead to a decisive shift in its function. The pedestal no longer functions as the primary bearer in material or ideological terms, it is now a rhetorical figure. Particularly within the framework of institutional critique, the pedestal experienced a general revision that elevated it to the status of a multiply coded exhibition element, one which forms the basis for its various new formulations today. The practical *demountable pedestal,* as proposed in the *Manual of Travelling Exhibitions,* was already an anachronism at the time from the perspective of avant-garde art, as it insisted on a strict separation of presentation and work. As an exhibition piece, however, it fulfils a function that has a great deal to do with conveyance and addressing the viewer, and is also bound with what we now recognise under a broader sense of the term *display:* a structure that goes beyond its presentational function; one that produces meaning and norms and thus communicates ideological concepts; one that establishes object-space and object-viewer relationships and enables contextualisation. By placing emphasis on the functional and the mobile, however, as is implicit in the *demountable pedestal,* these aspects are paradoxically brought to the fore—precisely because they aren't supposed to play any role at all. The pedestal's transportable construction, its simple, cubic form, and its classical height (classical in reference to traditional, smaller-scale sculptures) make it into a universally deployable presentation device. But appearances are deceiving. Traditional pedestals have a complex relationship to the space in which they are situated: on the one hand, they elevate the presented object from the space they are in and transfer it into another, higher realm, as it were; on the other hand, they are visibly integrated into the space itself. Pedestals literally serve as a foundation for contemplating artwork, as they define the viewpoint and thus the viewer's relationship to the work. Besides a physical elevation, the pedestal also creates an ideational elevation of the presented work and keeps the view at a distance. The pedestal defines a separate terrain, so to speak, and places the work in relation to both the viewer and the surrounding architecture. Like the picture frame, it mediates between the realm of representation and the realm of reality. This realm of reality brings a very tangible reference value into play: a pedestal and the work presented on it should be placed in relation to the surrounding space—if only, with polite disregard, to delineate this relationship as a non-relationship. All the exhibition displays shown in the appendix of *Manual of Travelling Exhibitions* are more interesting and more flexible than the pedestal proposed as the ideal presentation module. In fact, this module is suitable for very few objects. It presents things/objects at eye level, at least this impression is given, if a certain amount of proportionality is required. You can walk around it—i.e. it doesn't have a dedicated front side—but then again pays little heed to what is presented on it. It stipulates a strong attachment to materiality and a conventional object character. However, to a certain degree it fetishises the display itself, and shows similarities to contemporaneous forms of product display—like how the fundamental development of innovative exhibition design in post-war America ran parallel to the refined product presentation in the shop windows and department stores. This tendency has less to do with the increasing commodification of art than with a very American desire for its democratisation, a separation of the art exhibition from the sphere of the bourgeois elite. The demountable pedestal thus stands for an exhibition concept related to the idea of mobility, one that demands a healthy pragmatism and consciously places itself above the conservative rigor of museum presentations. The idea behind the demountable pedestal can be reduced to this simple maxim: art leaves the museum and makes its way to the people. Works are didactically presented at eye level, which is consistent with the notion of dehierarchisation. The presented object, no matter what it may be, offers an invitation to participate in a dialogue. That the universal readability of art and the associated immediacy of knowledge transfer only function if the pedestal's complexity regarding spatial contextualisation and art historical tradition is dismissed, can thus be attributed to the zeitgeist of post-war modernism and its desire for a universal artistic language. This is particularly noticeable when compared to today's approach to tall, narrow pedestals, like the one put forward in the *Manual of Travelling Exhibitions.* Isa Genzken, for example, frequently displays her work on stem-like pedestals, specifically constructed for each individual piece. Here, the pedestal is an explicit component of the work in terms of its narrative and rhetoric: it is a keeper of distance, ennobles something that deliberately plays with the aesthetics of the everyday, and determines a precisely defined position for the viewer. Isa Genzken presents her works in the style of architectural models in which the height of the pedestal transforms the view from above onto a model into a side view into a model. The white pedestal, with its white surface, functions like a stage for that which takes place upon it. It creates a model situation through which the sculpture itself takes up a state of exemplary symbolisation. The very fact that an entire series of Genzken's sculptures seeks direct contact with the ground underlines the significance of the pedestal as a conscious stance. Deciding for or against a pedestal, and choosing its height and size, are aligned to the respective work and its subject matter. Genzken's works are at once aware of the achievements of minimal art and incorporate the viewer's involvement produced by a simultaneous activation of the entire space. They contain the history of the pedestal, its disappearance, and its metaphorical expansion into the surrounding space—a reflective space for its own artistic development and an indicator of a self-conscious positioning within the historical field of art.

I CAPTURE YOU, YOU CAPTURE ME

GITTE VILLESEN WITH HELENE HERMANN

The vitrine for the installation *I Capture You, You Capture Me* is part of an installation based on a dialogue between Helene Hermann and myself. The objects in the vitrine were all collected or produced during our working process. After Helene Hermann had suggested that we should make a vitrine, she designed it and organised its production. All the label texts in the vitrine are written by her. The work is partly a portrait of Helene Hermann and partly about our mutual process and discussions while making it. We have each in our own way dealt with representation and staging before, she as a scenographer and I in my videos. This work specifically focuses on issues of how you represent someone else and how you stage or present yourself. Beside the vitrine, the work consists of a 2-channel video projection, 10 photographs and a hand-out. The work was produced for the Danish Pavilion, 51st Venice Biennale in 2005. A second version of the vitrine with a different selection of items was produced for the National Gallery of Denmark in 2007.

Fig. 15 *I Capture You, You Capture Me,* Gitte Villesen with Helene Hermann, Portrait of a dialogue between the scenographer Helene Hermann and artist Gitte Villesen. National Gallery of Denmark, 2007.

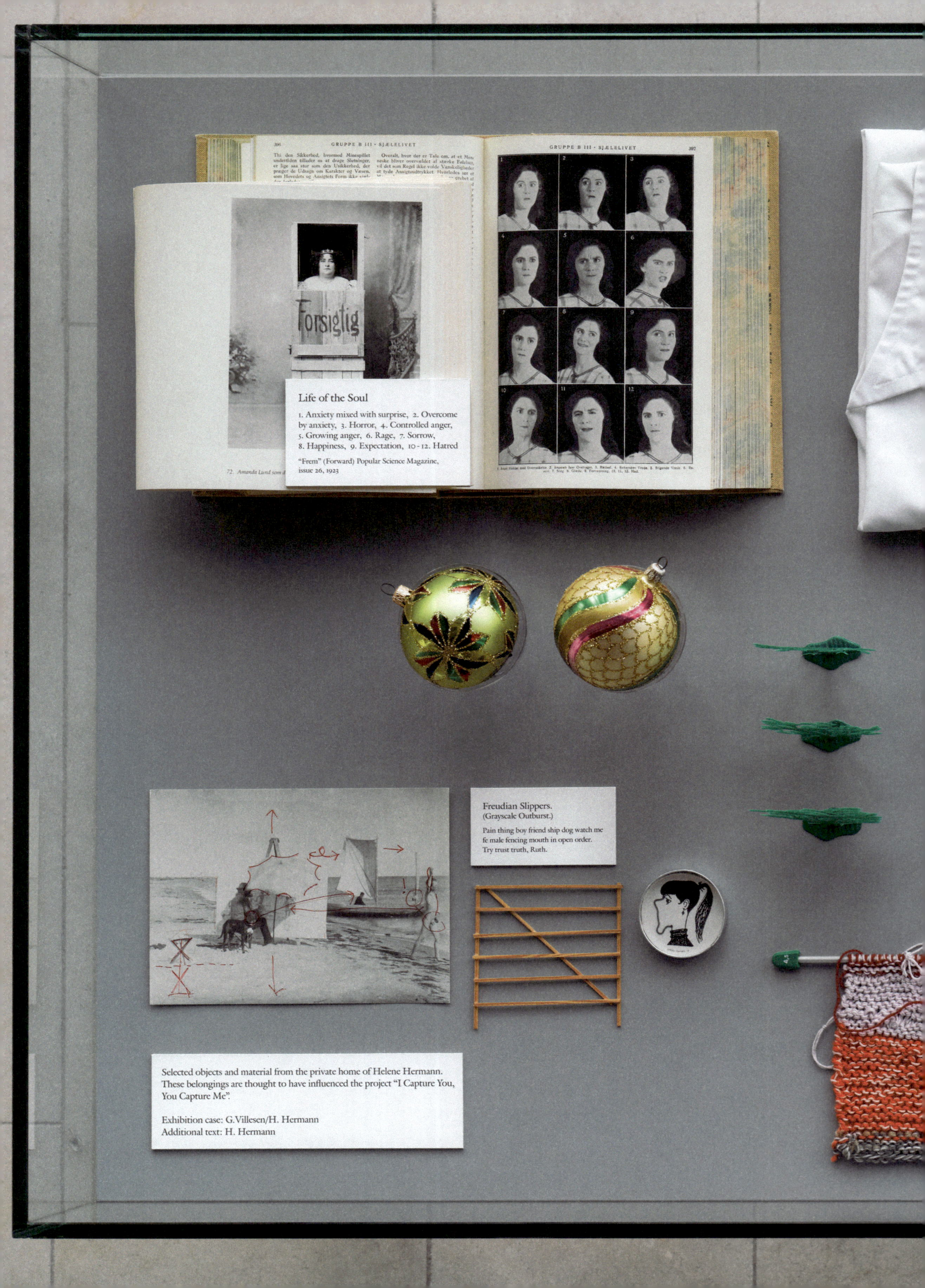
GRUPPE B III · SJÆLELIVET
Forsigtig
Life of the Soul
1. Anxiety mixed with surprise, 2. Overcome by anxiety, 3. Horror, 4. Controlled anger, 5. Growing anger, 6. Rage, 7. Sorrow, 8. Happiness, 9. Expectation, 10-12. Hatred
"Frem" (Forward) Popular Science Magazine, issue 26, 1923
Freudian Slippers.
(Grayscale Outburst.)
Pain thing boy friend ship dog watch me fe male fencing mouth in open order. Try trust truth, Ruth.
Selected objects and material from the private home of Helene Hermann. These belongings are thought to have influenced the project "I Capture You, You Capture Me".
Exhibition case: G.Villesen/H. Hermann
Additional text: H. Hermann

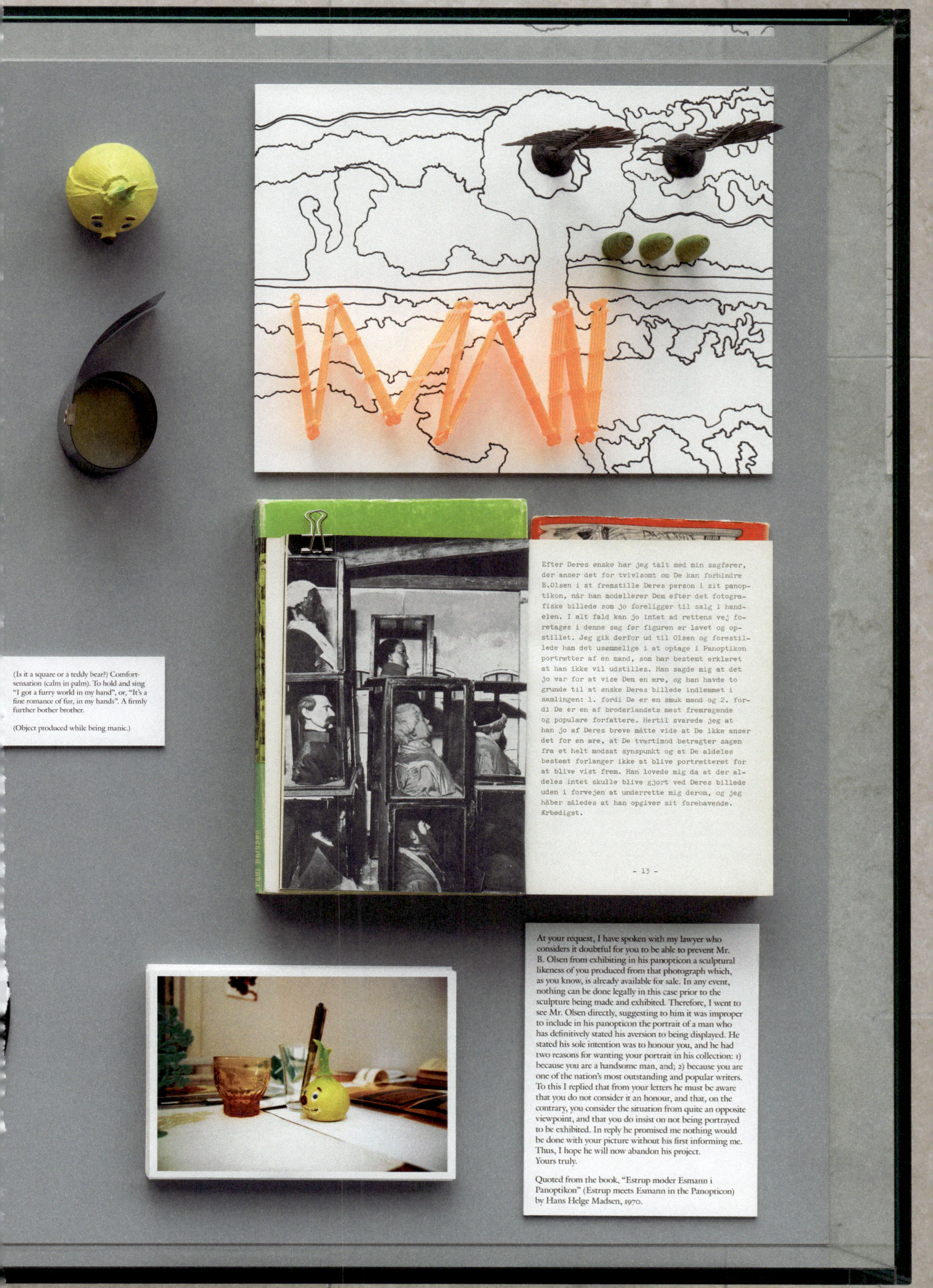

(Is it a square or a teddy bear?) Comfort-sensation (calm in palm). To hold and sing "I got a furry world in my hand", or, "It's a fine romance of fur, in my hands". A firmly further bother brother.
(Object produced while being manic.)
Efter Deres ønske har jeg talt med min sagfører, der anser det for tvivlsomt om De kan forhindre B.Olsen i at fremstille Deres person i sit panoptikon, når han modellerer Dem efter det fotografiske billede som jo foreligger til salg i handelen. I alt fald kan jo intet ad rettens vej foretages i denne sag før figuren er lavet og opstillet. Jeg gik derfor ud til Olsen og forestillede ham det usømmelige i at optage i Panoptikon portrætter af en mand, som har bestemt erklæret at han ikke vil udstilles. Han sagde mig at det jo var for at vise Dem en ære, og han havde to grunde til at ønske Deres billede indlemmet i samlingen: 1. fordi De er en smuk mand og 2. fordi De er en af broderlandets mest fremragende og populære forfattere. Hertil svarede jeg at han jo af Deres breve måtte vide at De ikke anser det for en ære, at De tværtimod betragter sagen fra et helt modsat synspunkt og at De aldeles bestemt forlanger ikke at blive portrætteret for at blive vist frem. Han lovede mig da at der aldeles intet skulle blive gjort ved Deres billede uden i forvejen at underrette mig derom, og jeg håber således at han opgiver sit forehavende.
Ærbødigst.
- 13 -
At your request, I have spoken with my lawyer who considers it doubtful for you to be able to prevent Mr. B. Olsen from exhibiting in his panopticon a sculptural likeness of you produced from that photograph which, as you know, is already available for sale. In any event, nothing can be done legally in this case prior to the sculpture being made and exhibited. Therefore, I went to see Mr. Olsen directly, suggesting to him it was improper to include in his panopticon the portrait of a man who has definitively stated his aversion to being displayed. He stated his sole intention was to honour you, and he had two reasons for wanting your portrait in his collection: 1) because you are a handsome man, and; 2) because you are one of the nation's most outstanding and popular writers. To this I replied that from your letters he must be aware that you do not consider it an honour, and that, on the contrary, you consider the situation from quite an opposite viewpoint, and that you do insist on not being portrayed to be exhibited. In reply he promised me nothing would be done with your picture without his first informing me. Thus, I hope he will now abandon his project.
Yours truly.
Quoted from the book, "Estrup møder Esmann i Panoptikon" (Estrup meets Esmann in the Panopticon) by Hans Helge Madsen, 1970.

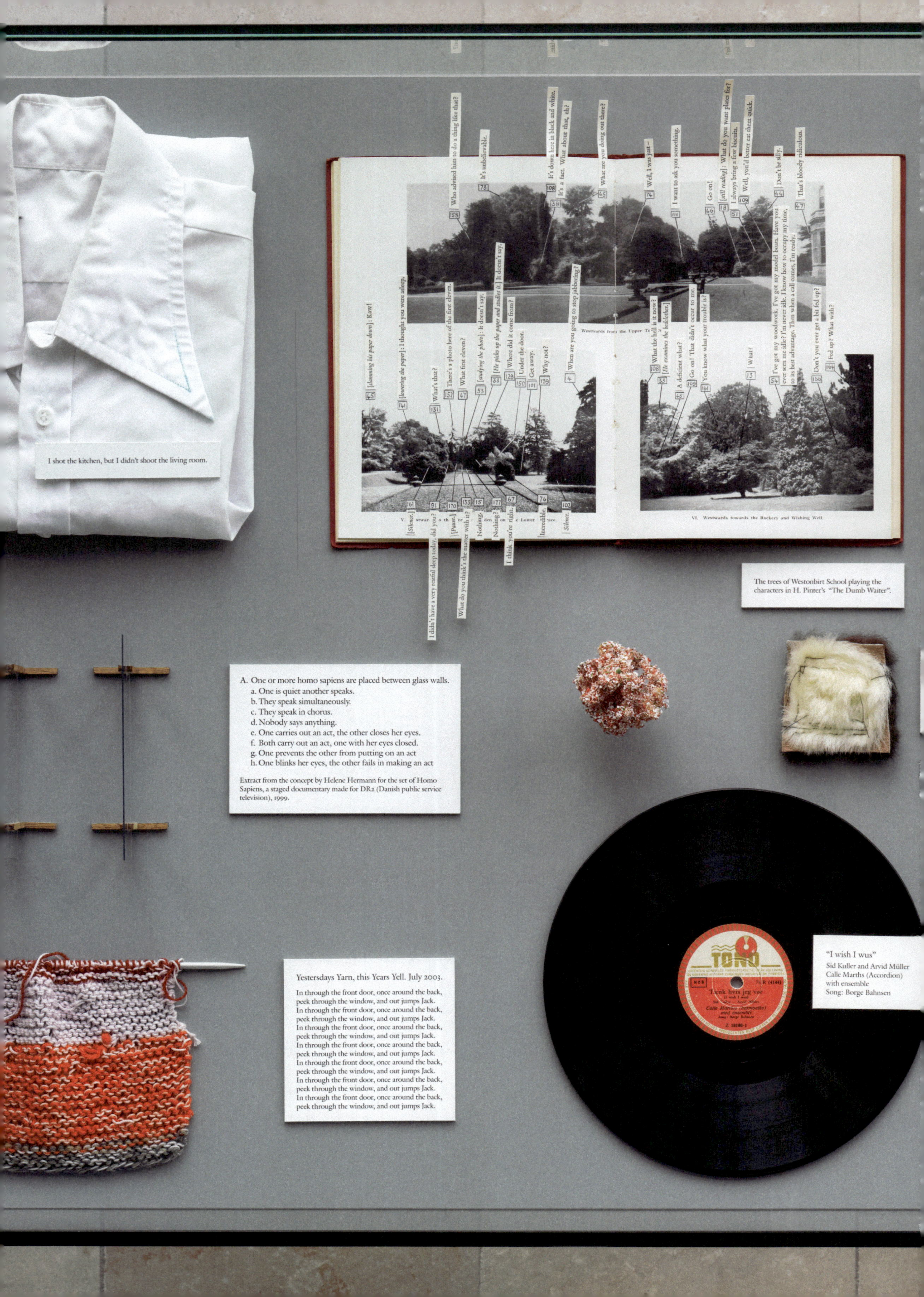
I shot the kitchen, but I didn't shoot the living room.
The trees of Westonbirt School playing the characters in H. Pinter's "The Dumb Waiter".
A. One or more homo sapiens are placed between glass walls.
a. One is quiet another speaks.
b. They speak simultaneously.
c. They speak in chorus.
d. Nobody says anything.
e. One carries out an act, the other closes her eyes.
f. Both carry out an act, one with her eyes closed.
g. One prevents the other from putting on an act
h. One blinks her eyes, the other fails in making an act
Extract from the concept by Helene Hermann for the set of Homo Sapiens, a staged documentary made for DR2 (Danish public service television), 1999.
Yesterdays Yarn, this Years Yell. July 2003.
In through the front door, once around the back, peek through the window, and out jumps Jack.
In through the front door, once around the back, peek through the window, and out jumps Jack.
In through the front door, once around the back, peek through the window, and out jumps Jack.
In through the front door, once around the back, peek through the window, and out jumps Jack.
In through the front door, once around the back, peek through the window, and out jumps Jack.
In through the front door, once around the back, peek through the window, and out jumps Jack.
In through the front door, once around the back, peek through the window, and out jumps Jack.
"I wish I wus"
Sid Kuller and Arvid Müller
Calle Marths (Accordion)
with ensemble
Song: Borge Bahnsen
TONO

SOME DEFINITIONS RELATING TO DEMOUNTABLE FRAMEWORKS

MARTIN BECK

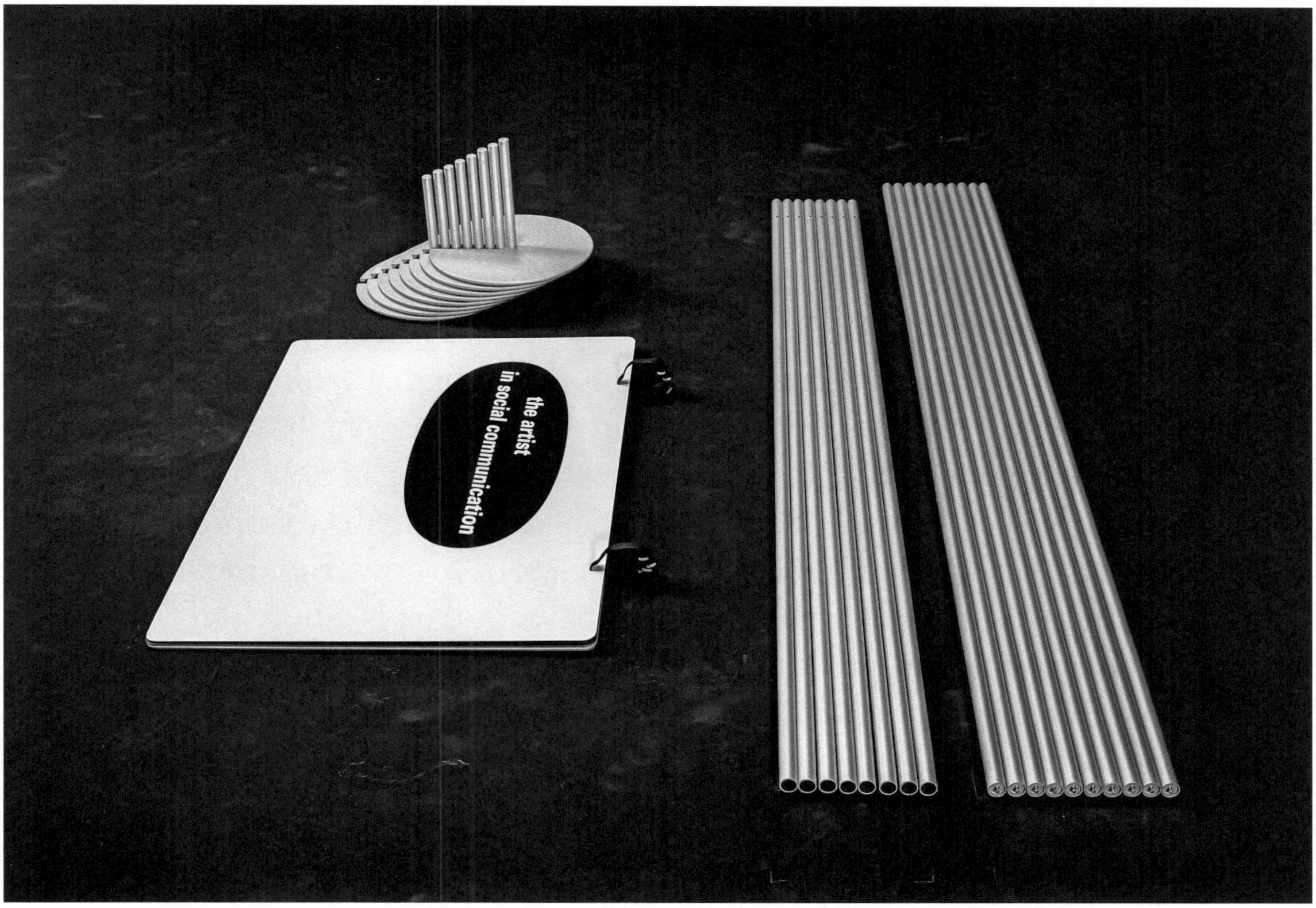

16

Fig. 16 Martin Beck, *Panel 1, Social Abstraction,* 2007–08, Framed C-print

1. To demount means to move from a position on a mounting or other support. To move means to change in position from one point to another. A position relates to the way in which something is placed. A mount is something that serves as a support, setting, or backing. A support is a fixture for holding something in position so as to keep it from falling, sinking, or slipping. To place means to put something in a particular position. A setting is understood as the context and environment in which a situation is set; a backing is a support or aid. To hold means to carry or support in a certain position. A fixture is something securely fixed in place. To fall means to drop or come down freely under the influence of gravity; to sink means to fall or drop to a lower level; to slip means to slide out of place…

2. A framework is a structure for supporting or enclosing something else, especially a skeletal support used as the basis for something being constructed. A structure is something made up of a number of parts that are held or put together in a particular way. To support means to hold in position so as to keep from falling, sinking, or slipping. To enclose means to contain. Skeletal means relating to, forming, or being of the nature of a skeleton. To construct means to form by assembling or combining parts. A part is a portion, division, piece, or segment of a whole. To relate means to establish or demonstrate a connection between parts; to form means to organise or arrange. To assemble means to bring or call together into a group or whole; to combine means to exhibit in combination. A portion is a part of a whole; a division is one of the parts, sections, or groups into which something is divided; a piece is a thing considered as a unit or an element of a larger thing; a segment is any of the parts into which something can be divided. A skeleton is a supporting structure or a framework…

BRÂNCUȘI ANECDOTE

FLORIAN WALZEL

"Import and export regulations frequently tend to obscure instead of encourage the movement of cultural material from one country to another." This succinct sentence can be found in Chapter III of the *Manual of Travelling Exhibitions,* under the section *Ocean transport.* Exactly how unyielding the disagreements between the art world and the customs authorities could be, is exemplified by an episode that happened over 25 years earlier in New York. The court case Brâncuși vs. the United States went down in history as one of the most captivating, and in retrospect amusing, confrontations on the differences between freight and cultural artifacts. In 1927, during the import of bronze sculptures by Constantin Brâncuși, including his work *Bird in Space,* US customs officials refused to declare them as art under the 1922 Tariff Act, thus denying them their duty-exempt status. Instead, the Port Authority levied the standard tariff: "manufactured objects of metal: 40 percent of sale price". Brâncuși refused to pay the sizeable sum, and the sculptures remained under lock and key. By passing an ultimate judgment on what is and what isn't considered art, the customs office had unwillingly made a decision that went far beyond administrative routines. The ruling came at a sensitive moment, and the story made the rounds in New York—rising to the status of an art scandal in the press. Faced with the prospect of making fools of themselves, the customs department called in art historians, and under the curious classification "Kitchen Utensils and Hospital Supplies" allowed a temporary release of the works. After the sculptures were successfully shown in the Brummer Gallery (NYC) and the Arts Club in Chicago, and had found buyers, the customs office annulled this temporary classification and reverted to its original demand for a 40 percent taxation rate. The dispute between the customs office and the art world flared up again, and was further exacerbated by the fact that prominent figures were among the buyers, for example photographer and later director of the Department of Photography at New York's Museum of Modern Art, Edward Steichen. Many renowned artists and critics also rallied to support Brâncuși. The audacity of the customs officials in judging modern art using their restricted, administrative categories prompted a lively public discussion on the question of "What is art?". In an almost comical manner, the contrasting positions were summed up in the remarks of Marcel Duchamp and F.J.H. Kracke, the U.S. Federal Customs assessor. On February 23rd, 1927, Kracke went on record with the *Evening Post,* saying, "If that's art, hereafter I'm a bricklayer". In response, Marcel Duchamp, friend and advocate of Brâncuși, countered in the *New York Times* on February 27th, by declaring: "To say that the sculpture of Brâncuși is not art is like saying an egg is not an egg". Eight months later, Brâncuși was eventually able to prevail in the US Customs Court: his works were declared tax-exempt. The judge's ruling set a precedent, replacing the previously valid definition of artworks as "imitations of natural objects [...] in their true proportions". From 1927 onwards, at least in the eyes of the US tax authorities, art no longer had to be figurative.

THE TRAVELLING OF MANUAL EXHIBITONS

MAXIM WEIRICH IN CONVERSATION WITH TINA KÖHLER

For 28 years, Tina Köhler has been the head of Exhibitions Coordination at the Haus der Kunst in Munich. During this time she has helped organise over 200 exhibitions, supervised numerous travelling exhibitions, and collaborated with a wide range of artists, curators, museums, and national and international institutions. In this interview, she talks about the logistical and technical complexity of contemporary travelling exhibitions, technological changes in the field, risks associated with transporting art, and the impact of increasing digitalisation on certain stages of production.

MW: What is the main difference between a travelling exhibition from the time of the *Manual* and a travelling exhibition today?

TK: Today, the motivation behind travelling exhibitions is completely different to then. In the 1950s and 60s, travelling internationally was expensive and only affordable for a small section of the population. For this reason, touring exhibitions were important because they allowed artworks to be taken to the public, and in doing so delivered cultural ideas. American exhibitions of abstract expressionism, for example, conveyed a new world view – that of a free America. This world view was also exported to postwar Germany, where there was a shortage of contemporary artistic positions, as many of them had been declared degenerate and banned during the Nazi dictatorship. From the 50s onwards, these previously banned works could finally be shown in Germany.

Nowadays, the main reason for travelling exhibitions is a financial one. Exhibitions have become so expensive that individual institutions are often unable to finance them alone. With a jointly conceived travelling exhibition, costs for restoration and organisation can be shared. This includes curatorial research visits and the developing of the exhibition concept, which is incorporated as intellectual property into the shared expenses. The costs for the transport crates can also be split. Popular exhibitions represent a good source of income for the institutions involved, which makes participating in a touring show or borrowing individual works – that can be shown in combination with one's own collection – an interesting prospect.

MW: Has the visiting public changed?

TK: There's a crucial difference between then and now: In the postwar era, there was an idealistic attempt to make cultural goods available in countries where they weren't accessible. Travelling exhibitions were an opportunity to provide people with access to work they wouldn't have otherwise been able to see in the original. Today, on the other hand, a wider public can travel to the location where the work is on show.

MW: So, do travelling exhibitions now have the distinct potential to bring works from many different collections together into an exhibition, that would otherwise be spread throughout institutions and collections across the world?

TK: Exactly. You devise an exhibition using content-based criteria and aim to borrow the necessary works for it to be able to tour. It can also be retrospective shows that concentrate on a specific aspect of an artist's œuvre. In the touring exhibition *Louise Bourgeois: Structures of Existence: The Cells* it was the *Cells* – a series of installations that are self-contained but can be seen into and sometimes even walked through. The fact that so many of these cells were together in a touring show is something that probably won't happen again any time soon. The exhibition was shown in the Haus der Kunst in Munich, Garage in Moscow, the Guggenheim Museum in Bilbao and the Louisiana Museum in Humlebaek.

MW: How do collaborations with other institutions arise?

TK: That's when our director's network comes into play. Through his work as a curator, Okwui Enwezor works on many international exhibition projects across the world. These curators also talk with their colleagues about potential joint projects. Such cooperations can be proposed and discussed during official trips, visits to other institutions, or meetings at international events such as biennials and art fairs. Therefore, it's always important to know exactly what other institutions are showing, what the focus of their collection is, and which artists and subject matters could be of interest to them or complement their collection. Having a feeling for this is crucial: What content matter do they work with? What's an appropriate, meaningful location for the exhibition? Who has the relevant facilities? Who has the money?

MW: Does the entire exhibition always go on tour?

TK: Sometimes a travelling exhibition needs to be adapted to accommodate different circumstances. There were two reasons for the changes we made to our choice of selected works: on the one hand, space; on the other, lender restrictions. For example, due to the strained political relations between Russia and the US, we had to contend with American restrictions on the lending of items to Russia—at the time, the Museum of Modern Art couldn't loan work to Russia. And other loan items couldn't be taken to Moscow because of space issues, or the owner had already agreed to other loans. The works that we couldn't exhibit in Moscow were temporarily stored at the Haus der Kunst and then reincorporated into the show in Bilbao.

MW: Could you go through the different production stages of a travelling exhibition with reference to the Louise Bourgeois show?

TK: First we receive the lists of work from the curators. This is followed by the loan requests; initiating correspondence with the individual museums, collections, and private lenders—the places where the works are located. Parallel to this, the budget is drawn up and logistics planning is begun. The established art shipping companies now have comprehensive databases, because they have transported such huge amounts of art to a wide range of destinations. Their estimates are fairly accurate, and in addition they give you important country-specific information to consider when planning international travel routes.

MW: Were there any country-specific aspects regarding the Bourgeois Exhibition?

TK: Yes, the journey through Russia was one—travelling from Munich to Moscow is not that easy. Due to the ongoing conflict in Ukraine, taking the direct land route through Poland and Belarus is advised against. So instead we took a shortcut with the ferry from Travemünde to Helsinki, and from there onward via St. Petersburg to Moscow. Another specific aspect was a law in Russia that states that a police escort is required when you transport art. This service, which is supposed to ensure your safety on the roads of Russia, has to be paid for by the contractor. The shipping estimates are devised by considering transport volumes and such regional details. We travelled with a total of ten trucks and trailers.

MW: How much preparation time does a touring exhibition of this scale usually need?

TK: The whole tour was planned about two years in advance, so two years before the exhibition was first set up in Munich. But at this point, the partners didn't know when the prior exhibitions were going to be taken down and shipped. I had to plan the delivery operations and the necessary interim storage locations, as well as asking for the timely creation of a hanging plan, which featured the positions of the work. The architecture of each location is different, and accordingly different works had to be delivered and installed first. But these weren't always the pieces to be shipped first from the previous location. Drawing up an efficient time plan for the delivery, installation, and temporary storage of the exhibition pieces was a massive challenge. The plans also had to factor in the limited operating hours of the shipping companies, and national and international driving restrictions for road freight on certain days of the week.

MW: How were the costs defined and divided between the institutions?

TK: At the same time as finalising the loan agreements with the lenders, we worked out the tour agreement, which included the shared costs. The organising institution sets a fee for the tour preparations, which encompasses costs for showing the exhibition, the curatorial concept, and the organisational input. Transport costs can easily be shared: for the Munich-Moscow-Bilbao-Humlebæk tour it made sense to split the shipping between all four partners. Apart from importing some work by air to Munich via Liège, and the return flight from Copenhagen to Liège on to New York, all shipping was done by road. Works that only appeared at three of the four locations were only paid for by these three partners. What proved beneficial was sharing costs for the transport crates, and collecting and shipping the works back to the lenders.

MW: How do the institutions cooperate with the shipping companies?

TK: The shipping company receives a list of works from the registrar and passes the request onto an

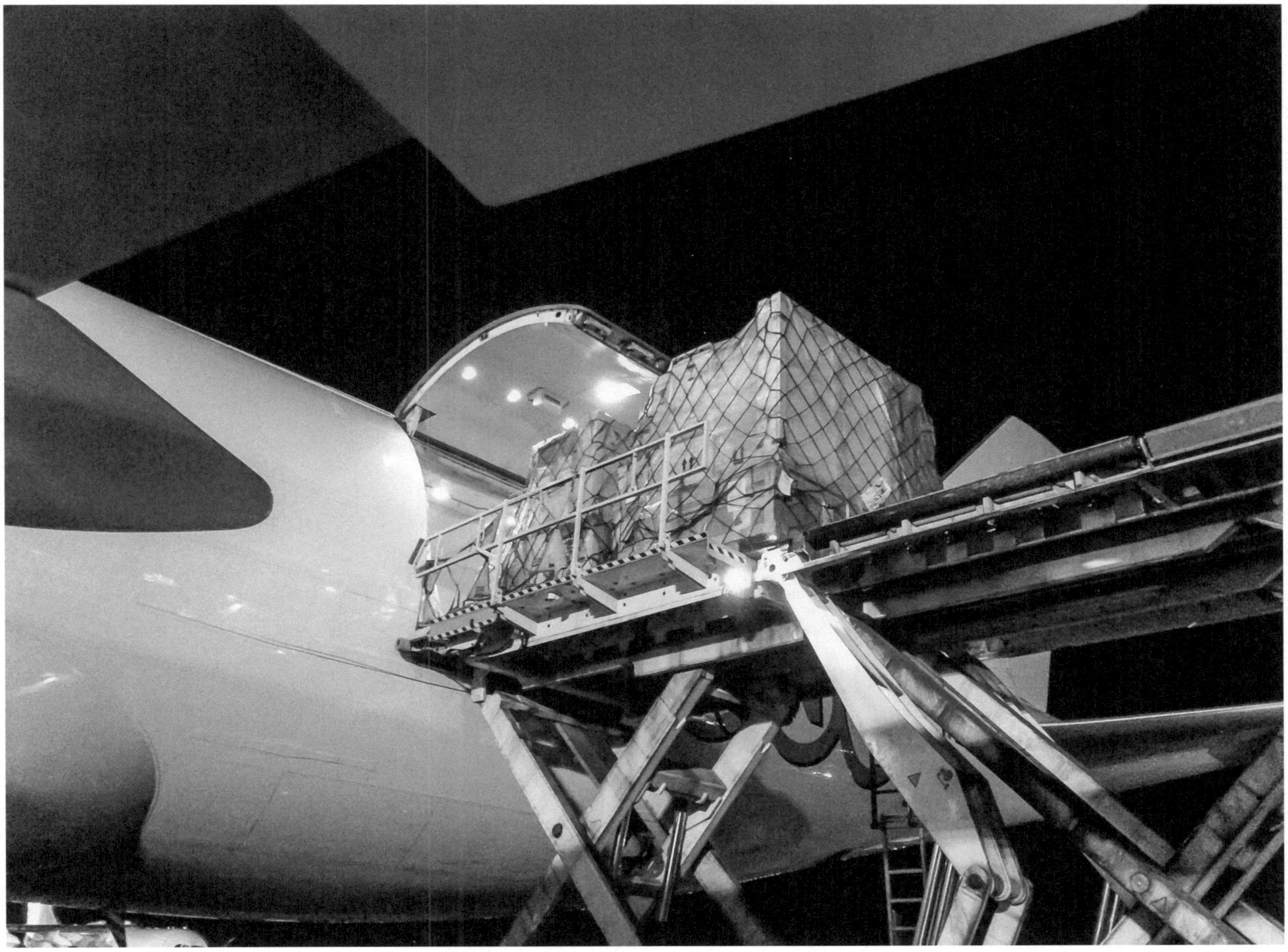

17

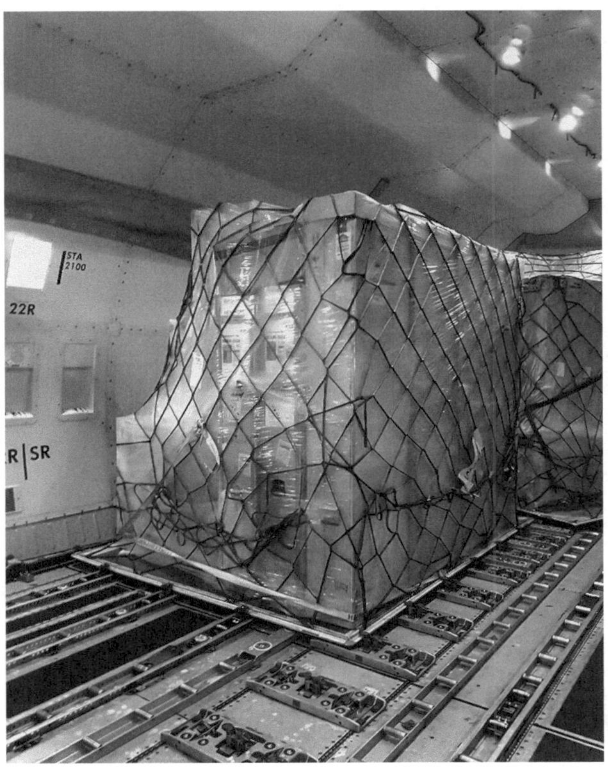

18

Fig. 17 – Fig. 18 Pictures from the export supervision report of the touring exhibition *Louise Bourgeois: Structures of Existence: The Cells,* ETD: 14.09.16, Flight no.: ICL310, Flight routing: LGG-JFK, Plates: E 3246 hdz (above), r 4412bbm (below).

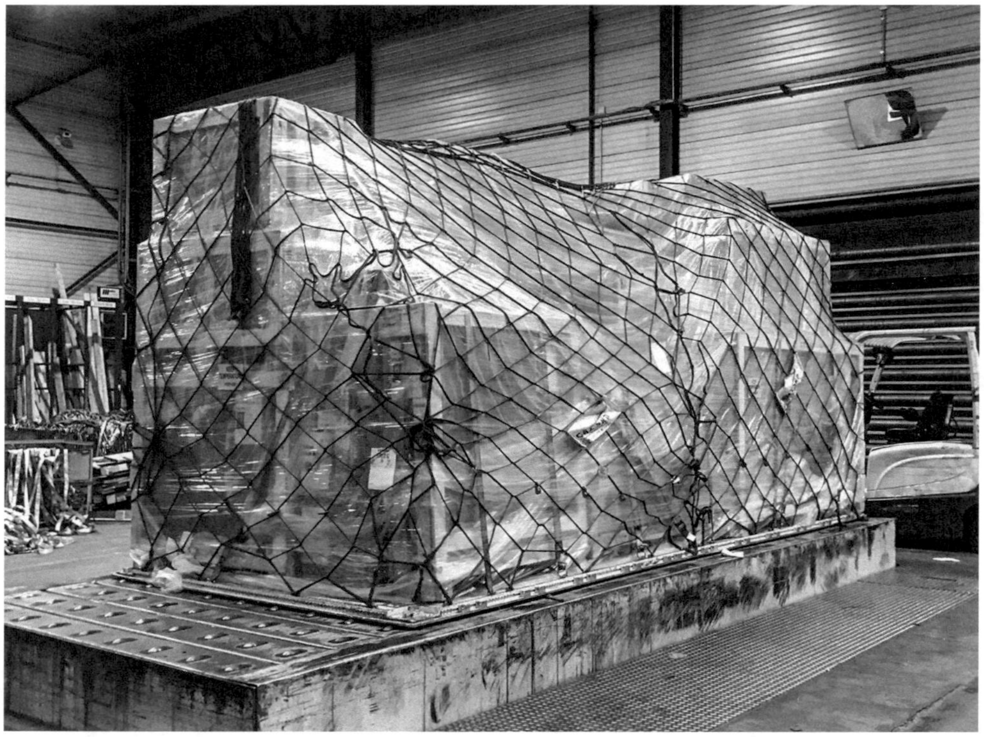

19

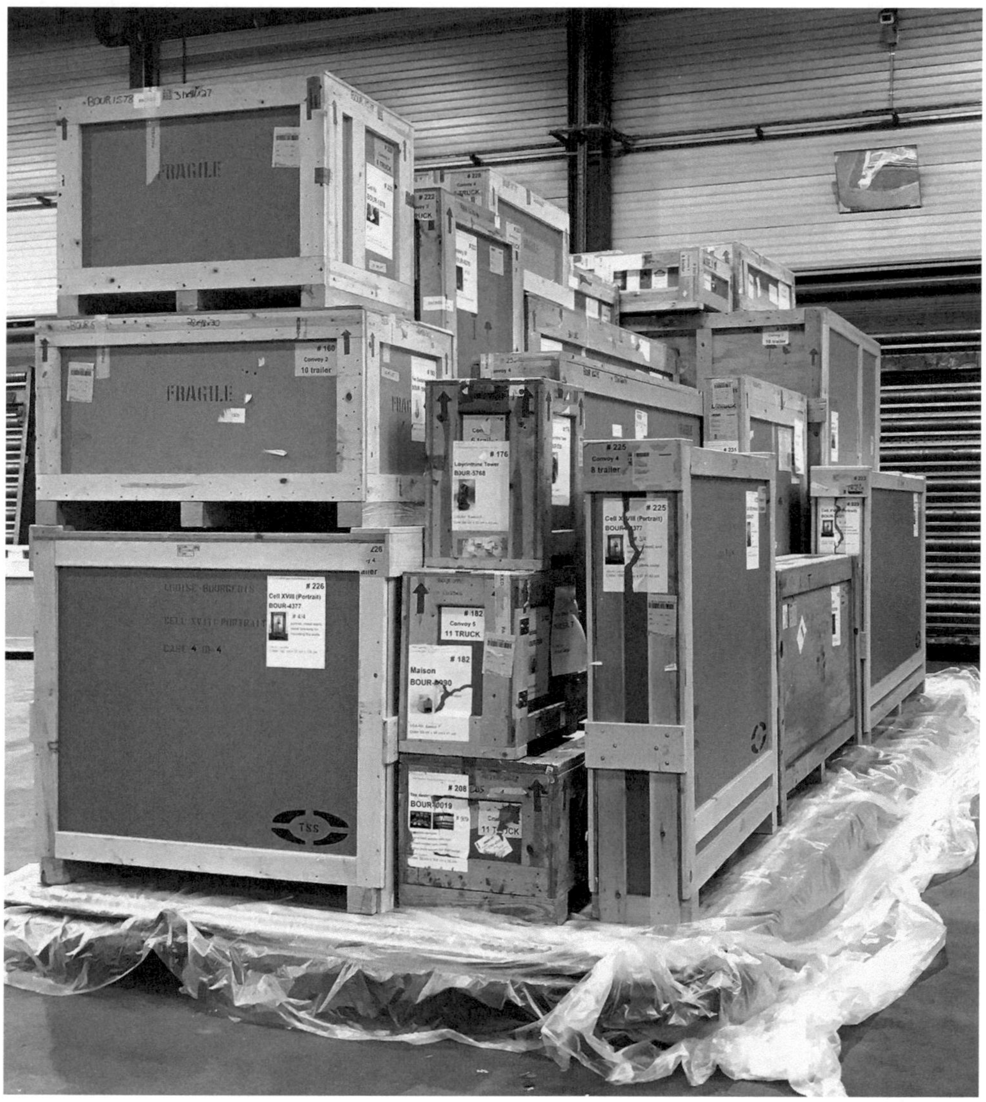

20

Fig. 19 – Fig. 20 Pictures from the export supervision report of the touring exhibition *Louise Bourgeois: Structures of Existence: The Cells*
ETD: 14.03.17, Flight no.: 5c310/14mar, Flight routing: ETD LGG-JFK, Pallet: P4M0044

agent abroad. The art shipping network is global, there are partner companies worldwide that are part of a large association of art forwarders. For instance, if I want to ship a work from Indonesia to Germany, the shipping company in Germany will ask their colleagues in Indonesia to examine the work there. They will go to the museum, or into the storage depot with the registrar or restorer, and then send us their opinion and a corresponding offer. The lending institution prescribes the packaging requirements: How should the work be padded? What type of container—climate-controlled or standard? Is sea freight permitted? Does a courier have to accompany the piece?

In addition to this, the agent in that country will provide information about the necessary bureaucratic procedures like export procedures and customs. Countries outside the EU have many different laws and directives regarding the export of artworks. In such cases, the overseas agent is a vital contact and is responsible for filling out the appropriate forms and speaking to the relevant authorities.

MW: Who insures the artworks?

TK: Either by our own insurance, the owner's, or that of the other institution. We have a *nail to nail* insurance for artworks in our exhibitions, which means that the pieces are insured for the whole loan period until they are returned to their original place—including transport, storage, and the duration of the exhibition. The type of transport is always explicitly agreed upon with the insurance company. Shipping by sea must be specifically requested and approved, as art isn't really supposed to be transported by sea: it's too damp and risky, there's no 24-hour surveillance in the harbour, and the weather at sea is unpredictable. But some works are simply too big to be carried by air, and then there's no other option than by sea.

MW: How do you assess the insurance costs of the works on loan?

TK: Generally, you accept the insurance value the owner states in the loan agreement. In some cases, however, the fluctuating art market causes problems: if a new record value is reached at auction, lenders sometimes orientate themselves to this new market price and increase the insurance value. This creates an additional uncertainty when calculating the insurance premium. In the planning phase of an exhibition you estimate the insurance premium, which consists of insurance value, materials, and shipping route. The more fragile the freight, the more expensive the insurance. Then, based on a risk analysis, further fees are specified for certain countries—for example the insurance for shipping by road through Russia is more expensive than by air from Munich to New York. The frequency of instances of damage to works within an institution also plays a role.

MW: Do you escort transits?

TK: We only accompanied the Louise Bourgeois exhibition from Munich to Moscow. Courier escort is only usually necessary with very valuable loans or on complicated routes. The responsibility you have for the loan item as a borrower should be fulfilled to the best possible level. Transporting items through the Russian winter undoubtedly had its risks, like the bad weather and the incalculability of the waiting times on the Finnish-Russian border. The couriers that travel with us are an added security measure who also ensure that the whole process—including unloading on arrival—is carried out with due care. The most important thing in transporting art is that it's done in a slow and cautious manner.

MW: Who assists you?

TK: I have a team of around 25 freelancers. They are all artists, and most have additional vocational qualifications. I have two co-workers who have helped set up three documentas and who have an extremely broad knowledge of all kinds of artworks—our freelance art handlers. On top of this, we also employ freelance restorers, a full-time registrar, a project-based assistant, and often an intern.

MW: How do you prepare for the installation of an exhibition?

TK: The basis for planning the installation starts with the artwork-specific documents, from the loan agreements and the list of works to the assembly instructions, the artwork manuals. When it comes to painting exhibitions, you don't need to ask much regarding construction; with sculptures, on the other hand, all details are needed: weight, footprint of the pedestal, desired height of the pedestal. If there are insufficient details we will carry out research and try to find previous presentations of the work and recreate how to construct it.

MW: How was that in the case of the Louise Bourgeois exhibition?

TK: A few works had detailed manuals, but some didn't. One lender had never even set up the work themselves. We intended to place focus on documentation when we installed the artworks in Munich, so that we could pass on the information to the subsequent locations. For this we needed someone to professionally document construction of the pieces. As such documentation was also in the interest of the estate of Louise Bourgeois, they provided us with their photographer, and in this way the manuals contributed to the completion of their archives.

MW: How do you document the condition of a work?

TK: The condition of a work is given in its condition report. It's the document that determines whether the condition of a work has changed, and if there are scratches, tears, fingerprints, or other damage. The lending institution creates an outgoing condition report and, after unpacking the work, our restorer prepares an ingoing condition report. There is a special form for this, which includes the data and technical details of the loan item, and it is enclosed with an accompanying image of the work upon departure. Any conspicuous details will be highlighted on the image, and detailed photos of these areas included. After examining the loan item, our restorer will record any potential changes on this form. They also monitor every step at which the loan item is moved, in order to record any possible changes.

MW: How have technical innovations changed and simplified your work in the past 30 years?

TK: A huge amount of things have changed. When I started in 1984, we compiled an index card for every work in the exhibition, and added a copy of a catalogue image or a photograph of the work. At the time, these index cards were our database. Sometimes I think I'd like to go back to these old index cards, which contained all work steps and details. Digitalisation has massively sped up the whole process—today we send out loan requests by email, and receive an answer two days later. The rate and volume of these email exchanges actually necessitate more staff. And faster, more frequent communication often leads to less committed considerations, numerous alterations, and an underestimation of actual planning times.

I think it's hard for a lot of people today to differentiate between digital means—for example 3D simulations of exhibitions—and the fact that there is a very tangible exhibition, something very real. A digital exhibition always looks well-ordered and coherent. But the reality is different. In the real world you have to deal with the diverse ways in which light falls, the shadows, the unevenness of the walls and floors, the ventilation grilles and other site-specific factors. Working with artworks while installing an exhibition is a slow process—sometimes you need to think about it overnight before you find the right position for a piece. And even though digital exhibition models are highly sophisticated, time and again we find that the positioning doesn't work in the reality of the exhibition space if the works are to be allowed to reveal what it is that defines them: their individual aura.

PAGE SEVENTY-SIX

CLÉMENTINE DELISS

One year after the publication of its *Manual of Travelling Exhibitions,* UNESCO organised a conference at which French anthropologist Claude Lévi-Strauss gave a seminal speech. He declared that it was time for his colleagues to change their tack. He called upon them to refrain from collecting yet more statuettes and objects on their expeditions to far away lands, and to begin to analyse the cognitive and language-based evocations of meanings in other cultures.[1] Lévi-Strauss's declaration had devastating consequences. It effectively destabilised the legitimacy of museum anthropology's unbaiting and, often brutal, acquisition of the artistic production and innovation of other peoples, the authorship of which was to 99% undocumented. His statement was to bring about the inevitable demise of museum anthropology's focus on the artefact as a catalyst of knowledge and lead to the gradual dissolution of laboratories of research held within museums. Moreover, it would shift exhibitions from research-led exercises in interpretation to increasingly cosmetic displays founded on existing ethnographic documentation.

Since the late 19th century, anthropologists had endeavoured to understand how an ethnic group's material production might reveal the specificity of their vision of the world. Accordingly, man-made traps and tools would demonstrate the technicity of hunting, fishing and gathering daily nutrition. Objects made from woven plant fibres such as rattan or bamboo offered illustrations of the functional aesthetics of everyday life in the tropics, from the building of roof structures to the design of skirts, hats, and bags, not to mention various mystically charged paraphernalia. In the domain of ritual, these material embodiments of belief were for many Western collectors the pinnacle of desire. Eager to experience life's unknowns and witness the most extreme forms of human existence, anthropomorphic figurines and masks exposing layers of human remains from the traces of repeated touching and stroking, to blood, sperm, hair and bone, were gathered and traded in large quantities. Today, these same prized objects play a central role in the development of retention strategies based on toxicity. Claims are made that the microbiome excreted in ancient New Guinean penis sheaths, the dried, coagulated plasma found on the Boli from Mali, or the remnants of nail and hair on so-called fetish objects from Central and West Africa carry the potentiality of viral contamination. All the more reason, argue museums today, to keep them locked up and out of reach.[2]

Spanning a geographic arc from East to West, the photograph on page 76 presents a view of approximately 15 items from a national museum collection in the US. As the *Manual* indicates, schools are provided with these artefacts, which are installed under UNESCO-prescribed conditions. In this exercise in cultural mediation, headrests, combs, boxes, and small sculptures share a stage

1 See Claude Lévi-Strauss, "Place de l'anthropologie dans les sciences sociales et problèmes posés par son enseignement" in *Les Sciences sociales dans l'enseignement supérieur,* UNESCO, Paris (1954), 1958. Republished in Structural Anthropology.

2 For a detailed discussion on toxicity see the discussion between Frédéric Keck and myself in *South as a State of Mind* entitled "Occupy Collections", No. 2, documenta 14, 2017.

and inform the viewer that these various carved objects have been produced in Africa by way of the human hand. However, what one witnesses in this quaint mode of display is less the drama of a stage upon which objects play out the various protagonists than something much more pedestrian: the configuration of a market stand. The grouping together with the various object descriptives and boutique spot lighting, sets up different options: the student can choose their favourite item all the while recognising and comparing the functions of these objects and the skills of the unnamed craftsperson.

The trope of the market display evoked by the assemblage on Page 76 has traversed history from Renaissance curiosity cabinets with their panoply of the bizarre through to the didacticism of 19th and 20th century ethnographic museums. It is hard to dislodge, forming part of the polarity through which the contextual exhibition of ethnology is incessantly pitted against the pedestal power of the art exhibition. Page 76 lies somewhere between the two. It's neither bathed in rural terracotta ambience nor entirely prone to the white cube aesthetic. It's even charming, if seen from afar. Today, this idiom takes on a renewed formulation that reiterates the same obsession with multiple choice. With contemporary art practices from Africa, curators and institutions alike continue to favour a mixed bag of wares over serious art- historical surveys of individual artists. Where are the in-depth and contextualising retrospectives of the older generation of painters and sculptors from the African continent? What is preventing such presentations from being more widely developed? Why are bodies of artistic production repeatedly dismembered, as if only parts, thrown out now and again, were sufficient to quell the desires of a purportedly mainly European audience? What is behind this market-stall approach to Africa's aesthetic practice? Even though exhibitions have shifted from the ethnography museum to the spaces of contemporary art, the focus on presentation and display dominates intellectual debates and museological initiatives. New forms of display—so the argument goes—can create new audiences, resolve demands for restitution, and by extension successfully obfuscate any urgency to the rights of access to these works currently held in European museums. Indeed, the history of museum anthropology is that of a battle of taxonomies, modes of classification and retention. Could it be that formats such as the UNESCO handbook from the 1950s continue to exert an implicit impact even in 2017?

MOBILE MUSEUMS

ANDREAS MÜLLER

The ultimate travelling exhibition should travel complete with its enclosing exhibition space. In the 1950s and 60s many museums around the world experimented with mobile museums as a part of their outreach programmes. The examples of mobile museums shown here range from existing vehicles that were appropriated and sometimes redesigned for the display of exhibitions to specifically designed and engineered complex machines. Their size was defined by road regulations—unless expandable solutions allow for larger spaces—and their display forms were often developed as a creative response to these limitations.

088

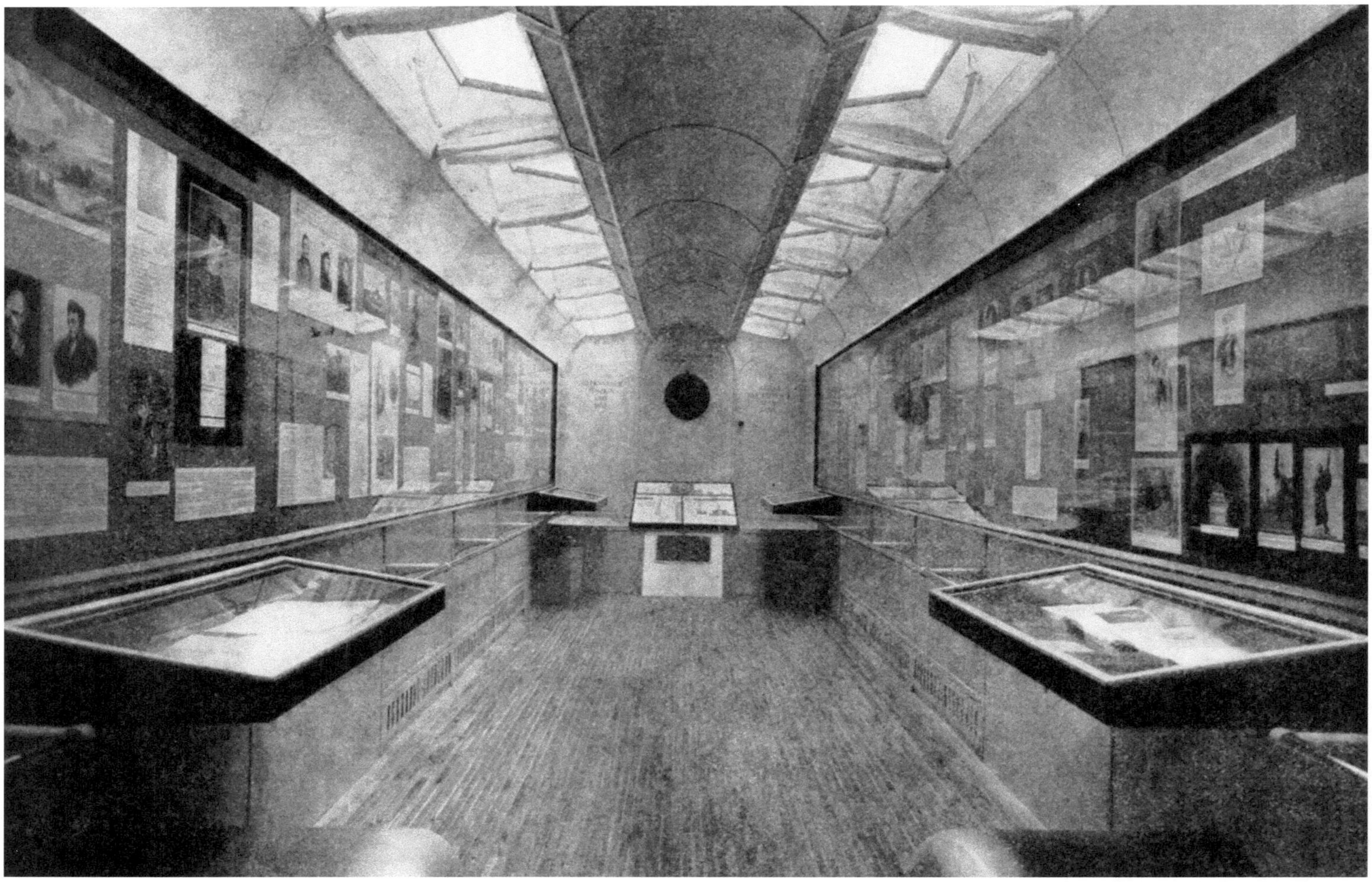

21

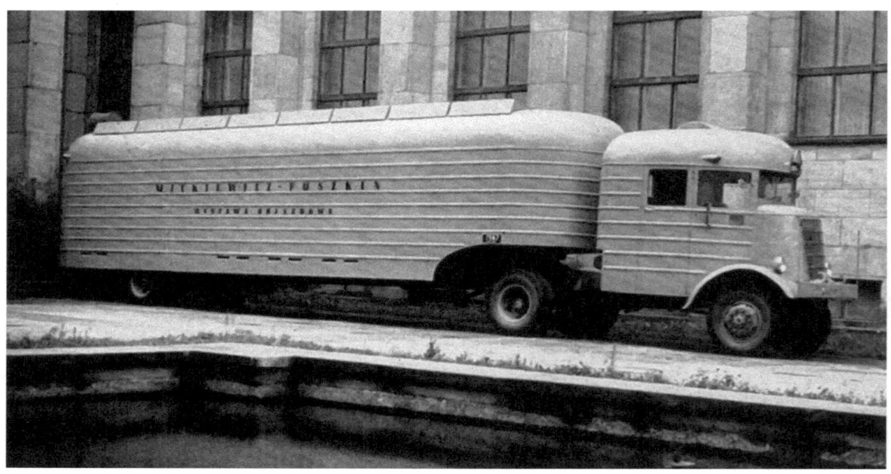

22

Fig. 21 – Fig. 22 National Museum Warsaw, Poland
In 1949 the Polish National Museum in Warsaw designed an experimental vehicle that was in itself a mobile museum. This motorised museum showcased exhibitions organised by the National Museum, travelling from one rural settlement to the next. The first exhibition that toured the country was devoted to the Polish poet Adam Mickiewicz; it included drawings, photographs, books and autographs, and between August and the end of November 1949, this vehicle toured through 111 villages and smaller settlements. The vehicle had audio equipment installed, and while the exhibitions were on view, content-related recordings were broadcasted.

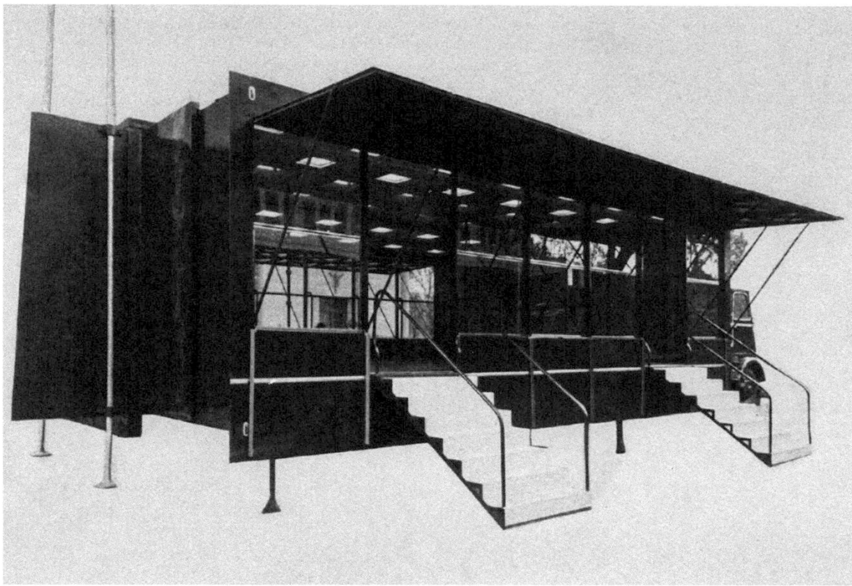

23

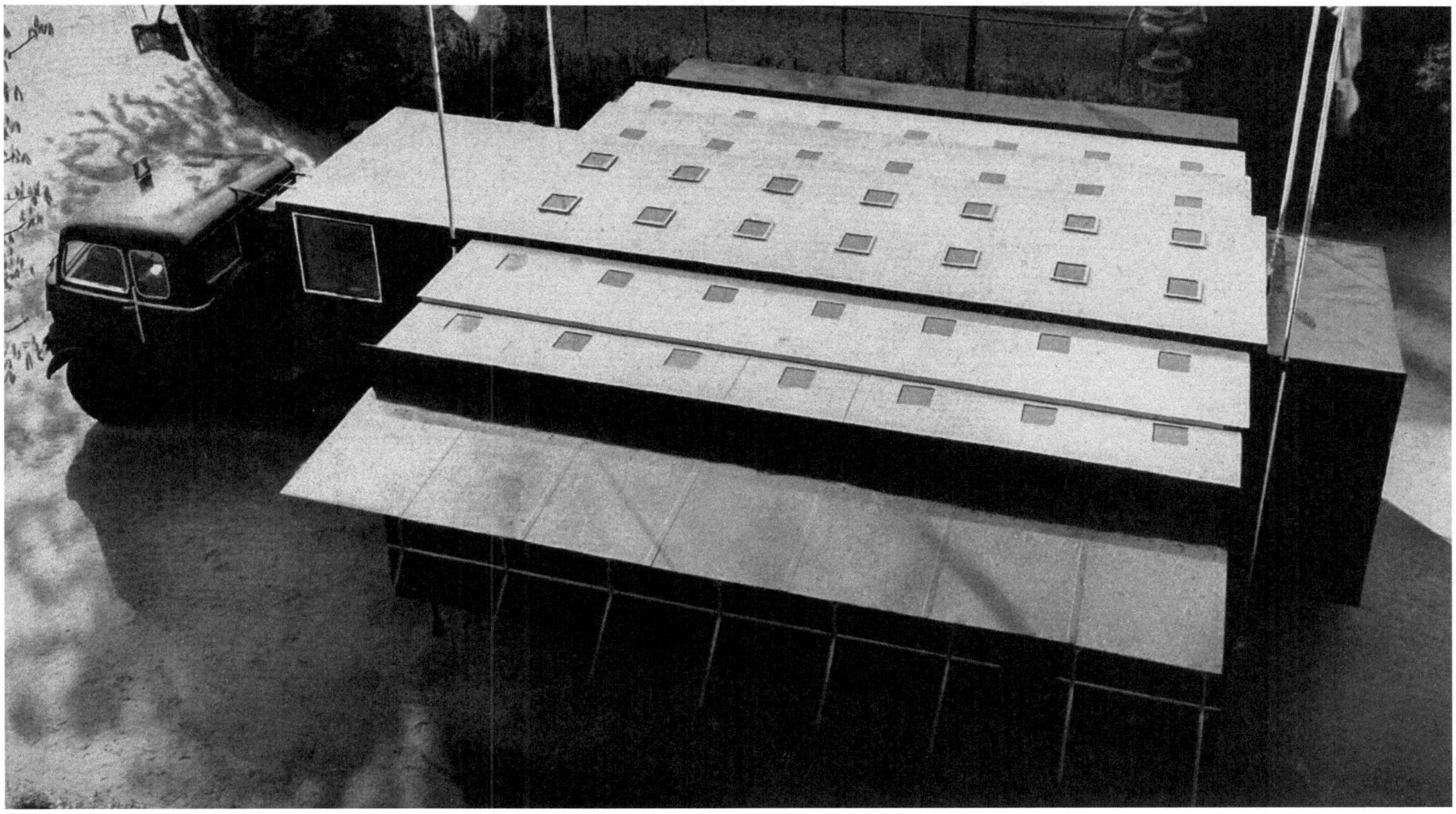

24

Fig. 23–Fig. 24 Economic Cooperation Administration, France

The architect Abraham Beer developed the Mobile Exhibition Unit as a prototype for the Economic Cooperation Administration (ECA), a US government agency set up in 1948 to administer the Marshall Plan in Europe. The unit consisted of a tractor and a trailer that could be expanded to three times its transport size; this offered an open plan exhibition space available to various arrangements of display structures. Based on this prototype the ECA's Visual Information Unit designed the exhibitions *Europe Builds* and *Productivity,* both exhibitions toured through several European countries in the mid-1950s. Abraham Beer went on to design variants of this unit, each suitable for different climate zones.

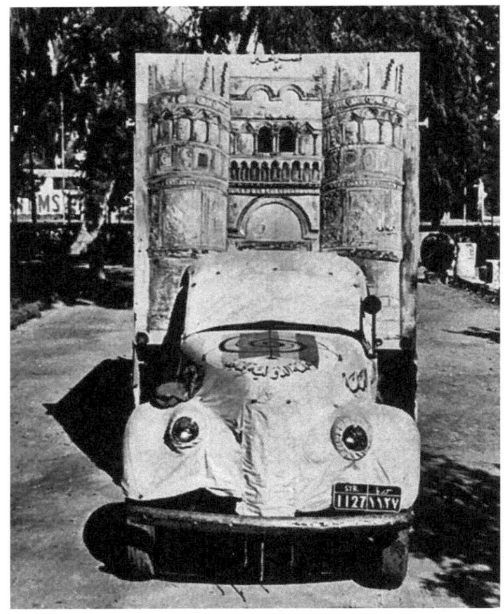

25

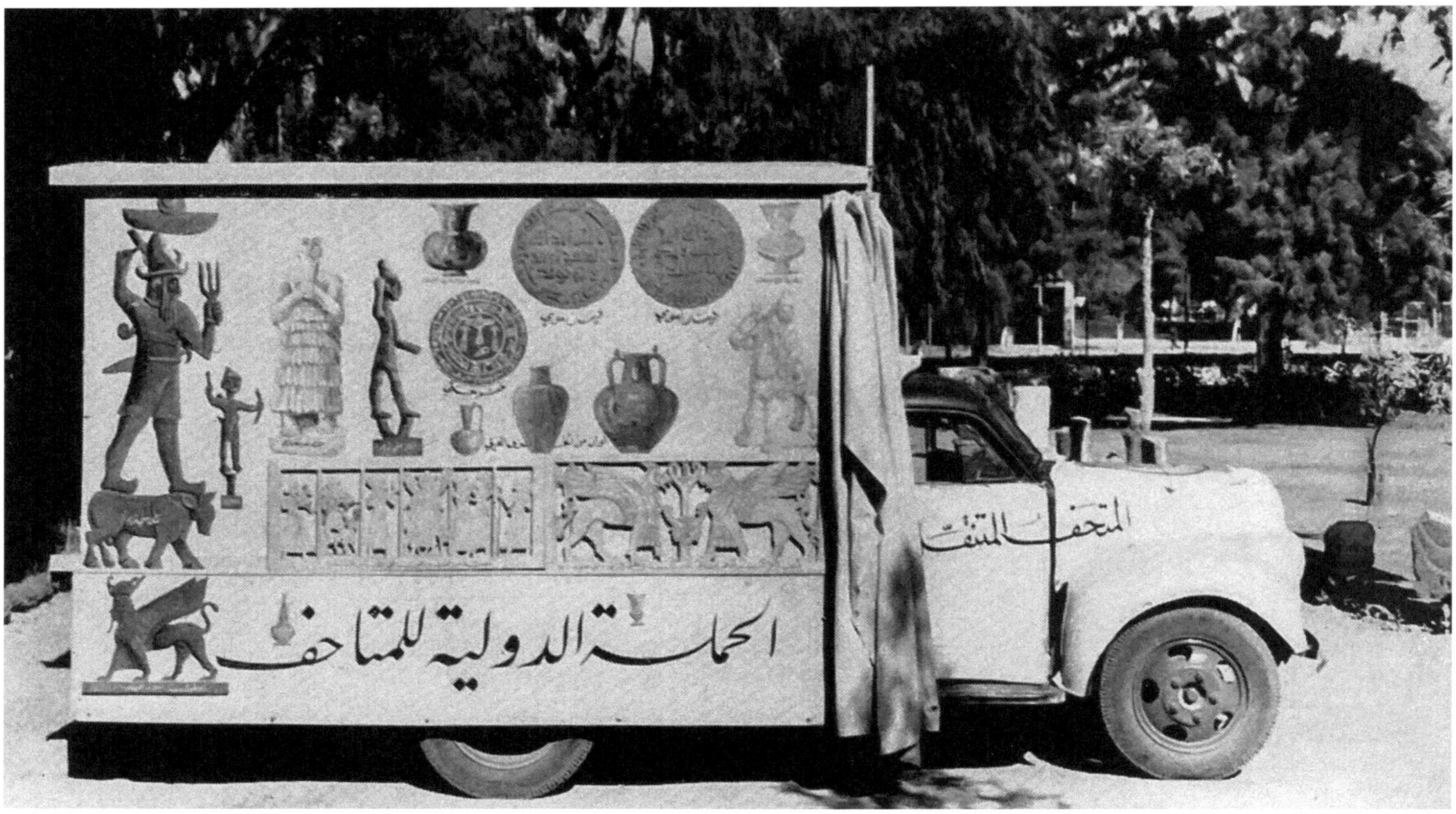

26

Fig. 25–Fig. 26 National Museum of Damascus, Syria
In 1958, the National Museum of Damascus equipped a travelling museum to tour the towns and villages of Syria, it contained an exhibition of archeological objects displayed in illuminated show-windows. The exterior of the vehicle was decorated with reproductions of famous monuments, with the front of the vehicle displaying a reproduction of the Qasr al-Hayr al-Sharqi, a castle built in 729 CE in the Syrian desert near Palmyra. Added to the UNESCO World Heritage List in 1999, it was looted and vandalised in the Syrian Civil War.

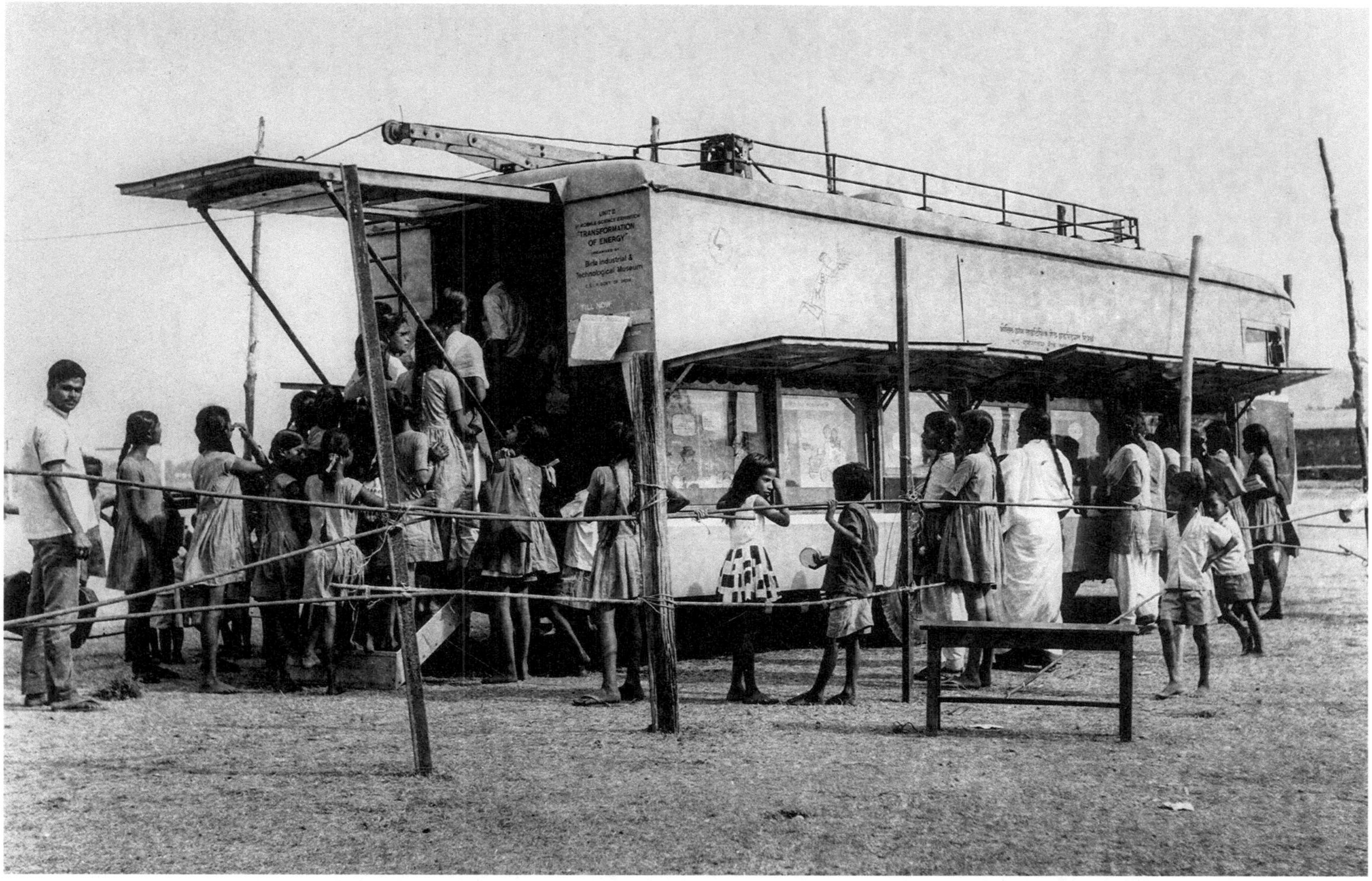

27

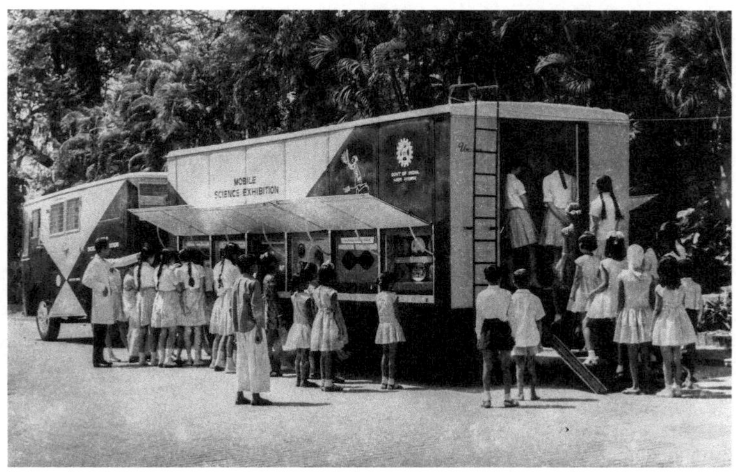

28

Fig. 27–Fig. 28 Birla Industrial & Technological Museum, India

The Indian National Council of Science Museums experimented with mobile museums in the 1960s. With a low literacy rate, particularly in the rural and remote areas, science museums were considered an effective platform for a non-formal science education. A specially designed *Museobus* was built by the Birla Industrial & Technological Museum, with a total of twenty eight exhibits on Transformation of Energy being devised. The project was inaugurated in the village of Barsul near Kolkata in 1966. The *Museobus* was designed for tours from four to six weeks and travelling during nine months of the year.

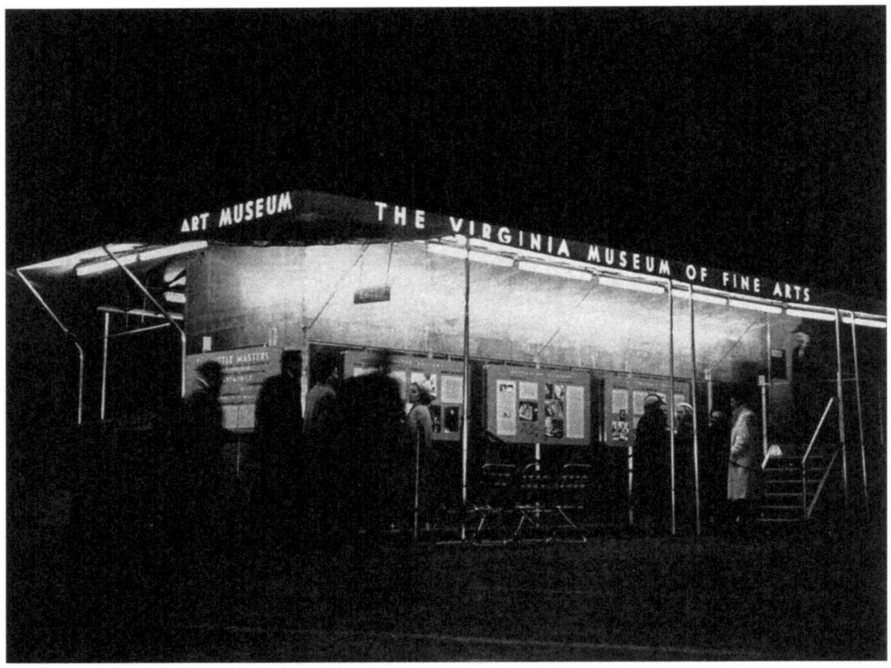

29

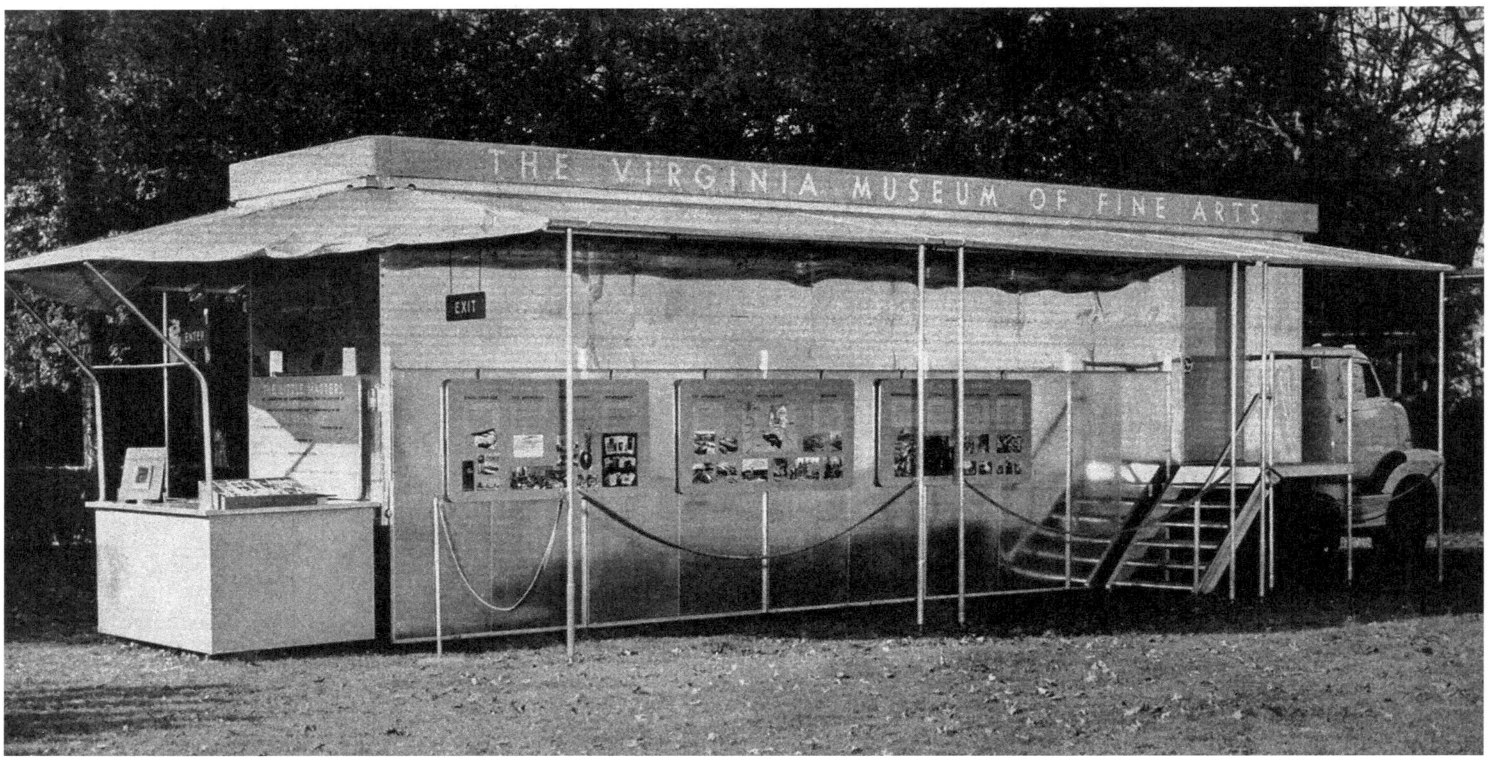

30

Fig. 29 – Fig. 30 Virginia Museum of Fine Arts, US

As early as 1953 the Virginia Museum of Fine Arts in Richmond had developed a mobile museum. As an educational project, the Artmobile presented original paintings accompanied by educational materials, such as information panels on the exterior of the trailer. These panels used photographs, captions and brief texts to communicate the nature of the exhibition (16th and 17th century Flemish paintings), their historical backgrounds, and the materials and techniques employed by the painters.

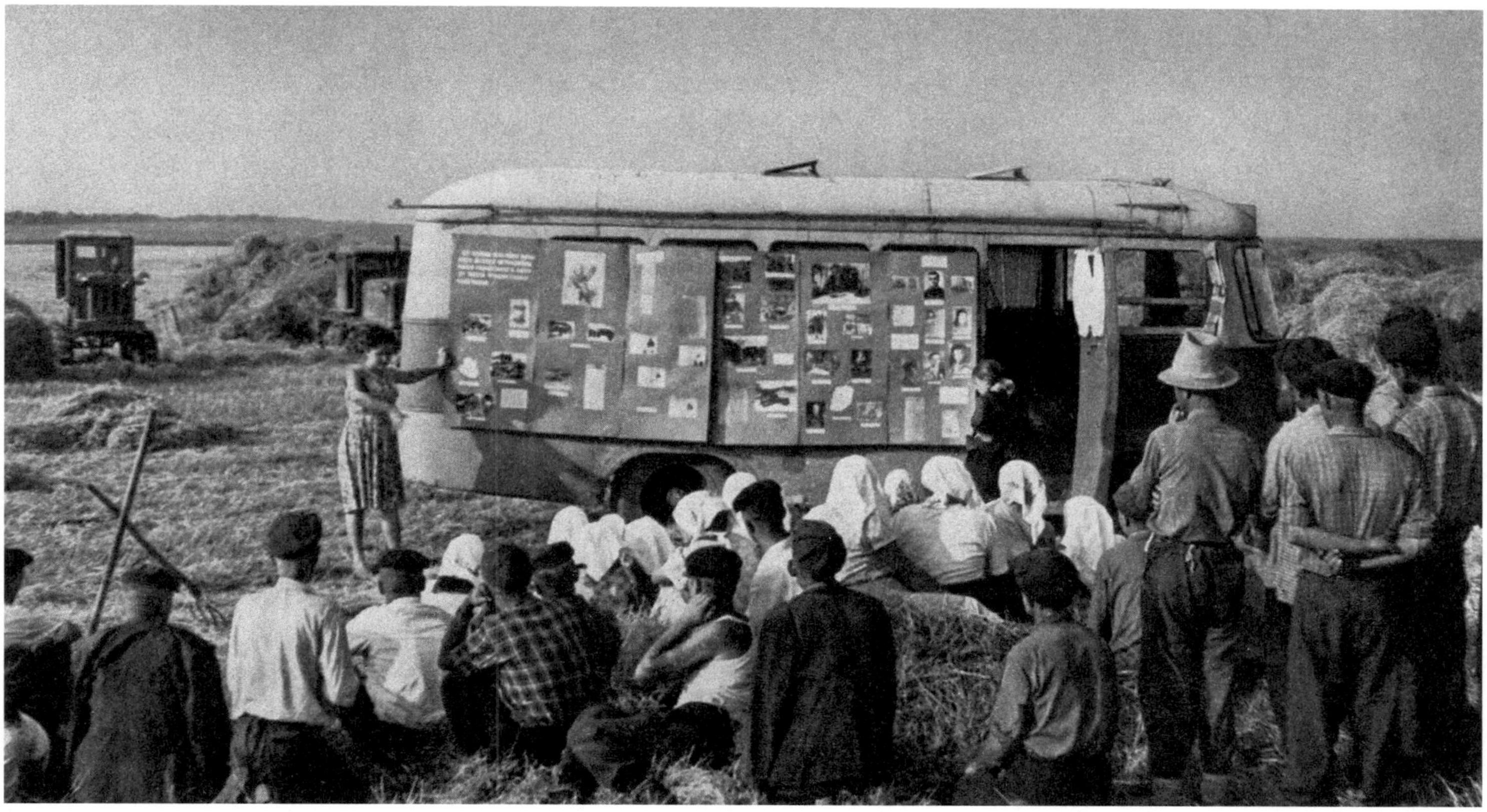

31

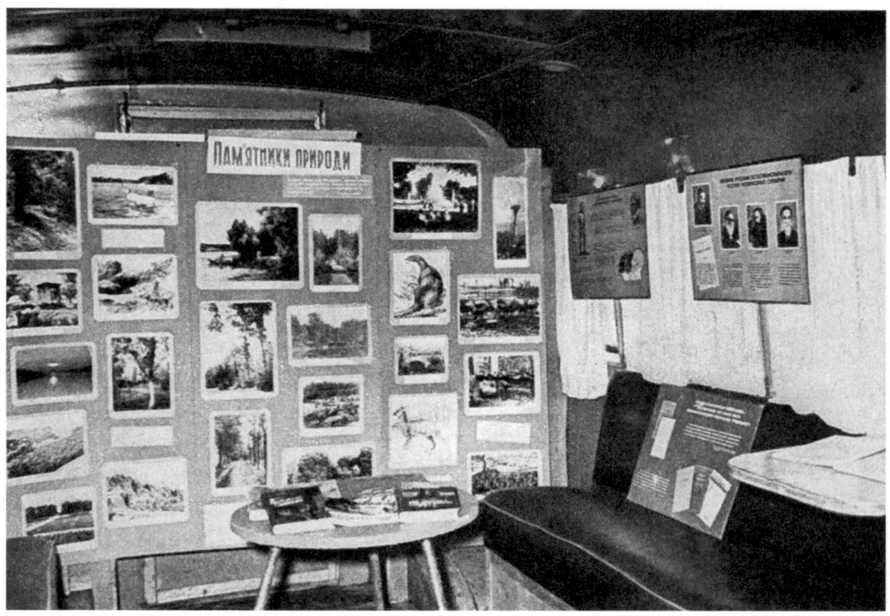

32

Fig. 31 – Fig. 32 Regionale Museum Yampil, Ukraine
In the 1960s some Ukrainian museums sent exhibitions to small settlements and even to kolkhozes or sovkhozes (collective or state operated and owned farms). The bus of the museum in Yampil, Ukraine, toured the regional villages and its staff gave lectures to local farmers, using simple displays of objects to provide a background to their talks. Inside, the museum bus had an exhibition and reading room.

EXPANDING MOBILE EXHIBITION UNIT II

SOPHIE LICHTENBERG

Based on the idea that travelling exhibitions disseminate information by way of their visual appearance, the *Manual of Travelling Exhibitions* describes them as tools of universal communication, and makes no distinction between the exhibiting art and the displaying of purely informative content. In the context of this de-hierarchisation, it not only composes a practical guide for the preparation of a travelling exhibition from concept to realisation, it also gives a history of the adapted transport and exhibition techniques. For example, under the caption *"Economic Life in Sweden"* there is a photograph that depicts the medium of the mobile exhibition: A converted and repurposed bus that had visited over 200 places in Sweden. An encounter with a foreign body that has integrated itself into the existing urban landscape and, as we're led to assume, interrupted its physical structure for a while.

Around the same time, at the beginning of the 1950s, the Visual Information Unit of the American Marshall- Plan administration in Paris, under the direction of the architects Peter G. Harnden und Lanfranco Bombelli Tiravanti, developed the *Expanding Mobile Exhibition Unit I.* Devised with the architects Abraham Beer—a colleague of Max Bill—and Peter Yates, as well as the graphic designers Ernst Scheidegger and Gérard Ifert, it was an exhibition vehicle in the form of a shell construction, with versatile display possibilities that could be used for many different types of exhibitions. A room in permanent motion that could be constantly adapted, both inside and out, to correspond to its contents and surroundings—a space with democratic potential.

While the example shown in the *Manual* makes way for an instance used in a new context—here a specially conceived exhibition vehicle—the question of a translatable form arises. How could the concept be modernised for today's age? How do previous developments influence the format of the mobile exhibition? Which new technological innovations and ideas could contribute to redefining the constantly changing, modifiable form of the exhibition and, based on already-considered ideas, create something new?

A collection of images and texts, created in 2015 in the context of a mobile home trade fair, records the details of current modular elements and the potential benefits of each component. Forms of integrated display systems serve as visual aids dedicated to a new, fictional state of the travelling exhibition—when rooms are taken on a journey. Images and texts, composed in a specific narrative, attempt to capture technological moments in order to generate a practical guide. A new, bigger picture formed from the conglomeration: an exhibition construction capable of temporarily breaking up the urban structure, and with its abundance of technology and innovative design capable of evoking new spheres of interaction.

Let us imagine that almost 60 years later, inspired by the American model, a new version of the travelling exhibition construction ensues, entitled *Expanding Mobile Exhibition Unit II.*

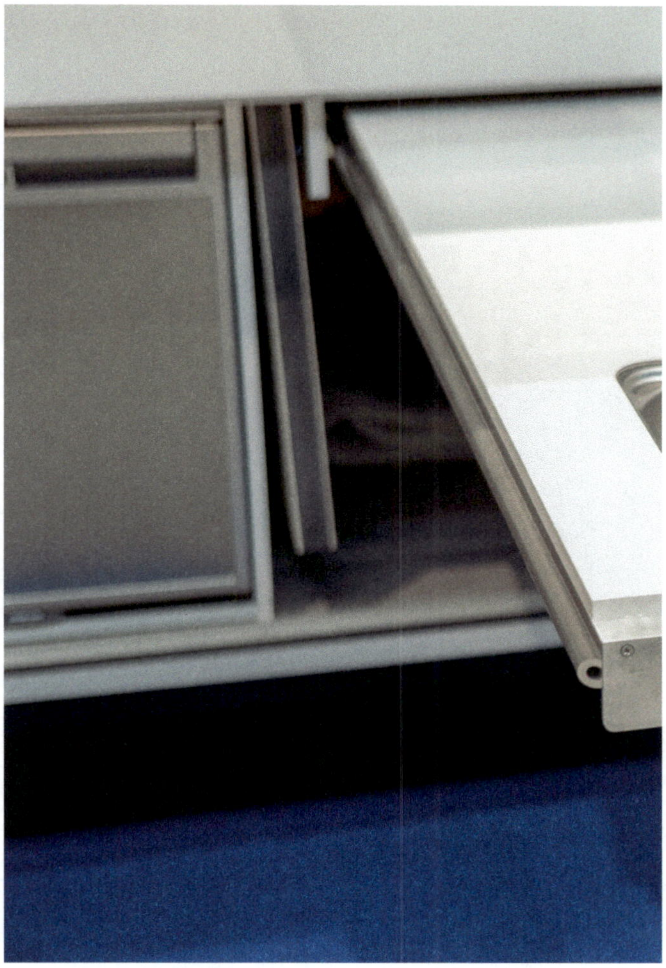

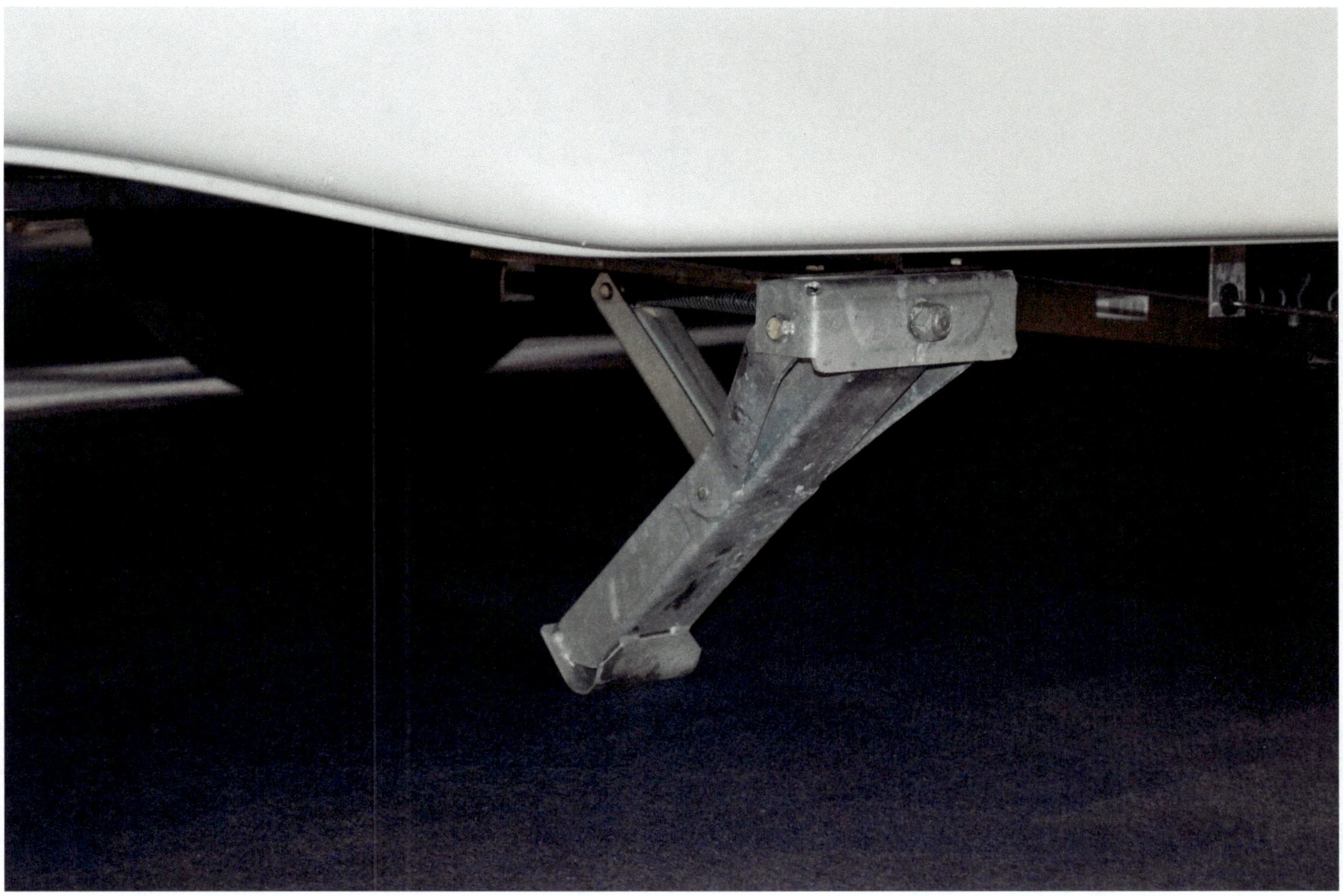

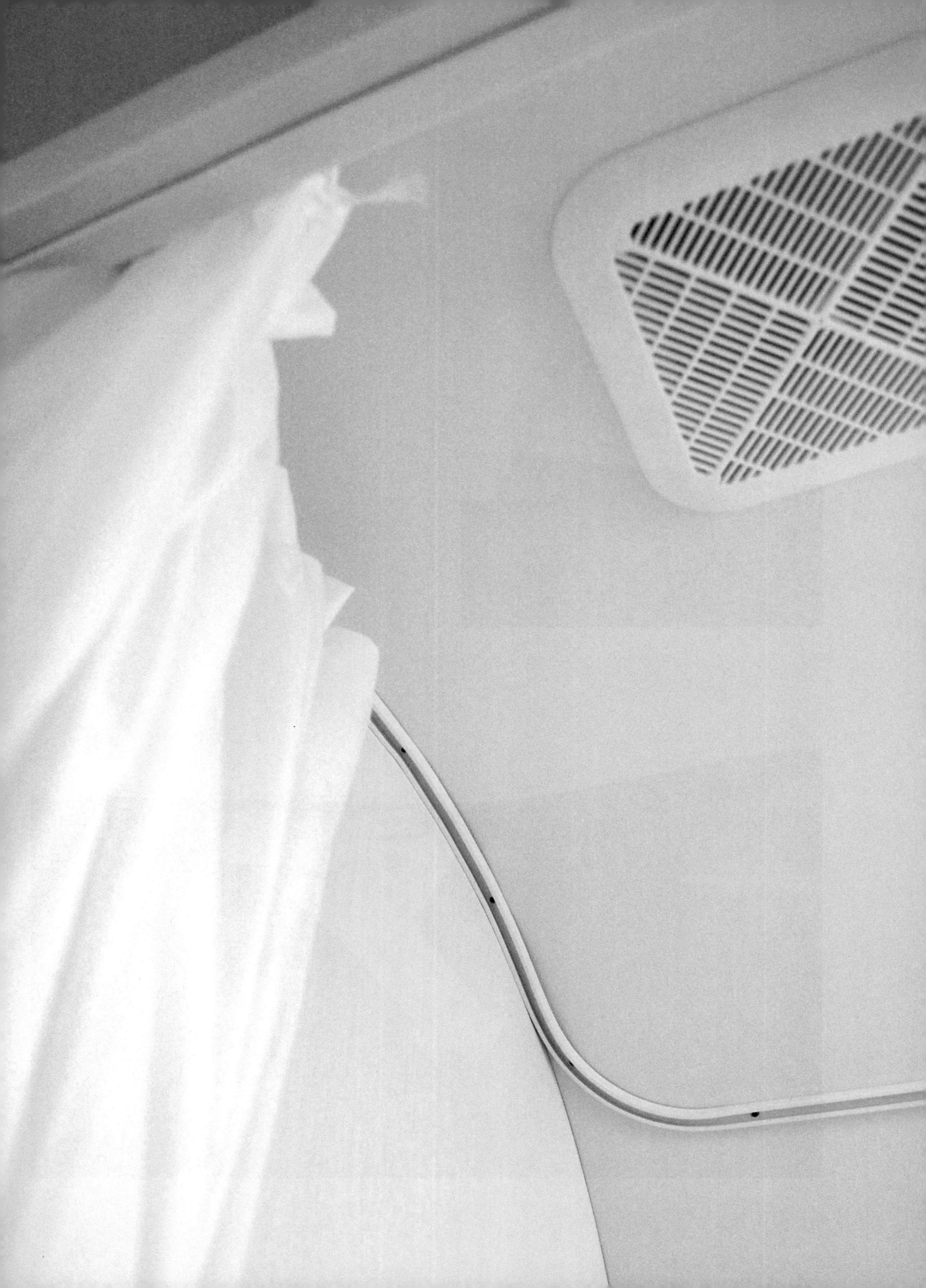

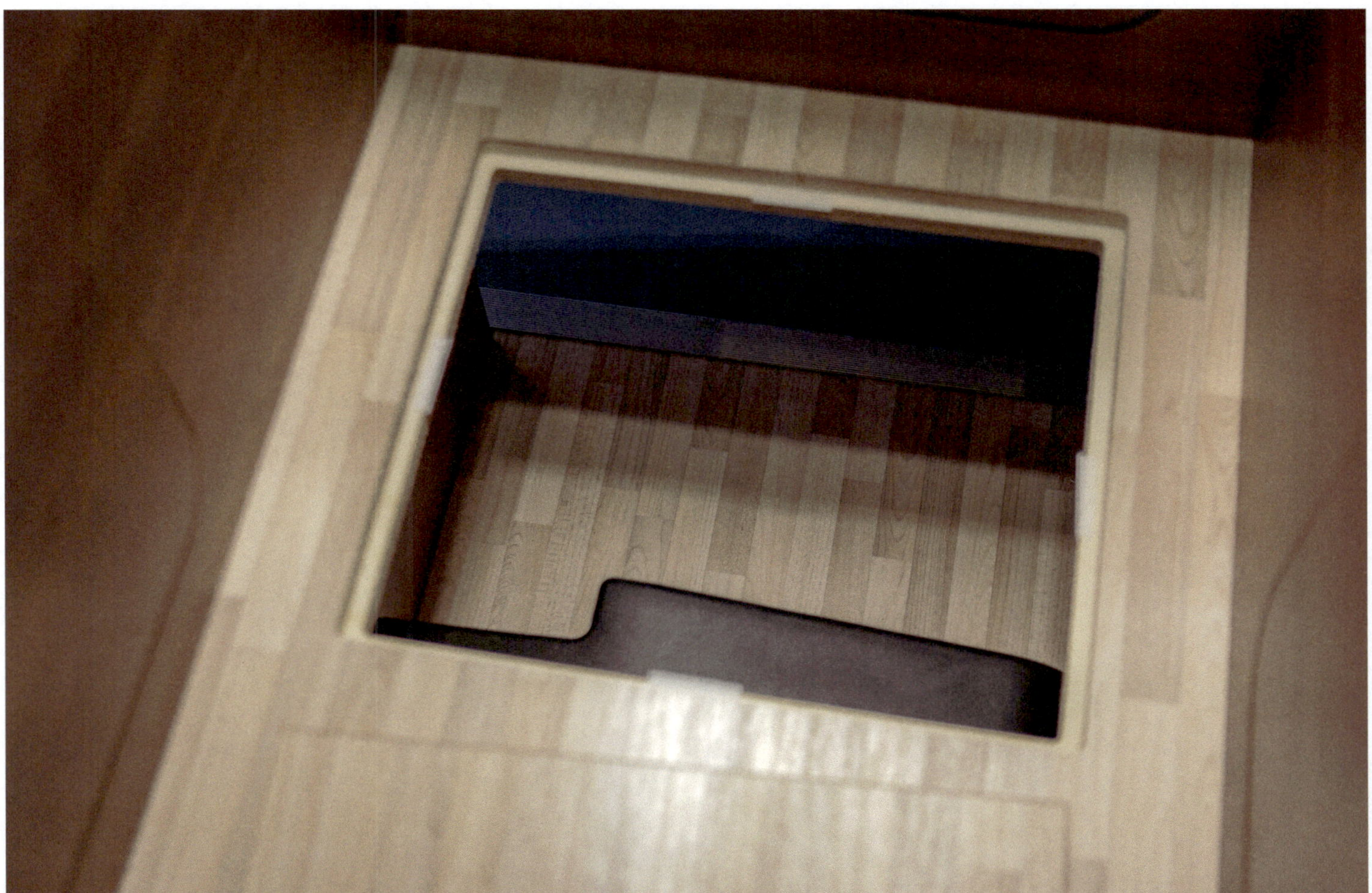

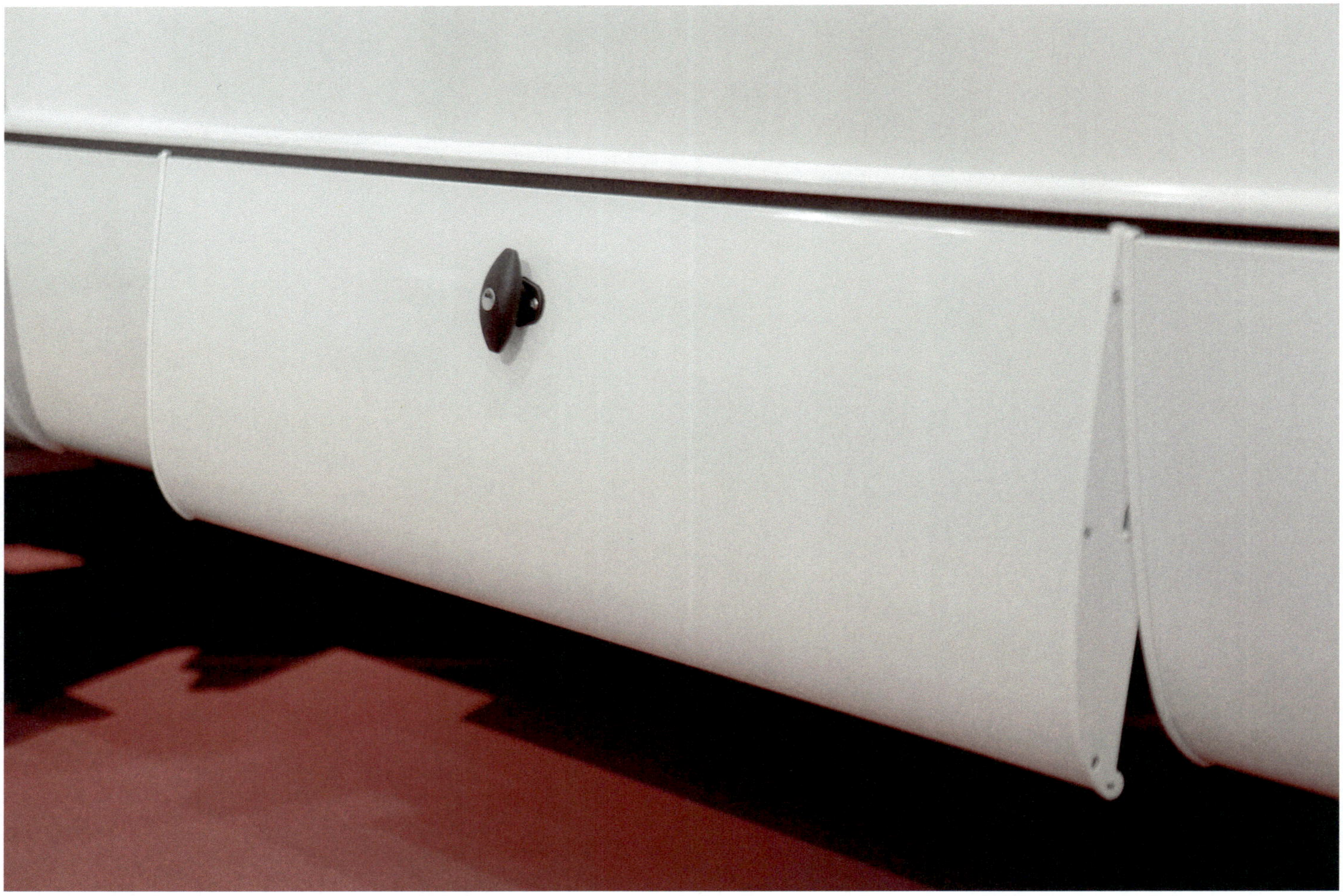

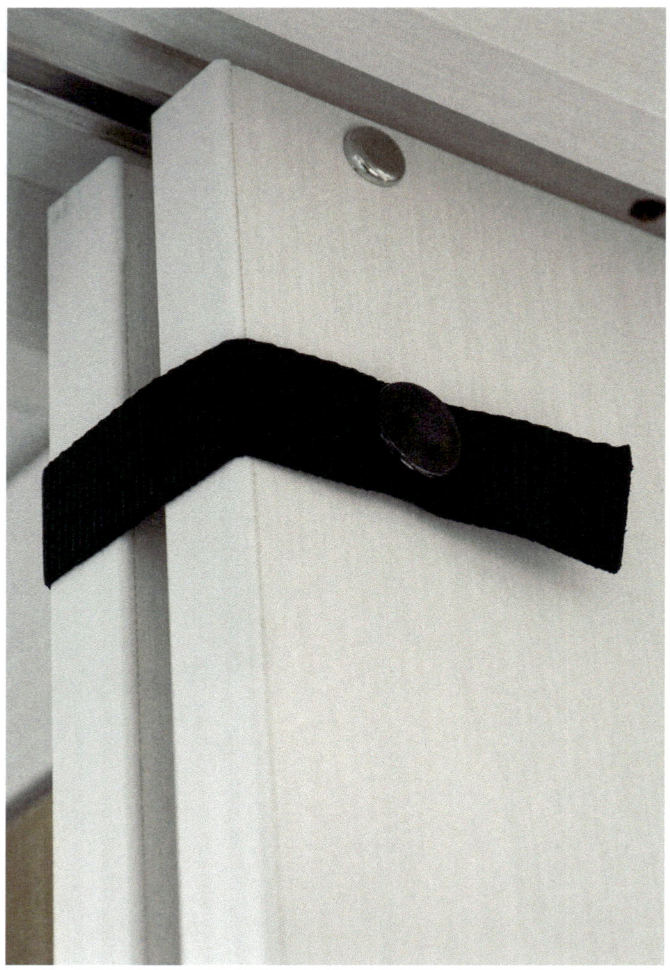

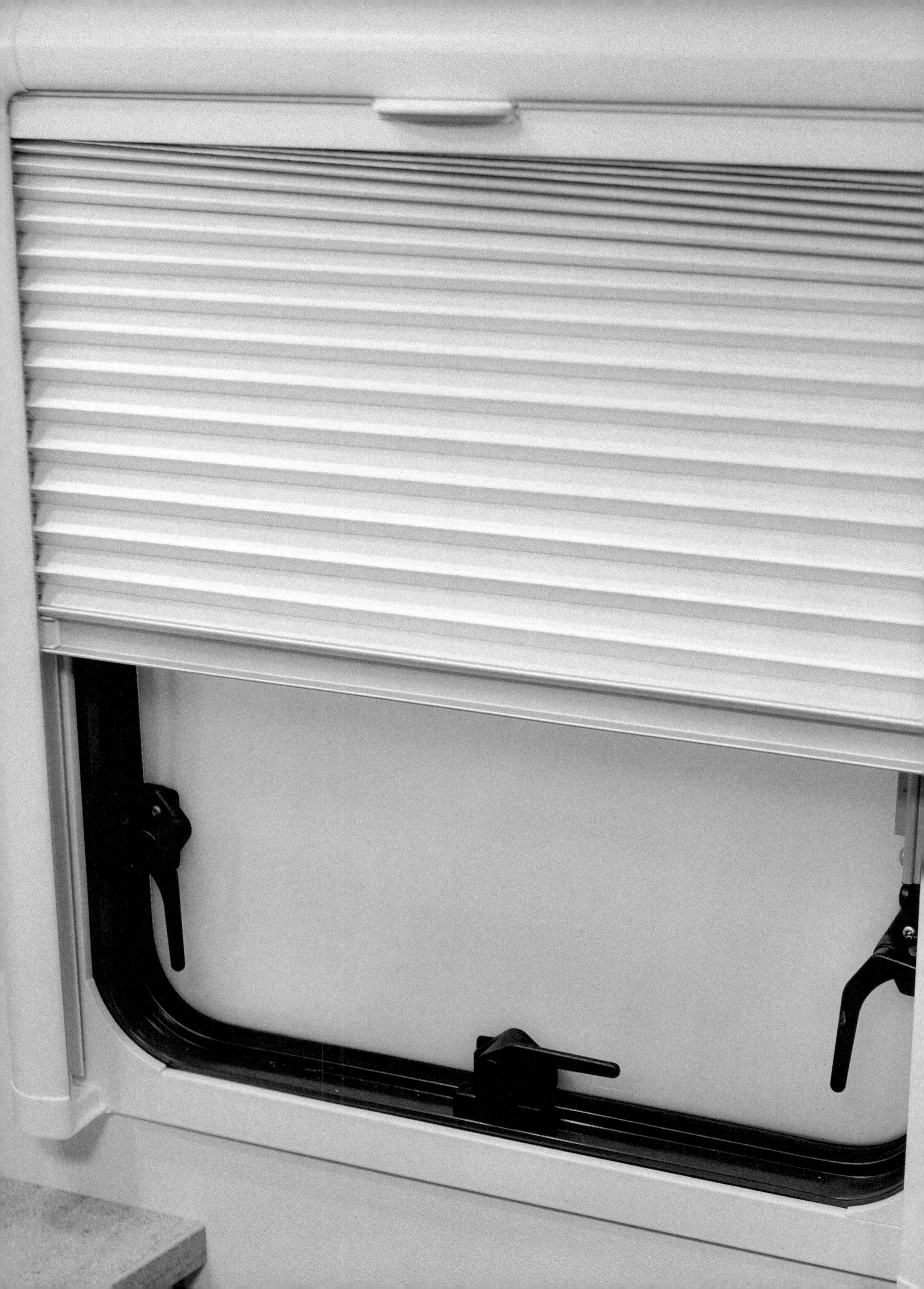

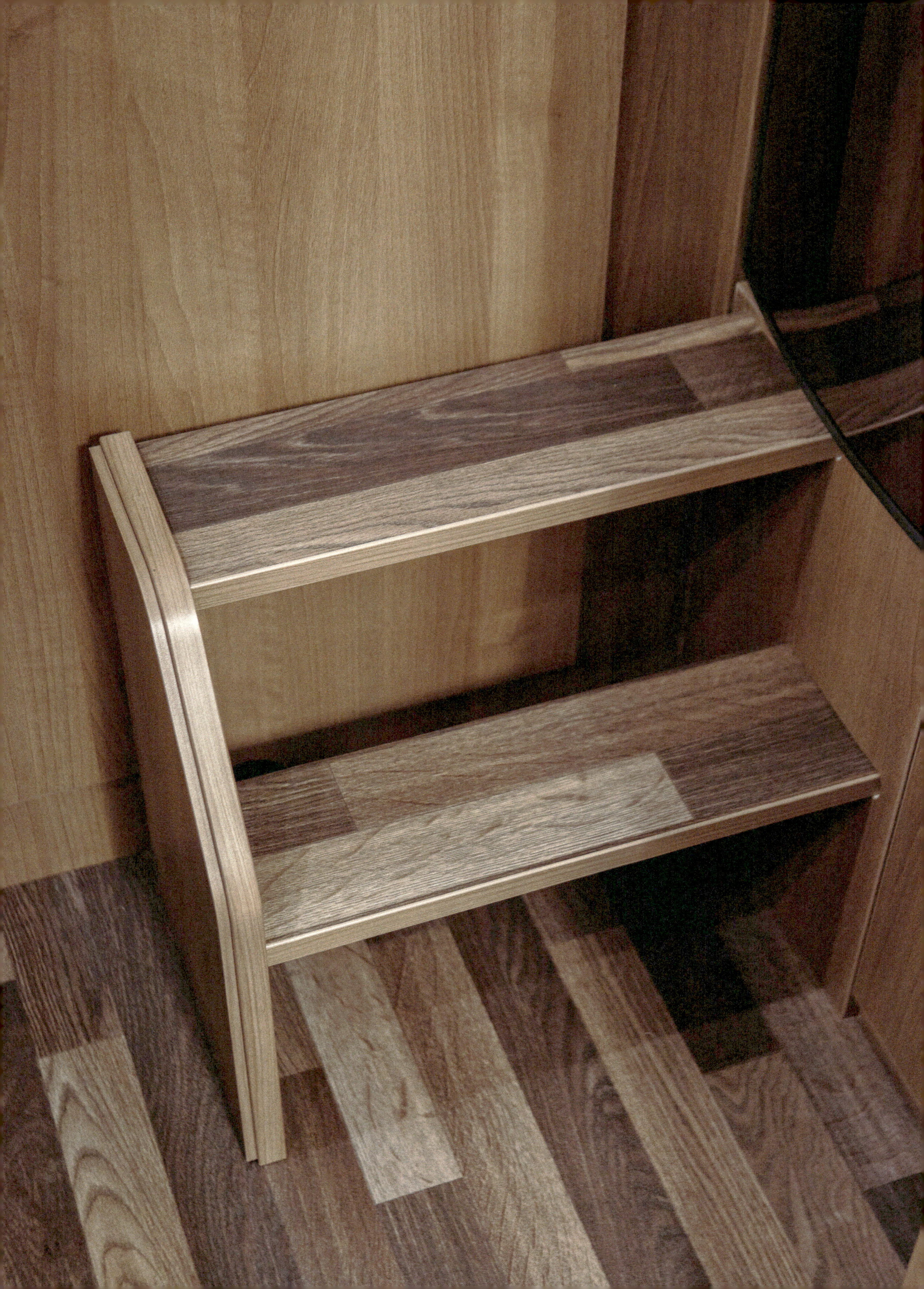

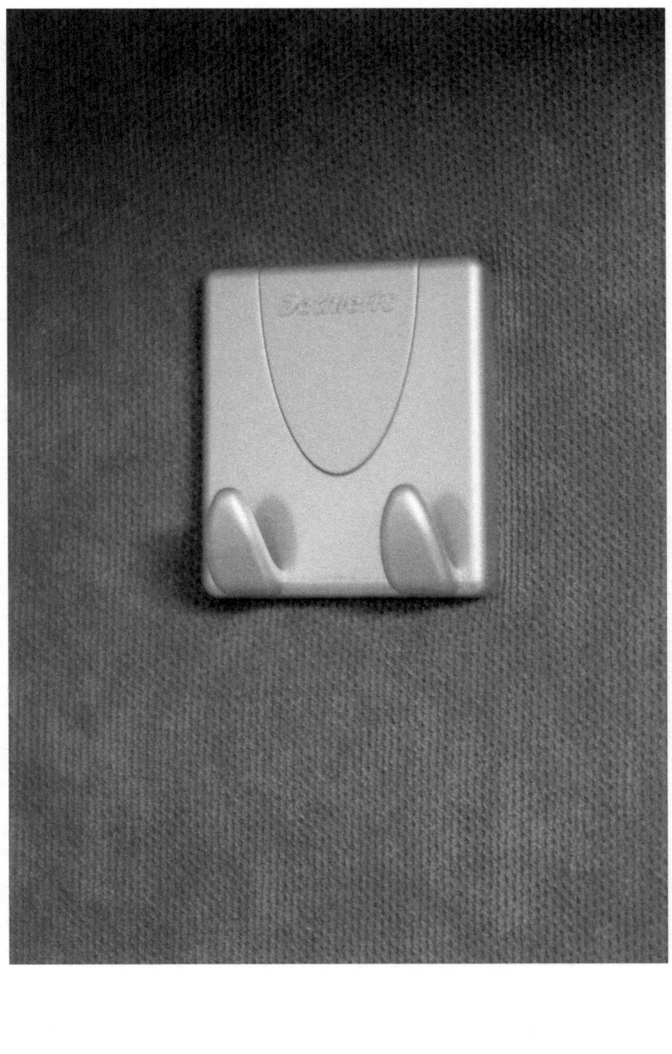

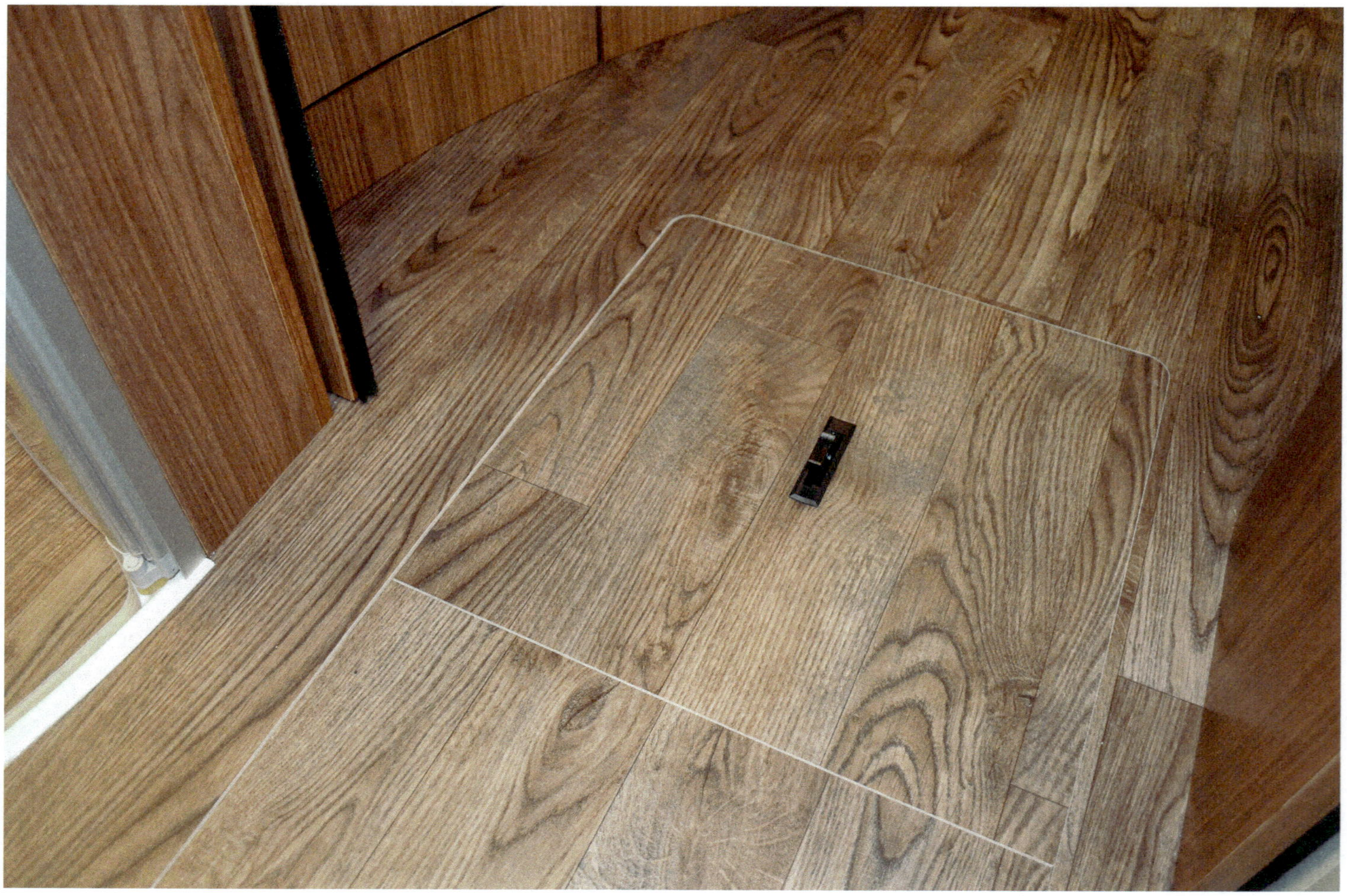

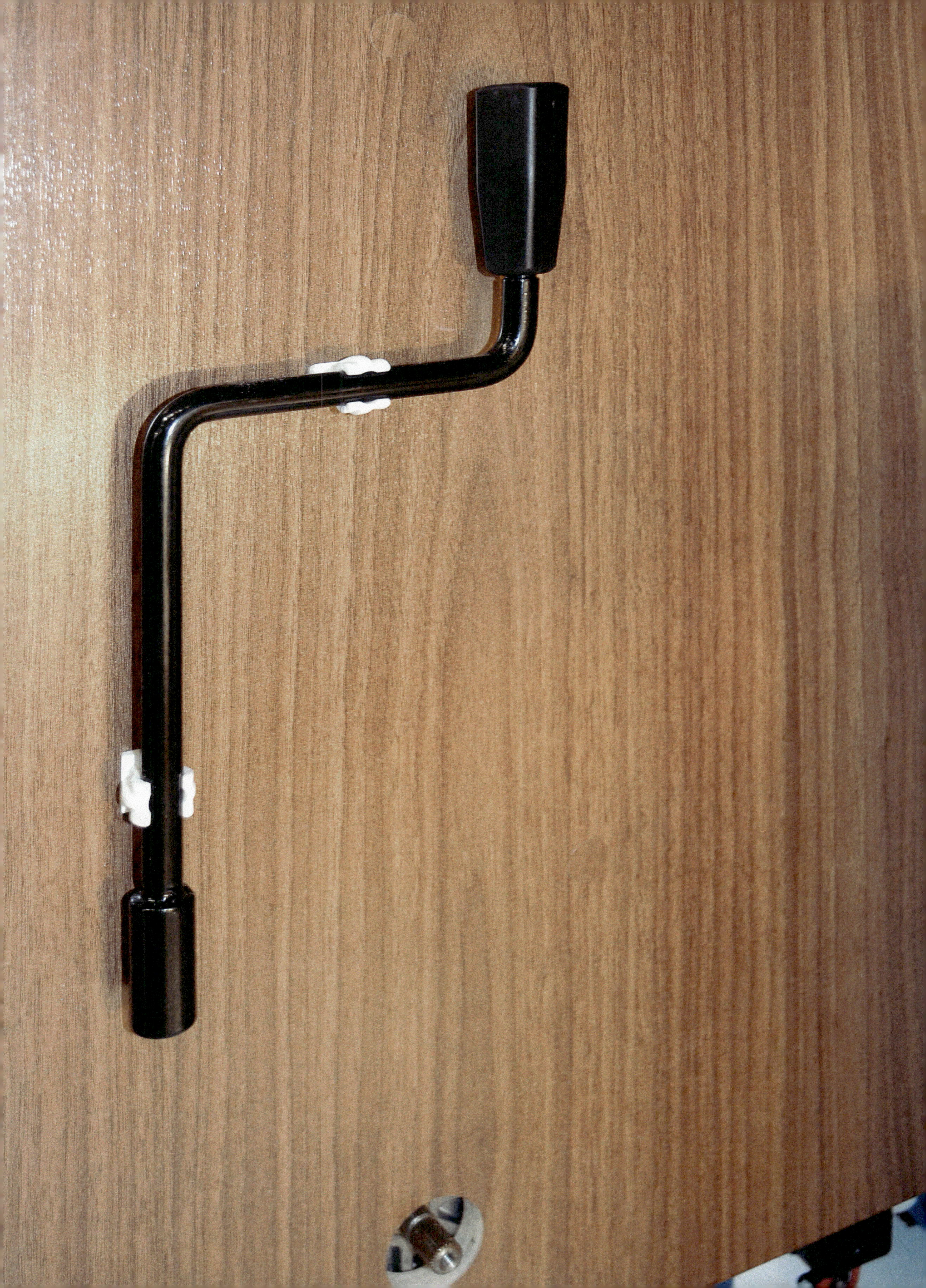

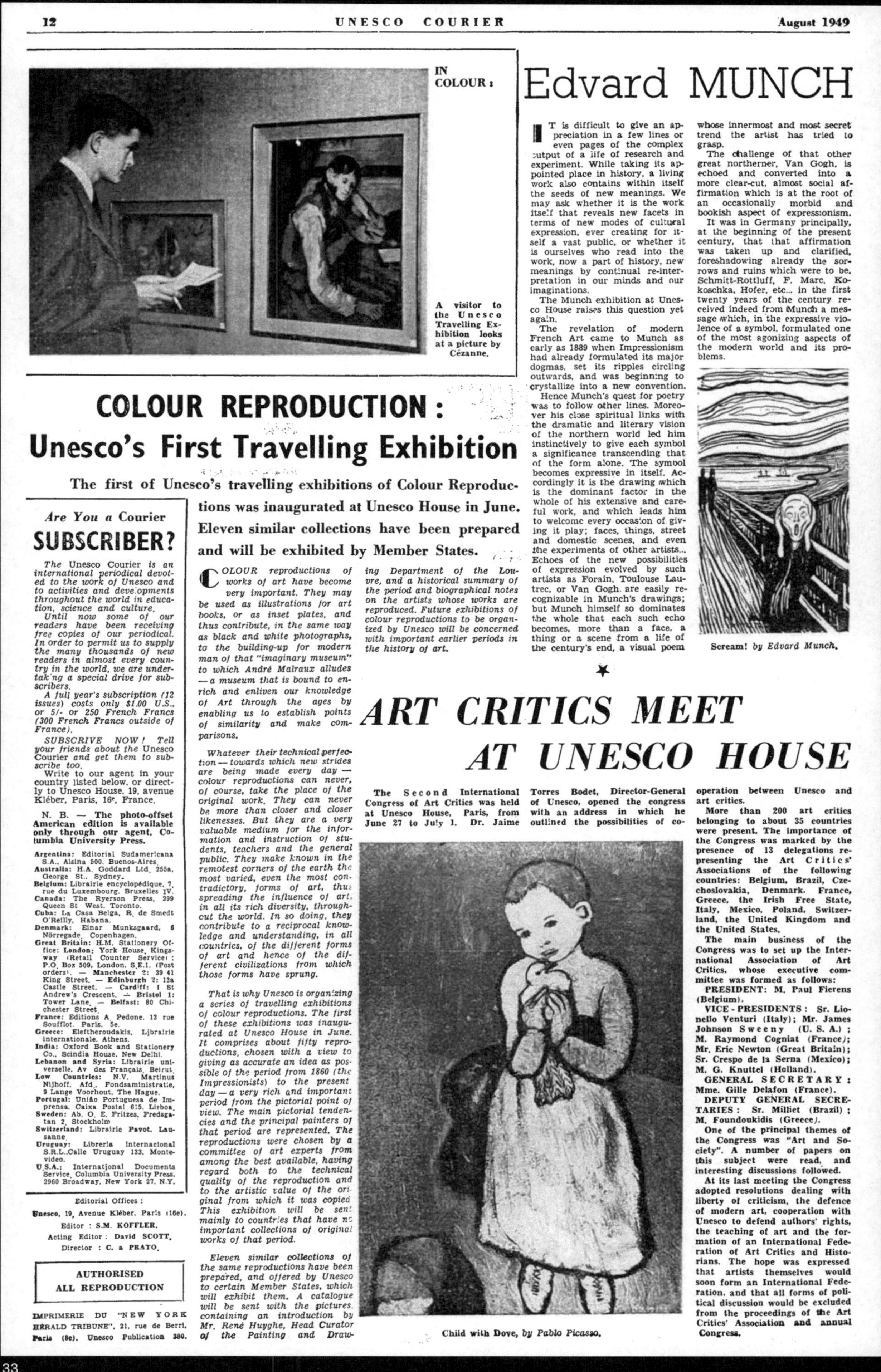

IN COLOUR :

A visitor to the Unesco Travelling Exhibition looks at a picture by Cézanne.

COLOUR REPRODUCTION : Unesco's First Travelling Exhibition

The first of Unesco's travelling exhibitions of Colour Reproductions was inaugurated at Unesco House in June. Eleven similar collections have been prepared and will be exhibited by Member States.

COLOUR reproductions of works of art have become very important. They may be used as illustrations for art books, or as inset plates, and thus contribute, in the same way as black and white photographs, to the building-up for modern man of that "imaginary museum" to which André Malraux alludes — a museum that is bound to enrich and enliven our knowledge of Art through the ages by enabling us to establish points of similarity and make comparisons.

Whatever their technical perfection — towards which new strides are being made every day — colour reproductions can never, of course, take the place of the original work. They can never be more than closer and closer likenesses. But they are a very valuable medium for the information and instruction of students, teachers and the general public. They make known in the remotest corners of the earth the most varied, even the most contradictory, forms of art, thus spreading the influence of art, in all its rich diversity, throughout the world. In so doing, they contribute to a reciprocal knowledge and understanding, in all countries, of the different forms of art and hence of the different civilizations from which those forms have sprung.

That is why Unesco is organizing a series of travelling exhibitions of colour reproductions. The first of these exhibitions was inaugurated at Unesco House in June. It comprises about fifty reproductions, chosen with a view to giving as accurate an idea as possible of the period from 1860 (the Impressionists) to the present day — a very rich and important period from the pictorial point of view. The main pictorial tendencies and the principal painters of that period are represented. The reproductions were chosen by a committee of art experts from among the best available, having regard both to the technical quality of the reproduction and to the artistic value of the original from which it was copied. This exhibition will be sent mainly to countries that have no important collections of original works of that period.

Eleven similar collections of the same reproductions have been prepared, and offered by Unesco to certain Member States, which will exhibit them. A catalogue will be sent with the pictures, containing an introduction by Mr. René Huyghe, Head Curator of the Painting and Drawing Department of the Louvre, and a historical summary of the period and biographical notes on the artists whose works are reproduced. Future exhibitions of colour reproductions to be organized by Unesco will be concerned with important earlier periods in the history of art.

Are You a Courier

SUBSCRIBER?

The Unesco Courier *is an international periodical devoted to the work of Unesco and to activities and developments throughout the world in education, science and culture.*

Until now some of our readers have been receiving free copies of our periodical. In order to permit us to supply the many thousands of new readers in almost every country in the world, we are undertaking a special drive for subscribers.

A full year's subscription (12 issues) costs only $1.00 U.S., or 5/- or 250 French Francs (300 French Francs outside of France).

SUBSCRIVE NOW! Tell your friends about the Unesco Courier *and get them to subscribe too.*

Write to our agent in your country listed below, or directly to Unesco House, 19, avenue Kléber, Paris, 16e, France.

N. B. — **The photo-offset American edition is available only through our agent, Columbia University Press.**

Argentina: Editorial Sudamericana S.A., Alsina 500, Buenos-Aires.
Australia: H.A. Goddard Ltd, 255a, George St., Sydney.
Belgium: Librairie encyclopédique, 7, rue du Luxembourg, Bruxelles IV.
Canada: The Ryerson Press, 299 Queen St West, Toronto.
Cuba: La Casa Belga, R. de Smedt O'Reilly, Habana.
Denmark: Einar Munksgaard, 6 Nörregade, Copenhagen.
Great Britain: H.M. Stationery Office: **London:** York House, Kingsway (Retail Counter Service); P.O. Box 509, London, S.E.1. (Post orders). — **Manchester 2:** 39 41 King Street. — **Edinburgh 2:** 13a Castle Street. — **Cardiff:** 1 St Andrew's Crescent. — **Bristol 1:** Tower Lane. — **Belfast:** 80 Chichester Street.
France: Editions A. Pedone, 13 rue Soufflot, Paris, 5e.
Greece: Eleftheroudakis, Librairie internationale, Athens.
India: Oxford Book and Stationery Co., Scindia House, New Delhi.
Lebanon and Syria: Librairie universelle, Av des Français, Beirut.
Low Countries: N.V. Martinus Nijhoff, Afd., Fondsaministratie, 9 Lange Voorhout, The Hague.
Portugal: União Portuguesa de Imprensa, Caixa Postal 615, Lisboa.
Sweden: Ab. O. E. Fritzes, Fredsgatan 2, Stockholm
Switzerland: Librairie Payot, Lausanne.
Uruguay: Libreria Internacional S.R.L., Calle Uruguay 133, Montevideo.
U.S.A.: International Documents Service, Columbia University Press, 2960 Broadway, New York 27, N.Y.

Editorial Offices :
Unesco, 19, Avenue Kléber, Paris (16e).
Editor : **S.M. KOFFLER.**
Acting Editor : **David SCOTT.**
Director : **C. a PRATO.**

IMPRIMERIE DU "NEW YORK HERALD TRIBUNE", 21, rue de Berri, Paris (8e). Unesco Publication 380.

Edvard MUNCH

IT is difficult to give an appreciation in a few lines or even pages of the complex output of a life of research and experiment. While taking its appointed place in history, a living work also contains within itself the seeds of new meanings. We may ask whether it is the work itself that reveals new facets in terms of new modes of cultural expression, ever creating for itself a vast public, or whether it is ourselves who read into the work, now a part of history, new meanings by continual re-interpretation in our minds and our imaginations.

The Munch exhibition at Unesco House raises this question yet again.

The revelation of modern French Art came to Munch as early as 1889 when Impressionism had already formulated its major dogmas, set its ripples circling outwards, and was beginning to crystallize into a new convention.

Hence Munch's quest for poetry was to follow other lines. Moreover his close spiritual links with the dramatic and literary vision of the northern world led him instinctively to give each symbol a significance transcending that of the form alone. The symbol becomes expressive in itself. Accordingly it is the drawing which is the dominant factor in the whole of his extensive and careful work, and which leads him to welcome every occasion of giving it play; faces, things, street and domestic scenes, and even the experiments of other artists... Echoes of the new possibilities of expression evolved by such artists as Forain, Toulouse Lautrec, or Van Gogh, are easily recognizable in Munch's drawings; but Munch himself so dominates the whole that each such echo becomes, more than a face, a thing or a scene from a life of the century's end, a visual poem whose innermost and most secret trend the artist has tried to grasp.

The challenge of that other great northerner, Van Gogh, is echoed and converted into a more clear-cut, almost social affirmation which is at the root of an occasionally morbid and bookish aspect of expressionism.

It was in Germany principally, at the beginning of the present century, that that affirmation was taken up and clarified, foreshadowing already the sorrows and ruins which were to be. Schmitt-Rottluff, F. Marc, Kokoschka, Hofer, etc... in the first twenty years of the century received indeed from Munch a message which, in the expressive violence of a symbol, formulated one of the most agonizing aspects of the modern world and its problems.

Scream! *by Edvard Munch.*

★

ART CRITICS MEET AT UNESCO HOUSE

The Second International Congress of Art Critics was held at Unesco House, Paris, from June 27 to July 1. Dr. Jaime Torres Bodet, Director-General of Unesco, opened the congress with an address in which he outlined the possibilities of co-operation between Unesco and art critics.

More than 200 art critics belonging to about 35 countries were present. The importance of the Congress was marked by the presence of 13 delegations representing the Art Critics' Associations of the following countries: Belgium, Brazil, Czechoslovakia, Denmark, France, Greece, the Irish Free State, Italy, Mexico, Poland, Switzerland, the United Kingdom and the United States.

The main business of the Congress was to set up the International Association of Art Critics, whose executive committee was formed as follows:

PRESIDENT: M. Paul Fierens (Belgium).

VICE-PRESIDENTS : Sr. Lionello Venturi (Italy); Mr. James Johnson Sweeny (U. S. A.) ; M. Raymond Cogniat (France); Mr. Eric Newton (Great Britain); Sr. Crespo de la Serna (Mexico); M. G. Knuttel (Holland).

GENERAL SECRETARY : Mme. Gille Delafon (France).

DEPUTY GENERAL SECRETARIES : Sr. Milliet (Brazil) ; M. Foundoukidis (Greece).

One of the principal themes of the Congress was "Art and Society". A number of papers on this subject were read, and interesting discussions followed.

At its last meeting the Congress adopted resolutions dealing with liberty of criticism, the defence of modern art, cooperation with Unesco to defend authors' rights, the teaching of art and the formation of an International Federation of Art Critics and Historians. The hope was expressed that artists themselves would soon form an International Federation, and that all forms of political discussion would be excluded from the proceedings of the Art Critics' Association and annual Congress.

Child with Dove, *by Pablo Picasso.*

UNESCO Courier, vol. 2, no. 7, 1949.

READINGS OF AN INSTALLATION VIEW

RIKE FRANK AND GRANT WATSON

The 1949 Anni Albers show at the MoMA was the first exhibition dedicated by the museum entirely to textiles. Organised by Philip Johnson and Edgar Kaufmann from the Department of Architecture and Design, it included Albers' works from the Bauhaus, fabrics for décor and industry, as well as several pictorial weaves, *art textiles* inspired by her teacher at the Bauhaus, Paul Klee, which Albers usually displayed in frames, therefore inviting contemplation rather than use. The image of this exhibition included in Elodie Courter Osborn's *Manual of Travelling Exhibitions* shows a variety of approaches to displaying Albers' works, always a tricky question when it comes to textiles, it includes at the centre of the image a chair mounted on a plinth tilted forward to emphasise its upholstery. In the background of this photo, lengths of fabric are displayed on dowels (carried over from the displays at the Bauhaus) and to the side of the chair a set of room dividers, produced by Albers especially for this exhibition. These last displays could be seen to occupy an ambiguous position, vis-à-vis their status as functional or purely aesthetic objects. Albers developed textiles relating to architecture at the Bauhaus, notably her 1929 wallcovering for the Trade Union Building in Bernau, cleverly designed to both reflect light and insulate sound, and according to Virginia Gardner Troy, these works made for the MoMA show were inspired by Albers' trips to Mexico where she saw mats being hung as a way to demarcate interior spaces. But in formal terms and in their construction, they also appear as modernist tapestries, precursors of the studio weaving movement that would emerge in the United States in the 1960s, which in part was inspired by Albers herself, including through her teaching, as well as from other Bauhaus trained weavers such as Marli Ehrman in Chicago and Trude Guermonprez in Oakland, California.

The exhibition *Textiles: Open Letter* that took place at the Abteiberg Museum Mönchengladbach in 2013 was named after one of Anni Albers' pictorial weaves, produced in 1958 and consequently not in the 1949 MoMA show. Principally through the medium of weaving, this exhibition explored the line traversed by textile practitioners in relation to the gallery, and the porous divide between the fine and applied arts. Although the Bauhaus's weaving workshop aligned with the school's move towards modern industrial design, the workshop kept their hand looms in order to produce more experimental works. Contemporary artists appear to have easily incorporated textile materials into their works, concepts and processes, whereas for mid-century artists working with textiles, the status of their practice as art was something felt to be contentious and problematic, because the mere fact of this has always been brought into question. This fact is outlined in the introductory essay from Mildred Constantine and Jack Lenor Larsen's 1971 book *Beyond Craft: The Art Fabric.* In it the authors trace a history of textiles as an art, and its use as a medium by artists leading up to the emergence of the fibre art movement of the 1960s. For artists working within this genre, like their Bauhaus predecessors, the abstract qualities of material and structure were important considerations, but in fibre art these were often explored on an even greater scale. Likewise, the spatial possibilities of textiles, which for designers like Otti Berger and Anni Albers was understood in relation to architecture, for the fibre artists pointed towards the autonomous sculptural possibilities of weaving. Crucial in this respect was the question of how fibre art works were displayed. Constantine and Larsen describe the "electrifying effect" that Polish and other Eastern European textile artists such as Magdalena Abakanowicz had at the Lausanne Biennial in the late 1960s, when they broke with the conventions of tapestries traditionally hung flat against the wall, by introducing multi-dimensional woven forms into the gallery space. This was a moment when the fibre artists found success on both sides of the Atlantic, including through seminal shows such as *Wall Hangings* at MoMA in 1969, *Deliberate Entanglements* at the UCLA Art Galleries in 1971, the Lausanne Biennial, which ran from 1962 to 1991, and a series of landmark exhibitions at the Stedelijk Museum in the 1960s and 70s among them *Perspectief in Textiel* in 1969 and *Structuur in Textiel* in 1977, not to mention fibre art exhibitions taking place in Eastern Europe, Latin America, and Japan.

The exhibitions at the Stedelijk were notable for the sculptural sensibility brought to the hanging of works as is evident in photographic documentation. In an interview, Liesbeth Crommelin, curator in the Department of Applied Arts at the Stedelijk from 1964, recalls the importance of hanging fibre art in a manner that reflected the status of individual works as being autonomous.[1] Instrumental to this was the influence of Wil Bertheux, head of Applied Arts at that time who had a background as an interior architect trained at what is now the Gerrit Rietveld Academie. The exhibition *Perspectief in Textiel* which featured work by leading fibre artists including Magdalena Abakanowicz, Sheila Hicks, Claire Zeisler and Elsi Giauque, was according to Crommelin the first time that Bertheux's "skill in the display of those big works became evident".[2] Correspondence between Bertheux, Crommelin, and the fibre artists reveals how carefully the contextualisation of fibre art works was taken by both the museum and the artists themselves. According to Crommelin, Bertheux even made drawings of the galleries and the space which was needed for every single work. When the artist arrived, he discussed with them all the possibilities but on the whole they felt he understood their work and agreed with his proposal to "hang them so that you never see one piece in the way of another".[3] This was in stark contrast to more conventional textile displays where fabrics are often shown as lengths or swatches in groups, sometimes alongside elements such as furniture, tableware or accessories, or even the Albers exhibition at MoMA, which maintained something of the Bauhaus tradition of product display.

Responding to this level of respect for the woven textile as a work of art earned plaudits from Constantine and Larsen, who in their book describe Bertheux's efforts for *Perspectief in Textiel* as "without peer"[4] and praise the curator for "supporting the lean intellect expressed in the work" and the way that he "achieved a serenity in the isolation of each piece and of one artist from another". Despite the fact that fibre art was installed as autonomous sculptures at the Stedelijk, it was still accommodated within a design context and shown in separate galleries from the fine arts. Terminology used in relation to these artists and their work is also revealing. A letter from museum director Edy de Wilde to Abakanowicz, refers to her works as "Gobelins", the French term used for tapestry, a medium from which she had self-consciously liberated herself.[5] Perhaps a desire not to be pigeonholed within an applied arts milieu is why the artist Lenore Tawney, a leading figure in American fibre arts, refused to participate in *Perspectief in Textiel.* Tawney stated that her "constructions, collages and drawings" had nothing in common with the other artists in the exhibition.[6]

In the summer of 1975, Anni Albers had her first solo show in Germany at Kunstmuseum Düsseldorf and the Bauhaus Archive in Berlin. The exhibition's subtitle—*Picture weaving, drawing, printing*—referred to fine art and its artistic techniques rather than to applied arts and crafts, a programmatic gesture (in the sense of a deliberate distancing) that also seems to have influenced the choices for the visual organisation of the accompanying catalogue. This is especially true of the plates (preceded by

1 Interview between Liesbeth Crommelin and the author, 1.10.2012.
2 Ibid.
3 Ibid.
4 Constantine and Larsen, *Beyond Craft: the Art Fabric,* Van Nostrand Reinhold, New York 1972, p. 57.
5 In a letter from Edy de Wilde to Magdalena Abakanowicz, 1967; archive of the Stedelijk Museum, Amsterdam.
6 In a letter from Lenore Tawney to Wil Bertheux, 12.09.1967.

an introduction to the artist's work by art historian Friedrich W. Heckmann): just three early weavings from the 1920s, from the Bauhaus Archive in Berlin, are followed by around fifty illustrations giving a substantial cross-section of her screen prints and drawings made (mostly) in the 1960s and 70s. In dialogue with the art works, the catalogue also contained the first publication in German of "One Aspect of Artwork", a chapter from her volume of writings *On Designing* (1971). In this essay written in 1944 (clearly influenced both by her experience of Nazism and her teaching at Black Mountain College) Albers addresses the need for new models of teaching and learning to pave the way for a "forming" education, rather than a purely imitative approach. She stresses that art—the experience of giving form that is inherent in artistic and craft processes (and processes of formulating, as her practice of writing shows)—plays a specific role in this.

What prompted Elodie Courter Osborn to include Anni Albers in the *Manual of Travelling Exhibitions?* Could one argue that it is the shared interest in education that led her to the decision to include Albers' MoMA exhibition? The advocacy for art as educative, empowering aesthetic experience? "Moreover",—she writes in her introduction—"the diffusion of knowledge for education in all fields—natural science, history, health, science, art, etc.—can be accomplished effectively through exhibitions."↩ 019 and continues: "With this emphasis on the need for bringing fundamental education to all the peoples of the world."

And yet Anni Albers inclusion with the two pictures of her solo exhibition is a striking fact:[7] on the one hand because the MoMA show never toured outside of the United States, and because Albers, on the other hand, is not only the only weaver but also the only female artist included (with Matisse, Henry Moore and van Gogh, plus examples from the field of applied arts and crafts).

The role of the Bauhaus weaving workshop and, in particular, the female weavers, which had long been neglected, ignored and undervalued, has in recent years gained interest and recognition thanks to the research of female authors such as Magdalena Droste, Anja Baumhoff, Sigrid Wortmann Weltge or T'ai Smith as well as artists like Katrin Mayer, Judith Raum or Leonor Antunes—in particular because of the tremendous influence of the weaving workshop on other media and a current revision of the dominance of the optical, to quote T'ai Smith: "[...] what specified weaving was constantly pushing against the specificity of those other media. Weaving harnessed the vocabulary of other media only to show, in the process, that those other media were never so discrete in the first place. What was specific about weaving at the Bauhaus, it turns out, was that it could exploit the limits of each disciplinary domain as well. So for example, the expressionist ‹picture› could no longer be seen as a direct expression of the artist's soul out of the fluid application of paint through a brush to a canvas. Rather the picture had become a laborious, even mechanical transfer into thread. Suddenly the picture was tethered to an apparatus that evoked the complexities of the textile industry—an industry that had become 'feminised', as hordes of women entered the factories in the nineteenth century. And when it came to the relationship to photography, the textiles only highlighted the discursive inverse of the optical—the palpable materiality of wool or silk and the medium's explicit life as a tactile entity, something that the discourse around Neue Sachlichkeit photography depended on and dismissed simultaneously."[8] As a result, due to its optical-palpable qualities, Bauhaus textiles made it to the cover of the Bauhaus magazine in 1931. Yet the story of Anni Albers' exhibition documentation seems to confirm the dominant image policy that was above all concerned with marking textile's functional character—in service to the other arts and crafts.

Until the publication of the MoMA online archive in 2016, the illustration 17 in the *Manual*↩ 095—showing a chair on a podium tilted slightly forward, surrounded by a carefully choreographed hanging of space dividers draped with lengths of fabric—was the most reproduced and often the only installation view used to document Albers' exhibition. This even applies to the detailed analysis by Virginia Gardner Troy, *Anni Albers and Ancient American Textiles: From Bauhaus to Black Mountain.* However, the entries in the online MoMA archive indicate that, besides the well-known exhibition view, there still are a whole series of further shots. So does the focus on the chair, a Van Keppel-Green design, reaffirm the thesis that textiles were mainly presented as functional textures emphasising the good design? And to what extent does the fact that the chair,

7 The first part of the publication consists exclusively of technical drawings and reproductions of documents, with no pictures of works.

8 T'ai Smith, "Tactile Lessons", unpublished manuscript, lecture held in the context of the conference "Textiles: Open Letter—A Haptic Space: Praxis and Discourse", 12.2012, Academy of Fine Arts Vienna, organised by Rike Frank and Sabeth Buchmann.

9 Anni Albers: "Though some of the earliest weavings unearthed after thousands of years have the magic of things not yet found useful and later periods have shown us weaving as art, thousands of years of establishing and expanding the usefulness of woven materials have made us see in them first something to be woven, walked on, sat upon, to be cut up, sewn together again, in short, largely something no longer in itself fulfilled. To let threads be articulate again and find a form for themselves to no other end than their own orchestration, not to be sat on, walked on, only to be looked at, is the raison d'être of my pictorial weavings." in: Anni Albers, *Pictorial Weavings,* MIT, 1959, p. 3.

as the master checklist in the online archive shows, is a loan from the architect and curator of the exhibition Philip C. Johnson, re-emphasising that textiles are presented subordinate to other arts and male-dominated techniques? How is it, if indirectly though, that Philip C. Johnson occupies the centre?

At the same time these additional views also support the theory that the exhibition design—the hanging and presentation of the textiles—was influenced primarily by Albers' many trips to Mexico and her longstanding engagement with Latin American, and especially Peruvian, textiles. The photographs reinforce the impression that the exhibition's design was a deliberate attempt to move away from the pure functionality of the textile[9]—without quoting the display grammar of the Bauhaus show curated by Walter Gropius and Herbert Bayer a decade earlier *(Bauhaus 1919–1928)*. This exhibition was controversial on account of its display,[10] following the idea of a "field of vision",[11] whereas Albers' design seems to have been aiming for a far more haptic space, an experience emphasising body, process, and material—further underlined by the inclusion of educational practice materials.[12] The staging of both the Van Keppel-Green chair and the space dividers also marked the Bauhaus's turn towards architecture[13] and interior design in the weaving workshops—first under Hannes Meyer and later under the direction of Mies van der Rohe. The latter handed the post to exhibition- and interior designer Lilly Reich, whose revised 1932 curriculum bore the title *ausführung von textilien nach freiem entwurf und nach gestellten aufgaben in den verschiedenen materialien und techniken unter berücksichtigung des bedarfs der neuen raumgestaltung* [making textiles based on free designs and set tasks, using a wide range of materials and techniques, bearing in mind the needs of new interior design]. In 1929, while Meyer still retained the post, the weaver Otti Berger published her essay "stoffe im raum" [fabrics in space] in the Bauhaus magazine *RED*[14] and Anni Albers developed wall covering fabrics for the Federal School of the German Trades Union (ADGB) near Bernau, a complex designed by Meyer.[15]

The year the *Manual of Travelling Exhibitions* appeared also saw the publication of *Neue Ausstellungsgestaltung* [New Exhibition Design], a study compiled by Richard Paul Lohse (in 1973, Lohse's extensive monograph *Modulare und serielle Ordnungen* also included a text by Friedrich W. Heckmann). Along with Klaus Franck's *Exhibitions: A Survey of International Designs* (1961) and George Nelson's *Display* (1953)—to name just two of the many books published around this time—Lohse's book became a reference source on methods and materials for a generation of artists in the late 1980s and 90s who were discussing display-related questions and the inclusion of design, addressing the demarcations and interrelations that mention textiles as a source of inspiration while devaluing them in terms of method and material. As a curatorial practice, this problem is exemplified by Mary Anne Staniszewski's *Power of Display: A History of Exhibition Installations at the Museum of Modern Art* (1998): the book mentions neither textile exhibitions nor the name Anni Albers in its index, although the Bauhaus, design and "primitive art" are dealt with including examples, and although Staniszewski's foreword reflects explicitly on the mechanisms of historical amnesia and exclusion, asking: "What sorts of viewers, or ‹subjects›, do different types of installation designs create? [...] What kinds of art histories, exhibitions, and installations are produced if the installations of the past have been forgotten? What sort of collective cultural memories does an amnesia regarding exhibition design produce?"

A question also raised as a gendered reflection by the artist Katrin Mayer in her work *Screens* (2014)[16] for the Kunsthalle Bielefeld: commissioned to produce a contribution to the collection, she references the history of the Kunsthalle's exhibition design: the free standing wall system, that Philip C. Johnson, architect of the Kunsthalle (1966–1968), originally designed with textile covering. Though Anni Albers is not mentioned, the design clearly relates to their close and ongoing collaborations, for example the Rockefeller Guest House (1949) in New York,[17] built in the same year as Anni's MoMA show—curated by Johnson. In *Screens*, Katrin Mayer replaces the later applied plasterboard by a collection of ten different kinds of Bielefeld linen that she produced locally with the last operating weaving workshop Weddigen in Herford.[18] Like the installation view, the collection of Bielefeld linens for Kunsthalle Bielefeld's permanent collection offers many readings; in our context it is the return of textiles in exhibition design, the reconsideration of textiles as an artistic medium and the gendered impact on recognition, which were the focus of our reading.

10 Mary Anne Staniszewski, *Power of Display. A History of Exhibition Installations at the Museum of Modern Art*, 1998, p. 143.

11 Ibid.

12 MoMA press release: "The show will be a selection from her enormous creative output covering a wide range of expression including educational experiments using paper, corn, grass and string to produce textile effects; [...]".

13 Among many publications on this subject, I would like to point to the *Das Bauhaus webt. Die Textilwerkstatt am Bauhaus*, 1998, that, in the context of a study on the weaving workshops, documents chair designs by Bauhaus architect Mies van der Rohe and by Josef Albers.

14 See *Das Bauhaus webt. Die Textilwerkstatt am Bauhaus*, 1998, p. 16 and T'ai Smith, *Limits of the Tactile and the Optical: Bauhaus Fabric in the Frame of Photography*, in: Grey Room 25, 2006, pp. 5–31.

15 v. sup.

16 Katrin Mayer, *Screens*, 2014, A.1, A.2, A.3, A.4, B.1, B.2, B.3, C.1, C.2, C.3, C.4, D.1, D.2, D.3, D.4, D.5, D.6, E.1, E.2, E.3, E.4, F.1, F.2, F.3 Manufactured for Kunsthalle Bielefeld using ten types of Bielefeld Linen, woven at Weberei Weddigen in Herford. Technical realisation (sewing) by Dorothee Goerke, assisted by Franziska Fiedler and Ana Aguilera. An edition of 2000 posters, developed with strobo M. Friederich J. von Klier in the context of "Projekt 25/25/25–25 Jahre 25 Künstler_innen 25 Museen", Kunststiftung NRW in cooperation with Kunsthalle Bielefeld.

17 As part of her research Katrin Mayer conducted an interview with Lucy R. Chudson who published her thesis under the title *Modern Textiles as Modern Architecture: A Case Study of Anni Albers and Philip Johnson's Rockefeller Guest House*, 2012.

18 For further information see: www.katrinmayer.net/index.php/ausstellungen/screens/.

IN BETWEEN BOXES

LYDIA KÄHNY

The freight box is the most successful format of globalisation. From the intermodal container to the shipping carton—global logistics are conducted by box. But while it is now mostly viewed as the unsentimental, technical shell that served as the vessel for the smooth internationalisation of goods and cultural artifacts, the box has a history of cultural multi-functionality.

On page 95 of the *Manual of Travelling Exhibitions* ↩103, we view a pop-up display: a tightly packed box whose compact dimensions not only facilitate the transport of its contents, they are also part of its presentation. This image is remarkable, as it shows one of the smallest forms that an exhibition can assume. Similar to a suitcase, which embodies the meeting of the private and the public, the box has a dual role: it is simultaneously a piece of architecture and an exhibition. Its small size makes it transportable and limits the content, while the casing offers protection and choreographs the exhibits. By turning it inside out it is transformed into both architectural body and show—a museum without an archive and a library. Its mobility also affects a certain modesty; the contents are neither revered on a white pedestal nor furnished with dedicated lighting, their arrangement and representation gives more an impression of a lucky bag or something found in the attic. The theatrical quality is augmented by the miracle of the packing process, the box's construction, and how intelligently the material inside is ordered. When unpacking it, constructing it, and putting it away, the recipient becomes a protagonist, experiencing the contents performatively in a practical, palpable encounter.

Using the following prominent examples, I will present the various forms and modes that can be taken by the exhibition in a box. Besides the one shown in the *Manual, You and Your Neighbourhood,* I will comparatively discuss the *Werkbundkisten,* boxes made by the German Werkbund, and the *Boîte-en-valise* by Marcel Duchamp.

You and Your Neighbourhood

You and Your Neighbourhood was part of an education programme initiated by Victor D'Amico, founding director of MoMA's Department of Education. During his long term in office from 1937 to 1969, exhibition materials and educational articles were distributed around the public schools of New York in specially made, mobile boxes. At the time, the city didn't employ any art educators, and with this highly progressive scheme D'Amico tried to respond to this institutional gap on behalf of the museum. Pupils of all social tiers were to be given the opportunity to come into contact with art. A notable aspect in this was the exceptionally broad concept of art that formed the basis for the educational material created, which sought to present predominantly contemporary works, including architecture, popular art, and applied arts.

↩103 31, 31A, 31B. YOU AND YOUR NEIGHBOURHOOD

What began as an experiment in three schools in 1937 became a permanent project with 130 specially made sets (13 themes, ten copies of each). These transportable boxes were circulated in 60 schools and were seen by around 250.000 pupils yearly. A decisive factor in the success of the programme was its continuous evaluation and development in collaboration with schools and art departments. After every school year, the boxes were sent back to the MoMA, where they were restored and possibly improved using suggestions from the schools.

You and your Neighbourhood was just one of these 13 themes. Among the other mobile exhibition sets were titles such as *Poster Design, Cartoons of Yesterday and Today, Jackson Pollock, Design Teaching Model,* and *Colour Booth and Staging Model.* These were accompanied by publications made available to the pupils by MoMA, for example *What is modern Painting? How to make Objects of Wood* and *What is modern Architecture?*[1] The boxes' design was like a small cupboard on wheels, with drawers, pull-out trays, and panels hidden behind the double doors. Inside, each object had its place, in a well-ordered and intelligible layout. *You and Your Neighbourhood* revealed images, text, and diagrams featuring examples of successful and failed urban planning. These could be reconstructed using a model landscape, and pupils could simulate their own attempts in a planning game. The box was made more remarkable by the clearly recognisable ambitions of participative learning. *You and Your Neighbourhood* addressed the highly relevant problem of an urban reorientation in the cities of postwar America.

In 1944, the well-known architects and urban planners Oscar Stonorov and Louis Kahn published *You and Your Neighbourhood: A Primer for Neighbourhood Planning,* a treatise in the visual education tradition of Otto Neurath.[2] The exhibition set not only borrowed its name from the book,[3] it also had the same aims: the democratisation of knowledge and competence to achieve a successful management of urban planning. Due to immigration and population growth in the 1940s, the metropolitan areas of the US had become increasingly deficient. For Stonorov and Kahn, the demand for urban modernisation was linked to the recommendation for bottom-up planning: neighbourhood planning could only succeed when architecture and planning were justified by the formulated needs of the inhabitants. In contrast to later modernist planning methods that focused on a team of centralised professionals as the main actors, theirs was an urban planning model that emphasised the residents' needs and specific local factors. As such, the *You and Your Neighbourhood* exhibition set was a concrete continuation of democratic planning ideals. In the game, the pupils were supposed to learn to formulate their ideas of successful urban design, in the hope that later, as mature citizens, they would be able to participate in local planning committees.[4]

THE WERKBUNDKISTE

While D'Amico's rolling boxes symbolised a broad concept of art education, the *Werkbundkisten* produced in West Germany call to mind a different kind of exhibition: the sales show. The thematic arrangement of household utensils subtly resembles the format of the Tupperware party, a successful marketing model that began in the US in 1951.[5]

The *Werkbundkisten* were boxes containing thematically grouped product samples that were sent to schools in West Germany. In the 1950s and 60s, they served to promote the development of aesthetic taste, and were supposed to go beyond a pure cognitive understanding and make certain moral values physically visible and comprehensible. Developed by the Berlin Werkbund in collaboration with the Senate for Adult Education in West Berlin, the boxes—with different thematic areas and accompanied by instructions—could be ordered in four federal states. In 1954, the programme incorporated three boxes on the themes *The Office Desk, Kitchen Equipment* and *The Laid Table,* all containing objects from everyday life. Each of the plywood cases had a different colour, but they were all constructed of two boxes stacked on top of each other and closed with a lid. Handles on the sides of each box enabled them to be carried by multiple people (Fig. 34–Fig. 35). Formal aesthetic analyses and guides for tutorials and craft exercises in art lessons aimed to help pupils internalise the formal language.[6] The sample objects were individually explained in the accompanying booklets. Even if the overarching educational goal was to increase awareness of the practical and aesthetic qualities of these everyday objects, no attention was given to the obvious question of product comparison. Instead of providing variations of a single product type, the cases

1 MoMA Press Preview for *Art for the Highschool of New York City,* 18.03.1963.

2 Otto Neurath (1882–1945) was an Austrian economist and philosopher of science, who worked as an educator of adults and workers. He founded the Gesellschafts- und Wirtschaftsmuseum in Vienna, where he developed the *Vienna Method of Pictorial Statistics* in 1925, which is also known as *Isotype–International System of Typographic Picture Education.*

3 In *Exhibitions and the Development of Modern Planning Culture,* eds. Robert Freestone and Marco Amati, 2016, p. 235.

4 In 1944, the MoMA also addressed the postwar period and the approaching housing question in the *Look at Your Neighbourhood* exhibition.

5 Sarah Levy on Brownie Wise, "Tupperparty-Pionierin, Geschäftsfrau in Schüssel-Position", *Spiegel Online,* 24.09.2012

6 Stefan Jungklaus, "Werkbundkiste–Erziehung zum Vernünftigen Konsumenten" *in Kampf der Dinge—Der deutsche Werkbund zwischen Anspruch und Alltag,* 2008, p. 126 ff.

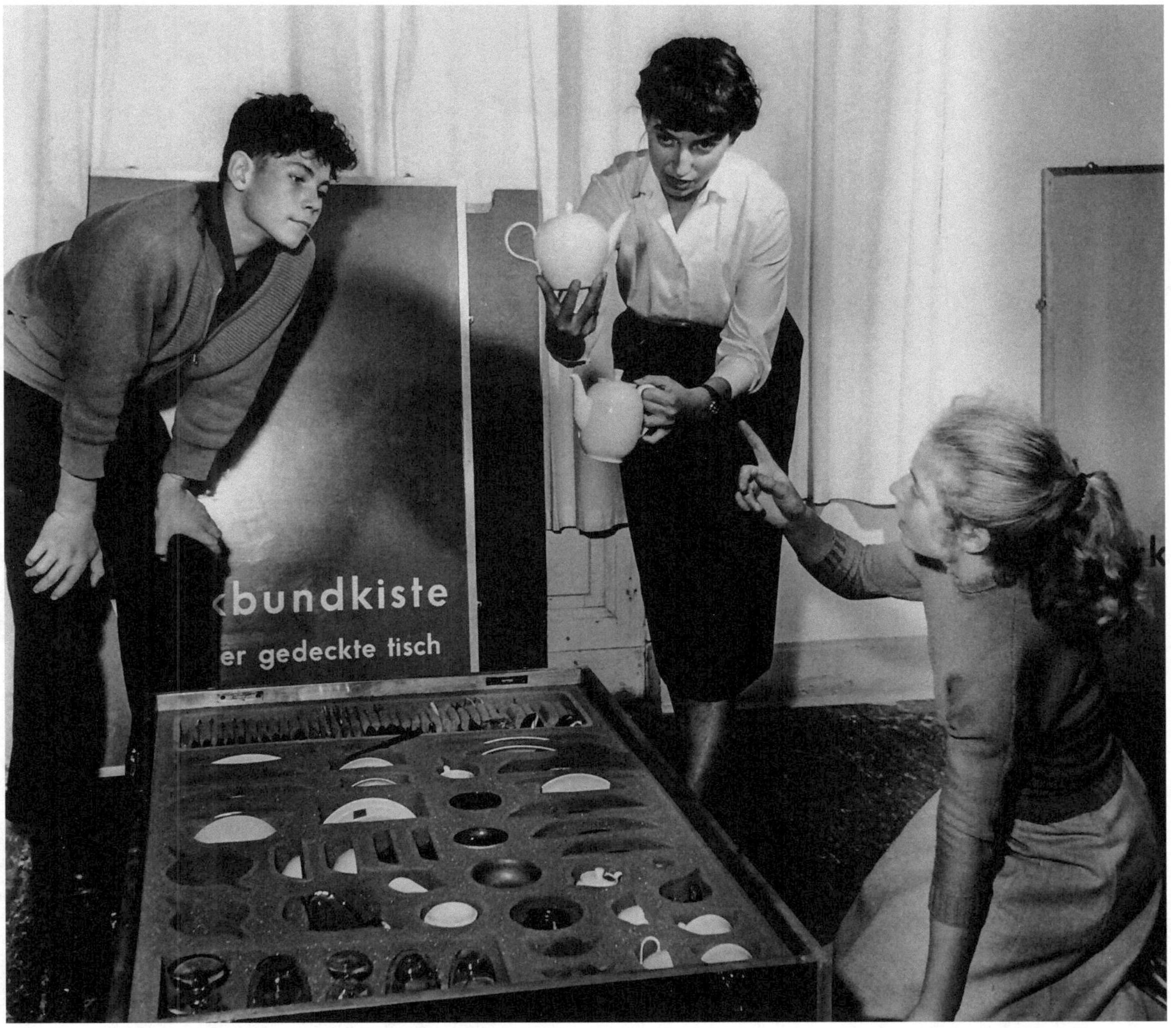

34

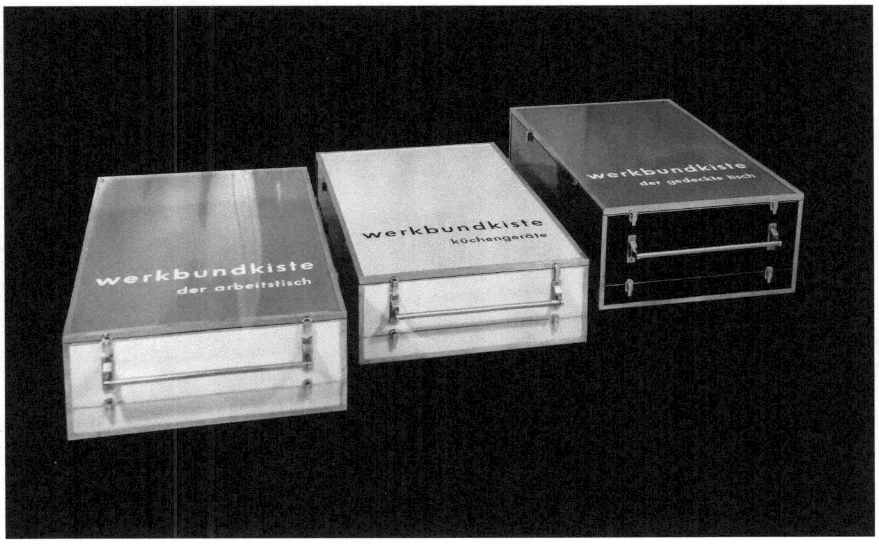

35

Fig. 34 Presentation of *The Laid Table,* at the Academy of Fine Arts in Berlin, photo: Fotostudio Orgel-Köhne, 1950s

Fig. 35 *Werkbundkisten, The Office Desk, Kitchen Equipment,* and *The Laid Table;* the image was produced for the journal of the Deutscher Werkbund: *Werk und Zeit,* No. 3

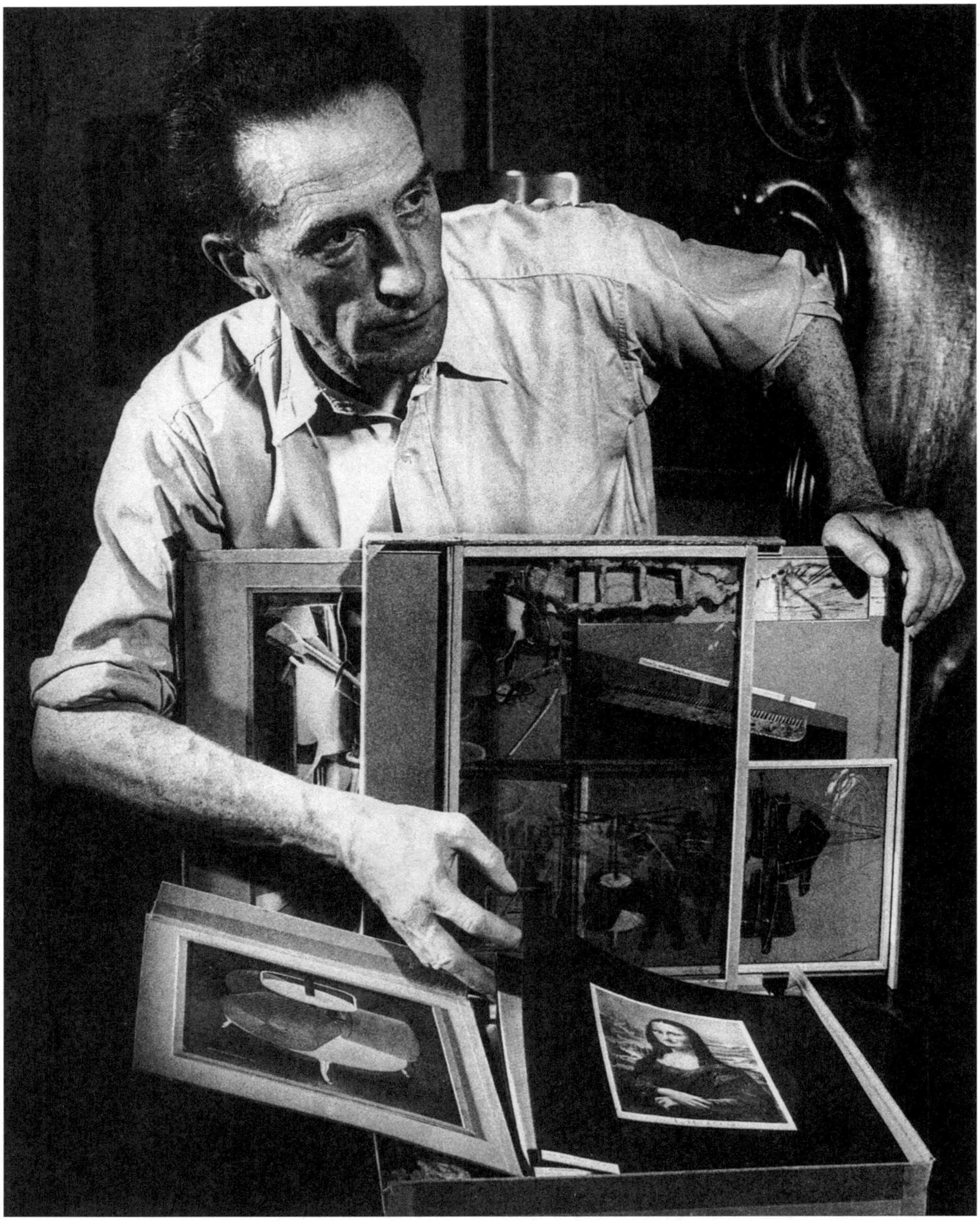

36

Fig. 36 Marcel Duchamp with a *Boîte-en-valise,* New York, 1942

contained single, purportedly model objects according to the criteria of the *Gute Form.*[7]

The information about the products in the enclosed booklets didn't read as a guide for the critical examination of the featured objects, but as a prompt to comply to the conclusive recognition of good taste. In an almost comical manner, unfounded utterances of praise—"beautiful form", "perfectly balanced", "plain, precise and light" alternate with interchangeable, largely banal usage instructions.

> "A vase whose form enables the arranging of flowers in such a way that the bouquet spreads freely in the upward direction. It is suitable for the decoration of the dining room table, without taking too much space or encroaching on visibility. It is effective even with very few flowers in it. The vase is reasonably priced."[8]

Passages like these can be read alongside illustrations of the corresponding object in the handbook to *The Laid Table:* The underlying notion of aesthetic education is dominated by ideals of hygiene, practicality, and cleanliness, while the description of the sensory experience of the objects amounts to nothing more than fussiness. The fact that the teachings also bore dogmatic traits was hidden by a veil of apparent objectivity. This way, the objects appear to prompt a certain, appropriate purchase and usage behaviour to which the morally upright consumer gladly complies. However, it fails to mention the fact that carrying out housekeeping and performing the activities of daily life could and should be rich in alternatives. Thus, there is an unresolvable conflict in the kind of aesthetic education as intended by the *Werkbundkisten.* On the one hand, the pupils were seen as subjects in need of help, and, unable to competently navigate the floods of products in the era of the new economic boom, thus they required critical schooling in order to deal with these new options of taste and consumption. On the other hand, the selection of products was clearly made in the interests of the critical examination.

With the beginning of the 1970s, a shift occurred that rendered the *Werkbundkisten* obsolete. The task of education had become increasingly politicised, and shifted from aesthetic education to consumer education. From this point, communicating the basic principles of usability was geared towards a critical consumer education. In addition, the lives and self-perceptions of the youth were suited less and less to the promised idyll of functional domesticity, which seemed nothing more than making the right choice between dessert spoon and teaspoon.

BOÎTE-EN-VALISE

Another box that is quite different is Marcel Duchamp's "portable museum", the *Boîte-en-valise* (Fig. 36). As the exhibition box is generally not considered to be an element of high art, but has its origins in the humble presentation methods of sales representatives, trade fair delegates, and travelling traders, its introduction into the ranks of artworks was a first. Between 1941 and 1971, the *Boîte-en-valise* was produced in an edition of 300, in the end consisting of seven series, each with slight variation. It was the size of a typewriter case and contained miniature reproductions of Duchamp's works. Production of the replicas was time-consuming, and sometimes took longer than the creation of the works themselves. The first 20 boxes were made of leather, and each included an original work. In 1941, the *Boîte* contained 69 items. In later versions, different coloured fabrics were used and the number of works inside varied. The box format allowed Duchamp's works to be gathered in one place, achieving a higher materiality than what was possible with images in an exhibition catalogue. Not much larger than a briefcase, these miniature collections also bridged the divide between the US and Europe: Due to World War II, Duchamp's œuvre was less known in Europe than it was in the US. As such, the boxes were primarily intended for sending abroad.[9] The *Boîte-en-valise* also brought together Duchamp's heterogeneous works, which had never been exhibited in its entirety; with the box, Duchamp had created an original way to realise his own complete retrospective. Above all else, Duchamp's *Boîte,* scaled and reproduced by the artist himself, symbolised the subversion of the museum—by purchasing it, anyone could become the proud director of their own diminutive museum. Against the background of Duchamp's own concept of artwork, this gesture is doubly ironic. With his ready-mades, Duchamp had already thematised the setting of art and highlighted the various conventions of the museum as an institution.

7 The idealistic approach of the *Gute Form* promised to enable the affordable basis equipment for all households through simply designed, high-quality products. The *Gute Form* became an established term through the book of the same name, published in 1957 by Max Bill (founding member of the Ulm School of Design, Germany). The idea of the pure form was accompanied by the notion that *Gute Form*—and good taste—could be learned. The concept was often cited in association with Functionalism to describe objective, functional, and timeless design.

8 Senator for Adult Education, Department for Schools, *Werkbundkisten Katalog,* accessible in the Werkbund Archiv–Museum der Dinge in Berlin.

9 Dieter Daniels, *Duchamp und die Anderen: Der Modellfall einer künstlerischen Wirkungsgeschichte in der Moderne,* p. 126 ff.

10 Ecke Bonk, *Marcel Duchamp: The Portable Museum, The Making of the Boîte-en-valise de ou par Marcel Duchamp ou Rrose Selavy,* Thames and Hudson, 1989, p. 9.

In other words, he had made the external aspect of art, all its practices of isolation, orchestration, and idealisation that are needed to constitute an artwork as an elevated object—into the actual subject of his art. In *Boîte-en-valise*, these conceptual and fragmented works of varying types of provocation weren't only presented like a stamp collection and reduced to a neat entirety—something against which his individual works had always strived—the reproductions inside were also much more elaborate than the original works. The ready-made was already a mass-produced object; to reproduce it again amounted to an absurd act. The artist Ecke Bonk summarised the *Boîte* thus:

> "The synthesis of his paradoxical principles, of his apparently—but only apparently—contradictory rationale. The manifold overlaps and cross-references in his work as a whole are reflected in the spatial construction of the *Boîte*, as well as in the arrangement of the reproductions. His artistic statement and achievements, in all their heterogeneous and many-sided profusion, are presented here by Duchamp as a carefully ordered whole."[10]

CONCLUSION

If you look at all three boxes, a certain relation can be seen in their portability and construction. All three establish an explorative and personal portal for their users, but the tone of their contents varies significantly. Through miniaturisation, Duchamp created an ironic overview with his *Boîte,* and while the *Werkbundkisten* contained 1:1 model products for the imitation of an ideal scenario, *You and Your Neighbourhood* encouraged users to create their own simulations with the aid of a planning game. Today, these three boxes are themselves showcase exhibits. And, as the choreographic and transformative features of these displays can only be experienced by a direct encounter, this historicisation causes a twofold removal from their original function. First, as stationary objects of information they are curtailed in their sense of mobility and distribution; second, they are no longer able to communicate the way they were originally intended to—in a practical fashion. There is no longer an inclusion of the user, who through their haptic interaction with the box should experience it as a coherent object and conceptually grasp its distinct orderliness. This detached perspective thus diminishes its biggest strength: the systemised transformation from transport box to exhibition display.

10 Ecke Bonk, *Marcel Duchamp: The Portable Museum, The Making of the Boîte-en-valise de ou par Marcel Duchamp ou Rrose Selavy,* Thames and Hudson, 1989, p. 9.

STANISŁAW ZAMECZNIK'S EXHIBITION DESIGN IN COMMUNIST POLAND

JONATHAN MAHO AND AARON WERBICK

Among the many case studies presented by Elodie Courter Osborn, a majority come from the United States and Great Britain. As stated by the author, it is due to the amount of experience gained by their respective institutions—for instance art galleries such as the Victoria & Albert Museum, having been involved in organising circulating exhibitions since the mid-nineteenth century. The other examples that were seen as worthy of being selected for her exposé are treated with less regard: while the book focuses on the work of specific American designers like George Nelson and Alvin Lustig, those coming from Poland, for example, weren't considered with as much interest. Little is to be found to support the choice of projects originating from this other UNESCO member.

The presence of Polish projects isn't only remarkable for the political regime of their country of origin—a nation which presented itself under the name *Polish People's Republic* at the time, according to its new Soviet constitution—but also for the fact that the given examples met very precisely the key principles listed by Courter Osborn. Light, flexible, reusable and easily combinable, the units made for the Muzeum Narodowe (the National Museum) in Warsaw belong to the most relevant pieces on view in her publication. Yet, nothing is said that could help to contextualise their noteworthy appearance, nor the work of the architects involved, since their names aren't even mentioned. Together with his colleague Tadeusz Pawluć, Stanisław Zamecznik (1909–1971) is only credited at the very end of the publication for the pictures 33, 33a, and 33b.

At the time the *Manual of Travelling Exhibitions* was published, Zamecznik had already developed an extensive and innovative design practice through his work at the Muzeum Narodowe, but also at the Warsaw Academy of Fine Arts. Thus, the presence of a Polish architect such as Zamecznik in this publication wasn't a matter of chance. As we are about to show, the accomplishment of exhibition designers in Poland, and especially that of this architect, was worth more than the anonymous presentation that was made in UNESCO's handbook.

THE SPECIFIC STATUS OF EXHIBITION DESIGN IN COMMUNIST POLAND

If the work of Polish architects such as Oskar Hansen or Jerzy Sołtan has been long acknowledged by their peers and academics worldwide, the specificities of post-war Poland itself—with regard to the political context in particular—is a matter that has been discussed less. Yet the papers of notes already available (such as these of Tomasz Fudala, curator at the Muzeum Sztuki Nowoczesnej w Warszawie [Museum of Modern Art in Warsaw][1]) are sufficient to comprehend the reasons why scenography received a great deal of attention in this country—both from the part of the architects and of the State.

1 We wish to thank Tomasz Fudala for the help and support he provided in preparing this paper.

↩105 33, 33A, 33B

In communist Poland, exhibitions were considered a mass medium and so, a political tool. Not unlike in the USA,[2] cultural events were used as a strategic media both for domestic and foreign politics. Thus, even when a show was organised at the initiative of a museum, the logistics, as well as the financial support were often provided by the Directorate of Museums and Monuments, under the auspices of the Ministry of Art and Culture. Among the most prominent examples of top-down propaganda exhibitions, one can mention *Warsaw Accuses,* initiated by the Office of Reconstruction of the Capital. Presented at Muzeum Narodowe in Warsaw in May–June 1945, it focused on the destruction of material culture by the German military during the occupation of Warsaw. Pointing at the foreign forces responsible for the Polish People's sufferings, it was mounted with the wish to arouse a feeling of national solidarity and support of the State. Tomasz Fudala explains that since the officials "us[ed] the persuasive and effective language of exhibitions" to "communicate with society", shows such as *Warsaw Accuses* "became a medium that the authorities needed as much as the people needed running water and public transit".[3]

The Polish government therefore became, with the national institutions it supervised, one of the main commissioners for architects and designers at the time. Indubitably, architects were not only needed by the communists for the construction of displays; their support was essential to rebuild the country and, as written by Fudala in his paper on Polish exhibition design after 1945, to "design a new architecture to convey new, socialist meanings".[4] Hence, in the case of town planning and housing projects, their involvement went along with creative constraint–architects being bound to the language of socialist realism imposed by the Soviets. Michał Woliński, a Polish curator, says that in the views of the authorities "the avant-garde was accused of formalism, and purist functionalism, as a Western invention, [and] officially fell into disfavour, even though some of its urban-planning postulates were actually employed".[5] For this reason, socialist realism was "decreed as the only officially sanctioned style in art and architecture" in 1949.[6] What's more, architecture projects had become extremely bureaucratic and strenuous to conduct due to the oversight of rigorous, centralised national agencies.[7]

Among the projects with which architects were both able to find work and enjoy artistic freedom, exhibition design remained one of these few areas (perhaps along with book illustration, as well as cover and poster design). In this field, creativity was more than just tolerated: the authorities saw innovation as an asset to foster a positive image with the shows that were presented abroad. Besides, experimentation was encouraged in order to find solutions that would allow the production of display units that could be used in different venues. For the institutions and agencies involved, getting reusable systems that could be shared among several partners helped to lower the price of upcoming shows. Thus, even if the exhibition wasn't meant to travel, the fact that the display units could be kept (and of use in the future) made the effort worth investing people and money. In this regard, the role of the architect as a provider of creative solutions was welcome. This motivated many of them to get involved in exhibition design, as well as to put their efforts in developing a new language–something which would have been impossible in architecture. As stated by Fudala and Zamecznik, "The temporary architecture became the practical ersatz of bolder, big-scale architectural concepts, which often remained unrealised in the architects' sketchbooks".[8] Consequently, exhibition design "constituted a niche wherein it was possible to implement the language of modern forms",[9] becoming a vehicle for westernist ideas otherwise disfavoured in any other areas by the Polish authorities.

What was true for architecture also applied to all the different creative fields. Thus, a shared frustration among professionals also fostered fruitful collaborations, making the best of ideas coming from different areas such as architecture and the visual arts, for instance. "The establishment of the bureaucratic supervision over architects and visual artists resulted in team activity becoming often the only way to survive for the individuals who were excluded for ideological reasons."[10] Although initially "created for one's own artistic needs", teamwork "aros[ing] from the shared sense of longing and need for a new expression, a new content structure" was beneficial to foster an innovative thinking, says the Polish painter Wojciech Fangor (1923–2015).[11] Laboratories such as the research units–co-organised by architect Jerzy Sołtan at

2 Jochen Eisenbrand, *George Nelson: Ein Designer im Kalten Krieg,* Park Books, Zurich, 2013, pp. 151–164.

3 Tomasz Fudala, "Architects on the Fringe. Polish Exhibition Design after 1945", in: Aleksandra Kędziorek, Lukasz Ronduda eds., *Oskar Hansen: Opening Modernism. On Open Form Architecture, Art and Didactics,* Museum of Modern Art Warsaw, p. 173.

4 Ibid., p. 173.

5 Michał Woliński, "Artificial Space Exhibitions and Pavilions", *piktogram,* No. 11, 2008, p. 132.

6 Ibid.

7 Fudala puts it like this: "as early as the late 1940s architects had to cope with a gradual nationalisation of the building-materials industry while they themselves had to submit their work to the rigors of state-owned design companies. The state design companies were under the supervision of various government agencies, each of which issued its own, often inconsistent, regulations, standards, and norms. Architects complained about the bureaucratic nature of the work, the constantly and inappropriately tightened norms, obstacles in coordination and supervision, and reductions in their incomes. Projects took twice as long to be approved than the construction phase." Tomasz Fudala, "A Dream of Prefabricated Houses", in: *Monika Sosnowska, Polish Pavilion, 52nd International Art Exhibition, Venice,* Zachęta National Gallery of Art, Warsaw, 2007, p. 28.

8 Foreword in: T. Fudala, M. Zamecznik (eds.), *Stanisław Zamecznik—The Space Between Us,* Museum of Modern Art Warsaw, Warsaw, 2010, n.p.

9 Ibid.

10 "A letter from a painter", *Wojciech Fangor—Spectra Art Space Masters, Starak's collection,* Fundacja Rodziny, Staraków/Spectra Art Space, Warsaw, 2015, n.p.

11 Ibid.

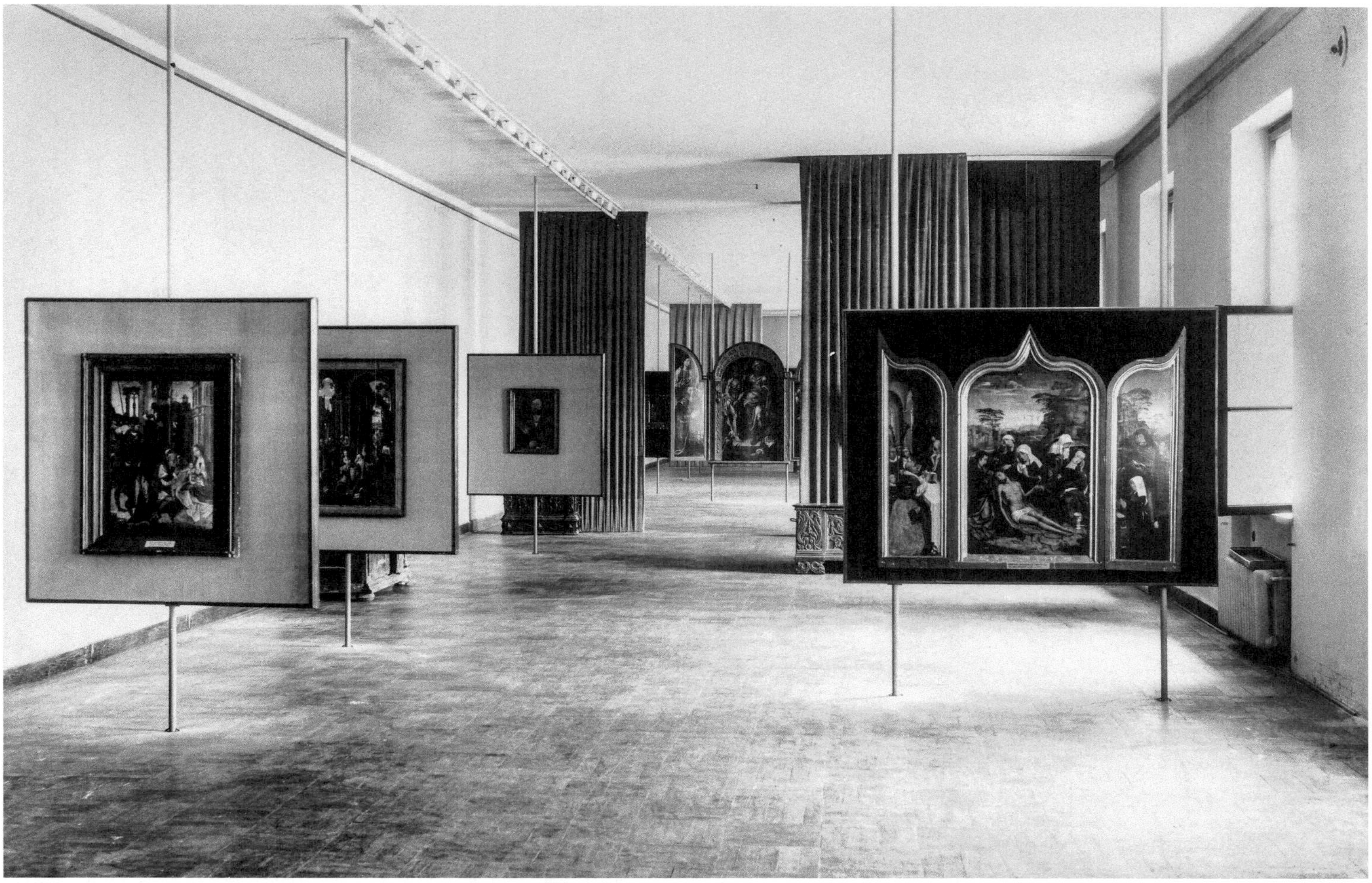

37

Fig. 37 Installation view, Muzeum Narodowe w Warszawie, c. 1950

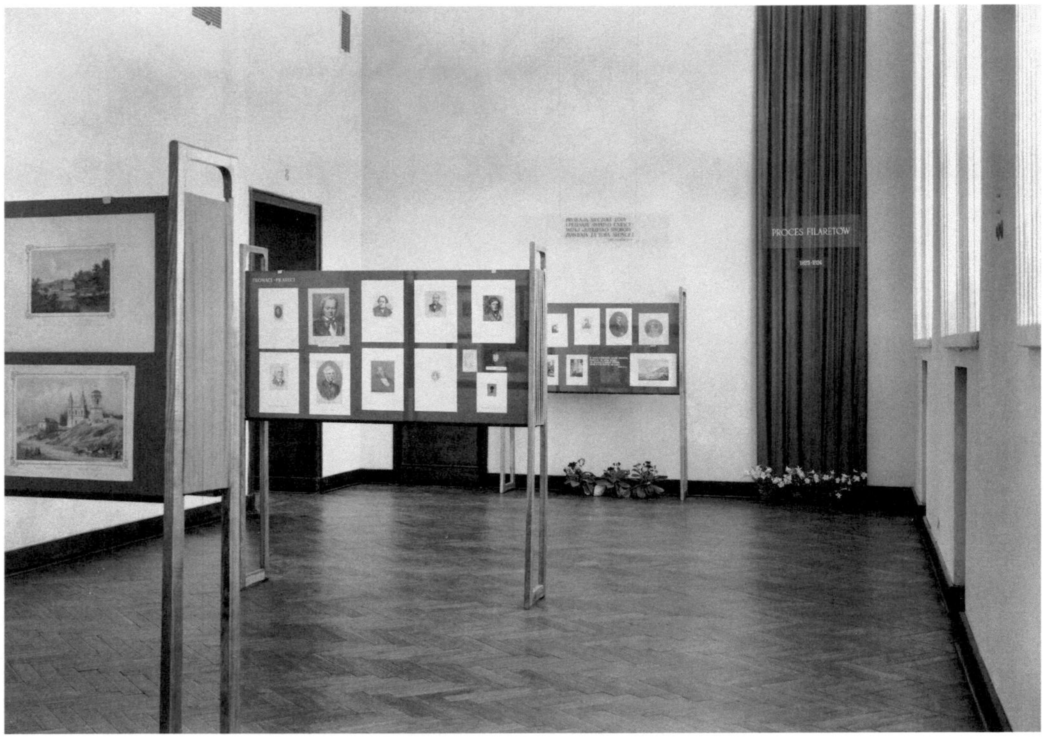

38

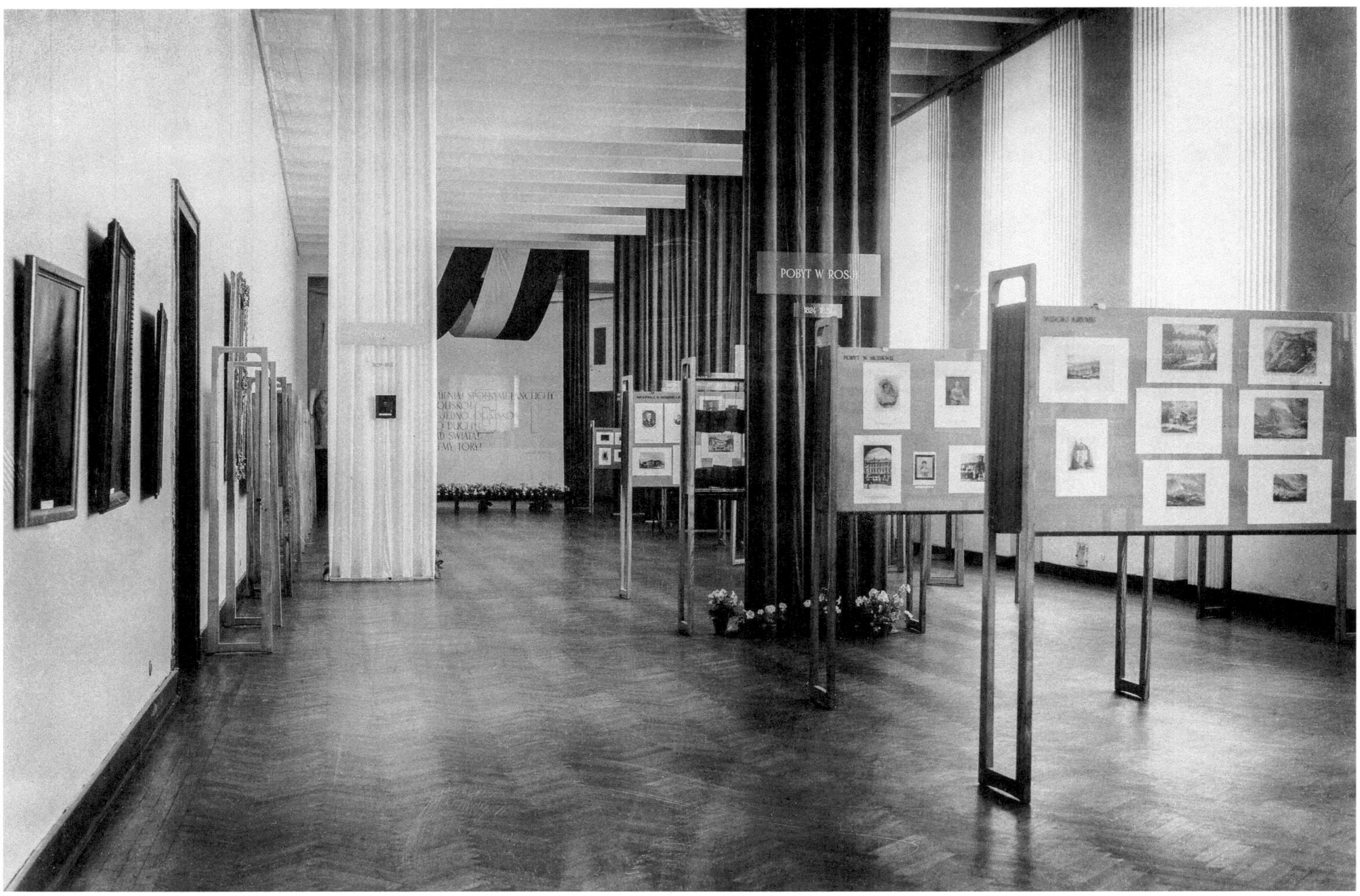

39

Fig. 38 – Fig. 39 Installation view of the Mickiewicz-Puszkin Exhibition presented in *Chronicles of Exhibitions,* National Museum in Warsaw, 1949

the Warsaw Academy—provided the needed meeting points to stimulate this kind of collective work between architects, interior designers, painters, and sculptors.

For all these reasons, Polish exhibition design was met with an enthusiastic response among people of knowledge outside the country. Already since the mid-1940s, it had been treated by foreign observers as a good example for travelling exhibitions, since innovative display solutions were also key to such projects. Of course, the reasons given for the inventiveness of the Polish exhibition design at the time were not due to these compensating creative restraints in other disciplines. Thus, when methods and means of display coming from Poland had been selected in 1950 for the journal on museography published by the UNESCO (in an issue taking as its subject "Museums and Circulating Exhibitions"), the author of a dedicated article focused rather on the importance of exhibitions as outreach to the Polish people. It goes without saying that no word was said about propaganda—which was what many circulating exhibitions were meant to serve in other UNESCO member states. In a text titled "Circulating exhibitions in the Museums of Poland", Kazimierz Michałowski (assistant director at Muzeum Narodowe in Warsaw at the time) evoked access to art for "people living at a distance from large towns and cultural centres".[12] He described the relevance of circulation shows in terms of social factors: "they are an effective means of fostering culture and art in every section of the population and every corner of the country. The scheme is based on the principle that [...] the propagation of art and culture is the best means of developing the new type of citizen-worker".[13]

Regardless, the justifications given to explain the importance of exhibitions in post-war Poland, the requirements in terms of design remained a universal matter of concern. As in the *Manual of Travelling Exhibitions*, the display units used by Michałowski to illustrate the related problematics in Poland were those of Stanisław Zamecznik. In the images attached to his article, the first one was of a feet-system arranged at the Muzeum Narodowe in an (undated[14]) exhibition of contemporary French painting; the 3 other pictures being of the very same mobile screens that would be presented in Elodie Courter Osborn's publication 3 years later. Michałowski described Zamecznik's panels as matching with the specific needs of circulating shows—their assemblage requiring "two men only" and "tak[ing] 6 minutes".[15] Michałowski goes on to write that "These screens are very light and can be easily transported, even in numbers. With them, it is possible to show a large number of exhibits even in a very small space", he wrote.[16] Like in the UNESCO practical guide, Zamecznik wasn't mentioned in its journal; his name was to be found at the end of the publication only, within the list of picture credits.

STANISŁAW ZAMECZNIK'S "ART OF SPACE"

As evidence by the presence of his display units in a journal published in 1950, Zamecznik's screens had been in use for several years when they were presented in the *Manual of Travelling Exhibitions.* He had been working for the Muzeum Narodowe since 1946. Among the important exhibition projects he had worked on, one should include the exhibitions presented elsewhere, in and outside the country. For instance, *The Recovered Territories* exhibition in Wrocław in 1948—a propagandistic machine intended to advertise for the work done by the State in the northern and western provinces that had become part of Poland after the war—but also the Polish Pavilion at the International Fair in Milan (in 1952, together with Henryk Tomaszewski). The design of the 1948 exhibition commissioned by the Warsaw Reconstruction Office was remarkable for its originality, with the use of curved panels in the Coal Pavilion arranged by Stanisław Zamecznik (together with Tadeusz Pawluć and his cousin Wojciech Zamecznik, under Jerzy Hryniewiecki's supervision).

Stanisław Zamecznik had studied architecture at the Warsaw University of Technology between 1929 and 1932. Later, he had been involved in projects such as the Polish pavilion at the 1937 Paris International Fair. After the war, his involvement at the Muzeum Narodowe was competed by a position as a lecturer of interior design at the Warsaw Academy of Fine Arts (Akademia Sztuk Pięknych w Warszawie), starting in 1950. The original approach characteristic of his teaching (Zamecznik being known for his laboratories of graphic experiments in the form of workshops) mirrored the innovative solutions developed in architecture at the Muzeum Narodowe. For instance in its painting gallery, he retracted the artworks from the

12 Kazimierz Michałowski, "Circulating exhibitions in the Museums of Poland", *Museum (UNESCO),* vol. 3, no. 4: "Museums and circulating exhibitions", 1950, p. 280.

13 Ibid., p. 282.

14 The exhibition was presented between 1945 and 1950.

15 Ibid., p. 280.

16 Ibid., p. 282.

wall and presented them on a set of rectangular panels attached to the floor and ceiling with a pair of metal pipes (a system independent from the exhibition space's walls, somehow reminiscent of the ‹Leger und Trager› system that had been introduced by Frederick Kiesler in Vienna in 1924). Placed in the middle of the room one after another in two rows, the stand-alone units not only altered the architecture of the galleries but also created a new circulation, making the visitors zigzagging from one artwork to the next (Fig. 37). Zamecznik's interest in defining new movements in exhibitions would quickly become one of his design's distinctive features. In the 1950s, he would become well known for sets relying upon large bent plywood panels. Those kinds of displays had the advantage of standing by themselves but also of making the viewers experience "a new reception of space"[17] while moving along curvy shapes.

Zamecznik "appreciated the freedom which working with exhibitions offered within the complicated, bureaucratic process of managing an architectural practice in the Polish People's Republic."[18] As he stated himself, "Here [in exhibition design], you can have less respect for the rules and instead have fun searching for systems."[19] Aside from the fact that it was a field free of artistic constraints, exhibition design was also carried forward by the changing role of museums at the time. Moving from housing permanent-collections to accommodating changing shows, they offered new opportunities for architects willing to get their ideas involved in concrete projects. While creating surfaces missing in museums initially built around permanent displays, professionals such as Zamecznik had the opportunity to implement concepts where panels mounted on vertical supports helped not only to increase the space available to exhibit art, but also to change the way it would be experienced.

The units presented in the *Manual of Travelling Exhibitions* served such a purpose. Created in the late 1940s, they allowed to double the background for the exhibited items but also to guide visitors throughout the room. As pictured in the UNESCO handbook, the stand-alone units could be placed in the centre of the gallery, arranged as one pleases. ↩ 105 Once installed, they inevitably shaped the viewers' movements in space, as well as directed their gaze—a real matter of concern for Zamecznik. Thus, although they were described by Elodie Courter Osborn as primarily "designed for travelling exhibitions in Poland", one can assume that the actual concept those units were meant to serve went beyond the idea of easing the organisation of circulating shows; in Zamecznik's view, they helped to alter the experience of space and art above all.

No matter what, the unit system consisting of cloth-covered plywood panels supported by two rectangular frames (to which they were hooked) would prove to be an excellent solution in any case. In galleries such as those of the Muzeum Narodowe, the additional (or alternative) surfaces that were created, enhanced the possibilities available for curators; in the event of a presentation elsewhere, the system's adaptiveness—consisting of stand-alone panels—made it a solution compatible with every venue. One exhibition illustrates this versatility: a show dedicated to the poets Adam Mickiewicz and Aleksander Puszkin, initially organised at the Muzeum Narodowe in Warsaw in 1949. In the *Chronicles of Exhibitions* (National Museum in Warsaw), one counts an installation view where Zamecnik's units are shown providing an alternative surface in the initial exhibition (the "real" walls of the room being left empty—(Fig. 38)); but one also finds pictures in which they are used as a complement so as to allow keeping artworks on the original picture rails (the paintings permanently displayed in the gallery, one can assume—(Fig. 39)). Later, the same units would then be used as the Mickiewicz-Puszkin exhibition travelled to Kraków, Wrocław, and then Poznań, allowing the exhibition to be compatible with different spaces, regardless the conditions under which it was to be shown once on site.

Another very similar system developed by Zamecznik would be used in such a variety of cases in the 1950s. As a more basic version than the one presented in the *Manual of Travelling Exhibitions*, it consisted of straight rectangular frames that could be (but not necessarily) combined with horizontal panels as well. Here again, these units would be used both to ease the transport and adaptivity of circulating exhibitions but also to provide alternative displays within the room. On one side, the wooden frames could be the display solution travelling with the show—for example to India, with a *Polish Arts Exhibition* presented in New Delhi, Madras, Calcutta, and Bombay in 1956 (and for which Zamecznik would travel to participate in the

17 S. Zamecznik in a letter to the editors of *Projekt magazine* in 1961.

18 T. Fudala, M. Zamecznik (eds.), *Stanisław Zamecznik—The Space Between Us*, *op. cit.*, n.p.

19 S. Zamecznik quoted by Tomasz Fudala in: "Ear for Space—The Architecture of Stanisław Zamecznik's Exhibitions", *Materialien zu Ausstellungsdesign und Szenografie*, vol. 2, 2016, p. 107.

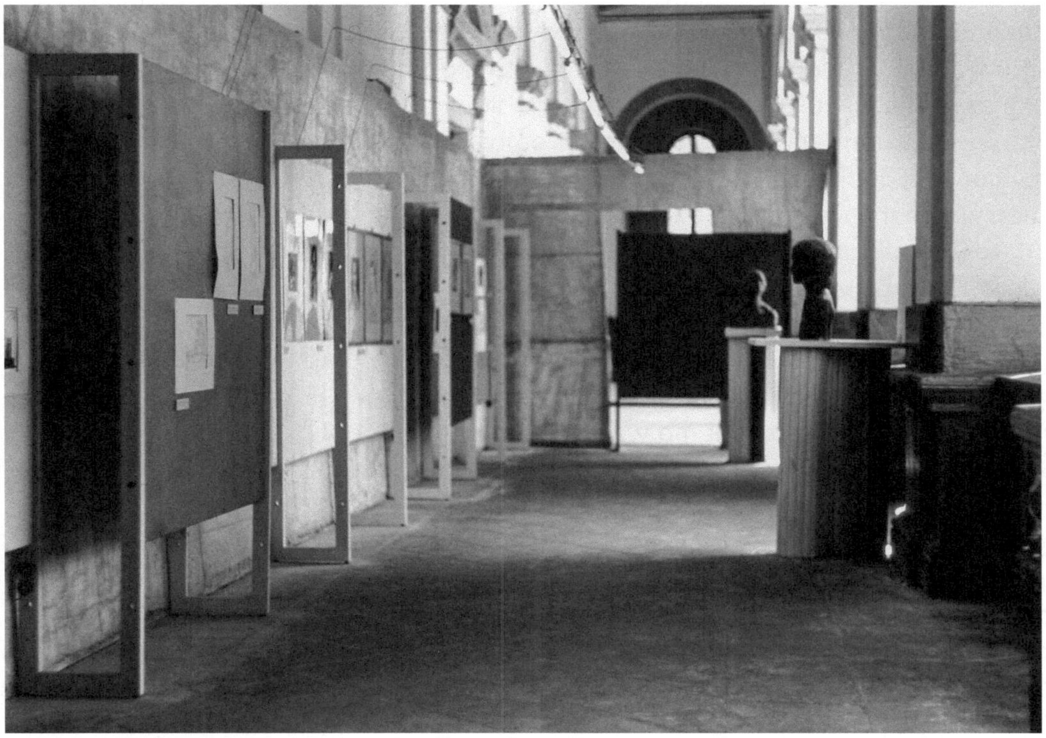

40

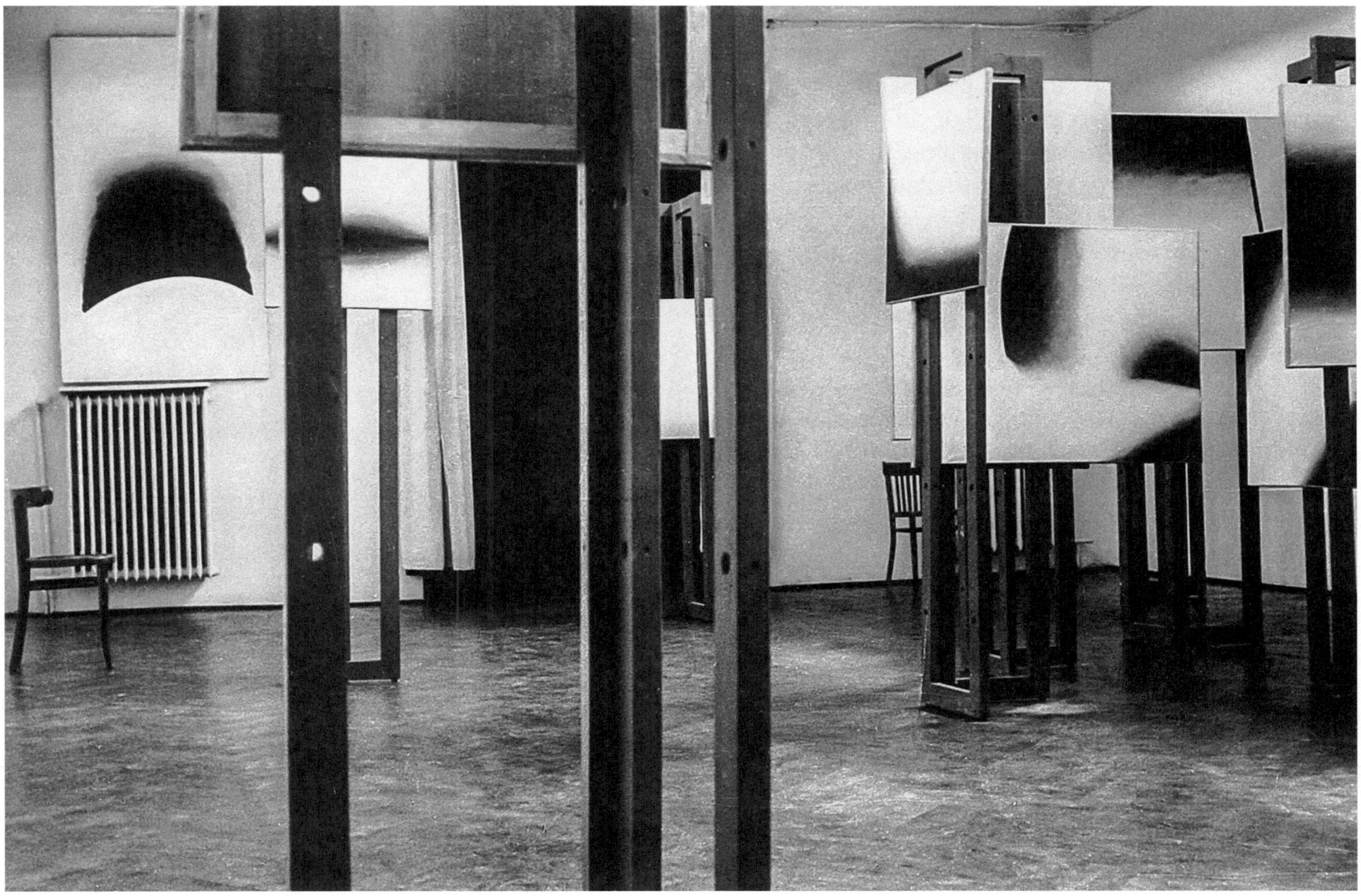

41

Fig. 40 *Polish Arts Exhibition* installation view (New Delhi), 1956
Fig. 41 *The Study of Space,* Salon Nowej Kultury, Jewish Theatre, Warsaw, 1958

installation – (Fig. 40)). There, the rectangular racks would be used in a row of several units connected to each other with perpendicular panels screwed on both sides. On another occasion, the very same frames would be arranged to build new display options as well as an original compartmentation of the room. In the summer of 1958, a joint experiment with the painter Wojciech Fangor led to the mounting of an exhibition where the system provided by Zamecznik helped to create space between the arranged artworks. Titled *Studium Przestrzeni* (The Study of Space, Salon Nowej Kultury, Jewish Theatre, Warsaw – (Fig. 41)), this show of 20 monochromatic optical paintings forming right angles with each other thanks to the wooden racks provided by the architect would be regarded later as one of the earliest environment exhibitions ever made.[20]

Thus if Zamecznik's design matched with the requirements listed by Elodie Courter Osborn – according to the quartet: light + reusable + sturdy + demountable – the ideas it was meant to serve corresponded to a vision that went beyond offering practical solutions to help disseminate and display art. As explained by curator Tomasz Fudala, "Stanisław Zamecznik was intrigued by the ‹labyrinth› of the exhibition and its reception by the moving viewer."[21] His interest in scenography regarded the visitors' movements and the spatial composition; he created shows that were defined as an "attempt to tell a story in space, to be received in time, in a form similar to the reception of music", as formulated by Zamecznik himself.[22] His design practice was in line with a broader movement according to which exhibition architecture was becoming an autonomous art form – what Zamecznik understood in his specific case as the "art of space". He organised shows that were less comprised of the exhibited items and display units themselves as of "the spatial zones generated by them", he said.[23]

Stanisław Zamecznik's presence in the *Manual of Travelling Exhibitions* doesn't only speak for the conditions under which creative professionals worked in the Polish People's Republic. One can consider the fact that his design was regarded as exemplary for the problematic that was raised in UNESCO's handbook as illustrating a growing interest in innovative exhibition forms at the time. If so much energy and talents were invested in scenography – and if one of its many earliest expressions found its way to a manual published by a symbol of the Western world that the Soviets were supposed to work against – it is due to a context in which political and ideological matters didn't count as the only upholders supporting the creative boom around exhibition design in the 1950s. This trend easily spotted worldwide assumed a universal meaning, going beyond the agenda it was supposed to serve on both sides of what was about to become the Iron Curtain.

If the reasons why display methods coming specifically from Poland weren't contextualised nor justified by Elodie Courter Osborn, and if Stanisław Zamecznik's name wasn't mentioned in her essay, it is maybe due to the very need of looking beyond the complex problematics that a publication such as the *Manual of Travelling Exhibitions* wasn't meant to address in the first place. Notwithstanding the treatment given to Zamecznik's accomplishment in 1953, he would remain an acknowledged designer among his peers in the years to come. When the exhibition *Family of Man* – organised initially by Edward Steichen at MoMA in New York – travelled to Warsaw under the auspice of UNESCO in 1959, Stanisław Zamecznik and Wojciech Fangor would be the ones commissioned for the exhibition's design.

20 Another exhibition considered as one of the earliest expressions of environment art, "Colour in Space", shown at Stedelijk Museum in Amsterdam and organised by W. Fangor, S. Zamecznik, and W. Sandberg, was presented in the autumn of 1949. As a matter of fact, it happened to be an updated version of the installation mounted a year before in Warsaw.

21 Tomasz Fudala, "Architects on the Fringe. Polish Exhibition Design after 1945", *art. cit.*, p. 182.

22 Stanisław Zamecznik quoted by Maria Matusińska in: M. Matusińska (ed.), *Stanisław Zamecznik 1909–1971*, Związek Polskich Artystów Plastyków: Centralne Biuro Wystaw Artystycznych, Warsaw, 1973, n.p.

23 Stanisław Zamecznik's commentary on his exhibitions with Wojciech Fangor (at the Salon Nowej Kultury, Warsaw and the Stedelijk Museum, Amsterdam), *Materialien zu Ausstellungsdesign und Szenografie*, *op. cit.*, p. 112.

THE POLITICS OF DISPLAY. EXHIBITION DESIGN IN THE COLD WAR

JOCHEN EISENBRAND

During the Cold War, the US government used cultural events, and the medium of the exhibition in particular, as instruments of propaganda and strategic tools of foreign policy.[1] From the early 1950s to the 1970s, the US government thus evolved into one of the most important clients for American exhibition designers. In this period, more than 150 designers participated in over 400 exhibitions commissioned by the US government. These exhibitions were shown in over 100 different countries and were seen by an estimated 300 million visitors.[2]

The designer George Nelson played a major role in this development. Between 1957 and 1972, Nelson contributed to a total of seven international exhibitions commissioned by the American government. Five of them were devised as travelling exhibitions and visited many different cities, sometimes even across different countries. Nelson was also the chief designer of the largest ever exhibition by the US to be presented outside of the country: the *American National Exhibition* in Moscow. Shown with resounding success in the USSR in 1959, as part of a cultural agreement between the two competing superpowers, the exhibition was by far the most extensive project Nelson was ever involved in with his studio.

These exhibitions were made possible by a specific political infrastructure developed by the US during the Cold War, which included two agencies that used the services of designers for their internationally focused activities: the United States Information Agency (USIA) and the Office of International Trade Fairs (OITF).

THE UNITED STATES INFORMATION AGENCY

In 1953, the year the USIA was founded, the Cold War entered a new phase. The Korean War, the first proxy war between the two new superpowers, ended in July after three years of fighting, and in both the USA and the USSR new heads of government came to power. In January 1953, Dwight D. Eisenhower replaced Harry S. Truman, and in March of the same year, following Stalin's death, Nikita Khrushchev became his successor. On August 1st 1953, one of Eisenhower's first official acts, was the founding of the USIA as the official propaganda apparatus of the American government. The new agency sought to centralise already existing overseas information programmes.[3] On October 22nd, the National Security Council approved the foundation of the USIA, and the president published a statement of its declared goals. It stated that the mission of the USIA was:

> "to submit evidence to peoples of other nations by means of communication techniques that the objectives and policies of the United States are in harmony with and will advance their legitimate aspirations for freedom, progress and peace".[4]

* *This article is based on outtakes from the book Jochen Eisenbrand, George Nelson. Ein Designer im Kalten Krieg – Ausstellungen für die United States Information Agency, Zurich 2014.*

1 For a history of propaganda in the Cold War, see Kenneth Osgood: *Total Cold War. Eisenhower's Secret Propaganda Battle at Home and Abroad,* Lawrence, KS, 2006.

2 Email to the author from Richard Suib, former head of the USIA Exhibits Development Division, 24.05.2011. See also Jack Masey/Conway Lloyd Morgan, *Cold War Confrontations. US Exhibitions and their Role in the Cultural Cold War,* Baden 2008, p. 11.

3 See the first in-depth examination of the history of the USIA, published in 2008: Nicholas J. Cull, *The Cold War and the United States Information Agency. American Propaganda and Public Diplomacy, 1945–1989,* New York 2008.

4 "Directive Approved by the President for the Guidance of the United States Information Agency", 28, 1953. Cited in Osgood, *Total Cold War,* p. 92.

For over 50 years, until its dissolution in 1999 under the Clinton administration, the USIA's main headquarters was on Pennsylvania Avenue in Washington, D.C. Employees of the USIA stationed abroad were in the service of the respective American embassy or consulate. While the agency as a whole was referred to as the USIA, at the time of its founding the existing 217 outposts in 76 countries retained the name of its predecessor, the United States Information Service (USIS).[5] The USIA had a wide scope and incorporated the following fields: operating the existing radio broadcaster Voice of America, producing and distributing magazines[6] and films abroad,[7] translating books from English into the respective national language, presenting performance art events, and, in Germany and Austria, maintaining the America House cultural institutions.

In the mid-1970s, 20 years after its establishment, the USIA had 10.000 paid employees and an annual budget of 240 million US dollars. At this time, the agency produced 66 magazines in 27 languages, ran 200 libraries in 83 countries, broadcasted 774,5 hours of radio programmes per week via Voice of America and took part in 46 international events with 264 political propaganda films.[8] An enormously influential apparatus, the impact of which can hardly be over-exaggerated.

From the very beginning, the USIA placed great importance on organising presentations on a wide range of subjects: cultural exhibitions on visual arts, architecture, and design, contributions to trade fairs, and educational exhibitions on everyday life in America, including industry and agriculture, the health system, and the peaceful application of nuclear energy.[9]

THE OFFICE OF INTERNATIONAL TRADE FAIRS

Besides the USIA, another government agency also engaged designers for the organisation of international exhibitions: the Office of International Trade Fairs (OITF), part of the US Department of Commerce. Whereas the work of the USIA was primarily educational and propagandistic, the mission of the OITF focused on nurturing tangible economic and commercial relationships. The borders between the areas of activity and the exhibition types of the two agencies, however, were fluid, and cooperations were frequent.

The reason for establishing the OITF was to enable direct competition with the Soviet Union in the trade fair sector. After the Soviet Union had taken part in 133 international trade fairs between 1950 and 1954 while the US "stayed at home", the American government saw the need for action. In 1954, President Eisenhower initiated a programme to promote the USA's official participation at international trade fairs. The programme was primarily intended to create incentives for American companies to participate in these fairs, and initially the budget was taken from the president's emergency fund, which Congress was required to authorise. Organisation of trade fair presence technically fell under the administration of the Department of Commerce, while the USIA was responsible for the political line.[10] The programme thus aimed to expand international trade relations as well as increasing political influence. Following this new field of work with interest, the magazine *Industrial Design* stated:

> "There is little doubt that measurable trade is only part of what the USA wants from its overseas exhibits. [...] the USA wants and needs to establish its influence in politically uneasy countries, to promote capitalism as a system superior to communism."[11]

The seat of the OITF was in Paris, and the first American trade fair appearance organised by the agency took place in Bangkok in December 1954.[12] Eighteen months later, in July 1956, the exhibition programme was declared permanent by Congress and given an annual budget of nearly four million US dollars. This allocation was earmarked as *seed money* respectively for the creation of a main exhibition, in which American industry could and should take part.[13] Within the first two years the USA had participated in 45 trade fairs. (Fig. 42)

For the designers commissioned by the OITF, exhibition work on behalf of the government was a completely new role, as the magazine *Industrial Design* observed:

> "The whole matter of U.S. participation in these shows is full of novelties. It has made the government an important client of the design profession; it has given industrial designers—who have done much to create the American scene—an enormous challenge in

5 For this reason, the USIA was also known as the United States Information Service (USIS) outside of the USA, an acronym that couldn't be used in the USA for risk of being confused with the United States Immigration Service. Masey/Morgan, *Cold War Confrontations,* p. 34f.

6 These included the magazine *Amerika,* published in the USSR, *Topic,* distributed in Africa, and the Arabic language *Al Majal*. Yale Richmond, *Cultural Exchange and the Cold War. Raising the Iron Curtain,* University Park, PA, 2003, p. 149.

7 The USIA's Motion Picture Service (MPS) cooperated closely with Hollywood. See Tony Shaw, *Hollywood's Cold War,* Edinburgh 2007, p. 174.

8 Ibid., p. 196.

9 More than 100 of these exhibitions are listed in: Jochen Eisenbrand: George Nelson, ibid. pp. 453–473.

10 Thomas C. Sorensen, *Auch wenn sie uns nicht lieben. Die Methoden der amerikanischen Propaganda,* Olten 1969, p. 116.

11 Jane Fiske Mitarachi, "Design as a Political Force", in: *Industrial Design,* 02.1957, p. 39.

12 Robert H. Haddow, *Pavilions of Plenty. Exhibiting American Culture Abroad in the 1950s,* Washington/London 1997, p. 41.

13 "U.S. Expands Role in Trade Exhibits", in: *New York Times,* 03.01.1957. Article partly reprinted in Fiske Mitarachi, "Design as a Political Force", p. 38.

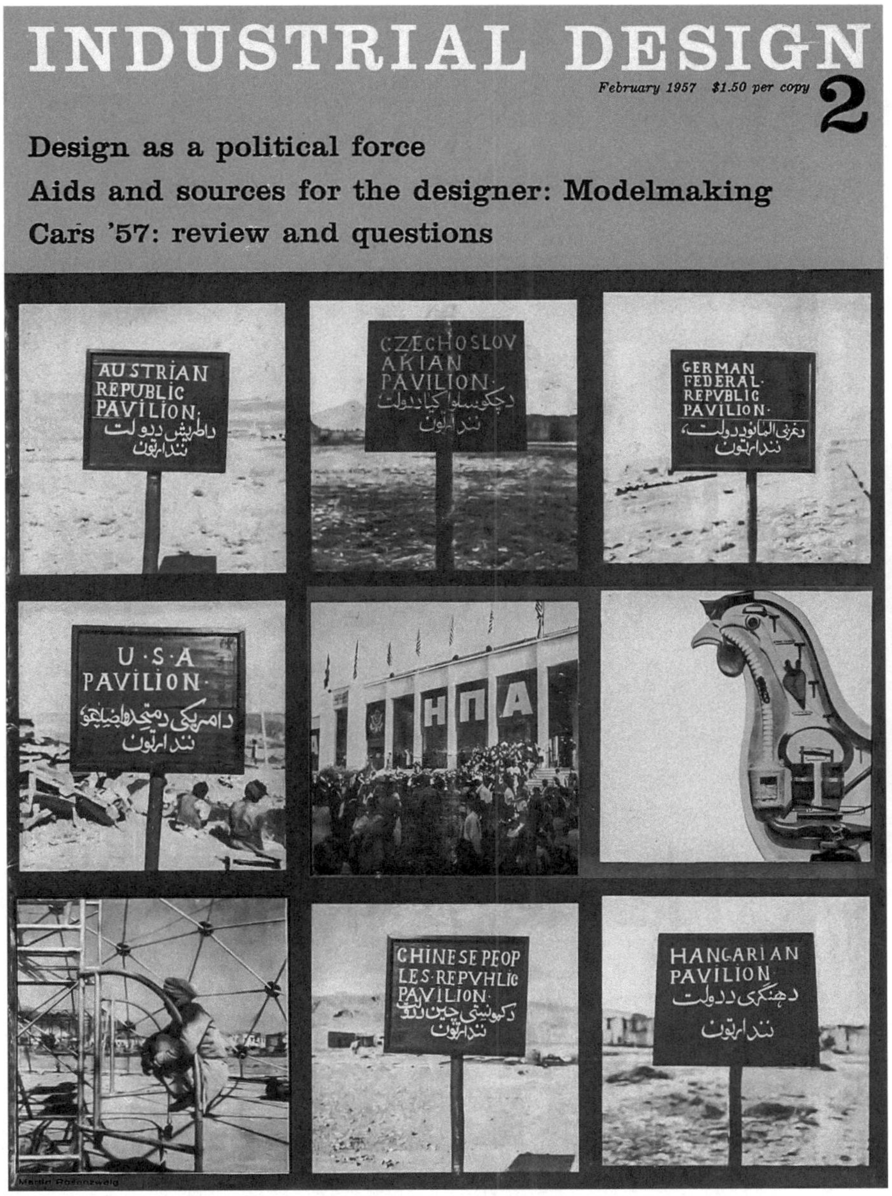
INDUSTRIAL DESIGN

February 1957 $1.50 per copy 2

Design as a political force

Aids and sources for the designer: Modelmaking

Cars '57: review and questions

42

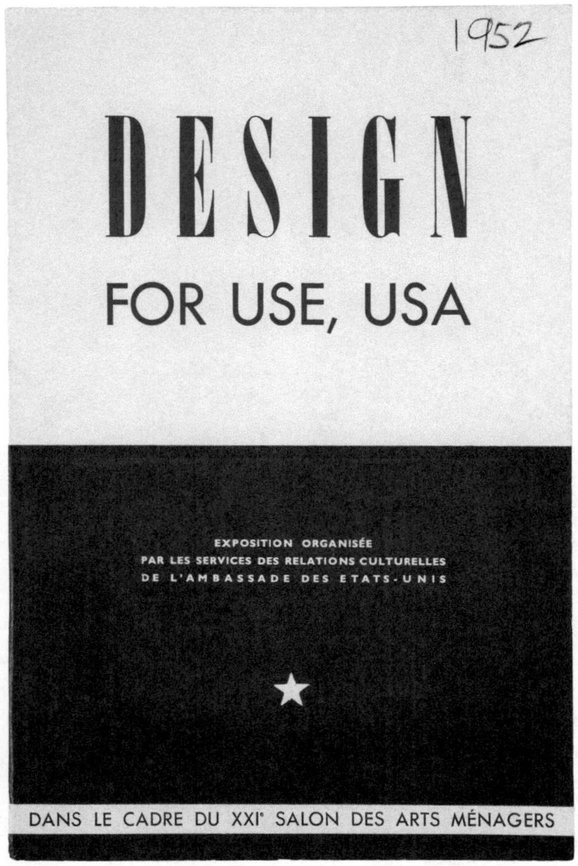
1952

DESIGN

FOR USE, USA

EXPOSITION ORGANISÉE
PAR LES SERVICES DES RELATIONS CULTURELLES
DE L'AMBASSADE DES ETATS-UNIS

DANS LE CADRE DU XXIe SALON DES ARTS MÉNAGERS

44

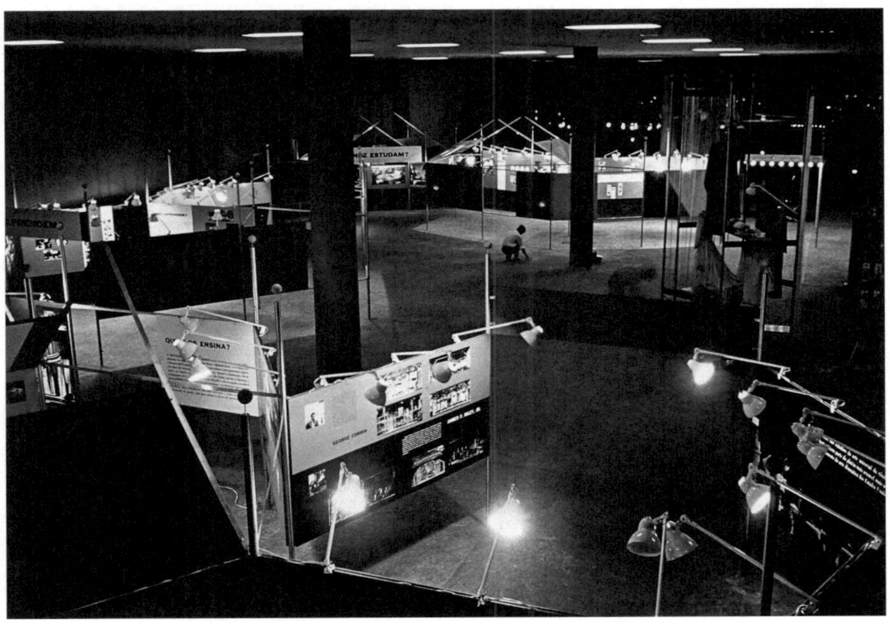

43

Fig. 42 *"Design as a political Force",* Industrial Design, February 1957

Fig. 43 *U.S. Education for Design for the Theatre,* São Paulo, 1957

Fig. 44 Catalogue of the exhibition *Design for Use,* organised by Edgar Kaufmann Jr. for the Museum of Modern Art, New York, and exhibited in Paris in 1952

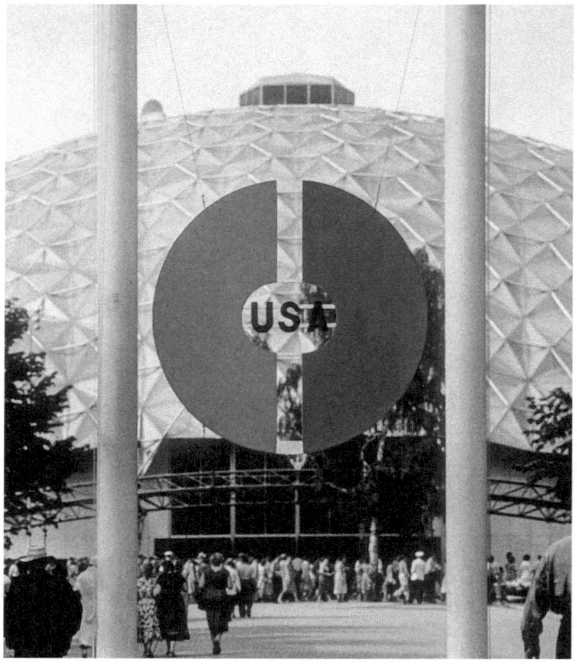

45

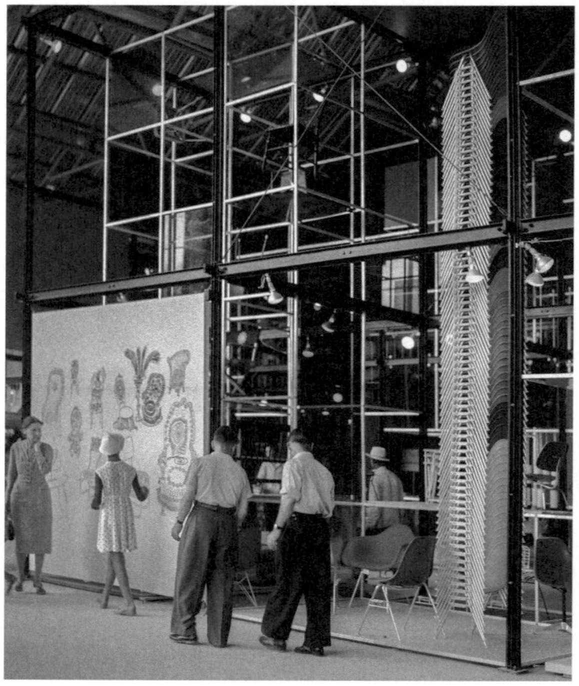

46

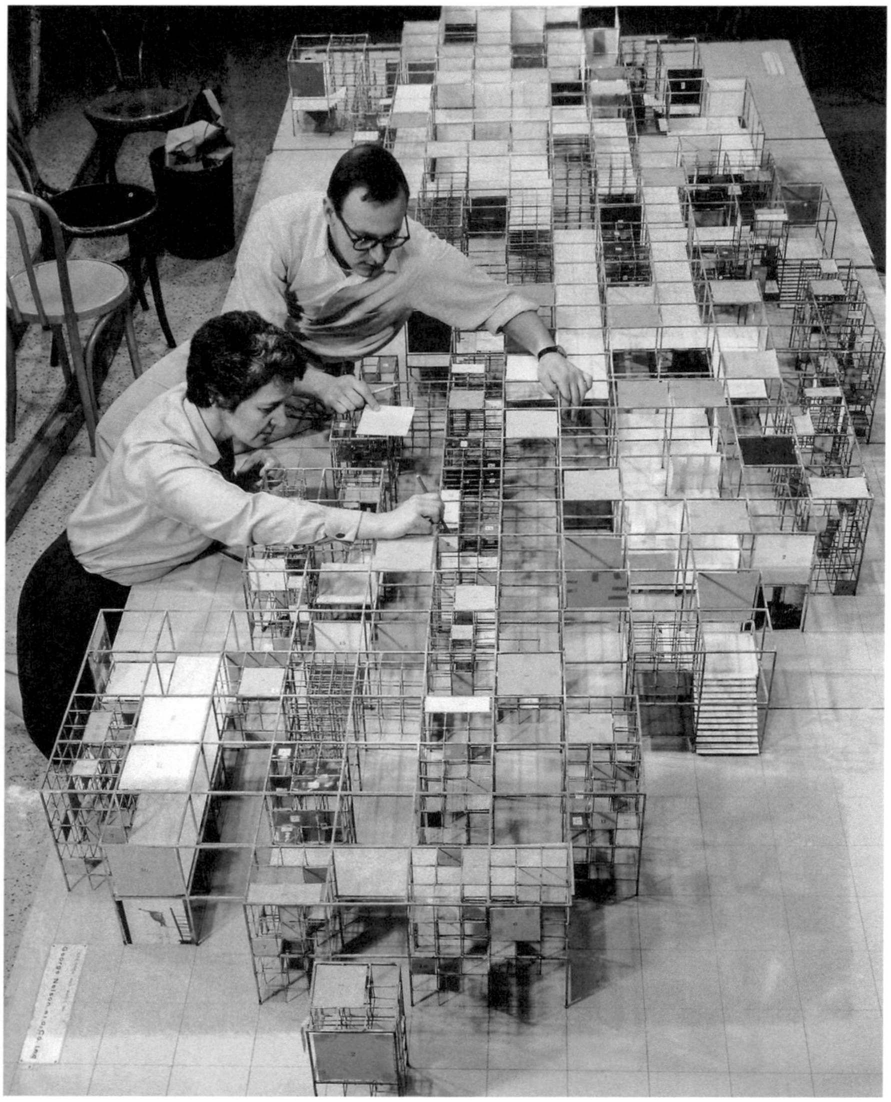

47

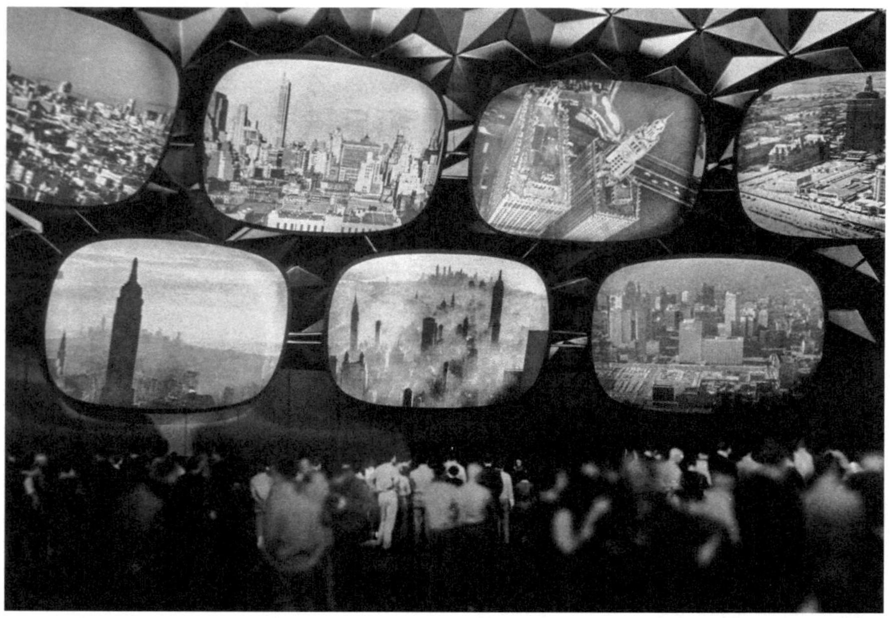

48

Fig. 45 Buckminster Fuller dome at the *American National Exhibition,* Moscow, 1959
Fig. 46 Support system for the *Jungle Gym* in the Welton Beckert pavilion, *American National Exhibition,* Moscow, 1959
Fig. 47 Model of Nelson's dismountable structure of the *Jungle Gym,* an exhibition system for the American National Exhibition in Moscow, 1959
Fig. 48 *Glimpses of the USA,* film installation by Charles and Ray Eames, American National Exhibition, Moscow, 1959

> presenting that scene to people abroad—a challenge verging at times on foreign policy planning. […] Designers were being asked to be propagandists; design became a tool of communication and the visual composition of an exhibition a secondary problem."[14]

Accordingly, focus was placed less on developing refined or avant-garde methods of presentation, and much more on the contents and the impact of the USA's self-representation, so as to be positively received by visitors in their respective countries. The question of which exhibits should be shown and with what accompanying information was more important than the question of how it should be presented—especially as the exhibitions had to be easy to transport and construct. The overarching theme of most of these exhibitions could be summarised by the slogan "Science, Industry and Technology in the Service of Humanity". Needless to say, a key factor was the implicit subtext that a free democratic society and a free market offered the best conditions to achieve this.[15]

Regardless whether the US exhibited at fairs in Bari, Vienna, Thessaloniki, Damascus or Zagreb, certain themes and types of exhibits always returned: fully furnished show apartments or even family homes demonstrating the country's high living standards; consumer goods, such as washing machines, kitchen appliances, and tools, emphasised how advanced technology could make life easier. Groceries were often presented in supermarket scenarios to convey how not only innovative industrial production techniques but also new distribution methods reduced prices for the consumer. Fashion shows organised within the context of trade fair presentations also proved very popular. DIY workshops equipped with the latest appliances illustrated the dissemination of the phenomenon that portended to embody a life shaped by self-determination. Children's playgrounds and kindergartens—which were actually populated by American children and teachers—vividly testified to liberal American educational methods that fostered the child as an individual. Another exhibition that addressed the subject of education as the foundation for individual self-realisation was *U.S. Education for the Theatre.* Shown in São Paulo in 1957, it was the first exhibition George Nelson organised for the United States Information Agency. In the framework of the second São Paulo Biennial, spanning an area of 500 square metres, the show presented the work of 30 American colleges whose students had trained in the field of performing arts.[16] (Fig. 43)

AESTHETIC EDUCATION AND PROPAGANDA

In Eisenhower's second legislative period, which began in 1956, and during which Nelson worked on his most important exhibitions for the USIA, the government placed increasing importance on such projects. After the uprisings in East Germany (1953), Poland (1956), and Hungary (1956), which were suppressed by the Soviet Union, the Americans changed their strategy regarding psychological warfare—from aggressive propaganda to a policy of small steps.[17]

Regarding foreign policy strategies, George Nelson made a note on the following extract from Eric Hoffer's 1951 book *The True Believer:*

> "The truth seems to be that propaganda on its own cannot force its way into unwilling minds, neither can it inculcate something wholly new, nor can it keep people persuaded once they have ceased to believe. It penetrates only into minds already open, and rather than instill opinion it articulates and justifies opinions already present in the minds of its recipients […] Where opinion is not coerced, people can be made to believe only in what they already know."[18]

To make the most of the invested capital and to increase their penetration, many USIA exhibitions went on tour, including design exhibitions that featured consumer goods. Between 1953 and 1955, the exhibition *American Design for Home and Decorative Use* was shown in Scandinavia, Belgium, and Italy. Organised by Edgar Kaufmann Jr. from the Museum of Modern Art, it featured around 300 exhibits by 150 different designers, including furniture, materials, ceramics, glassware, household utensils, and jewelry (Fig. 44). The show was the international offshoot of the *Good Design* exhibition, shown annually at the Museum of Modern Art and at the Merchandise Mart Chicago between 1950 and 1955.[19] The exhibition *Design Today in America and Europe,* in which the USIA played a decisive role, had a similar focus. Presented in India, it featured around 400 everyday objects chosen

15 As stated in Osgood, *Total Cold War,* p. 221: "Reversing Marxist claims that capitalism turned workers into cogs of the industrial apparatus, the American exhibits proclaimed that industry served the needs and aspirations of humanity".

16 "Art Honor is Shared. 4 Colleges in City are Among 30 in Gold Medal Exhibit", in: *The New York Times,* 27.10.1957.

17 Walter L. Hixson, *Parting the Curtain. Propaganda, Culture, and the Cold War,* 1945–1961, Houndsmill/London 1997, p. 86.

18 Vitra Design Museum, Estate of George Nelson (VDM GN) MAR-10446. Extract from Nelson's private literature notebooks. Hoffer's book *The True Believer* addresses the phenomenon of mass movement and fanaticism from a sociopsychological perspective.

19 Terence Riley/Edward Eigen: "Between the Museum and the Marketplace: Selling Good Design", in: John Elderfield (Ed.), Studies in Modern Art 4. *The Museum of Modern Art at Mid-Century. At Home and Abroad,* New York 1994.

by MoMA curators Arthur Drexler and Greta Daniels. MoMA's International Program—founded in 1952 and a major role model for USIA's exhibition work[20]—commissioned Nelson with the exhibition design and the catalogue, and the USIA assisted the project logistically and by providing a Buckminster Fuller dome, inside which the exhibition opened in New Delhi in February 1959. One of the main objectives of the project, for both the Museum of Modern Art and George Nelson, was the nurturing of an aesthetic sense by means of displaying well-designed products. At the same time, the exhibition also served the USIA's aim of promoting industrialisation and democracy in India, a post-colonial, non-aligned nation with a predominance of small- and medium-sized companies.

THE AMERICAN NATIONAL EXHIBITION IN MOSCOW

More than any other event, the *American National Exhibition* demonstrated the significance of exhibitions in the USA's international diplomatic endeavour during the Cold War. The show, which opened in the summer of 1959 in Moscow, was the pinnacle of American self-portrayal abroad (Fig. 45). It was a gigantic showcase for the American economy and the largest presentation of consumer goods the USA had ever organised beyond its own borders. A total of 3.000 tons of material was transported to Moscow, and its scale far exceeded the US pavilion at the Brussels World's Fair the year before. The focus wasn't placed on politics and ideology, but on everyday life and living standards in America, exemplified by household products from all areas of life: furniture, clothing, household appliances, toys, consumer electronics, books and records, cars, and even boats. The exhibition was intended to demonstrate to Russians how "America lives, works, learns, manufactures, consumes, and plays", and at the same time to subliminally convey two core messages: a) In the USA, freedom of speech and electoral freedom prevail; b) The unimpeded flow of goods and ideas not only has a formative influence on the economy, technology, and science, but also on the culture of the nation.[21]

George Nelson was recruited as the chief designer of the exhibition in the autumn of 1958. The main components of the exhibition were: a huge presentation of industry goods in a glass pavilion designed by Welton Becket and Associates, for which Nelson was responsible, and for which he created an extensive, flexible presentation system made of aluminum (Fig. 46, Fig. 47); a completely furnished prefabricated house; a Buckminster Fuller dome, in which Charles and Ray Eames—who Nelson had attracted to work on the project—showed their multiscreen film presentation *Glimpses of the USA* (Fig. 48); a Buckminster Fuller dome containing *Circarama,* a 360° projection by Walt Disney. Cultural impulses were provided by a MoMA architecture exhibition, a visual arts exhibition, and the *Family of Man* exhibition curated by Edward Steichen for MoMA.

The American National Exhibition was shown between July 24th and September 4th in Sokolniki Park in Moscow, and was visited by 2.700.000 citizens of the USSR, a visitor number given a modest B+ by the US government.[22] With the *kitchen debate,* the verbal dispute between Nixon and Khrushchev—a microcosmic version of the race between the two superpowers regarding consumption and living standards—the exhibition went down in history.

For Nelson, who subsequently organised four more exhibitions for the USIA, the *American National Exhibition* was one of the high points in his career as a designer.[23] He saw the exhibition as positively subversive, precisely because it concentrated on everyday life and universal human issues, and thus connected the people in the two countries despite their political differences.[24] In this way, he viewed the exhibition as a measure that promoted transcultural understanding, one that created a chink in the Iron Curtain. Much in the spirit of José Ortega y Gasset, a philosopher Nelson much admired and from whose book *The Revolt of the Masses* he noted the following:

> "History has brought out into the foreground the conflicts and, in general, the politics, that are always the last soil on which the seed of unity springs up; but whilst the fighting was going on in one field, on a hundred others there was trading with the enemy, an exchange of ideas and forms of art and articles of faith. One might say that the clash of fighting was only a curtain behind which peace was busily at work, interweaving the lives of hostile nations."[25]

20 Just four years after its founding, the MoMA established the Department of Circulating Exhibitions, which by 1952 had organised tours for over 400 exhibitions in the USA and Canada. Helen M. Franc, "The Early Years of the International Program and Council", in: John Elderfield (Ed.), p. 112. During World War II, the Museum of Modern Art explicitly supported propaganda exhibitions in the name of national concerns. These included the exhibition *Road to Victory* (1942), designed by Herbert Bayer, *Airways to Peace* (1943), and *Power in the Pacific* (1945). For a detailed description of these exhibitions and their reception at the time, see Mary Anne Staniszewski, *The Power of Display,* Cambridge, MA/London 1998, p. 209 ff.

21 George Nelson, typescript "Memo November 4 Meeting-Moscow Fair project-Department of Commerce-Annex No 3, Washington D.C., C. Robert Payne, Chairman", in: VDM GN MAR-00629. The *American National Exhibition* was not just the only USIA project, but also the only project of Nelson's office, to which all memoranda and protocols were archived and still remain intact.

22 Max Frankel, "American Exhibition Puts Ideas of U.S. Across, Analyst Finds", in: *The New York Times,* 5.09.1959.

23 These were the exhibitions *Atoms at Work,* shown in 1960 in Cairo; *Transportation* USA, which travelled through the Soviet Union in 1961 and 1962; *Industrial Design USA,* which stopped in the Soviet Union, Ukraine, and Romania (1967/68); and *Research and Development USA* (1970 in Budapest, Poznań, and Bucharest, 1972 a revised version in six cities of the Soviet Union).

24 Draft of the text from a tape recording of the remarks of George Nelson and Charles Eames at the Southern California Chapter, American Institute of Architects Meeting, 10 November 1959, Ambassador Hotel, Los Angeles, California. VDM GN MAR-10972, p. 28.

25 VDM GN MAR-10448 "Quotes O/S". Extract from Nelson's private literature notebooks. Cited here from the German edition: José Ortega y Gasset, Der Aufstand der Massen, Stuttgart und Berlin o. J., p. 197f. (translated by Helene Weyl. Original Spanish title *La Rebelión* de las Masas, published 1929).

GLOBAL DISTRIBUTION

The Manual of Travelling Exhibitions closes with an overview of countries and addresses of bookshops from which the publication at hand could be obtained. Below is a notation titled "UNESCO BOOK COUPONS". In order to promote the distribution of UNESCO publications internationally, with a focus on education, science and culture, a proposal was made in 1946 at a general conference of the UN, to launch the UNESCO BOOK COUPONS. In a resolution adopted in 1948, the "BOOK COUPON SCHEME" was directed primarily to countries with soft-currencies; nations with currencies that weren't comparable to those of most Western nations. The book coupons were understood as a unitary currency to purchase publications, published by UNESCO. Coupons at a value of 25¢, $1, $3 and $10 were purchasable. By these means the associated purchasing value, especially from cultural institutions, ought to be simplified and guaranteed. With the list of the distributors, it was possible to track the specific stores carrying the favoured book and to exchange the UNESCO BOOK COUPONS.

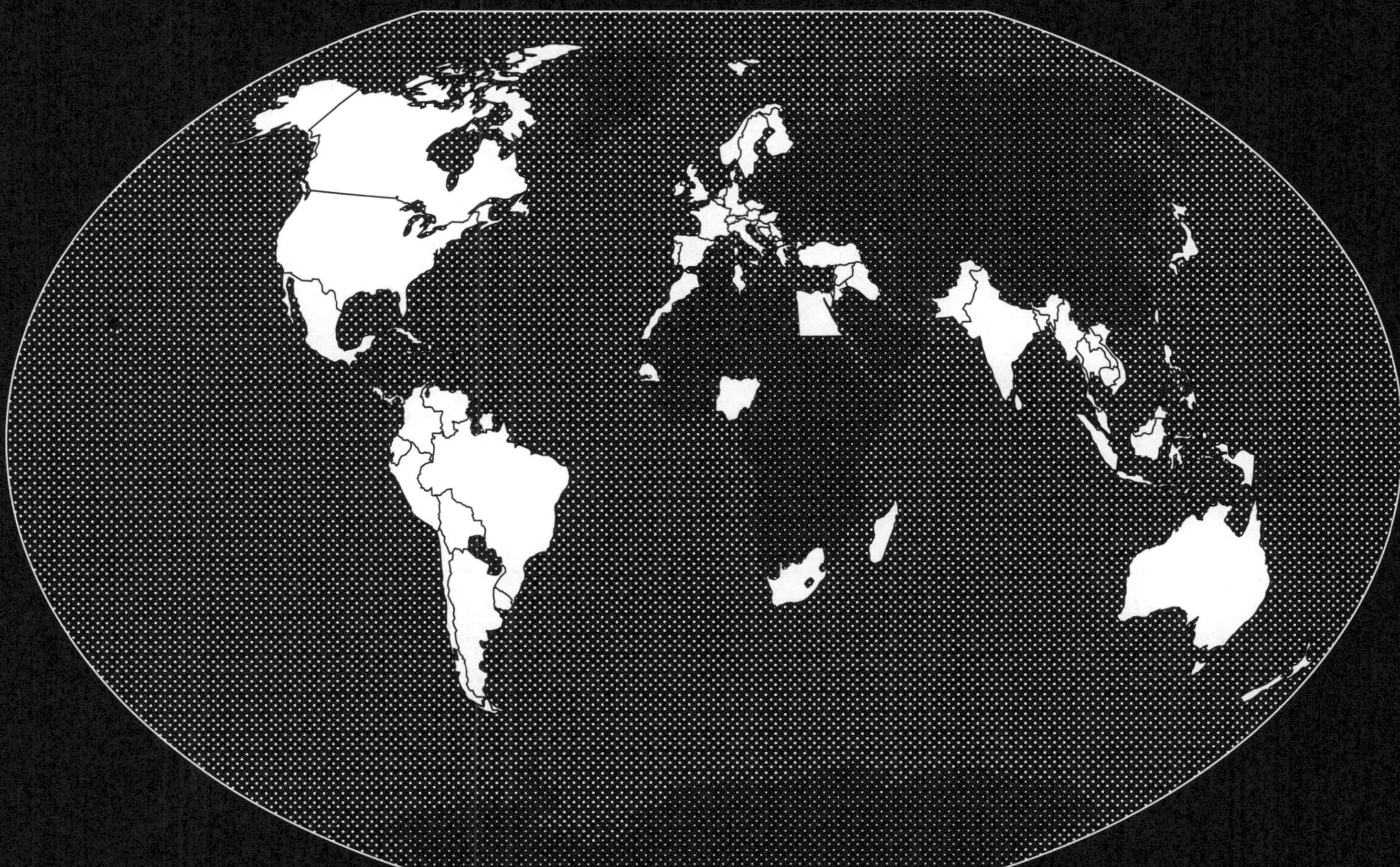

49

Fig. 49 This world map shows the countries listed in the *Manual of Travelling Exhibitions* which are included in the distribution network for UNESCO publications. With the exception of Portugal, which joined UNESCO in 1956, all the listed countries are UNESCO members, colonies or protectorates from UNESCO member countries.

LBA/ICHP/4

PARIS, 28 April 1948

UNITED NATIONS EDUCATIONAL,
SCIENTIFIC AND CULTURAL ORGANIZATION

UNESCO BOOK COUPON SCHEME

1. Definition.

The Unesco Book Coupon Scheme is proposed as a means of facilitating the purchase of educational, scientific and cultural publications across national frontiers and is designed especially to meet existing difficulties due to currency restrictions, and difficulties which "soft"-currency countries experience in obtaining publications from "hard"-currency countries.

2. History of the Scheme.

Following the recommendations of the First General Conference of Unesco (1), a draft Book Coupon Scheme was prepared and circulated widely to Member States of Unesco and to library organizations throughout the world. This proposal met with a very encouraging response, particularly from consumers in "soft"-currency countries. More specific proposals regarding the application of the scheme were submitted to the Second General Conference at Mexico (2), with the result that the Conference instructed the Director-General "to continue the exploration, and if possible begin the experimental application, of an International Book Coupon Scheme or other devices to permit institutions and individuals in "soft"-currency countries to buy publications from "hard"-currency countries;..." (Unesco 2C/129 Rev - page 15, 2.3.2.2.)

In execution of this Resolution, a meeting of experts was held in March 1948, in order to review the scheme as thus far presented and, in particular, to supply answers to a series of questions raised at the time of the Second General Conference. The Report of the Expert Committee is contained in document LBC D. 850 of 5 March 1948. The following outline or "work plan" is based on the conclusions of the Expert Committee. It cancels the previous Draft Proposal (Unesco Bib./2/1947).

3. Purpose of the Scheme.

The Scheme is designed to enable "soft"-currency countries to purchase internationally valid Coupons from Unesco for distribution to institutions and individuals of the country. The Coupons, which are to be used for the payment of publications purchased abroad, are redeemable in the currency of the supplying country, through Unesco.

---

(1) Report on the Programme of the United Nations Educational, Scientific and Cultural Organization, UNESCO/C/2, September 15th 1946, page 74.

(2) Unesco Book Coupon Scheme 2C/H/2.

LBA

50

Fig. 50 – Fig. 51 Unesco Book Coupon Scheme, Paris

UNITED NATIONS EDUCATIONAL,
SCIENTIFIC AND CULTURAL ORGANIZATION

BOOK COUPON
ORDER FORM

(To be completed by each purchaser who uses Unesco Book Coupons to purchase books and periodicals. No other order form is needed.)

(Write clearly in ink or use typewriter)

Notes for the purchaser

(a) The name and address of the bookseller abroad to whom this order is addressed. (Ask your Distributing Agency for the current list of booksellers authorized to accept Unesco Book Coupons.

(a) To: ....
....
....
....

(b) Quote author, title, place, date and price of publication(s). Prices are to be quoted in the currency of the supplying country. If you order through a local bookseller, who need not be authorized by Unesco, the price should not include any charges made by him, since these should be paid in your local currency. Any difference between the total price of this order and the total value of the accompanying Unesco Book Coupons is a matter for settlement solely between you and the bookseller named at (a).

(b) Please send the following publication(s) to the address indicated under (d) :

Author:	Title:	Place:	Year:	Price:
....	....	....	....	....
....	....	....	....	....
....	....	....	....	....
....	....	....	....	....
....	....	....	....	....
....	....	....	....	....
....	....	....	....	....

Sub-total: ....

Postage (usually does not exceed 5%) ....

Total: ....

(c) (Delete the inapplicable)

(c) I enclose signed Coupons to a total value of $ ....
I shall send the necessary Coupons after receipt of your pro-forma invoice.

(d) Mailing address

(d) The above publications are to be mailed to the following address :
Name of individual or institution ....
Address ....
....

(e) Need only be filled in if this address is different from the mailing address quoted under (d)

(e) Ordered for:
Name of individual or institution ....
Address ....
....

Name (in block letters)

.... Date .... Signature of purchaser ....

Note for the bookseller

This order form should be sent with the accompanying Unesco Book Coupons to :

Unesco,
19, Avenue Kléber,
PARIS, 16e,
France.

LBA

A WORD OF WARNING IS NEEDED. THE MANUAL AND THE UNIVERSAL

FLORIAN WALZEL

My first reading of the *Manual of Travelling Exhibitions*—I must admit—left me puzzled. On the one hand I could admire the kind of modern optimism that had recognised and fostered the possibilities of circulating exhibitions to democratise the riches of cultural heritage. On the other, I was strangely disappointed by the lack of cultural focus being discussed thereby. It is thus probable that everyone may also share this sense of disappointment, whoever misreads the title expecting the book on exhibitions to be about concepts and forms of mediation for things to be exhibited. But the *Manual* barely deals with the objects of concern other than in the abstract mode of cargo terminology. Except from the illustrations appendix that presents a rather loosely compiled set of photographic installation shots, it is a guide about dimensions, weight, potential weaknesses to be taken care of, and the insurance value of proxy matter. From a hands-on viewpoint of the practitioner this may seem understandable. If you wanted to transport a library for example, you would likewise prefer to know the physical weight of the books, rather than the weight of the thoughts contained therein. Still, I was irritated by being confronted with a pioneering handbook that had restricted its claim to technicalities: boxes, packages, packing material, joints, and prefab display systems plus some legal form sheets—in one word: externalities. Wasn't this book about culture? Where was this culture in terms of content? As important as the outward problem of how to manage, package and ship things may be, the inward problem of how to deal with the fact, that *placement essentially alters meaning* is not less, but rather more pressing. Apart from a laudable optimism "to make cultural values more readily accessible to all, without regard to social distinction or geographic isolation" 020 the *Manual* had little to nothing to teach about the cultural implications and limitations of its own ministry. If not for solutions one may well ask for notes on awareness towards the complex nexus of changing macro and micro contexts as well as different modes of perception and biases that objects have to meet, every time anew, in each new destination where they are exhibited. A sensibility that seems as important to the success of an exhibition project as the logistics budget.

I was about to put the book away. Carelessly I flipped pages just to reassure myself I hadn't missed something when I got to see it: the absence of discussion of any specific frame of reference *was* the cultural statement I was looking for. The reflection on contextual and situational challenges to travelling exhibitions had not been forgotten or spared, more likely, the author Elodie Courter Osborn must have assumed that cultural differences and inequalities were essentially caused by an educational and informational asymmetry between centre and periphery, and that after this gap was—with the help of travelling exhibitions—closed, deviance in view and interpretation would no longer persist.

The explicit strive to write a "general guide" ↩ 013 enlists the *Manual of Travelling Exhibitions* in the long record of modernity's universal design approaches. In short, the core of universal design programmes is the shared assumption that whatever was, that has proven good and workable here thus shall be good everywhere—proper execution presupposed. On a more theoretical level this concept builds upon the supposition that an abstract and universal virtue or goal can be reached everywhere alike since every local point is a priori included within the universal. Insufficiencies are thus *local* insufficiencies of means towards a uniform end justified by the general good it aims at. Delivering the deficient locus with the right means (re-)incorporates it into the moral and functional integrity of the whole.

This paradigm of universalism is central to modernist design, planning, and engineering.[1] Historically it can be traced back to Cartesian rationalism. Descartes' radical doubt devaluates what the senses tell us right here and right now, and permits the self-assuredness of cognition as the only starting ground for true knowledge; furthermore, cognition's destiny in his definition is the arrival at an ulterior and totalistic comprehension of everything. Not having reached this goal yet, leaves us in a deficient state.

An important lesson, maybe even *the* lesson from high modernism, we still haven't fully digested, is that this inherited version of universalism in terms of design and technology is a dubious concept. Many of the great promises of universal procedures from education over welfare to urbanism have failed or outrageously underperformed.[2] We may not forget; *the universal* is a concept after all. It is very different from a real place or entity, something that can neither be found here nor there but still claims to include every possible here and there. As it is abstract from any real place and condition, one may rightfully ask which properties become in fact abstracted to reach the purity of the idea of a global value set—and to which price.

I shall continue with the attempt of re-reading the *Manual of Travelling Exhibitions* as a form of delivering after some of the discussion of cultural context not being found in the first reading. It is Christopher Alexander who reminds us that "[w]e ought always really to design with a number of nested, overlapped form-context boundaries in mind".[3] This I try to examine in three short reflections.

DO TRAVELLING EXHIBITIONS MERELY EXPAND MUSEUMS?

Courter Osborn opens her introduction with the words "We tend to think of museums of mere static collections of objects" and points out that people were accustomed to the inert condition of museum practice, rather than this belonging to the phenomenon itself. Since about 1850, museums would also operate as promoters of circulating exhibitions or as hosts for these external shows in an increasing fashion. She argues that the reason why many collections hadn't travelled much before was thus logistical ineptitude and not out of necessity. By overcoming sluggishness and stasis of the depository by new means of logistics, the museum would be enhanced in reach and impact. The idea seems clear: removing spatial limitations would make the particular artwork or information object globally attainable and thus its value, be it aesthetic, epistemic or educational, it would be more widely regarded. The whole *Manual* is dedicated to this introductory thought. What is interesting here is that the practice of engaging travelling exhibitions is considered a mere extension of the museum's original scope. Though being a cultural standard narrative for the explanation of technical means, it is highly questionable whether the use of new means *only* extends the common ones. The motorised car is not just a faster horse carriage. Radio is not just an exclamator with a stronger voice. And the digital computer is barely comprehensible as a more powerful slide rule. Media apparatuses and technical means do not only expand known features but also reshape patterns of cognition, behaviour, and policies connected to their use. Rather than just to improve the supply for an existing demand, technical means typically feedback on the original ends and open up new possibilities for further and divergent ends. That technology exclusively expands in a vertical direction without lateral implications to the social edifice is a rare exception, and it is surely not true for the use of travelling exhibitions on the impact to the museum and its audience.

Sending out exhibitions instead of maintaining a space for people to come and see is a clear reversal of distribution logic from a pull to a push momentum. When it was the traditional purpose of the museum's depot to collect, conserve, order, and categorise, then the

1 In 1969 Buckminster Fuller published another Manual with the remarkable title *Operating Manual For Spaceship Earth.* It can be regarded as the great exclamation mark of high modernity's belief that local solutions belong to the past and have from now on to be mastered from the superior viewpoint of scientific understanding. Richard Buckminster Fuller, *Operating Manual For Spaceship Earth,* Carbondale and Edwardsville 1969.

2 An excellent study about the vast shortcomings of modern administrational ambition towards managing diverse cultural agendas can be found in: James C. Scott, *Seeing Like a State—How Certain Schemes to Improve the Human Condition Have Failed,* New Haven and London 1998.

3 Christopher Alexander, *Notes on the Synthesis of Form,* London 1970, p. 18.

standing exhibition constituted the public interface to these background tasks. With an intensive use of circulating exhibitions this interface changes: the museum becomes a broadcasting protagonist—which is something quite different than just a museum with greater reach.

Walter Benjamin has argued in his famous essay "The Work of Art in the Age of Its Technological Reproducibility" (1936) that this new broadcasting logic through technical modes of reproduction and displacement of the artwork from its primary context ultimately alters art's role.[4] Whereas the spatial bound artwork resolves in a ritualistic/religious and foremost contemplative way of viewing, the popularised object turns into a mundane and political thing. With ‹political›, Benjamin does not mean, that the work of art is now a state affair, but rather that worldly interests take part in its perception and interpretation. The artwork no longer spans a sphere of its own but becomes increasingly intertwined with the everyday policies of popular fashion, ideological decomposition, and negotiating market value. Though one might accuse Walter Benjamin to be quite sentimental about the artwork as the great other—was it truly that virgin and divine in the beginning?—it stays a precise observation that massive exposition and popularisation creates an alloy between art and special interest. Regardless if one conceptualises this as a pitiable alienation from the origin or merely as a settlement in a new realm, we can ask for some guidance in dealing with that issue, if we were yet inexperienced organisers of travelling exhibitions. The *Manual* is of little help here. Presuming the museum was a kind of phenomenological substratum that was immutable in its function, but nowadays just has more to do, the *Manual* proposes no policy directed towards sender responsibility. The questions are: who decides what is selected and worth to be shown abroad? Which preferences are to be set? What defines the leading narrative? Who might gain from this view? Who will be ignored? Who loses the right to set her or his mark?

Well, is that all too dialectical? By no means at all. Elodie Courter Osborn explains to us, that there was little knowledge in the world about how to set up circulating exhibitions. In this sense the decision making for content is a technicality, for techniques eventually cause altered modes of perception.

SHALL ALL OBJECTS BE TREATED ALIKE?

A second thing, I would like to move attention to, is the far reaching indifference against various types of exhibition objects. Autonomous artworks, objects of applied, or decorative art, industrial wares, or informational objects can all be subject to exhibitions, but within the book they are barely differentiated in terms of how they could be presented in their own right. The generalisation of the object as a unified "good thing worth showing" is again laid out in a very optimistic tone. Courter Osborn writes: "Moreover, the diffusion of knowledge for education in all fields—natural science, history, health, science, art, etc.—can be accomplished effectively through exhibition."↩ 019 A discussion is further missing of how to deal with these very different topics. While there is some beautiful egalitarian thought in treating all types of artifacts alike, for it could help to question unverified preconceptions—i.e. such as that the original artwork is in Western thought traditionally considered higher in cultural rank than the technical product, with very vague arguments—this sameness has to be asked of its own real-world properties. If everything from ancient pottery to modern factory wares, from ethnographic collections to contemporary scientific devices is shown in the same way, how does this universal and singular way come along? How is the presumed equal presentability finally mediated in pedestals, backgrounds, showcases, displays and so forth? As it turns out, the slightly too extensive thinking in logistical requirements didn't perform as expected in practice, as it produced a strong tendency to regard the common share of all these objects to be a *commodity.* As Clémentine Deliss proves in detail in her essay "Page Seventy-Six" ↩ 179, the *Manual* presents carvings from an ethnographic collection in the fashion of a market stand. Similar settings could be proven for other examples in the *Manual.* The technical capabilities thus define the object rather than the other way around: because it is *economically* sound to use equal prefab display tools etc., this swiftly holds the precedence over the much more complicated task of aligning the outer conditions to the demands of a sensible framing of the content. What gets lost this way is the challenge for visitors to engage in complex narratives and to co-investigate the problems that arise from certain objects the same way as the

4 Walter Benjamin, *The Work of Art in the Age of Its Technological Reproducibility, and Other Writings on Media,* London 2008, pp. 19–55.

museum's experts do. Isn't it a dubious universality in culture when the parameters of aesthetic layout in a travelling exhibition are barely distinguishable from the slick displays we see while window shopping?

SEMANTIC SPACE = EUCLIDIAN SPACE?

Last, we ought to consider the biases of the various audiences that exhibition objects may meet. Can we presume, that visitors see and respond in a fairly similar (universal) way to a given aesthetic object? In the core of the aesthetic discourse at least since Kant, the relation between the perceivable object and the subject who performs the aesthetic judgement is the troublesome third. If we believed an aesthetic object a priori had an intrinsic and defined value by its very self—meaning in aesthetic terminology being either beautiful or ugly—the subjective judgement would be rendered irrelevant because everybody felt automatically the same about a thing. It is obvious that this is not the case. Some people take great pleasure in looking at a painting by Pollock, others don't. Yet, if we assume on the other hand that the judgement was spoken by the subject alone, this would make any discussion about the value of a piece of art senseless, because there would not be enough objective substance to claim general reason for its foundation. Absolutely, perception is neither preconfigured in the object nor contingent on a subjective basis. This leaves us in the remarkable situation to value the hazy and fragile relation, as well as the context, where it is established as just important as a person or thing. One shall regard the aesthetic object therefore as the typical transitory object: it undergoes different perceiving acts, coloured both by cultural bias and individual sentiment. We might call this context semantic for it represents the decisive cognitive model underlying the perception.

Now, let's take a look at this semantic context in terms of macro and micro space as well as in terms of figurative and abstract, or conceptual art. A portrait of Napoleon—clearly a figurative piece—arguably might cause very different emotions shown in Paris, where the depicted might well be regarded as a figure of national grandiosity as in Moscow where it rather reminds of invasion and pillage. Still for a child or someone who has never heard of Napoleon, the portrait may just show a little man with a funny hat. So here we have very different perceptions regarding the national macro space of placement for a figurative piece of art.

Taking the micro context into consideration, another viewpoint arises. To come up with a very familiar example, Duchamp's famous provocation to claim a urinal a piece of art by simply signing and exposing it, works solely in the narrow context of a museum or art gallery. It strikes only in front of an audience well accustomed to the tradition of viewing art in this very institutional framework. Putting the ultimate non-artistic piece which is a) associated with low sanitary necessity and b) an industrial multiple lacking artistic virtue and have it exposed to the question of beauty is no similar offence anywhere else. While a cubist painting at least would be recognised as an artwork even in a department store, Duchamp's readymade would have most likely not. It would appear as one of the shop's products from the bath department that someone had tagged his own and then forgotten to pay for. So much about the particularities of the micro context of placement.

Every work of art thus underlies as many possible interpretations as there are perceiving subjects. Relative similarity in both perception and interpretation can only be assumed for audiences with relatively equal biases. The idea that semantic space can be as easily managed as euclidean space—by railway, truck and plane—is a superb underestimation of the role of the history of perception and bias, in other words: it is very modern.

CONCLUSION

At the end of this humble re-reading session of the *Manual of Travelling Exhibitions* we end up in a somewhat odd position. On the one hand the universal scope of the book seems too narrow to claim generality, on the other, some assumptions are far too broad to comply with relevant contextual questions to be literally universal. The *Manual* offers a too dense of a model for working institutions, as it does not consider that a change in mode of exhibition practice alters the change in responsibility for what is exposed upon a wide audience. Though in terms of assessing content, it is overly relaxed that particular intentions and interpretations of (Western) exhibition makers are congruent with the view of the rest. One may decide if the lack of capacity to process otherness within the assumption of universality is funny or tragic.

THE MANUAL AFTER THE MANUAL

In 1963, ten years after the *Manual of Travelling Exhibitions* had first been published, UNESCO launched another handbook named *Temporary and Travelling Exhibitions,* which includes parts from its predecessor. This new manual also contains a chapter by Hiroshi Daifuku with the remarkable title ‹Exhibitions in the technically underdeveloped countries›. It hosts—not without some paternalistic sound—some severe advices for exhibition makers to clearly regard their audiences, such as the hint, that not everyone in the world may understand, that a black and white photograph most likely depicts an initially coloured ambient.

As it seems almost impossible to trace back which feedback loops and iterations had taken place in the UNESCO headquarters after the first *Manual* that caused a premonition of this kind, we still may underline one of the new chapter's introductory sentences: "a word of warning is needed".[5] Universal practice is not ready beforehand, it results from what is eventually learned about the common good.

5 UNESCO, *Temporary and Travelling Exhibitions,* Paris 1963, p. 45.

CONTRIBUTORS

MARTIN BECK

Martin Beck is a New York-based artist whose works often draw from the fields of architecture, design, and popular culture. Recent solo exhibitions were presented at mumok, Vienna; The Kitchen, New York; Galerie für zeitgenössische Kunst, Leipzig (all 2017); 47 Canal, New York (2012 and 2015); castillo/corrales, Paris (2014); Kunsthaus Glarus, Switzerland (2013); and Leonard & Bina Ellen Gallery, Montreal (2012). Beck's books include *About the Relative Size of Things in the Universe* (2007); *The Aspen Complex* (2012); *the particular way in which a thing exists; Last Night* (both 2013); *An Organised System of Instructions;* and *rumors and murmurs* (both 2017).

ELODIE COURTER OSBORN

Elodie Courter Osborn (1911–1994) was an art historian and the first director of Circulating Exhibitions at the Museum of Modern Art in New York. In 1933, she joined MoMA's newly founded Department of Circulating Exhibitions as a volunteer and was named director in 1939, a position she held until 1947. In the 1950s she served as an adviser to the American Federation of Arts Exhibition Committee and vice chairman of its International Exhibitions Committee. She is the author of the *Manual of Travelling Exhibitions,* which was published by UNESCO in 1953.

CLÉMENTINE DELISS

Clémentine Deliss is a curator and cultural historian. She studied contemporary art and semantic anthropology in Vienna, Paris, and London and holds a PhD from SOAS, University of London. Between 2010–2015, she directed the Weltkulturen Museum in Frankfurt, instituting a new research lab with which to remediate collections within a post-ethnographic context. She was the publisher and editor of the itinerant artists' and writers' organ *Metronome,* which was presented at documenta X and 12. She has held several guest professorships, was a consultant for the European Union and is on the scientific board of the Musée du quai Branly. She is currently investigating the future of the global museum in Southeast Asia and curating exhibitions for the National Gallery, Hamburger Bahnhof in Berlin and the Centre Georges Pompidou in Paris.

KURT ECKERT

Kurt Eckert is a visual designer, based in Zurich. His career started at the Schule für Gestaltung in Zurich and continued as a lecturer for visual design and typography at the Zurich University of the Arts (ZHdK). From 2000 to 2005 he supervised together with Manuel Krebs and Marco Walser the Typoclub. He directed the master's programme for editorial design in conjunction with Matthias Michel from 2007 to 2013. His work as a designer is cooperating in the fields of architecture, film and art. He has designed several books in collaboration with Jonas Voegeli and was a jury member for The Most Beautiful Swiss Books in 2014 and 2015.

JOCHEN EISENBRAND

Jochen Eisenbrand is chief curator at the Vitra Design Museum where he curated the exhibitions *Airworld: Design and Architecture for Air Travel; Hidden Heroes: The Genius of Everyday Things* as well as major retrospectives on George Nelson, Louis Kahn (with Stanislaus von Moos), Alvar Aalto and Alexander Girard. His exhibitions have also been shown at other museums in Europe, the USA and in Asia. With a master's degree in cultural studies (1998), Eisenbrand received his PhD in design history at the University of Wuppertal in 2014. His dissertation *George Nelson: Ein Designer im Kalten Krieg* was published by Park Books in Zurich.

RIKE FRANK

Rike Frank is a curator, teacher, and writer based in Berlin and Oslo. She currently holds a position as an associate professor for exhibition studies at the Oslo National Academy of the Arts (KHiO). She was previously curator of the exhibition space at the Academy of Fine Arts Leipzig (HGB), was a member of the programme team at the European Kunsthalle and Ludlow 38, New York, head of the curatorial office for documenta 12, and curator at the Secession in Vienna. Publication projects include: *Textiles: Open Letter* (2015); *Textile Theorien der Moderne: Alois Riegl in der Kunstkritik* (2015); *Timing: On the Temporal Dimension of Exhibiting* (2014); *Sketches of Universal History: Compiled from Several Authors by Sarah Pierce* (2013).

HELENE HERMANN

Helene Hermann is an artist and scenographer based in Copenhagen. She studied graphic design at Portsmouth College of Art & Design, worked as an assistant for Cornelia Parker at Chisenhale Gallery in London, and graduated in scenography from the Royal Danish Academy of Fine Arts, School of Design in 1998. She has done several works such as the exhibition design for the group presentation *Kropsholder – 14 female furniture designers* at the Scandinavian Furniture Fair, the scenography and costumes for *Misantropen* by Molière at Malmö Dramatiska Teater, and the set for a staged documentary *Homo Sapiens* at DR 2 (Danish Broadcast Television). In 2005 Hermann collaborated with Gitte Villesen in *I Capture You, You Capture Me,* for the Danish Pavilion, 51st Venice Bienniale. Photography and painting are currently her main focus.

JOHANNES HUCHT
Johannes Hucht currently studies at the Karlsruhe University of Arts and Design, mastering in communication design, exhibition design and media theory.

LYDIA KÄHNY
Lydia Kähny holds a degree in vocational studies as a carpenter and a bachelor's degree of interior-architecture from Burg Giebichenstein University of Art and Design Halle. Subsequently she has worked as an artistic assistant in the rectorate and as a freelance interior designer. Currently she is studying exhibition design, media art, and art sciences at the Karlsruhe University of Arts and Design.

TINA KÖHLER
Tina Köhler is head of Exhibitions Coordination at Haus der Kunst in Munich. She has organised more than 200 shows over the last 28 years and has collaborated with artists, curators, and art institutions worldwide. With a background in cultural management and with professional work experience in the field, she has planned major exhibition tours like *Louise Bourgeois: Structures of Existence: The Cells,* mentioned in the interview of this publication. She has held lectures on cultural management and regularly consults art institutions.

MORITZ KÜNG
Moritz Küng is a curator, critic and book editor based in Barcelona, working mainly on the interface of architecture, visual arts and contemporary publishing. He has realised comprehensive solo exhibitions including monographs with architects as Arno Brandlhuber, Christian Kerez, OFFICE KGDVS, SANAA, Eduardo Souto de Moura, and artists such as Dominique Gonzalez-Foerster, Thomas Hirschhorn, Bas Princen, Joëlle Tuerlinckx and Cerith Wyn Evans. Recent publications include the catalogue raisonnés of Peter Downsbrough, *The Book(s)* (2011), and Heimo Zobernig, *Books & Posters* (2016), as well as George Brecht's Facsimile Reprint, *Book: This is the cover of the book* (1972/2017).

SOPHIE LICHTENBERG
Sophie Lichtenberg studied scenography, exhibition design, media art and art sciences at the University of Arts and Design in Karlsruhe. She is part of the theatre, performance and art collective RAMPIG based in Mannheim and is currently doing artistic research on the development of immersive role-playing situations executed for journalists by the German armed forces in case of crisis situations.

JONATHAN MAHO
Jonathan Maho is an art historian living in Berlin. He holds a PhD in English studies (focused on photography and exhibition history) from the Sorbonne Paris Cité University. For his dissertation, he worked on issues related to censorship in the context of the culture wars in the USA—addressing the limitation of the discourse surrounding the presentation of artworks dealing with sensitive topics. More generally, his research has addressed the status of performative images, as well as the impact of funding, exhibition design and art criticism on the reception of modern and contemporary art. He is currently working on a book dedicated to the Danish-Vietnamese artist Danh Vo.

GRACE MCCANN MORLEY
Grace McCann Morley (1900–1985) was an art historian and museologist. Starting in 1935, she was the first director of the San Francisco Museum of Modern Art, where she pioneered public educational programming on Modern Art, including guided gallery tours, an art rental gallery, and film and television programmes. In the 1950s she became the first director of UNESCO's Museums and Monuments Division and participated in the establishment of the International Council of Museums (ICOM).

VANESSA JOAN MÜLLER
Vanessa Joan Müller is an art historian and curator. From 2000 to 2005 she worked as a curator at the Frankfurter Kunstverein, Frankfurt am Main. In late 2005 she became the academic director for the European Kunsthalle project in Cologne, which explores different models for potential art institutions. From 2006 till 2011 she was director of the Kunstverein für die Rheinlande und Westfalen in Düsseldorf. Since 2013, she has been head of dramaturgy at Kunsthalle Wien. Numerous publications on contemporary art and art theory confirm her position as a curator with a strong interest in contemporary art and its social and philosophical contexts.

ANDREAS MÜLLER
Andreas Müller is professor of exhibition design at the Karlsruhe University of Art and Design. He studied architecture at the Berlin University of the Arts and was a founding member and editor of the magazine *An Architektur: Produktion und Gebrauch gebauter Umwelt.* He is part of the exhibition design studio Kooperative für Darstellungspolitik, based in Berlin. In his work, he investigates the communicative and transformative potential of designed spaces.

LENA THOMAKA
Lena Thomaka holds a bachelor's degree in art education from the University of Leipzig. She is currently studying communication design, exhibition design and art sciences at the Karlsruhe University of Arts and Design.

JENNIFER TOBIAS
Jennifer Tobias is the reader services librarian at the Museum of Modern Art, New York. She is a graduate of the City University of New York's art history programme. Her 2012 doctoral

dissertation is "The Museum of Modern Art's What is Modern? Series, 1938–1969". Tobias has curated several exhibitions at MoMA's Cullman Education and Research Building, including *Artifact or Idea? Photography in MoMA Exhibition Design, 1937–1979.* She has contributed to numerous publications, including *Cabinet, CAA Reviews,* and the *Journal of Design History.*

GITTE VILLESEN

Gitte Villesen is an artist based in Berlin. Her documentary videos and installations explore forms in which individuals or social groups shape their lives within the framework of their cultural possibilities. She illuminates how subjects and identities are constituted in the everyday micro-politics of gestures, habits, and rituals in the charged relationship between norm and deviation. She has taken part in numerous international exhibitions, including her participation with scenographer Helene Hermann for the Danish Pavilion at the 51st Venice Biennale in 2005.

NADER VOSSOUGHIAN

Nader Vossoughian is an architectural historian and curator based in New York and Berlin. He is an associate professor of architecture at the New York Institute of Technology and until recently a DAAD research fellow at the Bauhaus University in Weimar. He studied philosophy, cultural studies and German studies before obtaining his MPhil and PhD in architectural theory and history at Columbia University. He has curated exhibitions at Stroom Den Haag, MAK Centre for Art and Architecture, the AIA Center for Architecture, and the Museum of Applied Arts in Vienna, amongst others. He is currently working on a book about the standardisation of standardisation.

FLORIAN WALZEL

Florian Walzel studied communication design in Darmstadt and Portsmouth. He holds a master's degree in design studies from the Burg Giebichenstein University of Art and Design Halle. He is laureate of the Deutsche Studienpreis der Körber Stiftung (2006) and The Junge Akademie at the Berlin-Brandenburg Academy of Sciences and Humanities (2008) as well as scholar of the Internationales Forum für Gestaltung (IFG). He was guest lecturer for history and theory of design at the Zurich University of the Arts (ZHdK) in 2010; since 2012 he is an assistant lecturer at the University of Darmstadt. He is a founding member and editor of *Neuwerk – Magazine for Design Studies.*

GRANT WATSON

Grant Watson is a curator and researcher based in London. He is co-curator of "Migrant Bauhaus" a large scale project exploring the school's international reception to mark its centenary in 2019. Other current activities include the filmed interview series *How We Behave* commissioned by If I Can't Dance (IICD), exhibited with IICD in Amsterdam; The Showroom, London; Nottingham Contemporary; Middlesbrough Institute of Modern Art; State of Concept, Athens; the Whitechapel Gallery, London; and Extra City, Antwerp. Past projects include *Practice International* and *Tagore Pedagogy and Contemporary Visual Cultures* both of which addressed historical and contemporary cosmopolitanism. Watson is a tutor at the Royal College of Art and has a PhD in visual cultures from Goldsmiths College, London.

JOANNA WEDDELL

Joanna Weddell is a design historian at the University of Brighton, working as an editor and author. She has a background in architecture and is currently researching post-war design and museology at the Research Department of the Victoria & Albert Museum and the University of Brighton, UK. The investigation, *Disseminating Design,* examines the historic impact of V&A touring design collections and contributes to the Museum's regional strategy for design education.

MAXIM WEIRICH

Maxim Weirich is a freelance exhibition designer and researcher based in Karlsruhe and Berlin. He studied anthropology and media studies at The New School in New York and worked as an intern for the Museum of Modern Art (MoMA) in 2016 and 2017. He holds a pre-diploma in exhibition design and will graduate from the Karlsruhe University of Art and Design in 2018. Recently he has worked on exhibitions that focus on the display of historical objects in the realm of museums and art institutions (Badischer Kunstverein, 2015 and Badisches Landesmuseum, 2016).

AARON WERBICK

Aaron Werbick received his master's degree in architecture and design at the Academy of Fine Arts in Stuttgart Germany, his work moves between urban design and landscaping to exhibition design and scenography. In collaboration with renowned artists and architects he staged exhibitions at the House of World Cultures (HKW) in Berlin and the Museum of Modern Art (MMK) in Frankfurt. His main focus remains on churches, actively developing a method for the reevaluation of ecclesiastical spaces, as a result of social and spiritual shifts. Currently he is a research associate at the Karlsruhe University of Arts and Design.

INDEX

The index combines a selection of individuals, institutions, publications and artworks in the reading notes and essays.

SOURCES AND REFERENCES OF THE READING NOTES

1 Rupture Inaugurale: www.imprimerie-union.org/apollinaire-a-maeght/surrealistes/falerie-surrealistes
2 Imprimerie Union, Paris: www.imprimerie-union.org
3 Hans Rudolf Bosshard, Technische Grundlagen zur Satzherstellung, BST, Berne 1980; A Monotype Composing Machine, A Silent Film, 1925: www.typography.guru/video/a-monotype-composing-machine-1925-r93; A Monotype timeline: www.eyemagazine.com/feature/article/a-monotype-timeline
4 Stanley Morison: www.eyemagazine.com/feature/article/stanley-morison-changing-the-times; Typefoundry: documents for the history of type and letterforms: www.typefoundry.blogspot.ch/2011/04/garamond-or-garamont.html; Peter Gabor, Garamond vs Garamont: physiologie d'un caractère typographique, 2006: www.paris.blog.lemonde.fr/2006/09/21/2006_09_garamond_vs_gar; English translation: www.barneycarroll.com/garamond.htm
5 Hiroshi Daifuku, "Museums and monuments: UNESCO's pioneering role", *Museum International:* fiftieth anniversary issue, vol. L, no. 1, UNESCO, Paris 1998.
6 Imprimerie Union, Paris: www.imprimerie-union.org
7 Grace McCann Morley, "UNESCO's exchange of exhibitions programme: The first circulating exhibition", *Museum, Vol. 6,* no. 4, UNESCO, Paris 1953.
8 Hiroshi Daifuku, "Museums and monuments: UNESCO's pioneering role", *Museum International:* fiftieth anniversary issue, vol. L, no. 1, UNESCO, Paris 1998.
9 Grace McCann Morley: www.sfgate.com/entertainment/article/Grace-Morley-forgotten-pioneer-behind-SF-MOMA-3204269.php
10 Wolfgang Autenrieth, Xylographie: www.wp.radiertechniken.de/trockene-techniken/xylographie; Lueger: Lexikon der gesamten Technik, Autotypie 1: www.zeno.org/Lueger-1904/A/Autotypie+[1]; Autotypie: Fotos in der Massenvervielfältigung und fotografisches Bildgedächtnis: www.historischdenken.hypotheses.org/3428
11 see Susan Rossen & Charlotte Moser, "Primer for Seeing: The Gallery of Art Interpretation and Katharine Kuh's Crusade for Modernism in Chicago", Art Institute of Chicago Museum Studies, vol. 16, no. 1 (1990).
12 Giulio Carlo Argan, "Circulating and Educational Exhibitions in Italian Museums", *Museum, Vol. 3,* no. 4, UNESCO, Paris 1950.
13 MoMA, Machine Art, 07.–31.03.1938: www.moma.org/calendar/exhibitions/2927; MoMA, Machine Art, 05.03.–29.04.1934: www.moma.org/calendar/exhibitions/1784; www.moma.org/documents/moma_catalogue_1784_300061872.pdf
14 Leading and other Spacing Materials: www.britishletterpress.co.uk/letterpress-guides/composition/leading-and-other-spacing-materials
15 Alexander Tzonis and Liane Lefaivre, *Architecture of Regionalism in the Age of Globalization,* Routledge, London and New York 2012.
16 William Charles Richards, *Revolt and Reform in Architecture's Academy: Columbia and Yale in the 1960s,* University of Virginia, Virginia 2010.
17 Richard Paul Lohse, *New Design in Exhibitions: 75 Examples of the new Form of Exhibitions,* Verlag für Architektur, Erlenbach-Zürich 1953.
18 Library of Congress: Ekstasis, no. 2: www.loc.gov/item/ihas.200154181; www.dantebea.com/category/photographes/soichi-sunami/; Chris Sunami, Soichi Sunami: Modern Artist, The Pop Culture Philosopher (Blog), 2017: www.popculturephilosopher.com/soichi-sunami-modern-artist; The Seattle Camera Club: www.seattlecameraclub.com/soichi_sunami.html
19 Railway Express Agency, Inc.: www.britannica.com/topic/REA-Express-Inc
20 William Baker, Machine for manufacturing wood so as to be used as a substitute for curled hair in stuffing beds. Patent No. 2,654, 30.05.1842: www.google.com/patents/US2654?hl=fibers++wood+mattress
21 Wilhelm Lehmbruck, Standing Woman: armory.nyhistory.org/standing-woman

IMAGE CREDITS

Fig. 01, 02, 03 UNESCO Archives

Fig. 04 Elodie Courter Osborn, Director, Department of Circulating Exhibitions, The Museum of Modern Art, New York, with panels from the circulating exhibition *Elements of Design* (c. 1945). New York, Museum of Modern Art (MoMA). Gelatin-silver print, 7 1/4×7 5/8" (18.4×19.3 cm) Photographic Archive. The Museum of Modern Art Archives, New York. Cat. no.: A1079. © 2017. Digital image, The Museum of Modern Art, New York/Scala, Florence

Fig. 05 Panel 2 of the master set of installation photographs for The Museum of Art circulating exhibition *What is Good Design?* (1942–1945). New York, Museum of Modern Art (MoMA). Photo: Soichi Sunami (copyright unknown).
Department of Circulating Exhibitions Records, II.1.119.1. The Museum of Modern Art Archives, New York. Cat. no.: MA653. © 2017. Digital image, The Museum of Modern Art, New York/Scala, Florence

Fig. 06 Panel 15 of the master set of installation photographs for The Museum of Modern Art circulating exhibition *What is Good Design?* (1942–1945). New York, Museum of Modern Art (MoMA). Photo: Soichi Sunami (copyright unknown).
Department of Circulating Exhibitions Records, II.1.119.1. The Museum of Modern Art Archives, New York. Cat. no.: MA666. © 2017. Digital image, The Museum of Modern Art, New York/Scala, Florence

Fig. 07 Photo: Evi Künstle, Johannes Hucht & Lena Thomaka

Fig. 08 Open-display unit designed by the Victoria and Albert Museum, as published in Plate XXVII, Museums Journal, Jan. 1957, p. 243

Fig. 09, 10, 11, 12, 13 Peter Floud, Draft Script, MA/15/14, Circulation Department Administrative Papers, V&A Archives (n. d. c. 1948) © Victoria and Albert Museum, London

Fig. 14 Otto and Marie Neurath Isotype Collection, University of Reading

Fig. 15 Gitte Villesen with Helene Hermann; Photo: Anders Sune Berg

Fig. 16 Courtesy of Martin Beck and 47 Canal, New York

Fig. 17, 18, 19, 20 hasenkamp Internationale Transporte GmbH

Fig. 21, 22 Images from: Museum, Vol III, no. 4, 1950, "Museums and circulating exhibitions", p. 283

Fig. 23, 24 Images from: Museum, Vol V, no. 3, 1952, p. 186

Fig. 25, 26 Images from: Museum, Vol XI, no. 1, 1958, International Campaign for Museums, p. 68

Fig. 27, 28 National Council of Science Museums, Ministry of Culture, Govt. of India, 33 Block GN, Sector V, Bidhan Nagar, Kolkata 700091

Fig. 29, 30 Images from: Museum, Vol VIII, no. 3,1955, p. 125

Fig. 31, 32 Images from: Museum, Vol XIX, no. 3, 1966, "Museums in the Ukraine", p. 156

Fig. 33 *UNESCO Courier,* August 1949

Fig. 34 Presentation of *The Laid Table* at the Berlin University of the Arts, photo: Fotostudio Orgel-Köhne, 1950s, signature: ABD 7-132/55, Werkbund Archiv Berlin

Fig. 35 Landesarchiv Berlin, F Rep. 290 Nr. 0037468/photo: Willi Nitschke

Fig. 36 © Association Marcel Duchamp/VG Bild-Kunst, Bonn 2017; (photographer unknown)

Fig. 37, 38, 39 Courtesy of the Lissen and Piotr Zamecznik Estate

Fig. 40 Muzeum Narodowe w Warszawie

Fig. 41 J & S. Zamecznik/Archeology of Photography Foundation, Photo: Wojciech Zamecznik

Fig. 42, 43, 44, 45, 46, 47, 48 Vitra Design Museum

Fig. 49 Mercator world map after ISOTYPE, illustration: Johannes Hucht

Fig. 50, 51 UNESCO Archives

RE-READING THE MANUAL OF TRAVELLING EXHIBITIONS, UNESCO, 1953
The book appears in the series: Edition 76135 – Books from the HfG University of Arts and Design Karlsruhe

EDITORS
Andreas Müller, Aaron Werbick

COORDINATING EDITOR
Lydia Kähny

EDITORIAL TEAM
Johannes Hucht, Sophie Lichtenberg, Lena Thomaka, Maxim Weirich

GRAPHIC DESIGN
Johannes Hucht, Lena Thomaka

CONTRIBUTIONS
Martin Beck, Elodie Courter Osborn, Clémentine Deliss, Kurt Eckert, Jochen Eisenbrand, Rike Frank, Helene Hermann, Johannes Hucht, Lydia Kähny, Tina Köhler, Moritz Küng, Sophie Lichtenberg, Jonathan Maho, Grace McCann Morley, Vanessa Joan Müller, Andreas Müller, Jennifer Tobias, Gitte Villesen, Nader Vossoughian, Florian Walzel, Grant Watson, Joanna Weddell, Maxim Weirich, Aaron Werbick

TRANSLATION
Gareth Davies

PROOFREADING & COPY EDITING
Ames Gerould

LITHOGRAPHY
Ulf Beck, Christian Ertel

TYPEFACE
Garamond, Francesco Simoncini
Progress, Johannes Hucht

PAPER
Amber Graphic

PRINTING
druckhaus köthen

ACKNOWLEDGMENTS
AStA-HfG Karlsruhe, Matthias Görlich, Alejandra Janus, Elisabeth Kuon, Viktoria Langmann, Christiane Minter, Norina Quinte, Margit Rosen, Sereina Rothenberger, Jenny Starick, Regina Strasser, Céline Strolz, Marco Walser, Nadine Wietlisbach, Petra Zimmermann

We thank UNESCO for the generous permission to reprint the *Manual of Travelling Exhibitions* as well as various other UNESCO publications.

PUBLISHED BY SPECTOR BOOKS
Harkortstraße 10, 04107 Leipzig, www.spectorbooks.com

DISTRIBUTION
Germany, Austria
GVA, Gemeinsame Verlagsauslieferung Göttingen GmbH & Co. KG, www.gva-verlag.de

Switzerland
AVA Verlagsauslieferung AG, www.ava.ch

France, Belgium
Interart Paris, www.interart.fr

United Kingdom
Central Books Ltd, www.centralbooks.com

North, Central and South America, Africa, Asia
ARTBOOK | D.A.P
www.artbook.com

South Korea, Australia, New Zealand
The Book Society
www.thebooksociety.org

FIRST EDITION
PRINTED IN GERMANY
ISBN 978-3-95905-136-1